OF GODS, KINGS, AND MEN
The Reliefs of Angkor Wat

Photographs: Jaroslav Poncar
Text: Thomas S. Maxwell

SILKWORM BOOKS

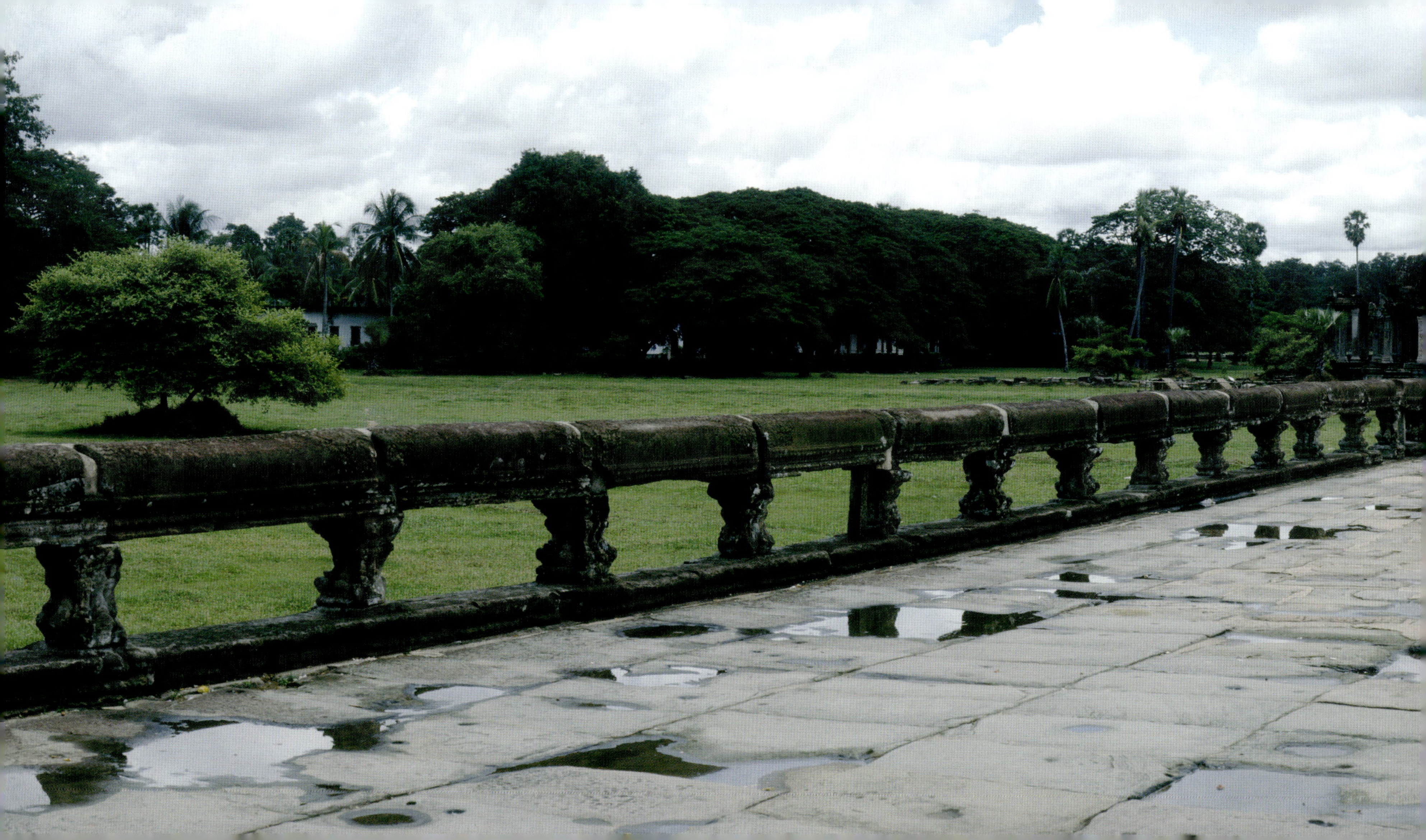

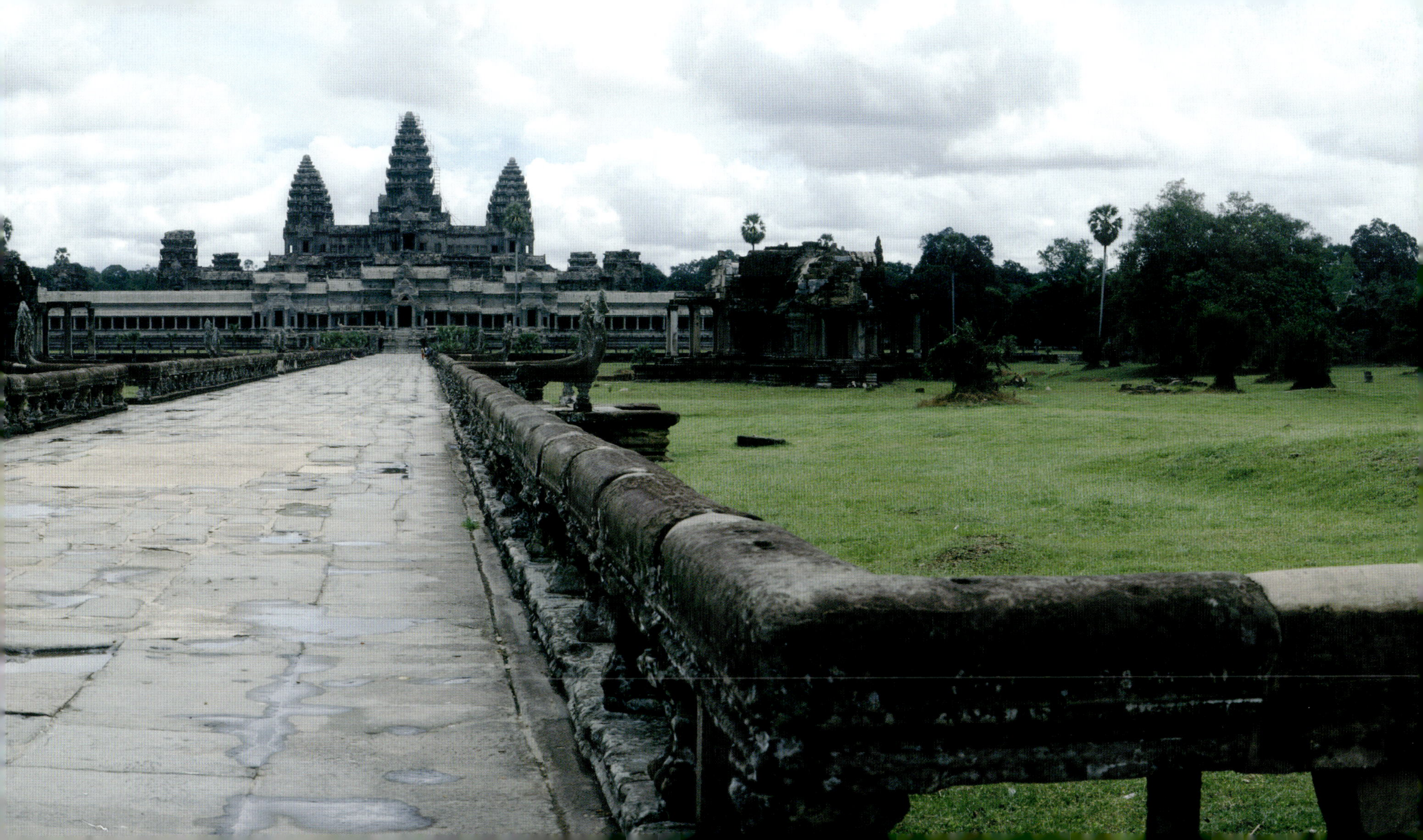

Images of Angkor Wat have become so familiar to us through the internet, television documentaries, educational compact disks, travel guidebooks, "coffee-table" books and tourism advertisements, that there might seem to be little left for us still to discover. In fact this is no more true of Angkor Wat than it is of any other Khmer temple. Even the most sumptuously illustrated art book cannot encompass the wealth of detail, architectural and artistic, that makes up these powerful expressions of ancient Cambodian civilization. But the urgent desire to see and understand all these details amounts to an imperative voice in many of us who are conducting new researches, using new technologies, at these temple sites; this exploration of the human past in terms of intellectual content has now become the serious and urgent concern of international agencies as well as national governments and universities. One of the tools we need for this work is the ability not only to mirror but also to reproduce the past's creations accurately. Attempts to record the two-metre high, five-hundred metre long reliefs on the walls of Angkor Wat's third enclosure already have a long history.

The first European reproductions of these reliefs took the form of moulages (plaster casts) made by Doudart de Lagrée in 1866. These were exhibited in Paris at the two Expositions Universelles of 1867 and 1889, after which all trace of them was apparently lost. A further, extensive selection of casts by Delaporte were housed in the Musée Indochinois du Trocadéro, and still more, representing the reliefs of the south gallery's west wing, were cast from estampages made by

Aymonier's mission and deposited in the Musée Guimet; in 1904, the Museum fuer Voelkerkunde in Berlin also acquired a fairly complete set of casts.

The first photographs of the reliefs were taken by a professional photographer, John Thomson, in 1866, just as Doudart de Lagrée was completing his work. Some of these pictures were published the following year in an exceedingly rare book entitled *Antiquities of Cambodia* (Edinburgh 1867). Poorly reproduced photographic plates subsequently appeared in the publications of such writers as F. Garnier (*Voyage d'exploration en Indochine,* Paris 1873), L. Delaporte (*Voyage au Cambodge,* Paris 1880), J. Moura (*Le royaume de Cambodge,* Paris 1883), Fournereau (*Les ruines khmères,* Paris 1890), and in E. Aymonier's monumental *Le Cambodge* (Paris 1900-1903). Attempts to understand the reliefs on the basis of inadequate visual material had understandably yielded rather superficial results. It was recognised, of course, that the Hindu epic tradition had inspired many of the scenes. In particular, the Indian *Ramayana* tradition was seen as the basis for the reliefs in the corner pavilions and on the northern half of the west wall, and the *Mahabharata* for that on the southern half; other scenes of fairly obvious content, such as the churning of the milk-ocean, the historic procession, the heavens and hells, and the sweeping battles between gods and demons, were identified as such but not yet fully analysed.

Not until forty-three years after Thomson, in May 1909, were all the gallery reliefs systematically photographed under the direction of Général de Beylié and the results officially handed over to the Académie des Inscriptions et Belles-Lettres in October of the same year. It was from this collection of 236 photographs that George Coedès worked on his first interpretation of the Angkor

Wat reliefs, which was published two years later in the *Bulletin de la Commission Archéologique de l'Indochine* (Paris 1911: 170-219); his article was entitled "Les bas-reliefs d'Angkor-Wat", and it was illustrated with a large number of de Beylié's photographs on thirty full-page plates. All subsequent research on these reliefs has been overshadowed by and indebted to this pioneering work. The text prepared for this book is based upon the brilliant photography of Jaroslav Poncar, carried out in 1995.

The temple that we refer to as Angkor Wat was built in the twelfth century by the Khmer king Suryavarman II, who reigned *circa* 1113-1150 AD, and dedicated to the Hindu god Vishnu. Suryavarman himself assumed the posthumous Sanskrit title of Paramavishnuloka, "He Who Has Gone to the Highest World of Vishnu", and it appears from a later inscription that the temple itself may originally have been named Vishnuloka, "The World of Vishnu", as if this massive structure was indeed regarded as an architectural symbol of its royal builder's final resting place in heaven. The complex occupies a site measuring some 1500 x 1300 metres and consists of an outer enclosure (1025 x 802 metres) surrounded by a moat, followed by three further concentric rectangular enclosures, all having a central gateway on each side and four corner-towers, with the principal temple standing like a mountain at the centre of the four innermost courtyards. The reliefs treated in this book are those carved on the walls of the third enclosure, a huge colonnaded stone continuum that separated the central sacred area of Angkor Wat from the surrounding city which, being built of perishable materials, has not survived.

Angkor Wat does not face the east, as do most Hindu temples throughout the world, but opens to the west. This reversal of the conventional orientation has no mysterious or especial esoteric significance, though it has given rise to much speculation. Most royal Khmer temples were dedicated to Shiva and faced east, but alongside this convention there existed another ancient Indian tradition of building Vishnu temples to face the setting sun, and this feature was taken up by Suryavarman's architects to proclaim the distinctiveness of the king's personal belief. The insistence on Vishnu - not Shiva - as the source and sustainer of righteousness in the universe is not only conveyed by this colossal reversal of the temple's axial direction, but is also everywhere stated in the visual content of the reliefs, as we shall see. Later, in the 12th and 13th century, another Khmer ruler, the Buddhist king Jayavarman VII, was similarly to insist upon the superiority of his personal religion in the layout and iconography of his great temples. This personal preference for one deity - Shiva, Vishnu or the Buddha - in which an individual elevates his chosen god or goddess (*ishtadevata*) above all others in the vast Indian pantheons, is a very ancient tradition and implies no disrespect toward other gods. As for the orientation of Suryavarman's temple, westward-facing Vishnu shrines were being built in northern India already in the Gupta and early post-Gupta periods (5th - 6th centuries; the Marhia temple at Deori in Madhya Pradesh and the Dasavatara at Deogarh in Uttar Pradesh are famous examples); and if we look further afield in Southeast Asia, beyond the India-Indochina axis, we find that Indonesian royalty had been building many of its Hindu temples to face the setting sun since the 9th century, based on a Javanese belief that the god should stand in the auspicious direction, the east, and that his worshippers should approach him from the west. In other words, the conception of Angkor Wat, though certainly unusual at Angkor, was conventional in terms of a wider Asian cultural horizon. To distinguish himself through his architecture, and so underline the individuality of his rule under the aegis of Vishnu, Suryavarman had only to select and emphasise certain Vaishnava elements of this far-flung temple-building tradition, the significance of which was undoubtedly known in ancient Cambodia. One of these points of emphasis was the westward orientation, and another was the pictorial content of the third-enclosure reliefs which stood at the boundary between temple and city, eternally depicting the greatness of Vishnu and the king as co-defenders of the universe and the state.

In order to understand these reliefs in ritual terms - that is, their role in the daily functioning of the temple - we have to look briefly at an Asian cultural phenomenon which is based on human movement in relation to a revered person or object. One of the most basic, and essential, forms of Hindu and Buddhist worship consists of walking in clockwise direction around a sacred object. In so doing, the right side of the body, which is considered pure, is always turned toward the object of veneration. In the case of a Hindu temple, the worshipper, approaching from the east, normally turns to the left in front of the entrance and completes a devotional tour of the peripheral shrines; only when this circular movement brings him back to the eastern door does he actually enter the temple. However, the clockwise direction *(pradakshina)* of this movement (East-South-West-North-East) only applies if one starts in the east. If the whole temple is turned around to face west, the direction of circumambulation is also reversed: the visitor turns to his right outside the entrance and proceeds counterclockwise *(prasavya)* around the structure (in the sequence West-South-East-North-West). The sequence of the reliefs at Deogarh, on one of the oldest west-facing Vishnu temples in the Hindu world, already indicates this, and most probably the same direction was still followed by Vishnu-worshippers circumambulating the third enclosure of Angkor Vat six centuries later. But a satisfactory explanation of

the logic behind the order in which the Angkor Vat reliefs are presented in the course of this circular movement has not yet been found.

Let us begin our search for a valid sequence in which to view these reliefs by reviewing the layout from a bird's-eye perspective. Approaching from the west - that is, from the front of the structure - the visitor is confronted by representations of two major battle scenes from Vaishnava mythology, in each of which the protagonist is one of the supremely revered incarnations of Vishnu: Rama at the battle of Lanka to the left (north) of the central gateway, and Krishna at the battle of Kurukshetra to the right (south). Along the south walls, extending from west to east, are depicted human beings, first in an historical procession and then in scenes from the afterlife. Parallel to these, along the north walls, first the Hindu gods in general and then Vishnu in particular are shown battling the demons. The reliefs on the two halves of the rear (east) wall show, on the southern stretch, one of the most famous moments from the Vaishnava creation-myth cycle (the churning of the ocean) and then, on the north, an eternally embattled Vishnu fighting off the onslaughts of a host of demons. The tone throughout is overwhelmingly dynamic and militant, in keeping with Suryavarman's restless energy and aggressive policies. At first sight, a continuous reading of the themes depicted in these vast reliefs, whether read in clockwise or counterclockwise sequence from the western wall, does not appear to yield a narrative logic.

The four sides of the enclosure seem rather to have been used to project out over the encircling city four aspects of Suryavarman's world-view seen through the prism of his Vaishnava belief. These aspects display four states

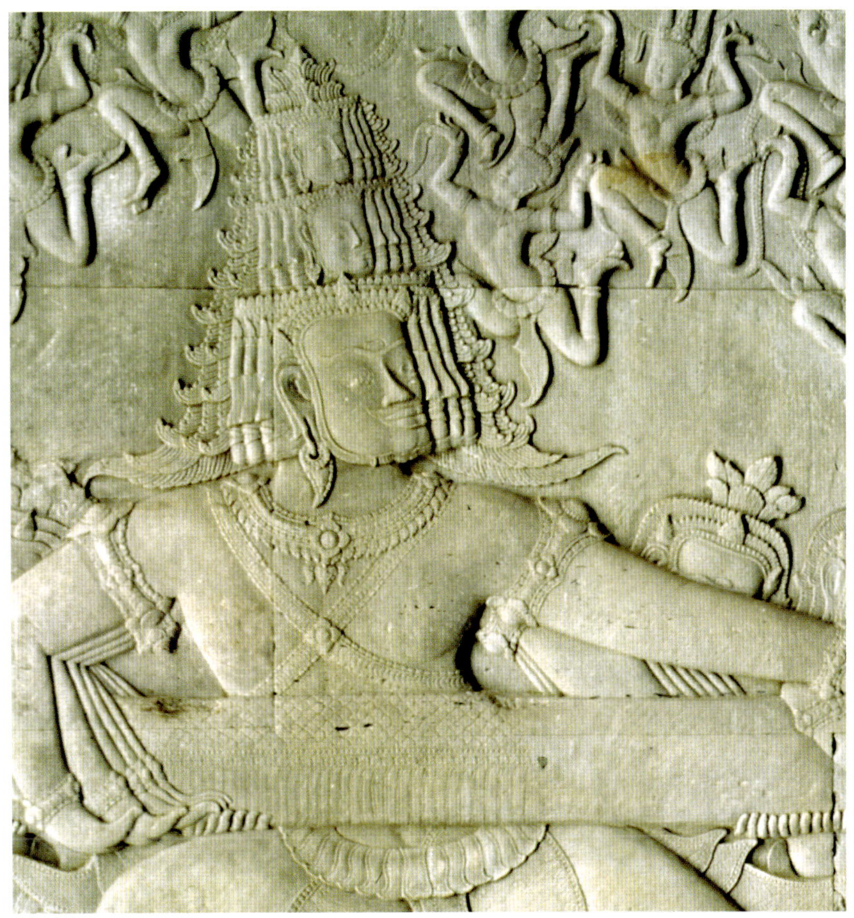

or levels of existence that are involved in the continuous struggle to maintain righteousness and order *(dharma)* in this world and throughout the universe. At the cosmic level, this struggle is believed to be eternally ongoing, between Vishnu and the forces of disorder, in spheres beyond our awareness; in this world, the struggle is periodic – each cataclysmic battle against disorder being waged by a particular incarnation of Vishnu – but also measurable in terms of human life, since every king has the duty during his reign to create and defend his realm in imitation of Vishnu. State policy can therefore be viewed as a reflection of the divine plan for the universe, and the king as a reflection of Vishnu himself.

Each of the reliefs, when regarded as a self-contained narrative, does not depend for its context upon a particular locus for the action; the reliefs are practically two-dimensional, and there are almost no backgrounds. The key to understanding such scenes is not their location in space, but in time. If the king and his army are represented in a procession leading from life to death, then clearly historical time, measured in human lifespans, is involved. If the semi-divine warrior *avataras* of Vishnu appear, the time-scale is a periodic one dependent on the balance between order and disorder in the world. If Vishnu appears waging war on the demons, we are in a time-scale that measures the life of the universe. And if Vishnu appears in a myth concerning the birth of the universe, we are being shown the beginning of time itself. These huge depictions of episodes in the history of existence are located in particular *yugas* – vast periods or aeons of time. There are in the Hindu conception four of these, known as the Krita or Satya-yuga, the most remote period, Treta-yuga, Dvapara-yuga, and Kali-yuga, which is the present. The events represented on the walls of Angkor Vat's third enclosure are set in these four *yugas*. Those on the east wall (the churning of the ocean) occurred in the first *yuga*, the Krita or Satya; those on the west wall in the second and third *yuga*, the Treta (Rama) and the Dvapara (Krishna); and finally those on the south wall (where the builder of the temple, Suryavarman, is depicted) in the fourth and current *yuga* – in which we also live – the Kali. There is, therefore, no doubt that in terms of Hindu time constructs executed under Suryavarman, but left incomplete, being finally sculpted only in the 16th century, by which time the original concept and specific meaning of the iconographic programme had undoubtedly been forgotten. Especially the location in the cosmic time scheme of the north-wall reliefs, and the mythological moments illustrated in them, therefore remains unclear. In keeping with the logic

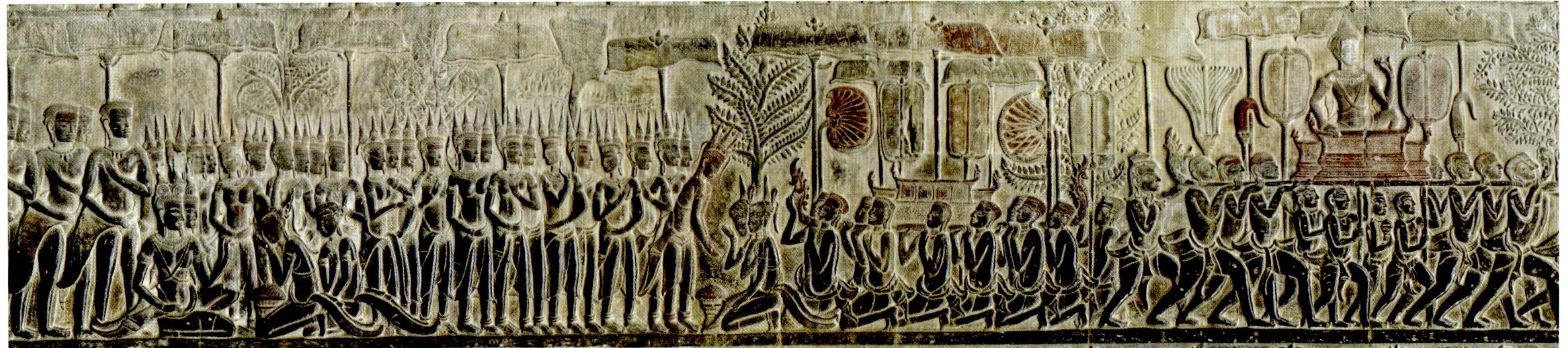

and Vaishnava cosmic mythology, these reliefs have to be viewed in counter-clockwise sequence, and that the circumambulation has to start, not in the west, but from the southeast corner, at the southern end of the east wall, where the depictions are lit by the rising sun.

Our perception of this time sequence is blurred only by the fact that the two reliefs at the transition from the east to the north walls were not of the other three sides of the enlosure, however, these events depicted on the north side can only have been set in the Treta Yuga. It certainly appears that a dominant theme of both the northern and the western reliefs was intended to be the judgement of kings, a concept that is parallelled on the south wall in the depictions of King Suryavarman, the judge of the dead, and the assignment of the deceased to heaven and hell. Toward the middle of the 12th century, among the ruling elite at Angkor, these were mighty themes, concerning a great king and his mortality, the continued defence of order in the kingdom and throughout the universe, and the measures of time through which gods and men are brought face to face with their origins and destiny. In forming his empire and building the temple of Vishnu, Suryavarman was concerned to establish his place and role in this cosmic scheme. This he did, as most Hindu kings had done before him, by defining his chosen god and his own world-shaping actions as the appropriate and effective response to the exigencies of the historical moment into which he was born. We should therefore not forget that the myths and legends represented in these reliefs were by no means simple-minded visualisations of stories from scripture, but politically interpretative versions of mythology intended to change and unify the existing world-view to conform with the strategic programme that Suryavarman set in motion for himself and for his subjects. There are moments in the reliefs at which this becomes very clear, but also certain other points, such as the later north-eastern reliefs mentioned above, at which we receive only a shadowy impression of the king's thinking.

As we have seen, the starting point of the cosmic time sequence represented by the reliefs around the outside of the temple enclosure undoubtedly lay in the east, not in the west. By locating the first relief on this side, the depiction of the creation of the world appropriately faces the sunrise, which marks the beginning of the ritual day in every Hindu temple. Let us now summarise all these scenes in the *prasavya* (counter-clockwise) sequence. 1: On the eastern walls, Vishnu appears first in the Krita Yuga as the foundation, axis and dynamic of the world's creation, in the form of turtle, mountain, and holder of the endless serpentine waters from which everything arose, including the secret of immortality. Further to the north on this wall, as sustainer of the created universe and defender of *dharma*, he fights alone against hordes of demons assailing him from all sides. 2: Along the northern walls, where we enter the Treta Yuga, Vishnu is seen in multiple transformations of himself battling the arch-demon Bana, son of Bali whom he conquered as Vamana, the dwarf, and then as the leader of the whole pantheon attacking the demons. 3: On the western walls the chief warrior-forms of Vishnu in this world, Rama and Krishna, are depicted, respectively fighting at the end of the Treta Yuga and in the early Dvapara in Lanka, stronghold of the demon-king Ravana, and in India at the transition from the Dvapara to the Kali Yuga, on the great northwestern plain called Kurukshetra. Like the king of Angkor Wat's present, these heroic incarnations of the legendary past also fought to preserve *dharma*; Suryavarman is thus pictorially linked into the chain of Vishnu's interventions in the affairs of this world. 4: Finally, the reliefs on the western part of the south wall depict mortals in the Kali Yuga: the king with his priests, ministers and generals meet on a holy mountain and then descend to the plain and proceed to the east, carrying with them the ritual fire which was believed to burn eternally, a tradition still maintained in many Hindu temples of India today. The eastern stretch of this wall shows the procession arriving before the judge of the dead, the god Yama (also known as Dharmaraja, King of Dharma) seated on his symbolic animal, the black water-buffalo. Here the flow of human beings, on entering the afterlife and being judged, separates into three streams: one of these continues into a series of hells reserved for those who have committed specific sins, while two ascend into heaven.

The four levels at which the struggle for *dharma* takes place are thus indeed laid out in a logical sequence: the universe at the creation of its miraculous contents, as perceived by Vishnu who created the universe itself; the achieved

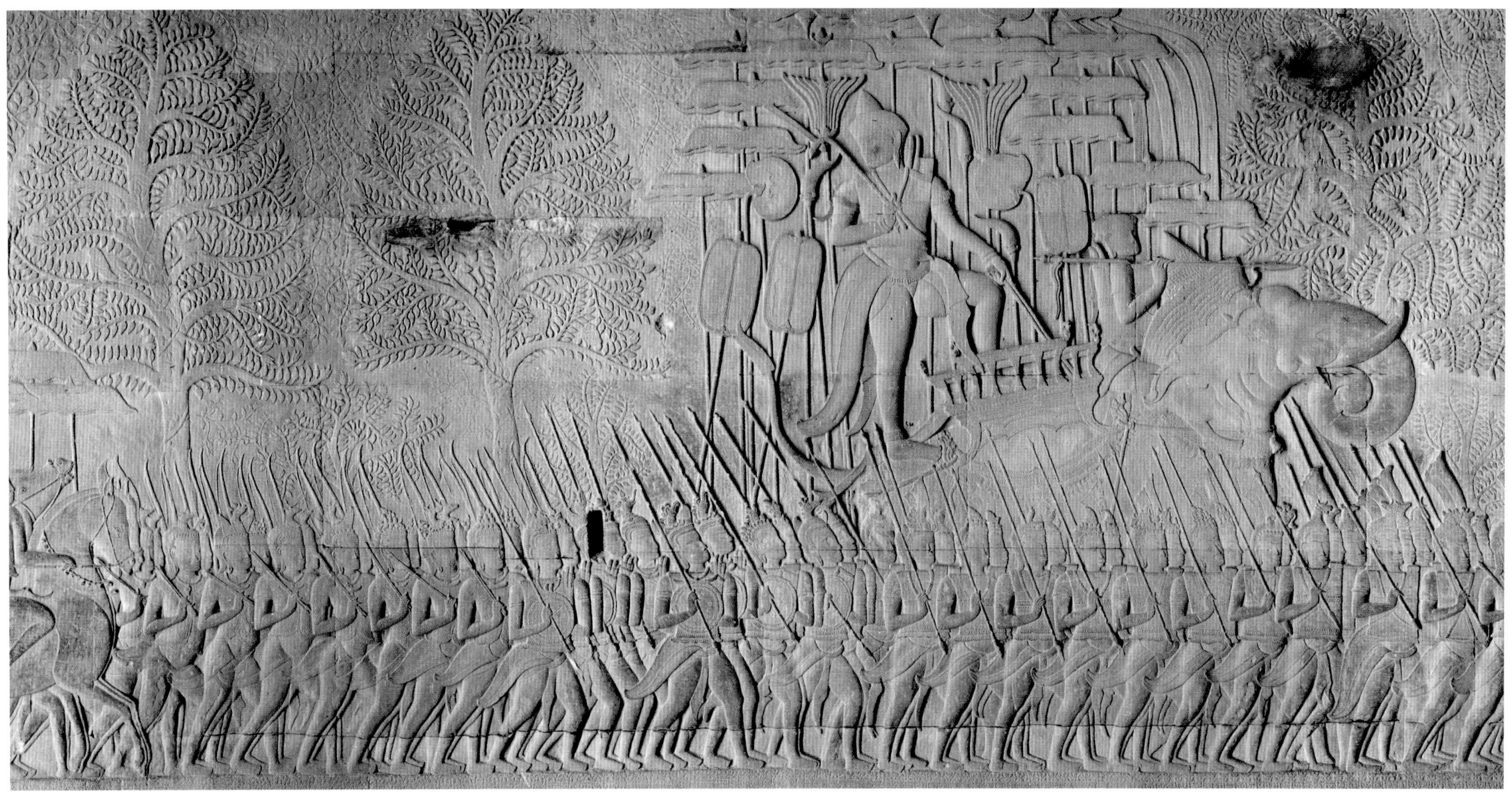

universe as the location of Vishnu's continuous struggle for the establishment and maintenance of order; the world of mortals, also conceived as a battlefield, but as seen from the standpoint of the incarnations of Vishnu when they intervene in its affairs to reestablish order; and the same embattled world as perceived by mortals themselves in their struggle to achieve order, in this life and the next. The first two series of reliefs represent the activities of Vishnu as creator and warrior at large in the cosmos, and the second two his activities in partly-divine human form in this world.

The reliefs are thus simultaneously a glorification of Vishnu the god, as self-transforming creator and defender, and a glorification of the king as one of the god's transformations. They identify the temple, for those who approach it from the city, as the palace of the god (it was known into the 16th century as Vishnuloka, "The World of Vishnu", as mentioned above), and the 12th-century inscriptions included in the southern reliefs identify the depiction of the king by his posthumous name of Paramavishnuloka or he who has departed for that world. The coherence of the reliefs is based on concepts operating at two levels: the conventional level, at which the traditional account of the sequenced ages of the universe is represented in terms of Vishnu's cosmic activities, and the meta-level of Suryavarman's official legend, in which he is both partially identified with these activities of his chosen deity, and regarded in death as inhabiting the eternal realm of that god. It is the depiction of this mystical connection between the king and his god that is the key to understanding the reliefs. They were not intended to constitute a detailed exposition of some unchanging theological system – the element of permanent continuity is provided by the yuga time-frame that starts in the east – but they were intended to represent the declaration of faith and

the mission statement of a powerful Vaishnava ruler who believed in war as his *kshatriya* duty, and in Vishnu as his warrior exemplar. And it was to experience this personal statement concerning the king that the reliefs had to be read in a sequence starting in the west. The visitor to the temple in this case turned right in front of the main entrance, passing the depiction of Krishna, with whom the Kali Yuga - that is, the present - begins, and then encounters the king and the theme of mortality along the south wall. The remainder of the reliefs, as explained above, then follow the *yuga* sequence from the beginning, providing the cosmic background to Suryavarman's deeds in the here and now.

It is therefore most probable that both of these circumambulatory sequences were employed in the ritual functioning of Angkor Vat. The priests who sustained the temple as a living place of worship would have observed a dawn ceremony in which the *yuga* sequence was invoked, starting in the east, whereby the temple was located within the time-cycles leading from creation to the present; while visitors to the temple from outside would have followed the same *prasavya* sequence but starting in the west, and in so doing would have encountered Vishnu through the eyes of the king, his principal devotee. For the purposes of this book the reliefs will be presented in the *yuga* sequence, beginning with the dawn of creation and ending with the afterlife of human beings, since this may be especially useful for readers encountering Hindu thought, and Angkor Vat, for the first time.

CREATION OUT OF CONFLICT:

VISHNU AT THE CHURNING OF THE OCEAN

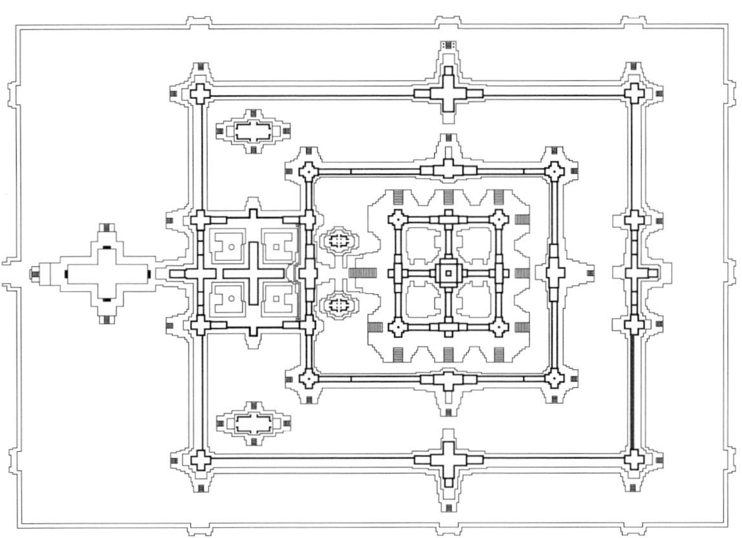

East Gallery, South Wing

CREATION OUT OF CONFLICT:
VISHNU AT THE CHURNING OF THE OCEAN
Krita Yuga

The Churning of the Ocean is not a creation myth in the sense that it deals with the origin of the universe. It is concerned with a mythic event in the history of the created world. That event represents a quest – as fascinating and motivating to many today as it was thousands of years ago – for freedom from disease and old age, for health and eternal youth: in a word, the quest for immortality. For this, as the myth so vividly portrays, the mortal gods will sacrifice wealth, the natural environment, and the lives of others. In the Indian stories, the pursuit of immortality involves the uprooting of mountains, the destruction of life in the sea and on land, the burning of forests, self-denial, deception, seduction, unholy alliances, war, and the mobilization of supernatural forces. Immortality, says the myth, is real, but it can only be won on these terms, and proceeds to tell the story of how, in a bygone age, the gods first set about winning it. The method they devise is to churn the ocean until the secret of immortality comes to the surface in the form of a potion. The strategy is to involve the demons in the churning, for the sake of their added strength, but later to deprive them of their share of the ambrosia.

The act of churning can be seen as a modified version of the ancient sport of tug-of-war, in which two teams of athletes pull on opposite ends of a rope in the attempt to pull their opponents over a central line. In the villages, milk is churned using the same principle, but with this difference, that in the centre the rope is passed around a pole which stands vertically in a pot containing the milk.

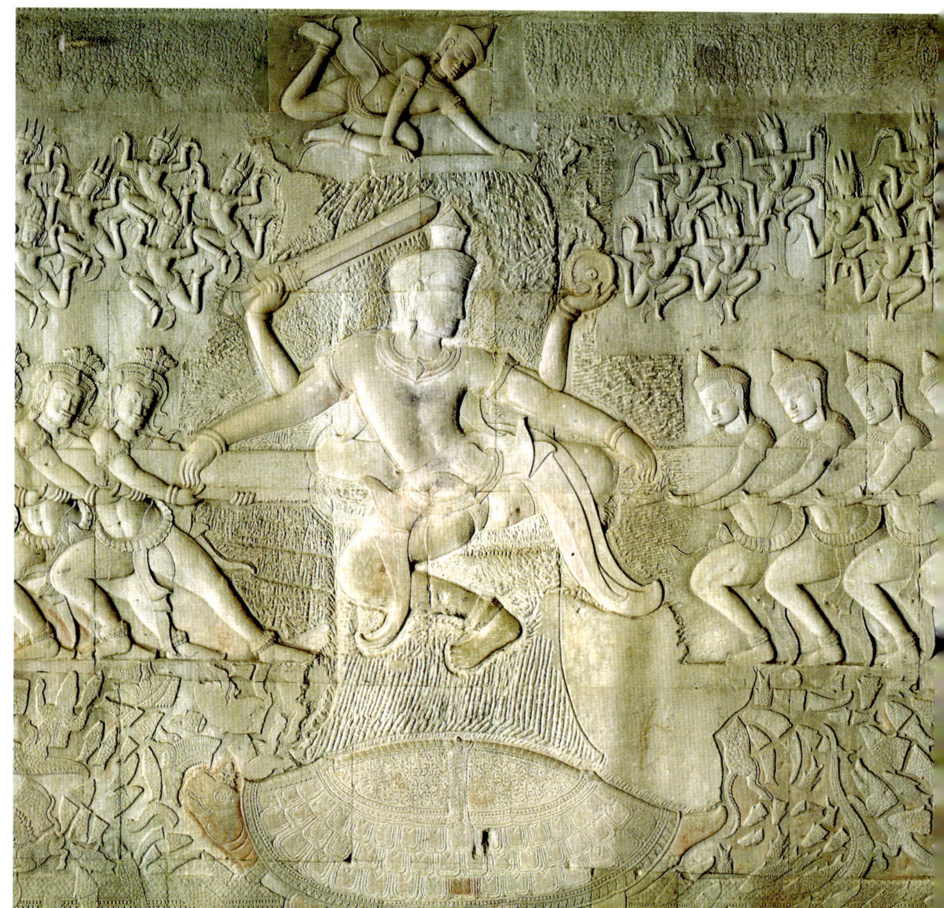

16

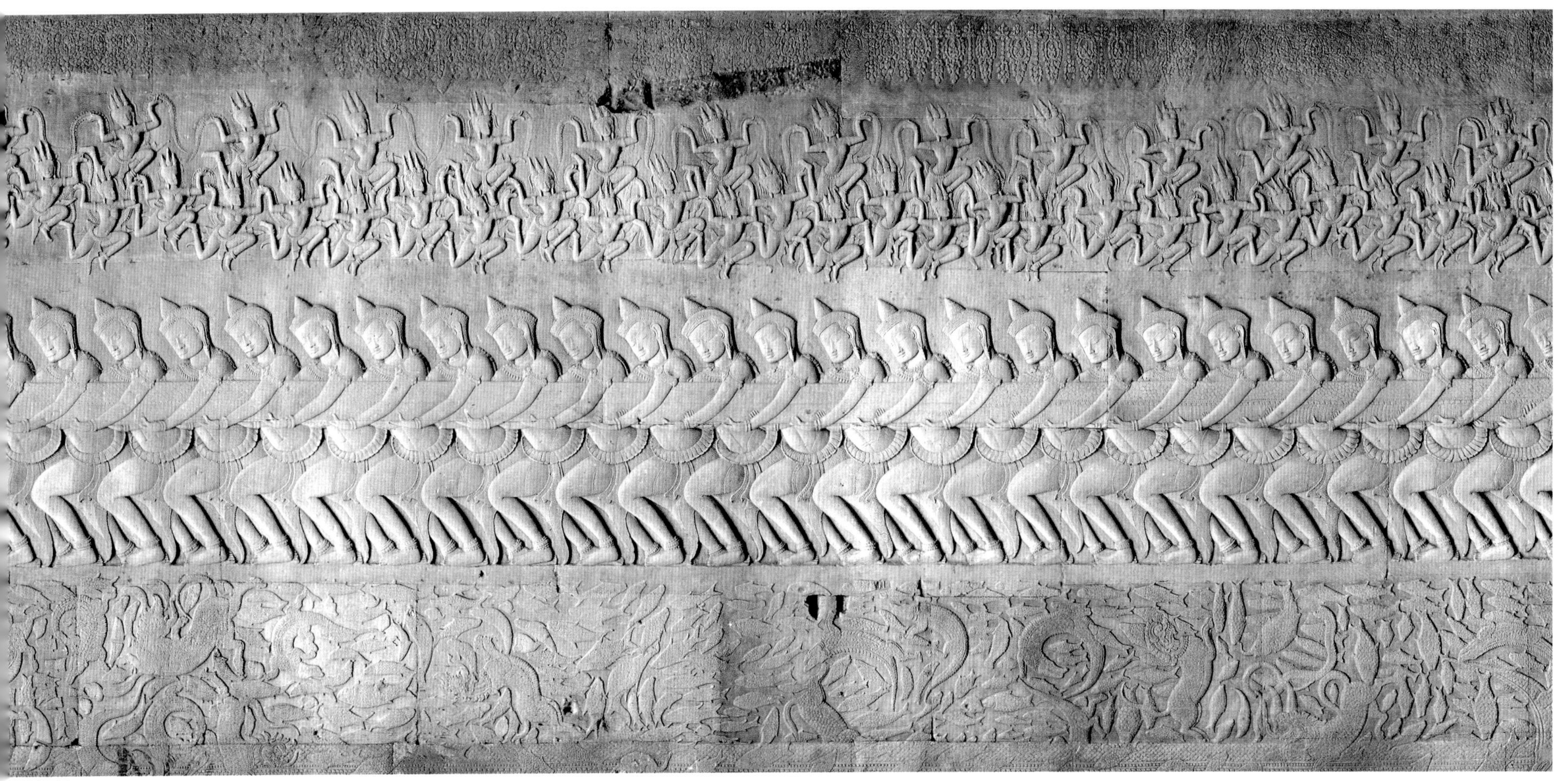

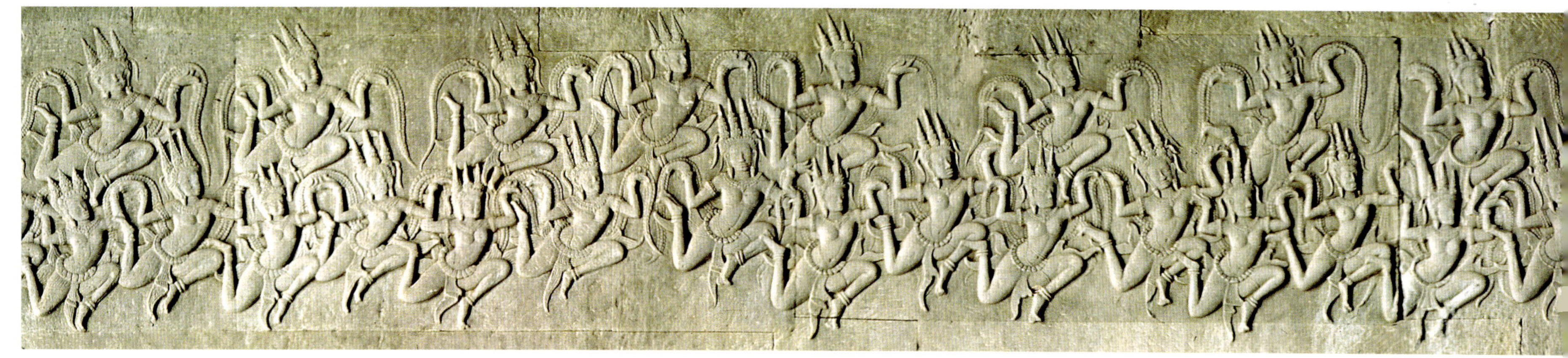

When two persons, usually women or elderly men, pull alternately on the ends of the rope, the pole rotates in the pot, and hence the milk is churned into buttermilk. The genius of the ancient mythmakers lay in the dramatic reinterpretation of this simple act as the mechanism for the creation of the world's miraculous contents. Within the developed story, the genius of the gods, especially Vishnu – renowned for his wily, Odysseus–like stratagems – lies in his introduction of an axis (identified with himself) in the form of a mountain as churning rod, into the eternal war between gods and demons, so that the energies of the two opposed groups are converted from antagonistic struggle to creative purpose.

But there is more than one story. The Hindu textual tradition preserves, in the form of carefully structured and dramatically narrated myths, numerous accounts of the creation of the universe and of the world with its miraculous contents. These variant versions were composed at different historical moments within the evolution of Indian thought and religion, so that each reflects a changed cultural horizon and operates on the basis of new sets of symbolic values. In this way each new version incorporated certain elements from earlier narrations, while interpreting them differently and also introducing original material. The story of the churning of the ocean began to assume the form in which we know it today during the period when the two great Indian epics, the *Ramayana* and *Mahabharata,* were being compiled (c. 300 BC – 300 AD), each epic poem developing a different formulation of the same basic concept. In this long epic phase, Hinduism as we know it today was still in the making. Its myths and legends reflect the dynamism of a new society forming itself out of a vast

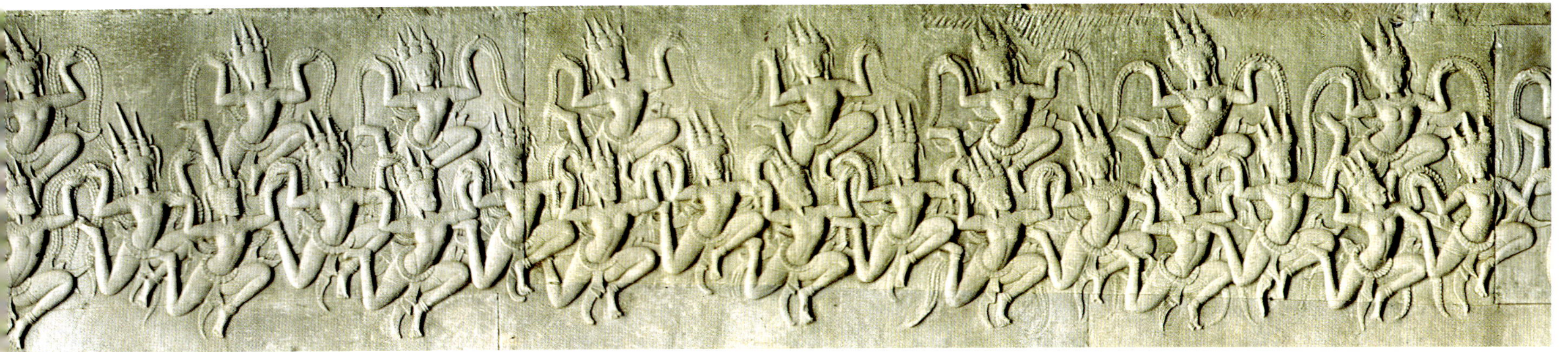

and ancient conceptual world, a world full of disparate perceptual and structural categories waiting to be reconciled with the challenges of the present. Those challenges included the perceived movement of society from a fragmented past toward a unified future, from a world of invisible forces controlled by ritual toward a pantheon of personal gods made visible and responsive to human needs. The depiction of the stresses involved in the attempt to weld everything together recurs time and again as one of the dominant themes of the mythology. The churning of the milk-ocean is no exception.

One of the earliest versions of the myth is recorded in the *Harivamsa*. In this story, the demons attempt to uproot a mountain named Mandara in order to churn the ocean with it. Finding themselves incapable of doing so, they turn to the omnipresent spiritual power, the god Brahma, for advice. It is he who directs them to enlist the additional strength of the gods in order to achieve their purpose. For a thousand years the gods and demons then use the mountain and the giant serpent named Vasuki to churn the sea, which is transformed from salt water into milk, and then from milk into the drink of immortality, in Sanskrit called *amrita*, the winning of which is the primary object of the whole operation. The drink thus produced is at first kept by the demons, but then won from them by the gods whose leader, the warrior-god Indra, acting on the advice of Brahma, presents it to the world. A similar early narrative, with significant variations, can be traced in the *Ramayana,* in which the ocean is regarded from the outset as a sea of milk. The first versions of the myth thus operated chiefly with the symbols ocean – mountain – serpent (conceived of as milk, churning-stick, rope), in a universe that was fraught with the opposition between gods and demons and in which the supreme power was the omnipotent but impartial Brahma, with Indra as commander of the gods who stood for order and the preservation of life. They dealt through metaphor with the theme of transformation in an old-world concept of the universe to which neither the god Vishnu nor his cosmic powers were relevant.

It is the great Indian epic, the *Mahabharata,* which records a more developed story, and this is the version which was to form the chief basis of the later and better-known narratives of the encyclopaedic Indian texts known as *Puranas*. At least a summary reading of the ten most significant elements in this key Sanskrit narrative is therefore necessary in order to understand the sources of the Angkor Vat relief. The epic formulates the story as follows. 1: The gods assemble on Mount Meru, axis of the worlds, to discuss ways and means of acquiring the *amrita,* so that they might become immortal. To assist them, Vishnu advises Brahma that both the gods and the demons together should churn the ocean, after all the precious stones and healing herbs of the natural world have been added to it to create the mixture - a kind of cosmic soup - from which *amrita* can be extracted. 2: But the gods are unequal to the task of uprooting Mandara, the mountain that is to serve them as the churning rod, so at the request of Vishnu and Brahma the Serpent King named Ananta ("Endless"), who lies at the very bottom of the world, performs this feat for them. 3: Gods and demons then ask the Turtle King, Akupara, and the king of the gods, Indra, to provide the lower and upper supports for the mountain, and the ocean itself agrees to

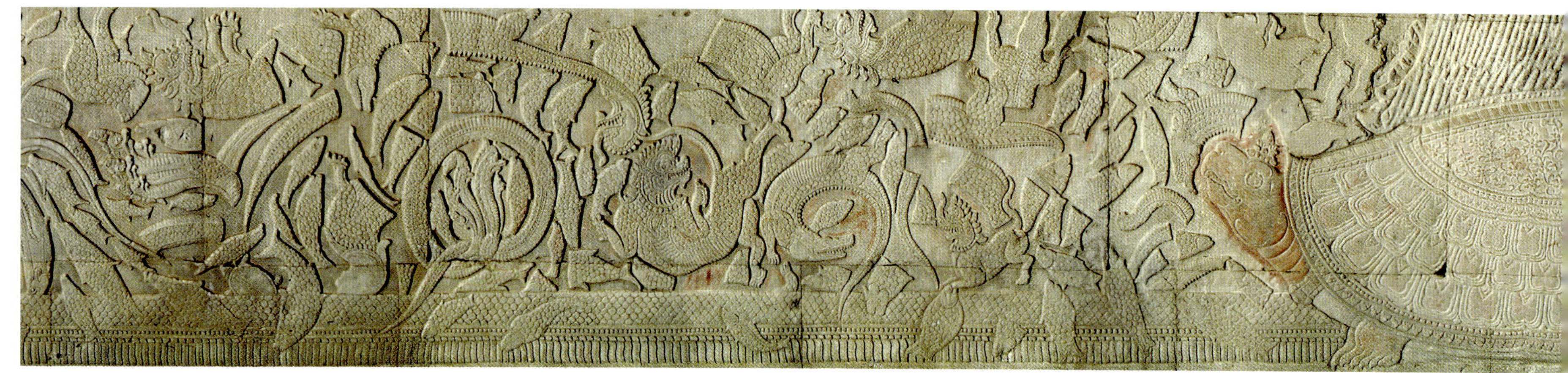

be churned on condition that it also receives a share of the *amrita*. 4: A second Serpent King, Vasuki, the brother of Ananta, is used as the rope to cause the mountain to revolve, the demons taking up positions at his head, the gods at his tail. 5: As they heave alternately on the serpent, both teams are covered with flowers shaken from the mountain. Fire and smoke emitted from the serpent's mouth in the course of the churning form storm clouds over the demons, but the ensuing downpour cools the gods, who are weakening. 6: The churning process is destructive: at the foot of the mountain, aquatic creatures in the ocean and in the underworld are destroyed by its violent rotation, while above, the creatures inhabiting its slopes perish as the whole mountain is engulfed in flame when the trees on its slopes fall and catch fire. 7: The juice of all the sap and molten gold flowing down from the burning mountain is charged with the power of the *amrita* which will change the gods into immortals, but as it enters the sea, it only turns the water into milk which, as the churning continues, becomes butter; there is still no sign of the drink of immortality. 8: At this, the exhausted gods protest to Brahma and declare that only with Vishnu's help can the *amrita* now be obtained. Accordingly, Vishnu confers the extra strength which the protagonists need to continue the churning. 9: As this proceeds with renewed vigour, the treasures at last begin to appear: the moon, the goddesses Lakshmi and Sura, the white horse called Uccaihsravas, the jewel named Kaustubha and, finally, the long-awaited *amrita*, contained in a pot held by Dhanvantari, the physician of the gods. 10: The demons struggle violently among themselves for their separate portions of the magical drink, but here Vishnu again intervenes, transforming himself into a deceptive female shape of such seductiveness that the bemused demons give

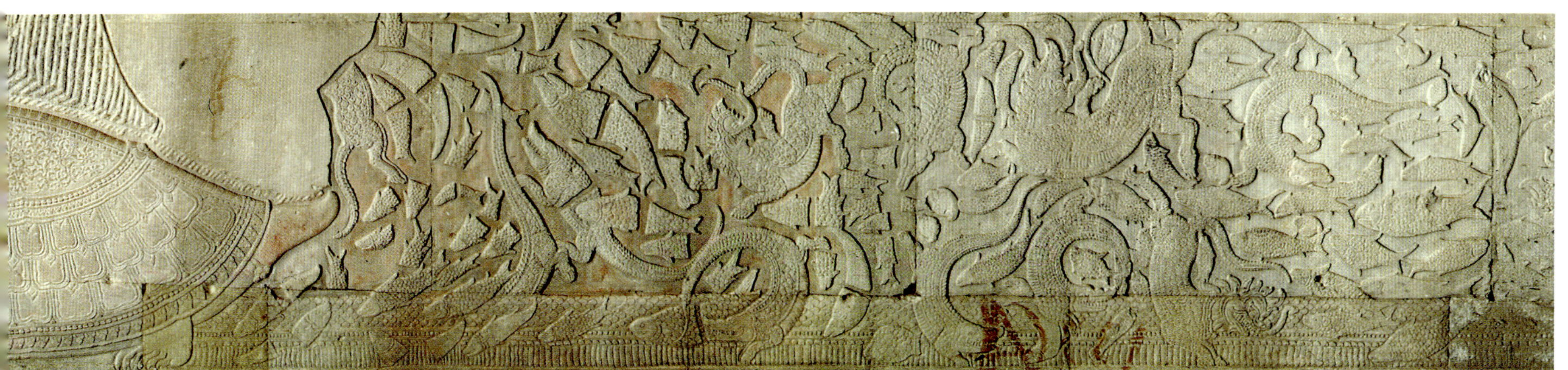

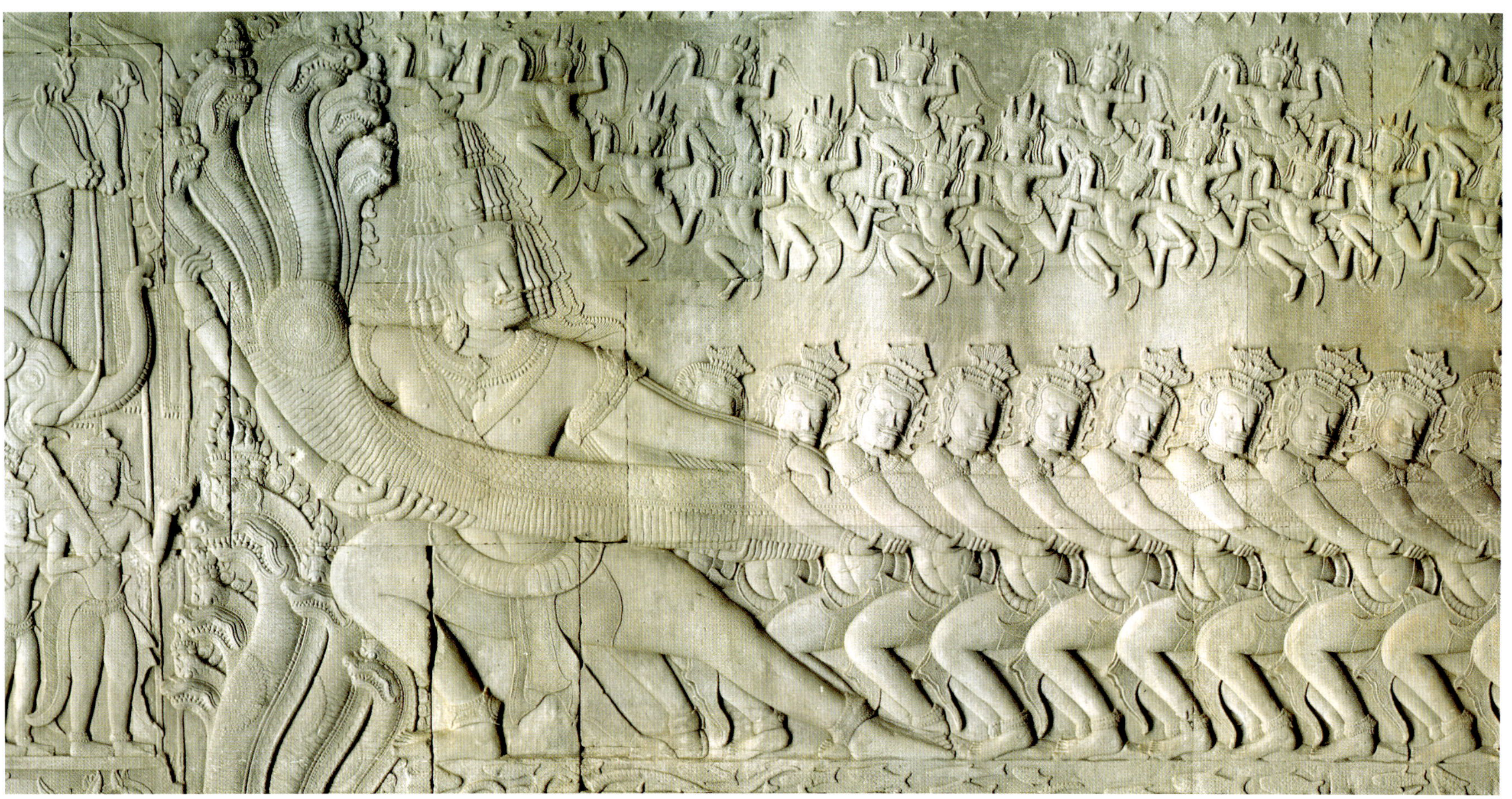

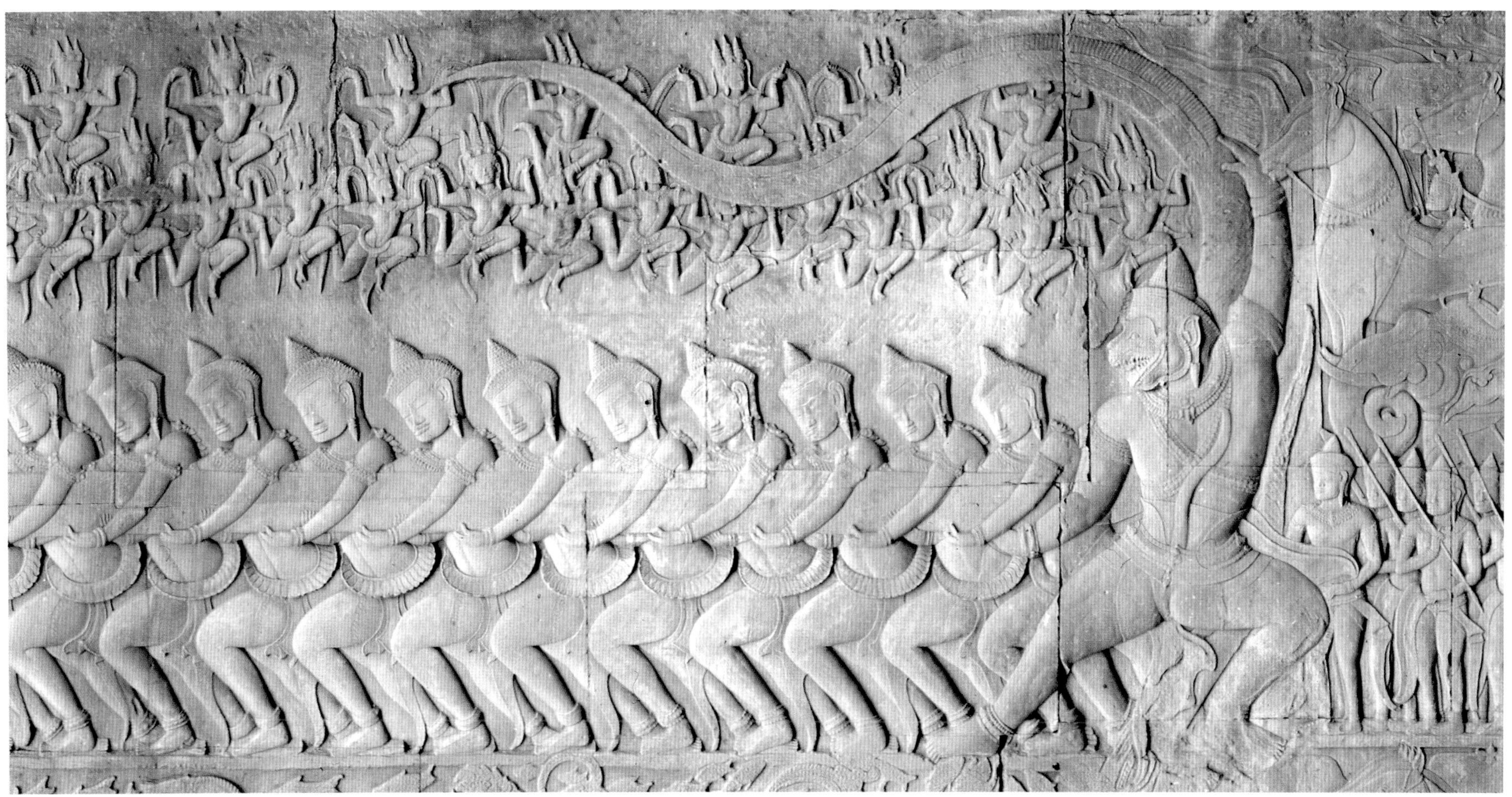

up the *amrita.* Vishnu presents the potion thus won to the gods, who drink it. There follows the episode concerning the demon Rahu's unsuccessful attempt to partake of it in the guise of a god, and a final battle in which all the demons are soundly routed, after which Indra hands the *amrita* back to Vishnu for safekeeping. But the complete Vishnuization of the Churning myth, based largely upon this *Mahabharata* narrative, is first recorded in the later *Vishnu-Purana,* where all the action is made to hinge on Vishnu himself, who usurps the roles played by other key figures in the earlier versions. Here, it is he who transforms himself into the Turtle to provide the mountain-axis with its basis. He also assumes further visible forms in order to lend his strength to both teams of protagonists, appearing in the midst of the gods, but also in the midst of the demons, as they pull in opposite directions on the body of Vasuki. In this version it is Vishnu also who holds the mountain firm from above, in a form invisible to both gods and demons.

The depiction of the scene – including Vishnu's metaphoric identification – is brilliantly achieved in the Angkor Vat relief. Both the anchor-man and the two captains of the demons are shown with towers of heads representing the uncontrolled rage that characterizes their ferocious nature; while the gods, urged on by the primeval aggression of a giant monkey, yet controlled by two unruffled captains, seem almost unaware of the titanic struggle in which they are engaged. The contrasting moods that the two teams represent, epitomise the iconographic distinction between *devas* and *asuras* that had already been a hallmark of Hindu art for some seven hundred years when this Cambodian relief was carved. The identities of these six larger figures, three in the row of demons and a further three on the side of the gods, has given rise to considerable speculation. The *Mahabharata* version of the myth, however, makes clear that they

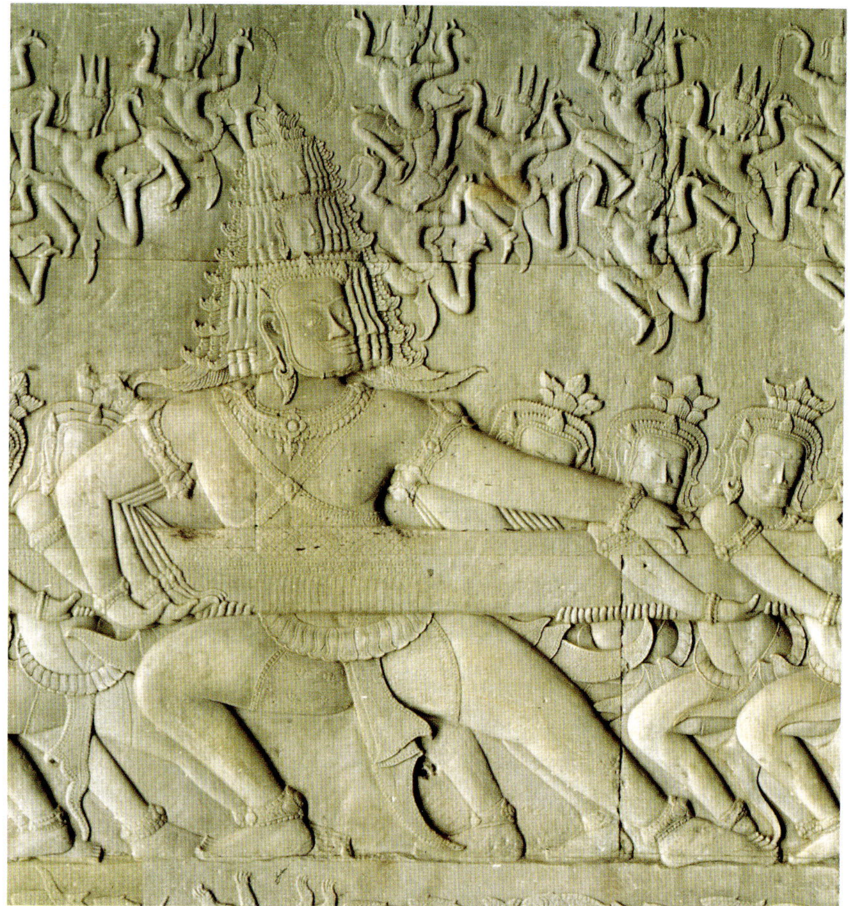

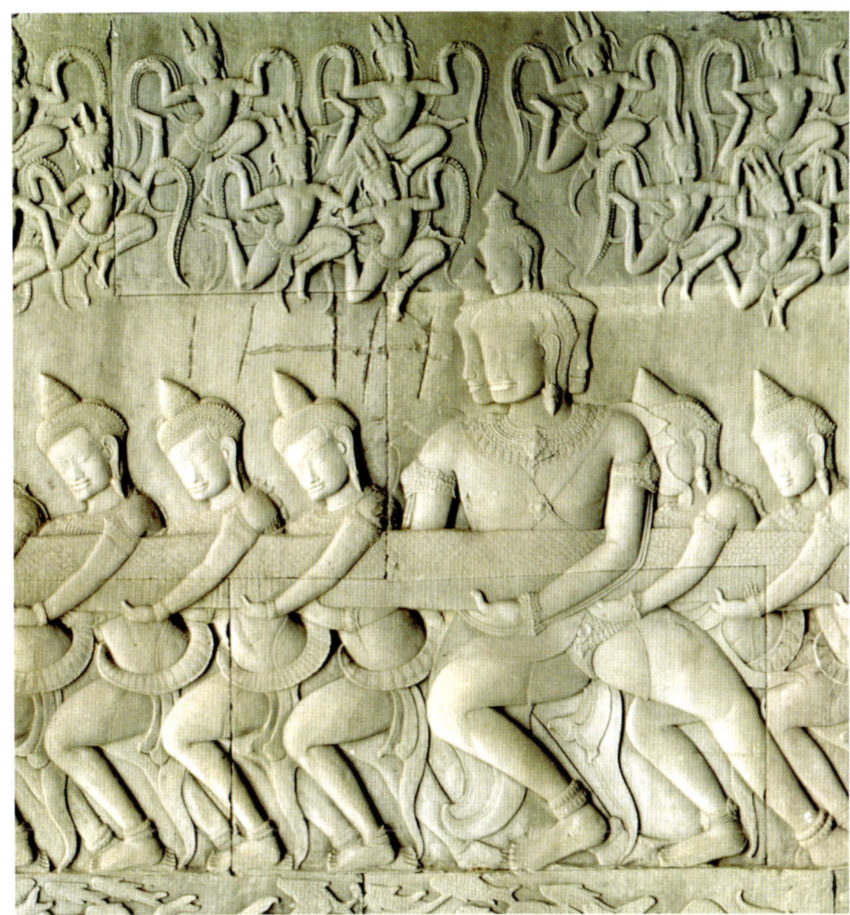

must be regarded as aspects of Vishnu himself, who transformed himself several times in order to participate in the churning on both sides. On the demonic side, these three giant figures are identical, each having twenty-one visible heads in three levels of seven. On the side of the gods, on the other hand, each of the three manifestations is different: the first from the centre has a single head, the second has four, and the third is the great ape. This visual distinction between uniformity and variety conforms to the old Vedic concept of the anti-gods striving for monolithic power, while the opposing gods stood for organised multiplicity. The identity of the monkey at the end of the line of gods in particular has been much discussed. This figure from the *Ramayana* can only represent Hanuman, the leader of Sugriva's monkey–army and ally of Rama, righteous and heroic incarnation of Vishnu. His image appears on the battle standards of no less than eight of the Khmer army generals in the relief of the Royal Procession (south gallery, west wing), sometimes in exactly the same posture as here, one arm stretched forward and the other raised above his head; a Hanuman standard is moreover carried in front of the sacred fire *(vrah vleng)* which precedes the king in the same relief. He therefore appears here on the side of the gods as a symbol of generalship and the martial defence of order. The depiction of him fanning the gods with the serpent's tail, which he wields like a huge banner, is a reference to the cooling winds that sustained the Devas during the churning: Hanuman was the son of the wind-god. Several versions of the myth speak of the contrast between the fiery atmosphere emanating from the heads of the serpent, where the demons were positioned, and the cooler environment at its tail, to which the gods were assigned. Regarding the serpent itself, this creature appears to be represented twice: once at the very base of the relief, and again, as churning rope, in the hands of the antagonists. Coedès interpreted these two depictions in terms of time: according to his interpretation, we see Ananta first before the churning, and then again during it. As we have noted, however, the *Mahabharata* version of the myth names two serpents: Ananta (also known as Sesha), guardian of the deepest levels of the underworld who alone can uproot the mountain, and Vasuki, his brother, who serves as the churning rope. It appears more likely that their relative positioning – beneath the base of the mountain and coiled around it – was intended to indicate that two serpent-kings with separate identities are depicted. The long horizontal axis of the relief, although at first perhaps appearing monotonous, as Coedès perceived

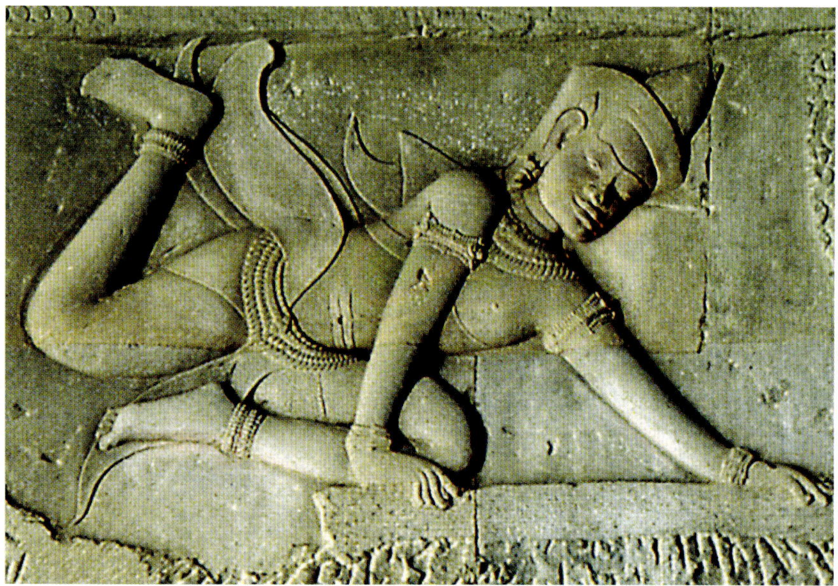

it, thus in fact contains many subtle references to the polarities and oppositions that generate the dynamism of the visual narrative.

At the centre of this relief, the elements of its vertical axis again derive directly from the Indian texts. The Turtle King, Akupara, as an incarnation of Vishnu yet wearing a lotus-bud crown in acknowledgement of his ancient royal status, supports the uprooted mountain on his shell. Mount Mandara itself is outlined, but no detail has been filled in. The head of the remarkable whirling figure of Vishnu superimposed upon it is also not completed, but his contorted anatomy was depicted by a master sculptor. The head is turned to the observer's right, to face the gods, the upper torso with its four arms is shown from the front, while the body below the waist and the legs are seen from the back, the left foot braced on the mountainside, the right leg bent up around it in a supporting embrace above the coiled body of the serpent. It is not possible to interpret this posture as turning in one particular direction, for the artist has used Vishnu's body as a symbol to represent his superhuman strength in holding up the mountain and simultaneously to personify it as an axis rotating first in one direction, then in the other. On his chest he wears the ocean-born Kaustubha gem, supported on a wide necklace, and his two upper hands wield two of his weapons, the sword Nandaka and the disk Sudarshana, their names signifying Rejoicer and Resplendent. In their forms and actions, these attributes express separately the two qualities of the mountain-axis which Vishnu combines in his body: the straightness of the sword and the whirling of the disk. Their innately destructive character as divine weapons – the pure sword of Brahma that defeats other metals, the all-consuming fiery disk of Agni – was used by Vishnu in his wars against the demons, and his display of these particular attributes

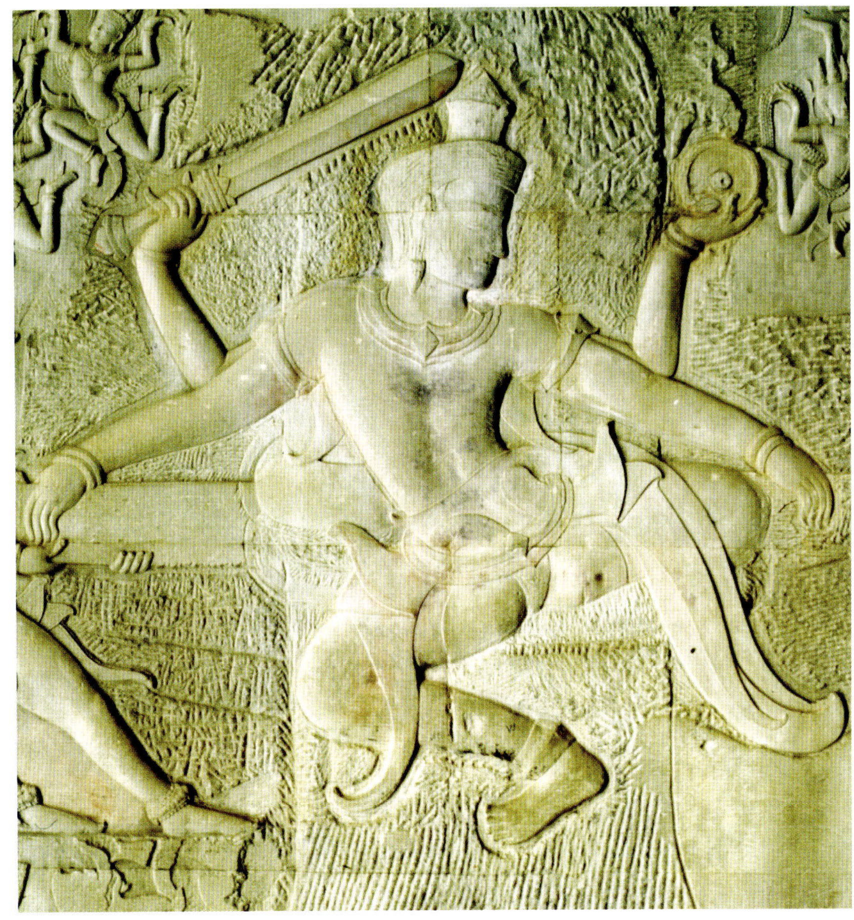

in his raised hands is a direct assertion of his alliance with the gods, belying the even-handedness with which his lower arms stabilize the churning-rope on both sides.

There is no doubt that the crowned figure depicted in the classical flying posture descending on the summit of the mountain represents Indra, king of the gods. In the *Mahabharata* narration he is specifically mentioned:

"The gods and demons said to the Turtle King, Akupara, 'You, Your Majesty, should be the foundation for the mountain.' The Turtle consented and placed it on his back, while Indra pressed down on the summit of the mountain with a *yantra*" (*Mahabharata,* Critical Edition, 1.16.10–11)[1].

Perhaps better known in the sense of *mandala,* this word *yantra* essentially means a support or tool for holding something fast, a stabilising construction. This the Khmer sculptors working at Angkor Wat interpreted as a flat block with which Indra is indeed shown pressing down on the peak of Mandara. Indra functions here as the counterpart of the turtle at the lower end of the axis, so that the mountain is stabilised both from above and below. Just as the turtle on the ocean floor is surrounded by fish, caught up in the turbulence and cut to pieces by the violent action of the rotating mountain, so Indra is surrounded in the serenity of his heaven by the seductive *apsaras* who, produced from the ocean by the churning, inhabit his court.

This tripartite axis vertically bisects three horizontal levels. They depict three different forms of tranverse movement – the anarchic and aimless

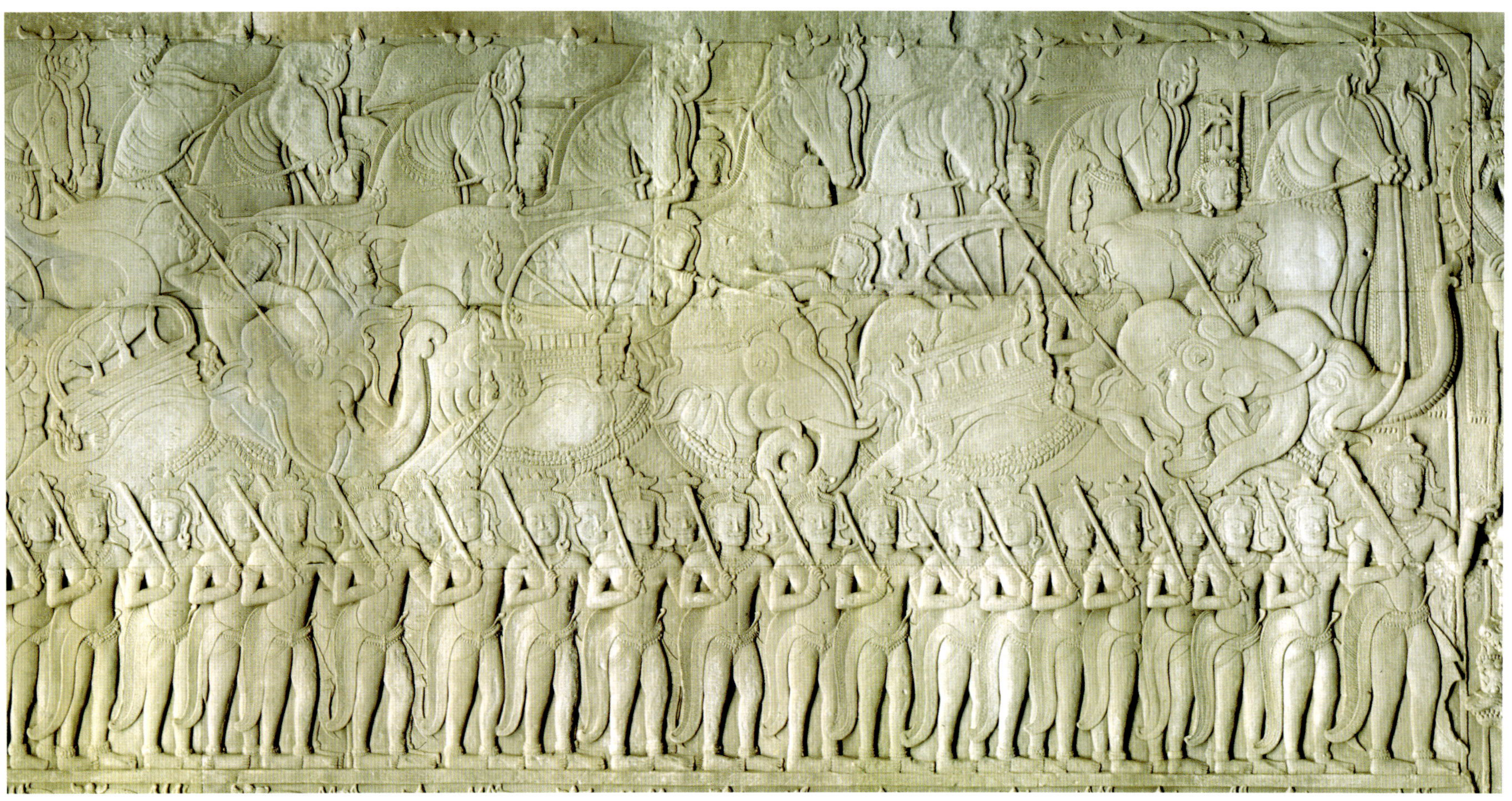

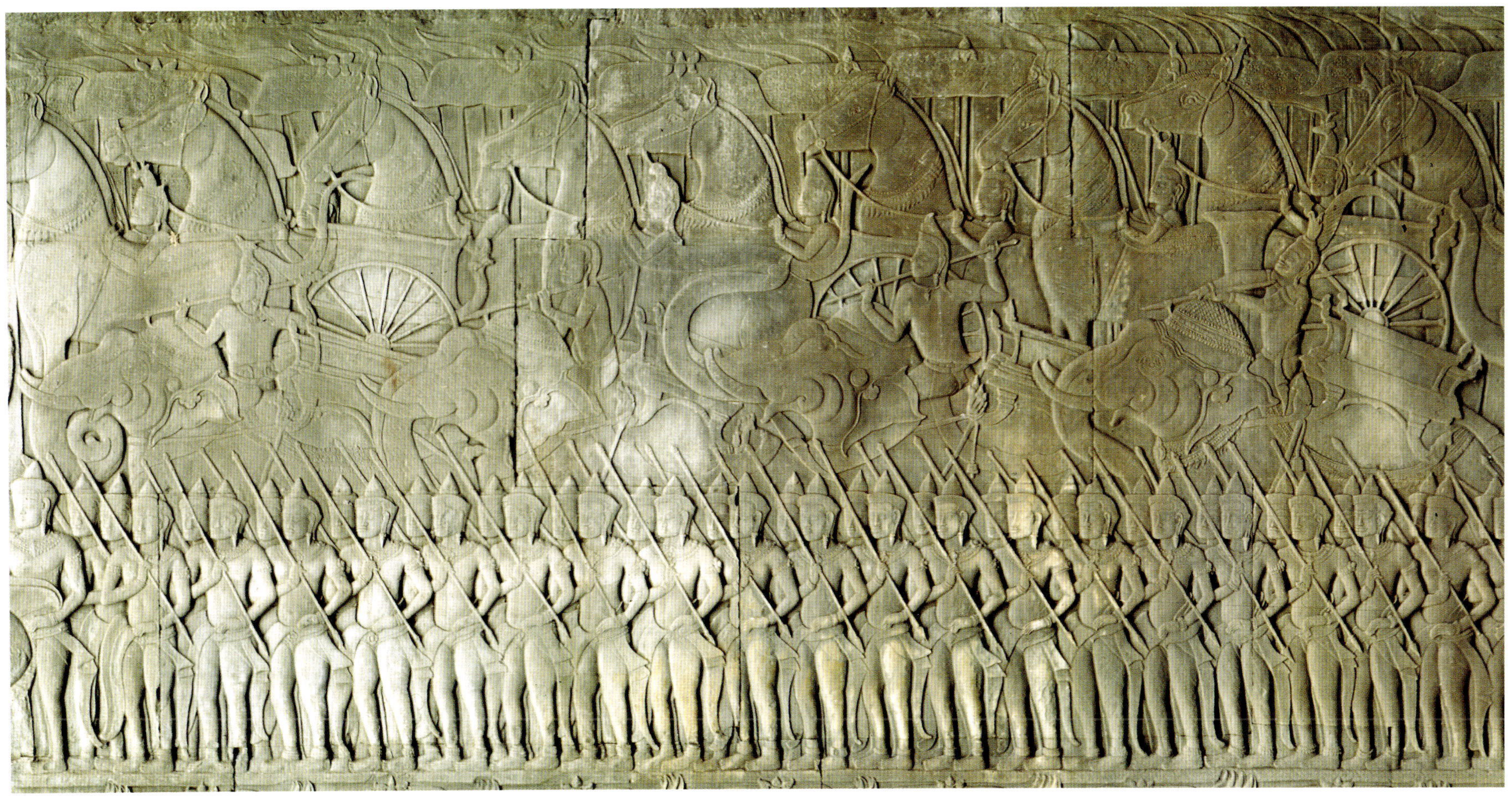

teeming of fish in the substratum (anarchy is defined in Sanskrit as *matsyanyaya,* "the law of the fishes"), the polarization of forces in the struggle between gods and demons in the middle level, and the perfectly ordered freedom of the *apsaras* flying above. The centreline, scene of the titanic struggle, divides pre-existent chaos from created order. These two conditions are conceived of as transparent elements, water and air respectively, symbolized by the fish and the *apsaras.* The defining middle ground, the vast horizontal axis of the whole composition, is the arena of combat. Its outcome can take the form of chaos (should the demons win) or order (should the gods prevail). Both potential results are vividly portrayed. It is to assure victory for the forces of order, for the gods, that the mountain rises as the vertical axis. Its function is to convert the endless opposition between antagonistic forces into a decisive result: the defeat of anarchy and the establishment of order as the cosmic law. The means by which this can be achieved lies in the metaphor of churning on which the story is based. If the gods relentlessly churn the obstructed seas of anarchy, the free skies of order will result, ensuring their own immortality: they will always defeat the demons, and hence order, not chaos, will become the fundamental rule governing the universe. The obvious parallels with human affairs make this mythological scene into an unmistakable political statement. The policies of state, directed by the king, will bring about an ordered society. The relief depicting the Churning of the Ocean provides this assertion with mythological background and religious authority, embedding it in a coherent narrative located in cosmic time and space. The king is Vishnu, and Vishnu is the conquest of death and disorder.

Seen in this light it becomes less surprising that elements of the central scene were left unfinished. The figures that in the myth were created by

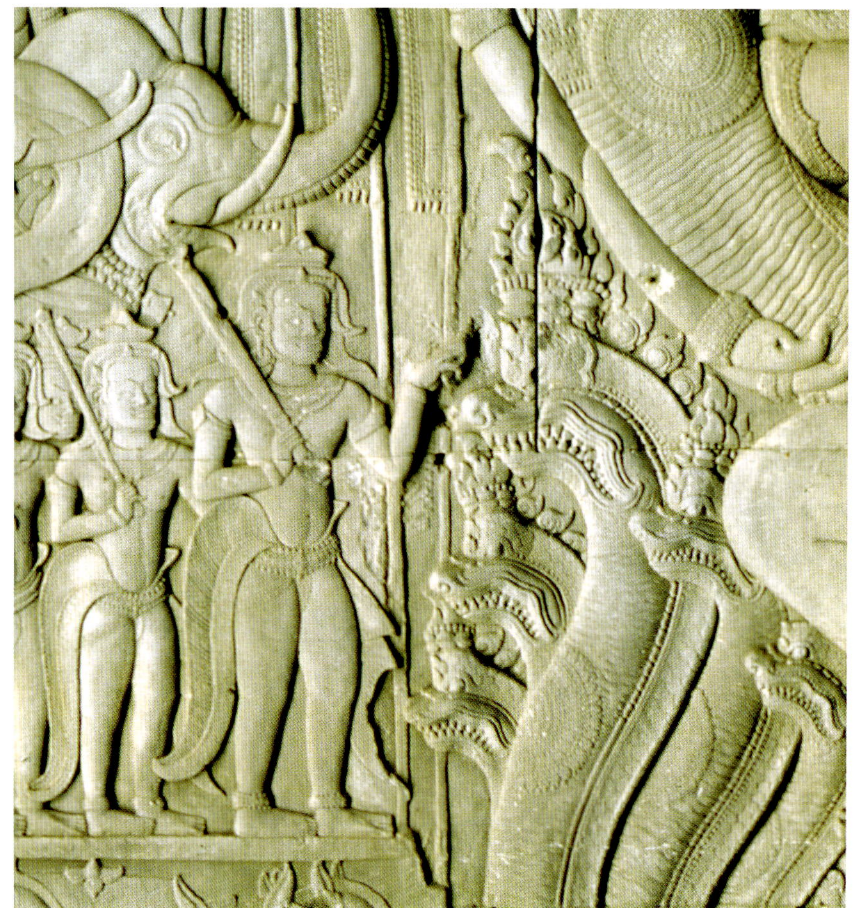

the churning – the celestial creatures and goddesses, and even the *amrita* itself – were either depicted in the relief as very small, accessory figures adjacent to the mountain, or not represented at all. Spaces were deliberately left or created beside the mountain, starting from the shell of the turtle (where some of the fish on the left side were cut off to make a workable surface) and extending up to its summit next to the first *apsaras,* in order to provide free surfaces on which they could be depicted, but the work stopped at that point. Mount Mandara, the very axis of the composition, was marked out and hatched as a column with spreading base and rounded summit (flattened by the pressure of Indra's *yantra*), but was never carved out in detail. Vishnu himself, although his anatomy was brilliantly planned and represented with extreme care, is also an incomplete figure, lacking definition in the depiction of his face and crown. Above and below him, on the other hand, the flying figure of Indra and the huge turtle Akupara were sculpted in intricate detail and are almost fully finished individual reliefs. There is no doubt, as we have seen above, that the Khmer sculptors had detailed knowledge of original Sanskrit narratives containing the story of the churning. So why this hesitation in depicting the results of it, and in defining the facial features of Vishnu? It looks very much as if the main statement was considered to have been made with the depiction of the ocean and the sky and of the struggle between them, and that the details of the outcome of the churning, which might seem so important to us, were regarded as mere accessory matter. They were certainly left to the last, yet the intention clearly was to show them, and a few experimental figures were indeed carved on the hatched area to the right of the mountaintop, as if to indicate the scale and placement of them when work should be resumed. This suggests that work was not stopped suddenly by unforeseen circumstances, but was halted deliberately and temporarily while awaiting new information.

The necessity for all three of these colossal figures – Akupara, Indra, and between them Vishnu himself – to lend their combined and different strengths to the vertical axis emphasises the perilousness of the undertaking: a mountain uprooted from its fundament and suspended in air while being driven in wild rotation by the hostility between the forces of order and chaos. In a Vaishnava temple, however, as in a Vaishnava text, these numerous gods and demons, the antithetic stresses inherent in the world, are all considered ultimately to be manifestations of the one supreme Vishnu, and from this knowledge springs the aesthetic tranquility and balance with which the stormy event is depicted.

THE BATTLE OF PRAGJYOTISHA:

VISHNU–KRISHNA AND THE ARMY OF NARAKA

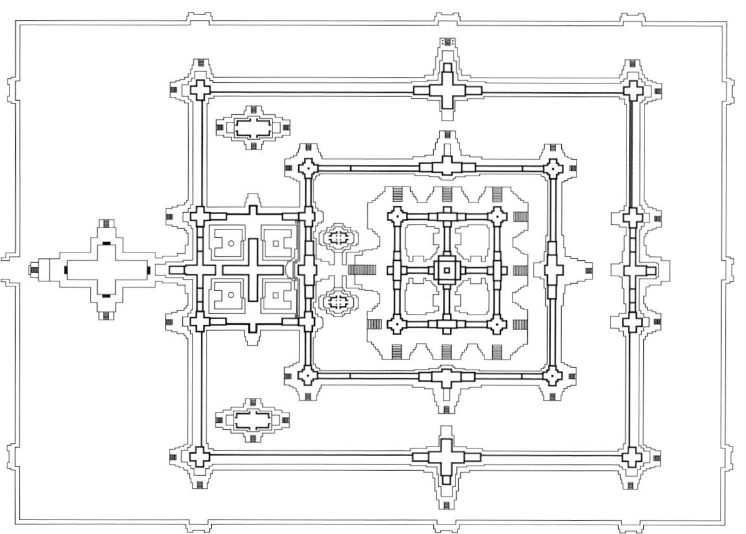

East Gallery, North Wing

THE BATTLE OF PRAGJYOTISHA:
VISHNU-KRISHNA AND THE ARMY OF NARAKA
End of the Krita Yuga, beginning of the Treta

There are two short inscriptions on the walls flanking the north-east corner of the third enclosure, and they refer specifically to the making of the reliefs on these walls, though not to their content. The inscription here on the east side is almost completely preserved, while that on the north is substantially damaged; the reading and interpreting of them, through new estampages and rubbings, is the work of George Coedès [2]. He published his results in 1962 in the *Journal Asiatique,* and they are still generally accepted. In his interpretation, the Khmer-language texts of these inscriptions run as follows:

East gallery, north side: "His Majesty Mahavishnuloka had not yet completed two panels; when His Majesty Brah Rajaonkara Paramarajadhiraja Ramadhipati Paramachakravartiraja ascended the throne, he charged Brah Mahidhara, of the royal artisans, with sculpting a narrative on the panels... in the 8th Saka year (of the decade), year of the Horse, Wednesday, full moon of Bhadrapada."

North gallery, east side: "His Majesty Mahavishnuloka had not yet completed two panels; when His Majesty Brah Rajaonkara Paramarajadhiraja Paramapavitra ascended the throne, he had a narrative sculpted. One strove to finish it in 1-4-8-5 Saka, year of the Pig, full moon of Phalguna, Sunday. The two galleries and balustrades were solidly completed (?) as in the past."

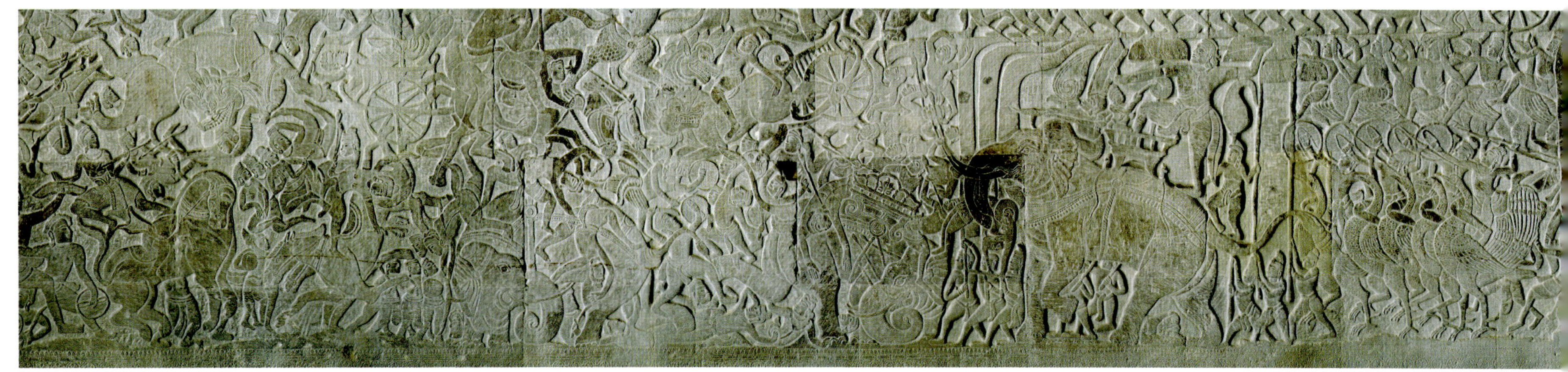

Both inscriptions begin with the statement that King Mahavishnuloka (recalling the name of Paramavishnuloka, the posthumous name of Suryavarman II, founder of Angkor Wat) had left these two panels (*phen byar* in the first text, *phdan byar* in the second) incomplete up to the time when a new king, represented by the lengthy string of Sanskrit titles beginning with Brah Rajaonkara in the first inscription, came to the throne. It was he, the later king, who then enjoined one of the royal sculptors *(rajasilpi),* named Mahidhara, to sculpt these unfinished panels anew (*punah chlak phen niyay; oy chlak niyay* in the second inscription). The two dates, marking the issuance of the royal command and the actual completion *(samrac)* of the two reliefs, define a period of some seventeen years in the 16th century: from Wednesday, 8th September 1546 to Sunday, 27th February 1564. The work was most probably initiated during the reign of the king known to the royal

Khmer chronicles as Ang Chan (*circa* 1529–1556 or later), who would correspond to the Brah Rajaonkara Paramarajadhiraja Ramadhipati Paramachakravartiraja of the first inscription. The "Paramapavitra" mentioned in the second inscription is not the personal name or title of a particular king, but part of a conventional expression *(samtec ta paramapavitra)* referring to the currently ruling monarch; this title could therefore indicate either Ang Chan or his son and successor, Paramaraja I, as the ruler during whose reign the new reliefs were completed. The dates of course indicate that the carving of the relief on the east side was undertaken first, that on the north side second; the work proceeded in counterclockwise direction.

The fact that these Hindu reliefs were supplied with inscriptions containing references to kings past and present, and precise dates, indicates the great

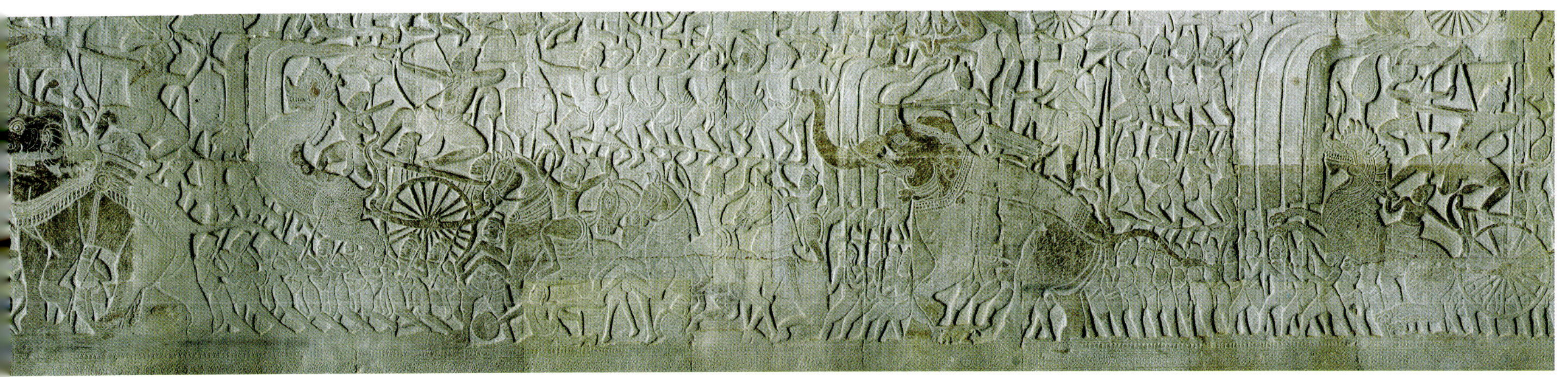

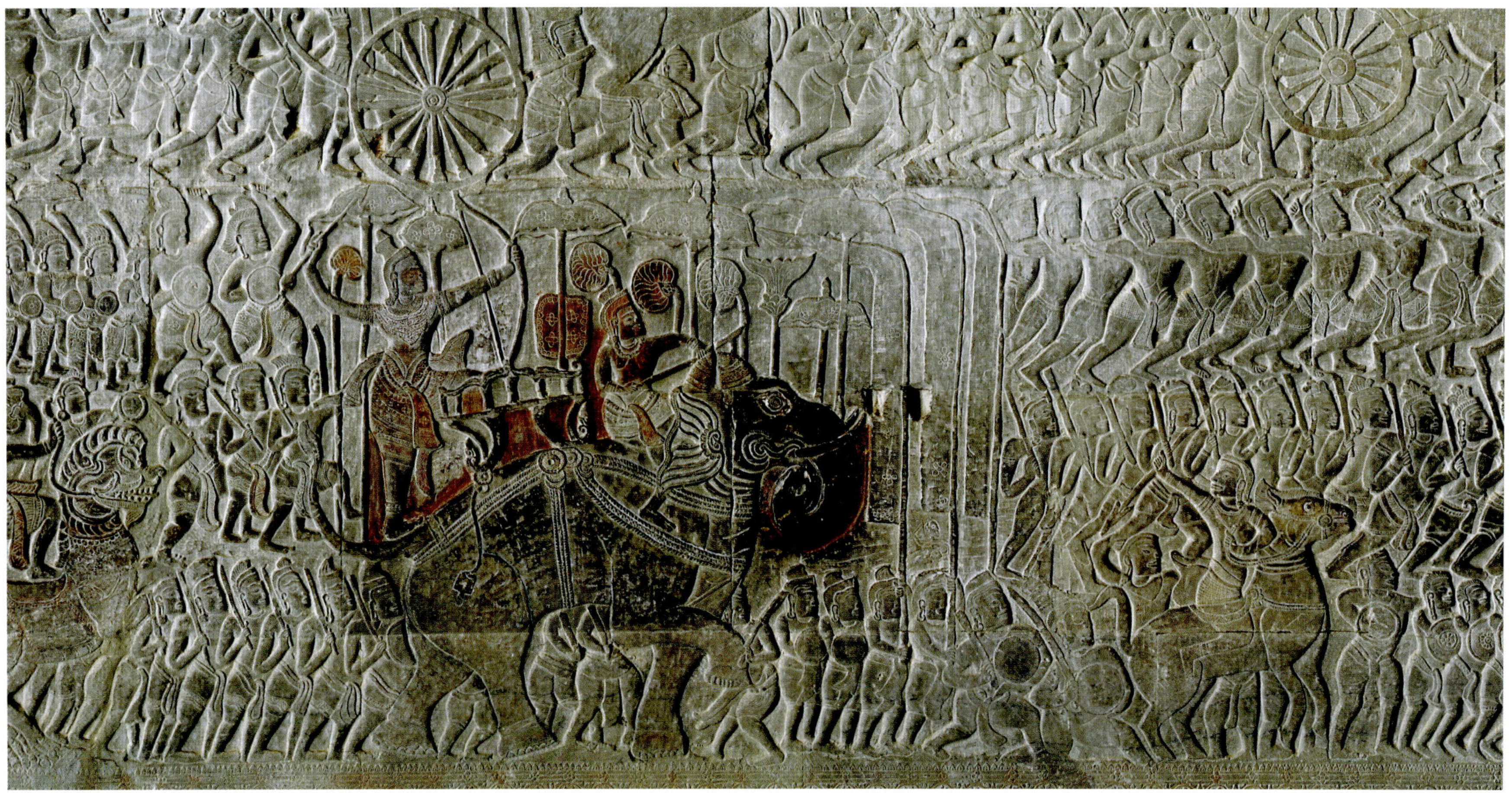

prestige and awareness of tradition that attached to this work in the 16th century. It was undertaken as a respectful act of restoration although Angkor had for several generations no longer been the capital, and despite the establishment of Theravada Buddhism in place of the earlier mixture of Hinduism and Mahayanism – contemporary and later inscriptions elsewhere in Angkor Wat itself testify to its use as a centre of Theravada piety, although it was still known to Buddhists as Brah Bishnulok, the Holy World of Vishnu, temple of the king who centuries before departed this life for that Hindu heaven. In the Theravada Buddhist society that Cambodia had become, the two missing north-eastern reliefs were supplied, in completion of the cycle of Vaishnava depictions of the 12th century, by Mahidhara at the command of Ang Chan, evidently as an assertion of national tradition. It is said that the incomplete panels first came to the attention of Ang Chan when he was in the Angkor region in 1540 to fight against a Thai invasion, which he successfully defeated; and that on a subsequent visit ten years later, while the work on the two panels was in progress, he rediscovered the ruins of Angkor Thom, royal city of Jayavarman VII centred on the Bayon, buried in the jungle to the north of Angkor Wat. One can well imagine the sense of shock that this confrontation with the colossal face-towers from the past induced in a king accustomed on the one hand to the relatively sober architecture of palaces and Theravada establishments, and on the other to the expansive elegance of Angkor Wat. It is interesting to note that, in the two and a half centuries between the reign of Jayavarman VII and Ang Chan's second visit to Angkor Wat, the enormous neighboring palace complex of Angkor Thom had so completely disappeared from Khmer memory that his viewing of Jayavarman's ruins ranked as a rediscovery. The sculpting of the new Angkor Wat reliefs to complete work left undone in the 12th century might therefore seem all the more unexpected. We might con-sider three reasons for this. In the first place, Angkor Wat – unlike most other ancient temples – had not disappeared from memory, but was in active use as a Theravada Buddhist establishment; secondly, Ang Chan's initiative conforms to the traditional concept of merit accruing to a king who restores the temples of his predecessors; and thirdly his work might also be seen as one aspect of a conscious desire to reclaim their heritage on the part of the Khmer élite, who evidently nurtured a sense of exile after the transfer of the capital from Angkor to the region south of the Tonle Sap.

It is against this background of social change and awareness of cultural loss that the aesthetic and iconographic shortcomings of the north-eastern reliefs have to be viewed. No stone temples had been erected at Angkor since the early 14th century, a period of more than two hundred years, when these reliefs were carved. It is not surprising to find that in the intervening period both the aesthetic sense and the sculptural techniques of the early 12th century, when the originals were created, had largely disappeared from memory and ability. It is, on the other hand, astonishing to discover that in a Theravada social context the Hindu mythological themes and their leading personae were still well remembered and could be depicted as narratives to bridge the long gap in the sequence between the Churning of the Ocean at the south-east corner and the great Battle of the Devas and Asuras in the north-west. These 16th-century reliefs broadly follow the same compositional principles and iconographic symbolism as the originals – they are divided into three horizontal registers and are punctuated at more or less regular intervals by identifiable chief characters - but despite the energy in the depiction of the figures the tense dynamic of the 12th-century works is no longer to be seen.

The fact that the two reliefs that were left unfinished were two which bracketed a corner is certainly significant. It appears that in considering the layout of their own temples, the Khmers thought, not in terms of whole sides, but of quadrants, each of which was divided into four equal squares. Thus in discussing the placement of sacred images, the inscriptions speak of corner areas described with reference to the intermediate directions. In the short shrine-inscriptions of the Bayon, for example, the rectangular courtyard structures, called *kutis,* are not called "the northern *kutis*" or "the western *kutis*", but (to take two examples) "the *kuti* in the north-west square of the north-west quadrant" *(vrah kuti uttaresanapaschima),* or "the *kuti* in the north-west square of the north-east quadrant" *(vrah kuti uttaresanapaschima)* [Bayon, inscriptions 5 (K) and 7 (M)][3]. In the relief galleries of Angkor Wat's third enclosure, the locations of the two unfinished reliefs would similarly have been thought of as *uttaresanapurva* and *uttaresanapaschima*: it was to the corners of the structure or complex that locational references were made, not to its sides. When we describe the Angkor Wat reliefs as being the "northern" or "eastern" reliefs, for example, we are applying our own spatial conceptions, not those employed by the Khmers, to whom they were "in the north [half]" *(uttara),* "of the north-east [quadrant]" *(isana),* "in the east [square]" *(purva)* or "in the west [square]" *(paschima).* This ancient conception of the location of the two unfinished reliefs in the north-eastern quadrant of the enclosure matches the locus of their narrative content: as we shall see, both depict the subduing of demonized kings ruling in the north-eastern territories of India. This has consequences for our understanding of the reliefs. Whereas each side of the rectangular enclosure represents a Yuga, each pair of reliefs bracketing a corner has a thematic unity. A corner stands for the juncture between two Yugas, and the two reliefs on each side of

that corner are to be understood as defining the transition from one Yuga to the next. In order to grasp the meaning of these reliefs it is therefore advisable to consider them in pairs, not only on each side of the enclosure, but also and more especially at the corners.

What we are shown in the first of these two later reliefs – in the eastern gallery's north wing, adjacent to the Churning of the Ocean – is Vishnu fully incarnated as Krishna mounted on his anthropomorphized eagle, Garuda, fighting alone against two armies of demons who converge upon him from opposite ends of the panel. It is difficult to relate the entirety of this scene to a specific mythological narrative in existing Hindu texts. Since the number of demons who are depicted being thrown down from their elephants to either side of the central Vishnu-Krishna figure is four, however, Coedès suggested that this battle most probably referred to an incident related in the *Harivamsa,* in which Krishna defeated the four Asuras Muru, Nisunda, Hayagriva and Pancanada before the city of Pragjyotisha[4]. This city lay to the north of the Lauhitya or Lohita river in Kamarupa (in modern terms, the Brahmaputra in Assam, in the extreme north-east of India between China and Burma), and was said to be ruled by a demon king named Naraka. The country of Kamarupa, being a remote and largely tribal border area, was regarded in the *Mahabharata* and *Ramayana* as a land of *mlecchas* – impure, non-Hindu foreigners – and demonized as an Asura kingdom. According to the *Kalika-Purana,* probably composed in the Assam valley, Naraka was born of the union between Prithivi, the Earth-goddess, and Vishnu in the form of his Boar incarnation (Varaha); yet as king, he took such a hostile attitude toward Hinduism and orthodox Vedic rituals that he even refused to worship the widely-renowned local goddess, Kamakhya-Devi. For this he was cursed by a

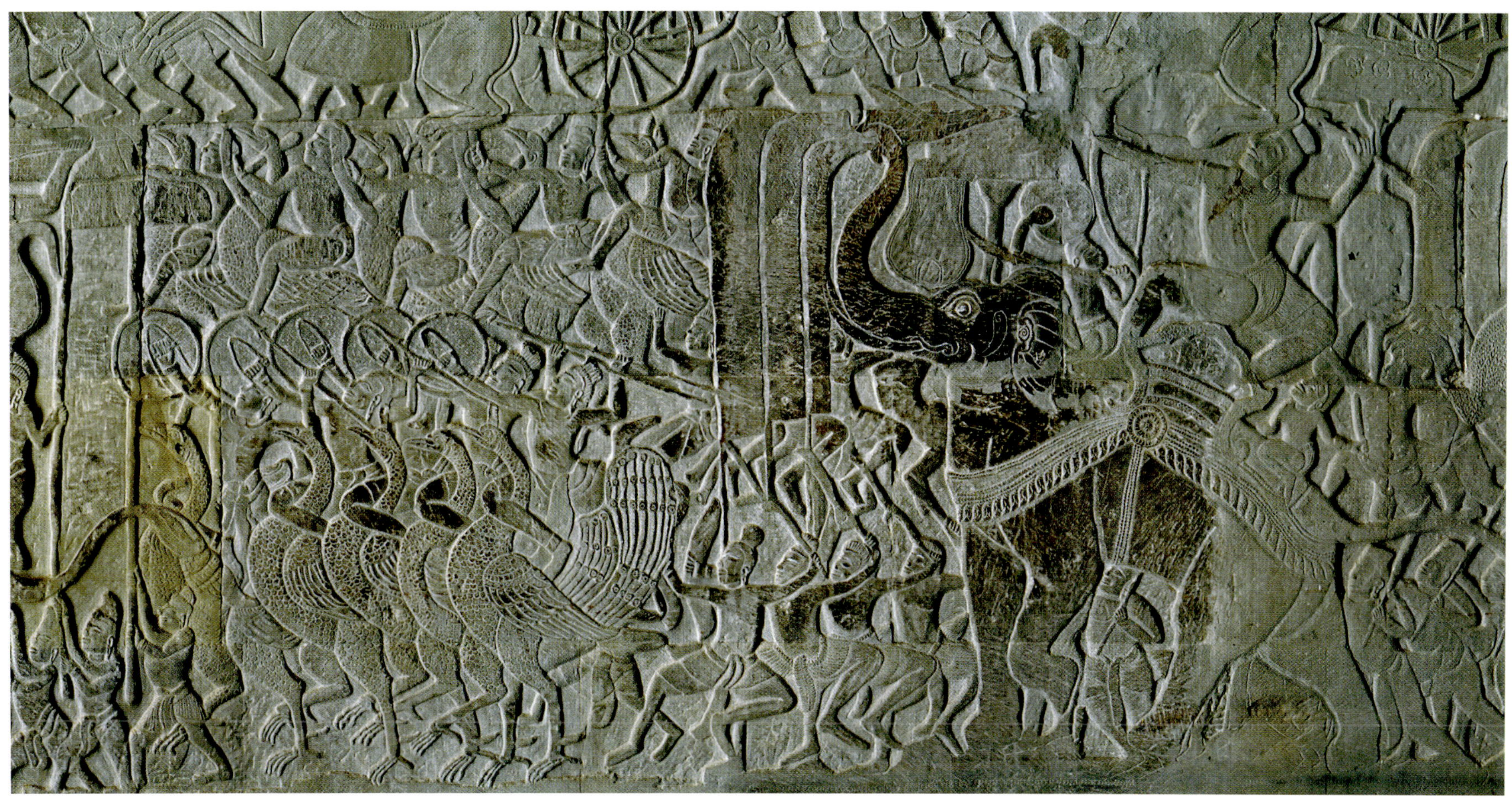

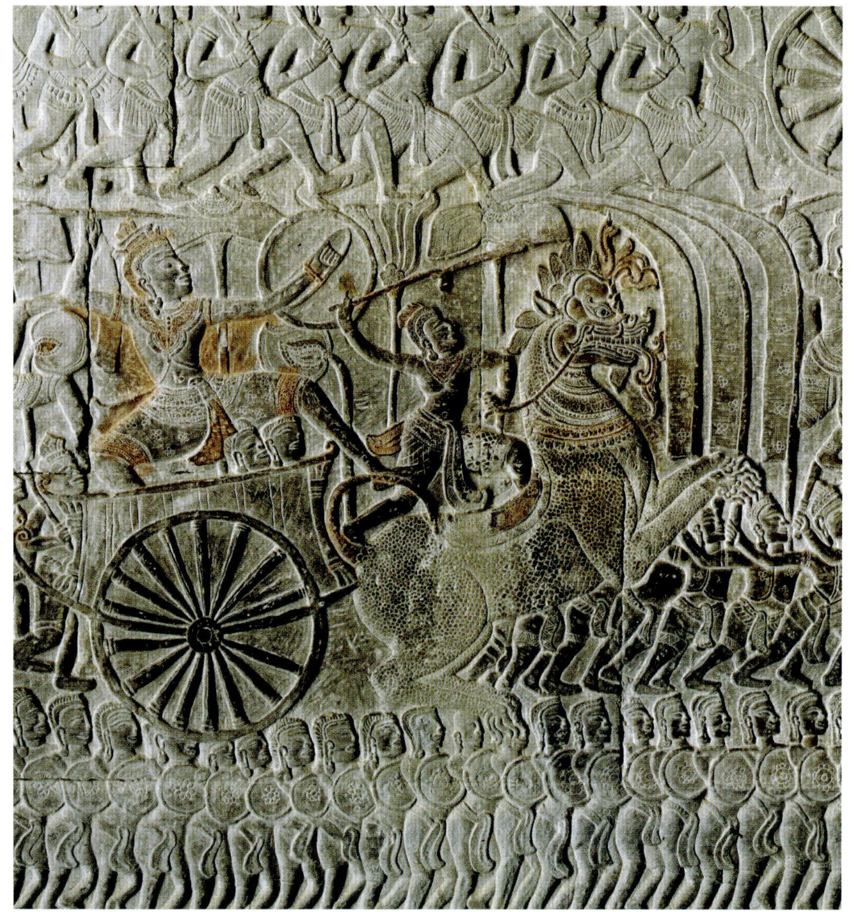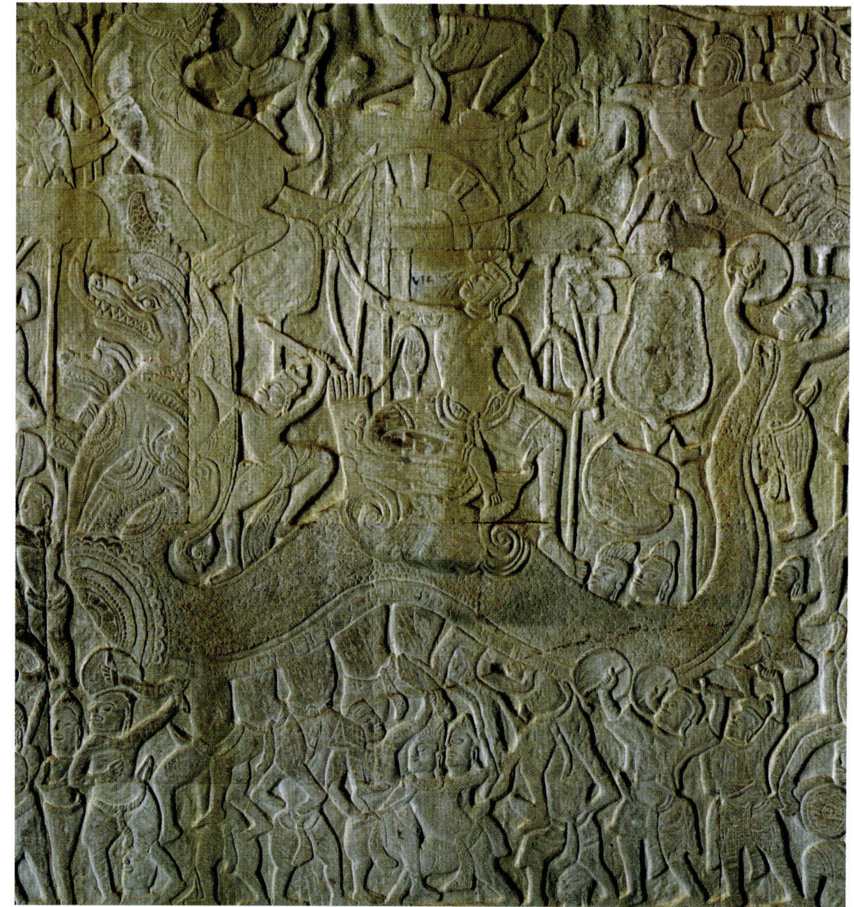

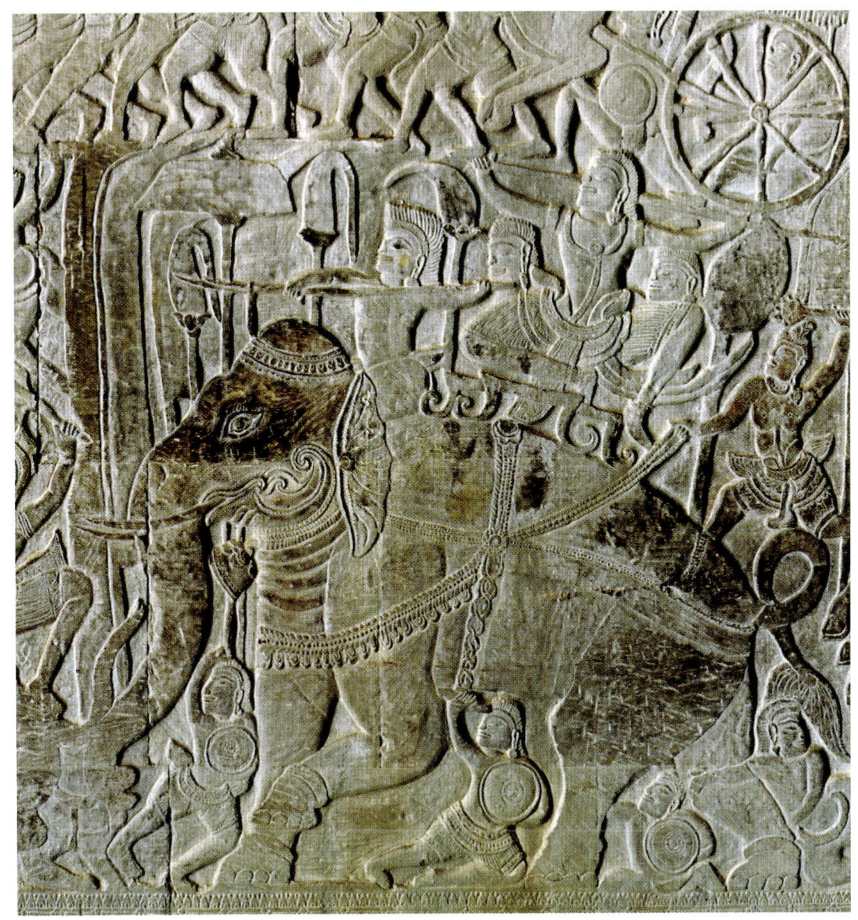

powerful *rishi* to die at the hand of his father. When, fearing for his life, he finally resorted to Kamakhya's temple, it was to discover not only that she had deserted her shrine, but also that his own parents were inaccessible to him. As his conquests increased, his mother, the Earth, complained to the gods that she could no longer bear the growing demon population and prayed to have this burden lifted from her. In fulfilment of the curse, the gods' reply was to send Krishna as destroyer to annihilate the demon horde – this is the subject of the present relief – and kill his son Naraka. It could well be the case that, Vishnu-Krishna being partly identified with the Khmer king, this scene was intended as a mythological reference to his battles against external enemies of the state – as we have seen, Ang Chan is said to have fought off a Thai invasion near Angkor shortly before these new reliefs were executed. In addition to the general assertion of Khmer national culture, which these reliefs certainly represent, a contemporary political statement may therefore also have been intended. Even if it is correct, as has been proposed, that Ang Chan's sculptors followed old original tracings or sketches left on the blank panels by Suryavarman's artists two centuries before, the symbolism and its relevance to the later political situation would still, like the mythological references, have been clearly recognizable.

The wider context in which this central defeat of the four leading demons takes place, consists of a furious convergence of variously mounted demons, none of whom can be identified in Indian terms. In their midst appears a group of four identical spear-bearers mounted on peacocks like multiples of the Hindu war-god, producing a particularly eerie effect. Their identity as Asuras is confirmed by their crested helmets but also through the infiltration of their battle formations, essentially consisting of war-elephants and horse-drawn

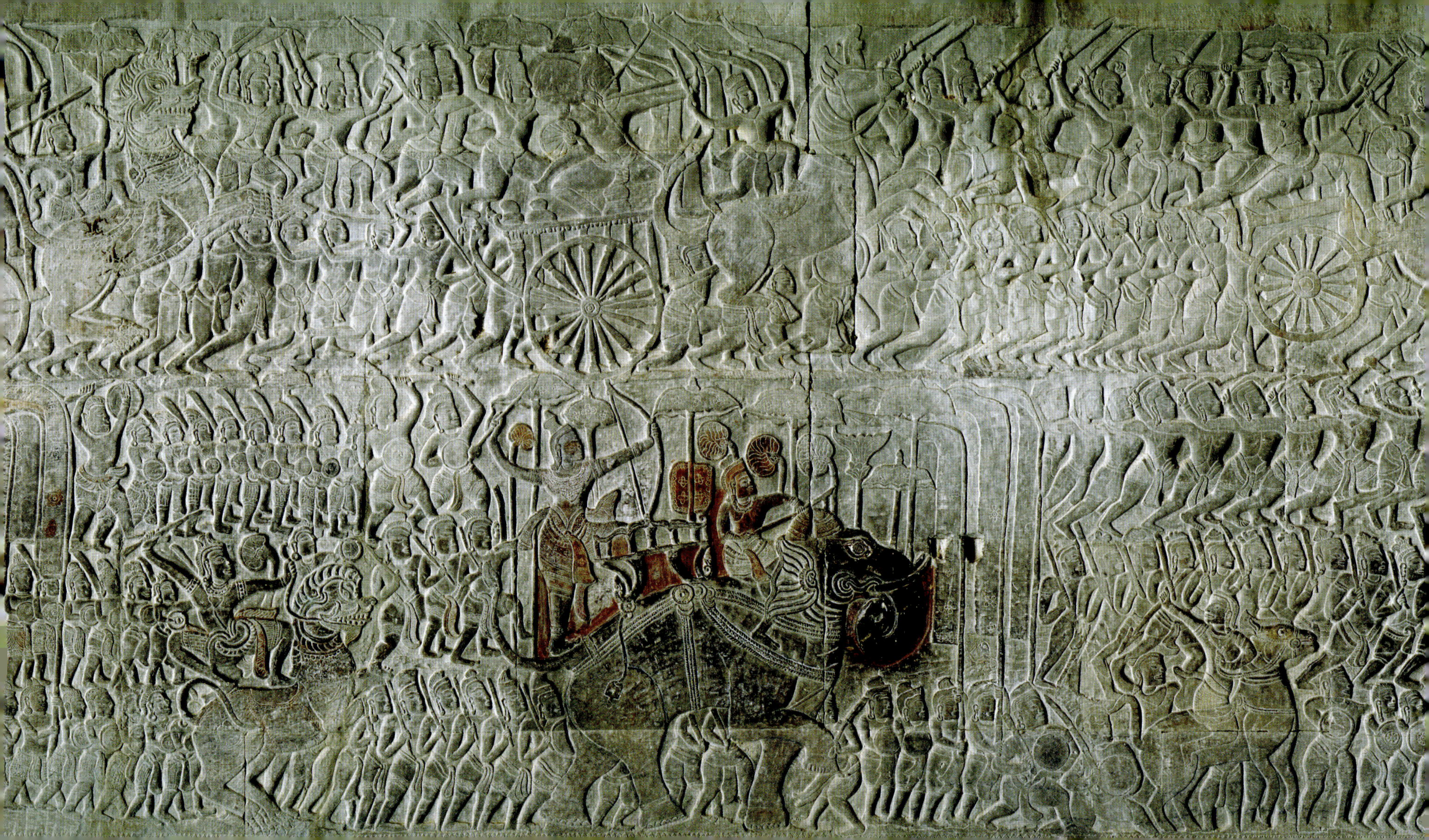

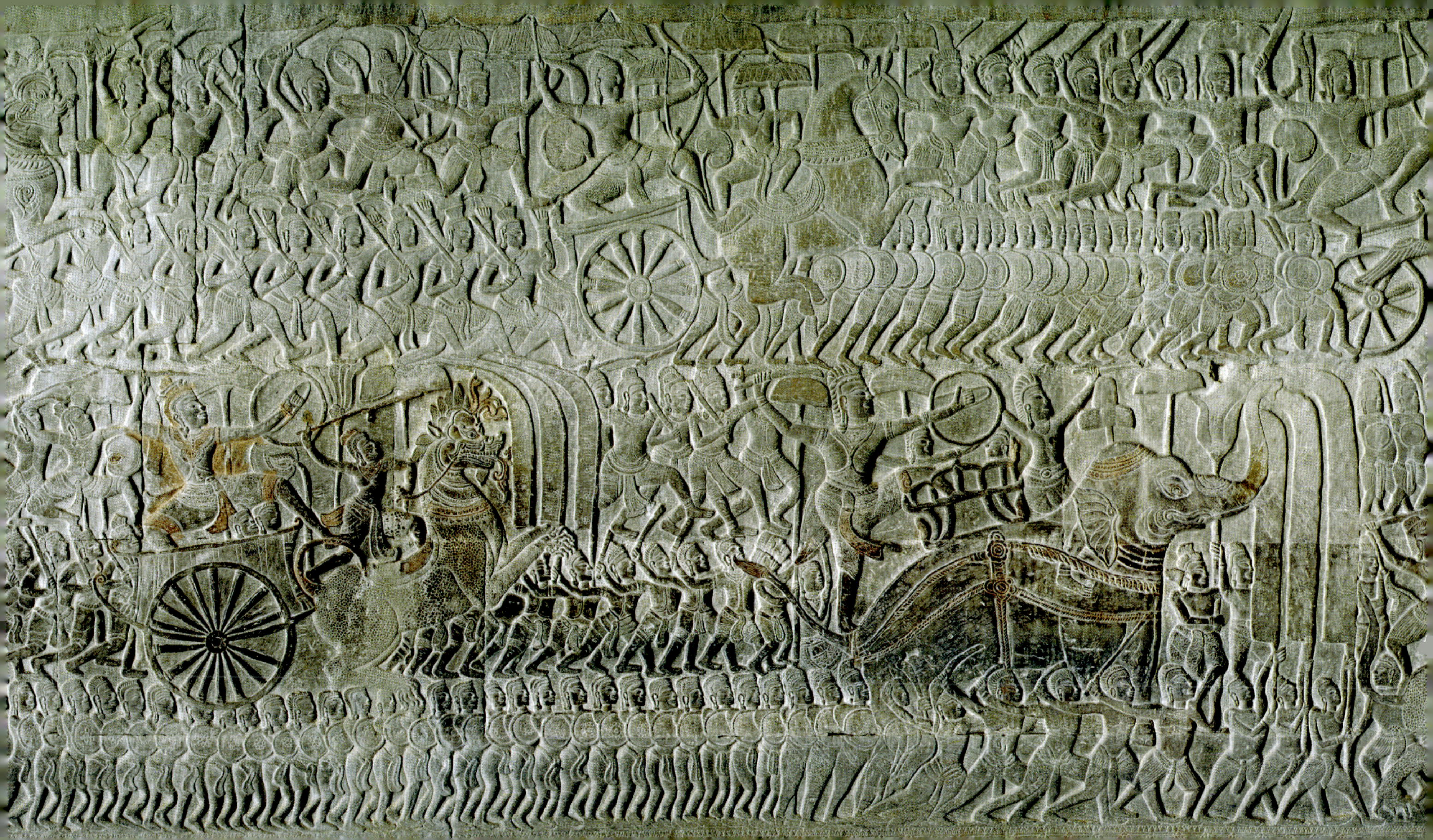

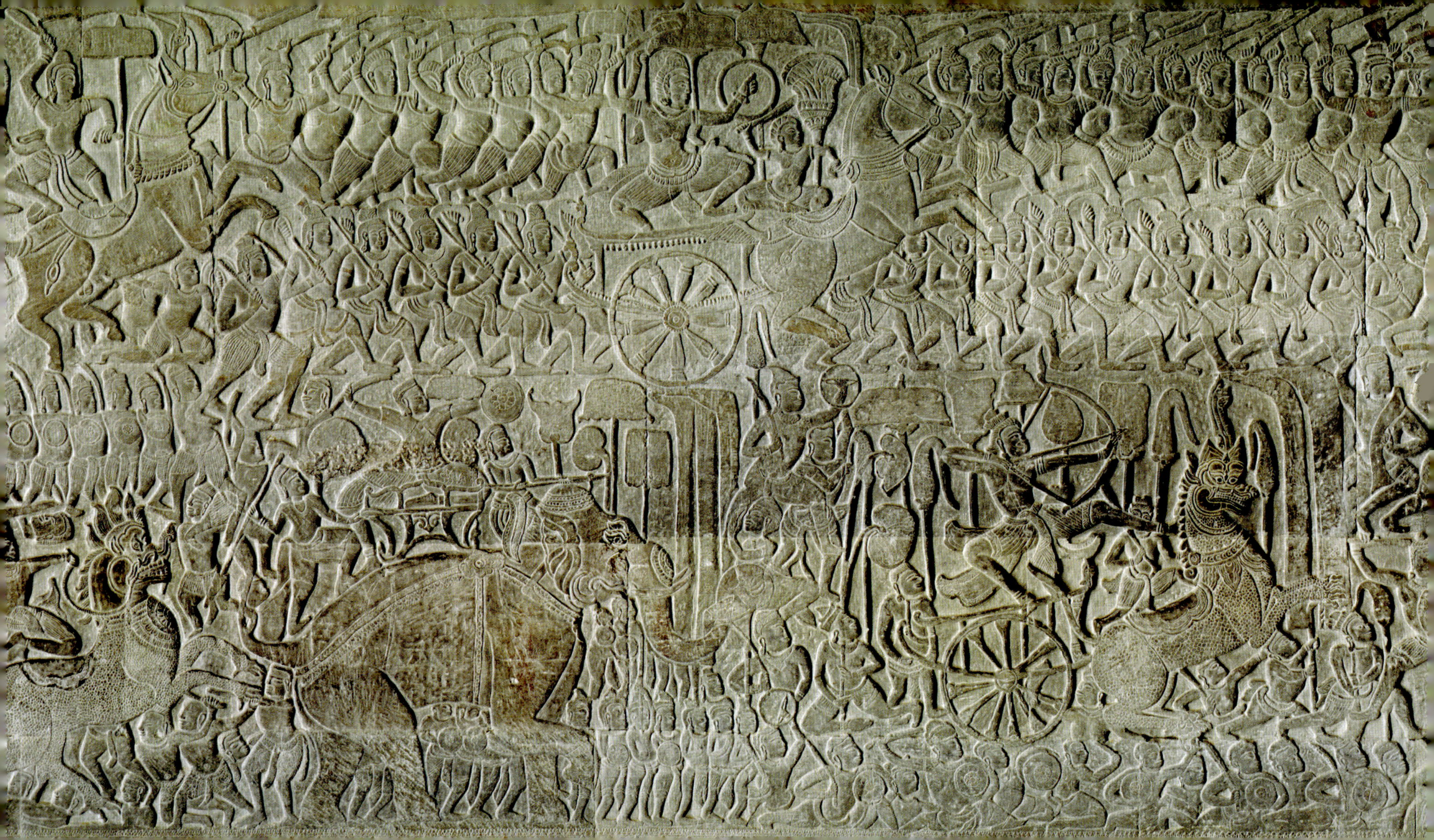

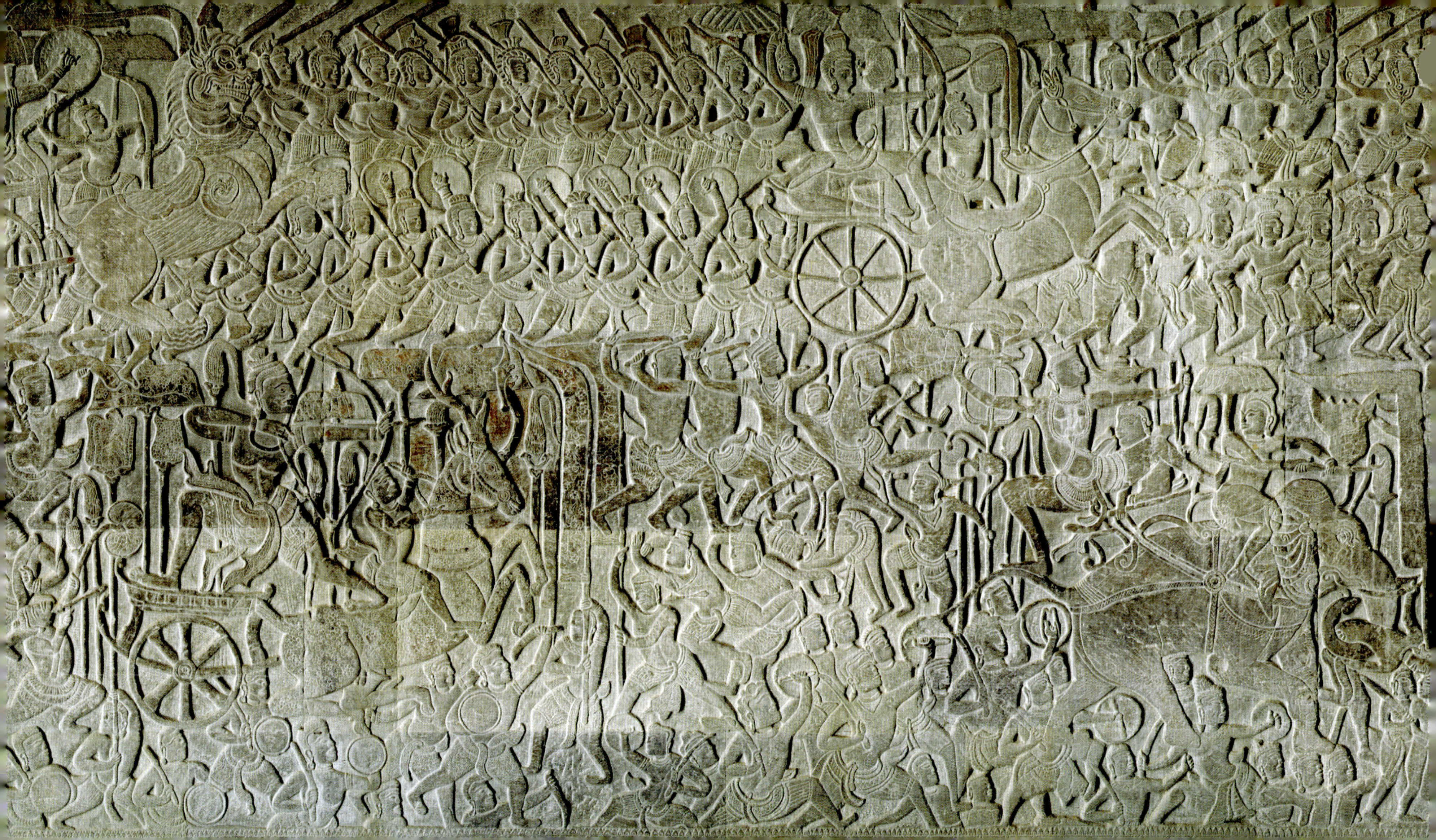

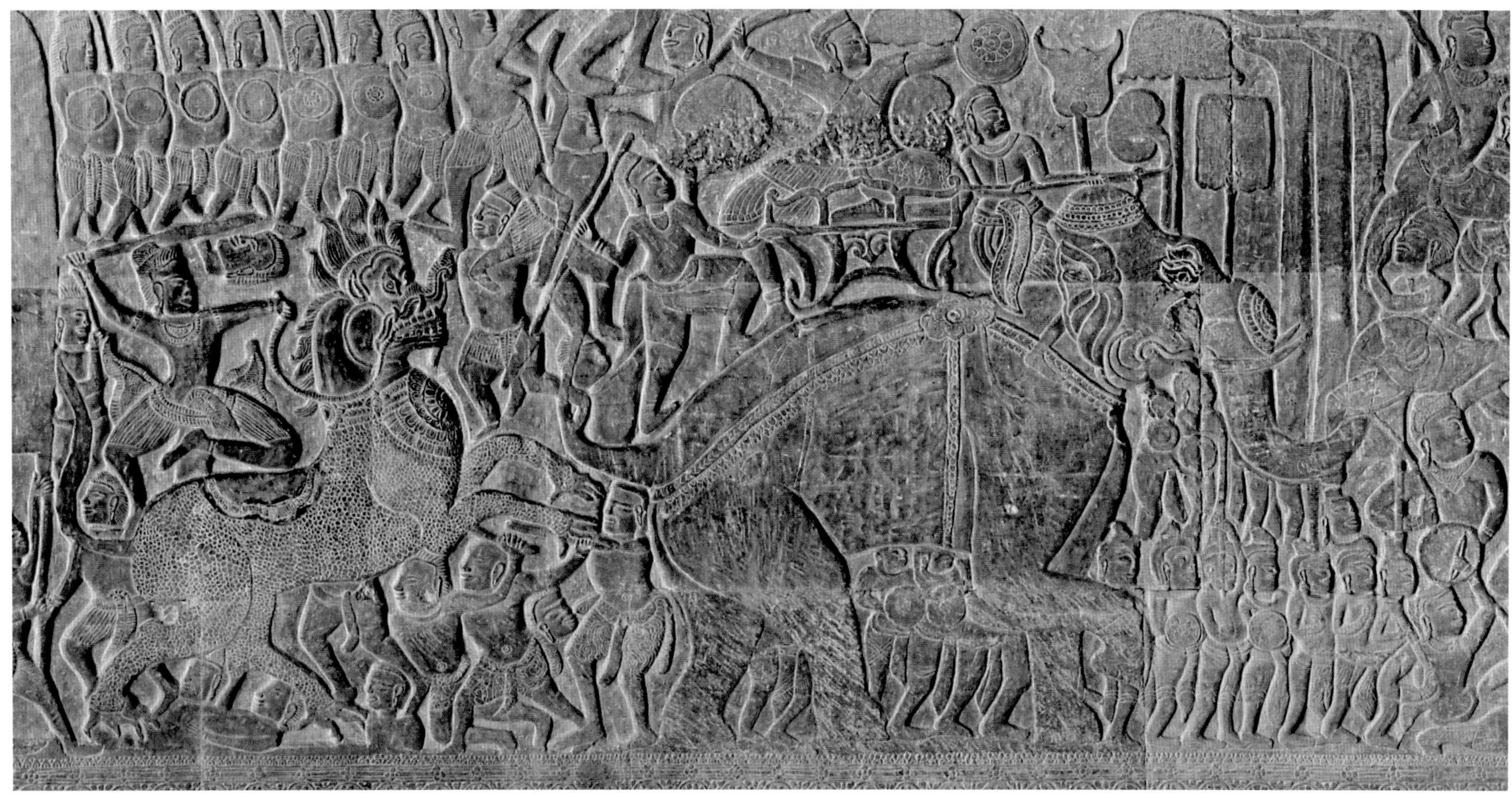

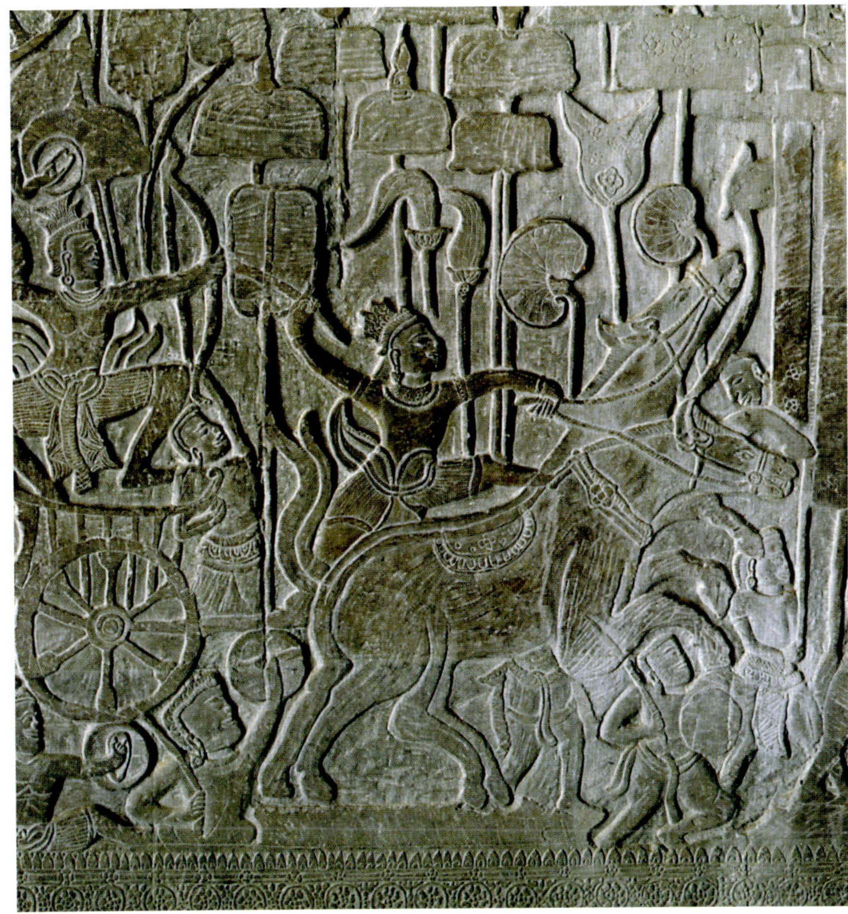

chariots, by monstrous creatures of the imagination, such as the lions of exotic design which draw certain of their chariots, their bodies covered in scales, their whiskers transformed into writhing snakes, some with elephant trunks and others with a serpent rearing between their ears. Defeated figures hoisted bodily into the air by the trunks of the charging elephants, are not depicted as gods, but are identical to the Asura warriors themselves, as if in the heat of battle these maddened creatures and their demon riders are unable to distinguish between their own foot soldiers and those of the enemy. As in the following relief, the subject is not the defeat or slaying of the archdemon, but the battle which preceded it. The message is contained in the struggle, not in its climax. It is an anarchic scene of carnage, its participants representing the two wings of Naraka's army erupting from Pragjyotisha to meet certain defeat at the hands of Vishnu–Krishna at the centre, like the fish at the base of the Churning of the Ocean, drawn inexorably into the maelstrom of Vishnu's central rotating mountain, there to be cut to pieces.

But the story does not end with this statement. For the continuation, we proceed to the next panel.

THE BATTLE OF SHONITAPURA:

VISHNU–KRISHNA AND THE ASURA BANA

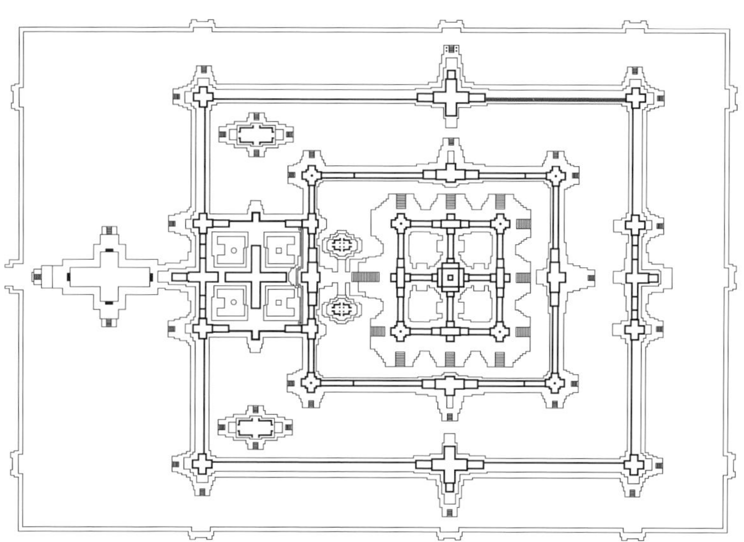

North Gallery, East Wing

THE BATTLE OF SHONITAPURA:
VISHNU-KRISHNA AND THE ASURA BANA
Treta Yuga I

Turning the north-east angle of the gallery by way of a corner pavilion - which was also left unfinished - the first scene encountered on the northern side is the second of the 16th-century reliefs, its completion dated by inscription to 27th February 1564. As with the previous panel, the textual source of its narrative appears to have been a version of the *Harivamsa*, though several episodes of the myth recounted in that text are omitted. Nevertheless, Vishnu as Krishna, his only full *avatara,* makes six appearances in the course of the battle narrative, always standing on the outstretched wings of Garuda, who also appears alone, without Vishnu-Krishna, at the beginning (far left) of the relief. At the end (far right), the god appears yet again, after the battle has been won, in a remarkable scene depicting him in respectful conversation with Shiva. The story that accounts for this composition, which is clearly divided into eight sequential episodes derived from the text version, concerns the battle against the Asura Bana.

Like Naraka, Bana is a particularly interesting figure in Hindu demonology. He was a worshipper of Rudra-Shiva and descended from the great god Brahma through a resplendent line which included such famous and infamous names as Marichi, Kashyapa, Daksha, Diti, Hiranyakashipu, Prahlada, Vairochana, and Bali, whose eldest son Bana was. He was a neighbouring king and friend of the Asura Naraka, whose city is the setting for the events depicted in the previous panel, and to whom Bana gave consistently negative advice, leading finally to his destruction at the hands of Vishnu. Bana's capital city, Shonitapura ("Blood City"), like Naraka's kingdom of Kamarupa, was believed to be situated in the far North-East of India, in modern Assam, two administrative districts of which are named after these ancient kingdoms, centred on the towns of Gauhati and Tezpur. There is abundant inscriptional evidence, from preangkorian times onward, for the naming of Cambodian sacred sites after such legendary landscapes in India. These beliefs, situating mythical events in real geographical locations and symbolizing them by the erection of temples, may account for the placement of the Naraka and Bana reliefs at the north-eastern corner of Angkor Wat's third enclosure. In the minds of the planners there appears to have existed a definite and complex thematic connection between these two reliefs.

As will become apparent from the wider context, only certain of the closing episodes of the myth concerning Bana are represented in the relief. The bare bones of the story are these. Bana travelled to the Himalaya and there meditated on Shiva and practised severe religious austerities. So gratified were Shiva and Parvati by his devotion and worship that they listened to his desire, which was twofold: to be considered their son, and to be given a thousand arms with which to defeat all his enemies. These desires were granted. Shiva indeed regarded him as his son (just as Naraka was the acknowledged son of Vishnu), as younger brother to Skanda the war-god, and with his many arms he was believed invincible. In consequence of this Bana then became an addicted warrior, fighting ceaselessly beneath the peacock standard of his brother, the Hindu god of war, until inevitably his last enemy was defeated. Aware of his dispiritedness at having no one left to fight, Shiva sought to help him by declaring the lowering of his battle standard to be the signal, not for a final end of hostilities, as

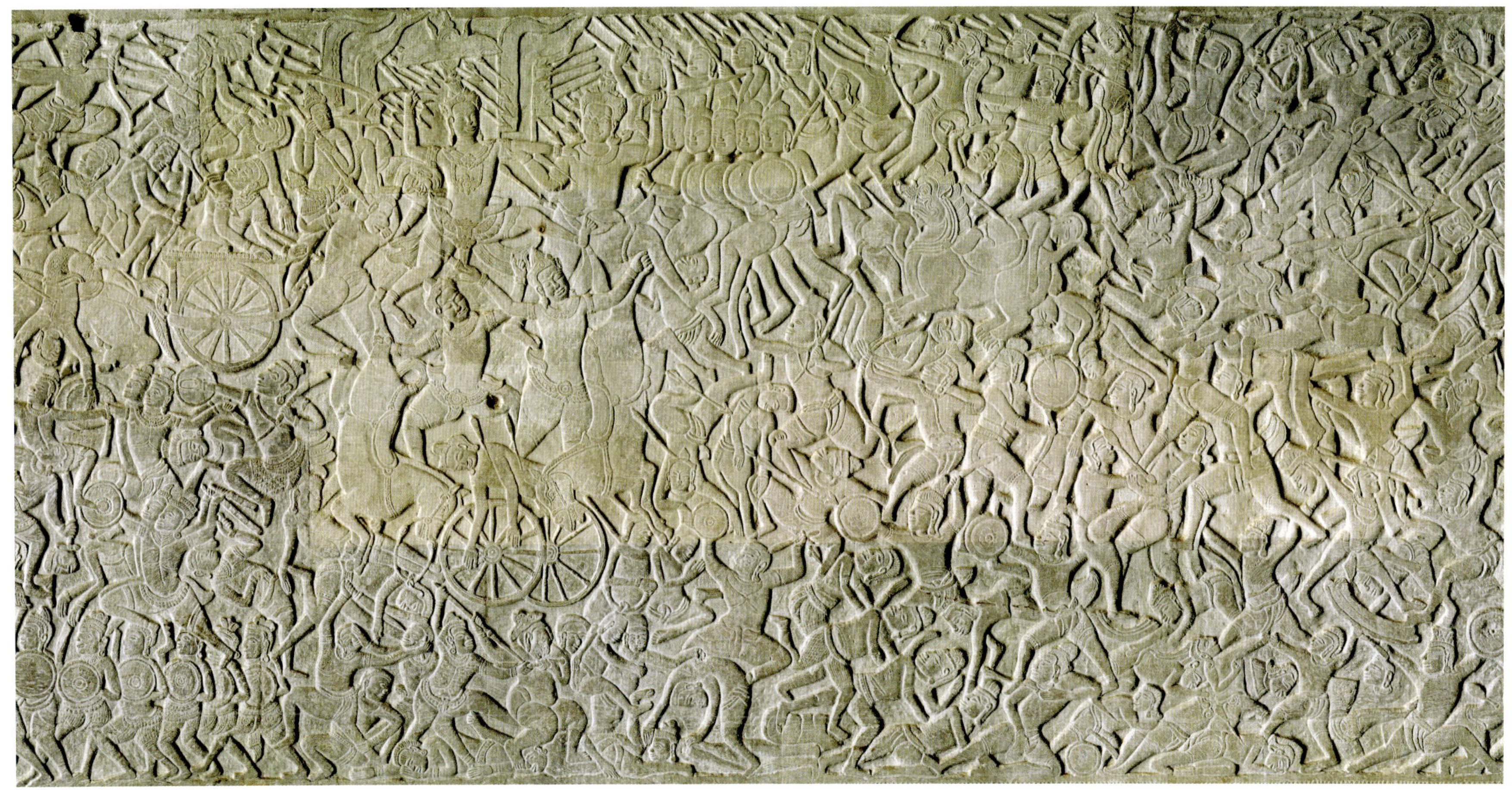

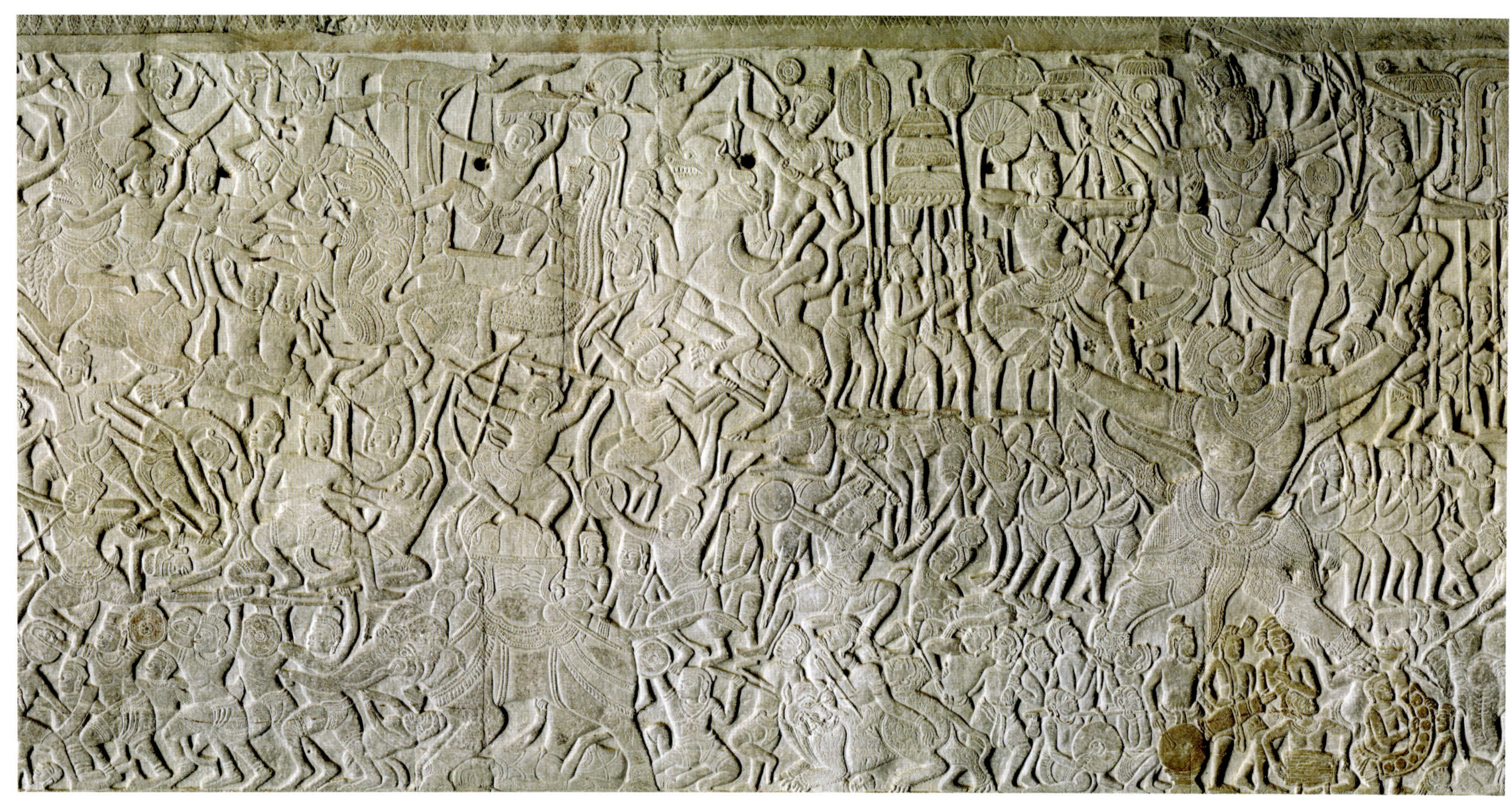

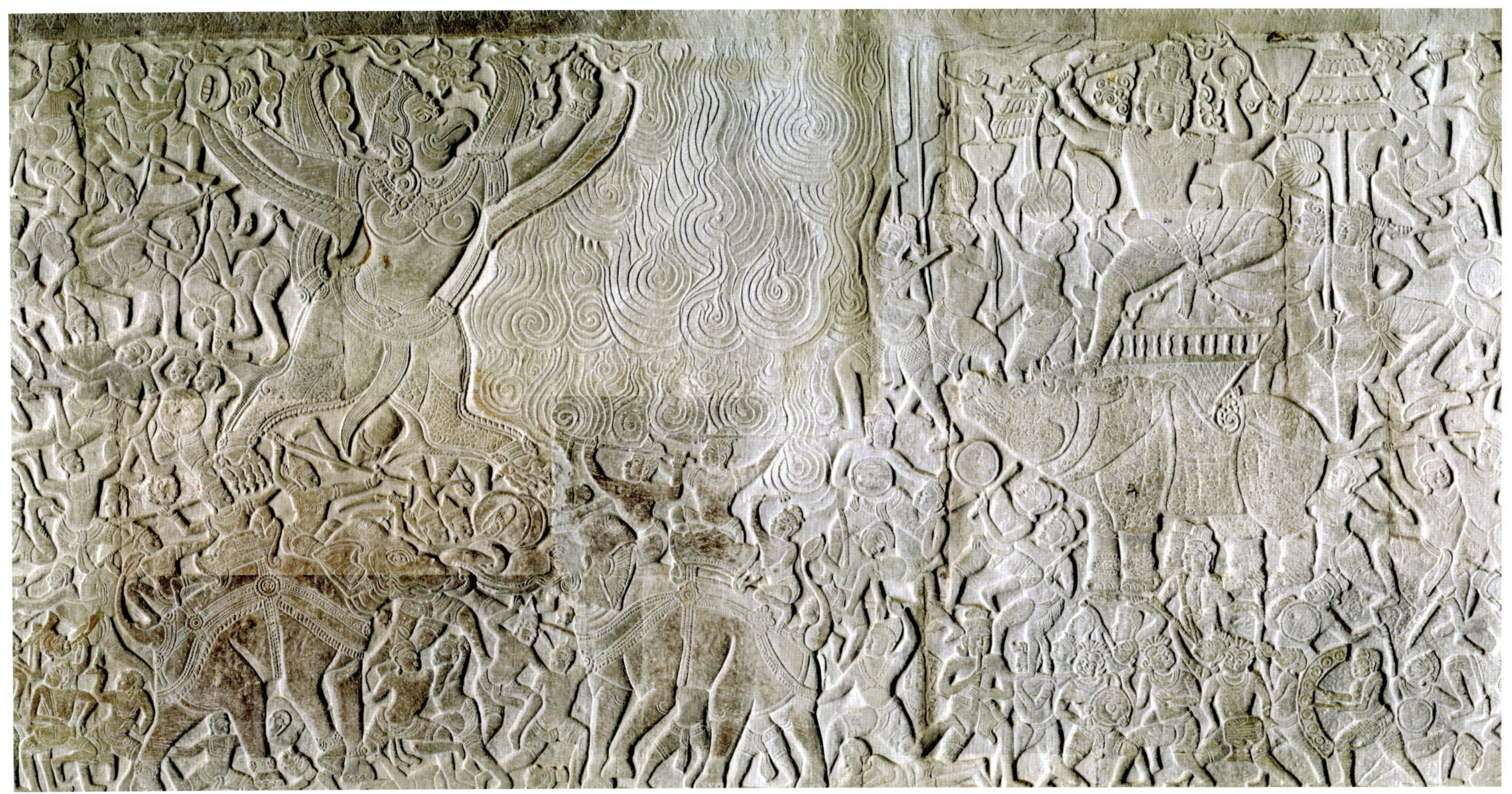

Bana feared, but for the beginning of a new war. Bana rejoiced in this prospect, but his minister, realizing what the gift of Shiva meant, correctly foresaw the impending disaster.

The subsequent unravelling of Bana's fate is a complicated story. His daughter, Usha (Dawn), in a dream fell in love with Aniruddha, son of Pradyumna and grandson of Krishna (Vishnu incarnate) himself, who was the ultimate sworn enemy of Bana. Acting as intermediary, a friend of Usha made the journey to Krishna's capital, Dvaraka (at the extreme western end of the subcontinent, on the coast of modern Gujarat), and brought Aniruddha back with her to Shonitapura. When Bana heard of the love affair, which the couple conducted in secret under his nose, he was furious and led his army against Aniruddha, but failed to subdue him; by resorting to magic, however, he succeeded in binding him with snakes. On learning then of his captive's identity, and realizing the danger into which his own actions had led him, Bana decided to spare Aniruddha's life and accept his relationship with his daughter as a *gandharvavivaha,* an unofficial marriage based on mutual consent. But it was too late. Krishna, informed of these developments, mounted Garuda and, accompanied by his elder brother Balarama and his son Pradyumna, sped to Shonitapura at the head of a great army. (Our relief depicts the events that now followed upon the arrival of Krishna in Bana's kingdom.) Seeing his adoptive son's troops trapped by Krishna's forces, Shiva himself now entered the battle, fielding his nightmarish hordes of Pramathas, demons of torment assuming numerous appearances. In consequence, the struggle now escalated into a confrontation between Vishnu-Krishna and Shiva, the two most powerful gods of the Hindu Triad. Such was the tumult that the Earth-goddess again appealed to the gods for rescue, whereupon Brahma spoke to Shiva, reminding him that ultimately he and Krishna were one and the same god, and counselling the end of hostilities. Shiva having obediently withdrawn, Bana renewed the fight alone and was defeated, all but four of his thousand hands severed by Krishna's disk, and his life saved only by the intervention of Shiva (the last of the events shown in the relief), who took him under his protection. Krishna, the victor, now organized the aftermath, entrusting the Shonitapura kingdom to Bana's minister, rescuing Aniruddha from his prison of snakes, and returning him, together with Usha, to Dvaraka.

The detailed phases of the battle shown in the relief begin with the encounter with a wall of fire which encircled the city of Shonitapura as its first line of defence. Garuda extinguished this by flying to the sacred Ganges (which joins with the Brahmaputra to the south-west of Shonitapura, in modern Bangladesh), swallowing vast quantities of water, and returning to the demon-king's city, where he regurgitated the holy water like rain on to the demon's ring of flame[5]. The fire is depicted confronting Garuda in personified form – beyond the flames Agni, god of fire, strikes a warlike pose on a rhinoceros (*khadga* or *khadgin;* the word also signifies "sword" or "sword-bearer"), which in Khmer iconography is his symbolic animal, replacing the sacrificial goat that serves him as vehicle in Indian religious art. In this scene Agni appears six-headed like the war god Skanda, and it may be that a dual identity for this figure is implied: in South and South East Asian tradition, multiheadedness can be used to represent the wrathful and violent transformation of an otherwise serene personality. The same feature is also applied to five of the six appearances of Krishna in the battle scenes: he is shown with a veritable tower of heads, indicative of his vehemently warlike mood, intent as he is on the destruction of Bana. This imagery harks back to the archetypal manifestation of Vishnu-Krishna as the ultimate god of war and death, which is described in the *Bhagavadgita,* where his uncountable heads devour the warriors on the battlefield of Kurukshetra. In this depiction of the battle of Shonitapura, he appears mounted on Garuda, flanked by the smaller figures of Balarama and Pradyumna who are carried on the giant eagle's wingtips. Only in his third appearance does Krishna fight alone, and here he is shown in his four-armed and single-headed form, aiming at the enemy with arrow and throwing-sword, his discus (the fire-*chakra* named Sudarshana) held in reserve to sever Bana's whirling mass of arms.

The figure of Bana, in attacking posture on a war chariot, is preceded by two shambolic monsters who presumably represent the Pramathas of Shiva; whether they are physically harnessed to the chariot is not entirely clear from the 16th-century relief, but this was probably the original intention, to portray Bana as fighting from Shiva's chariot, which was sent into the battle for him at one point in the textual narrative. In the horrific absurdity of their disorganized facial features, these grotesque figures recall the two "Bharata Rahu" monsters in the 12th-century reliefs of Banteay Chmar. Bana himself, located far to the right in the relief panel, facing the sequenced advance of Krishna, is depicted holding a spear, symbolic weapon of Skanda, and wielding a deadly circle of swords to represent his thousand hands, yet with a single head (his desire, granted by Shiva, concerned only his force of arms), the only figure to be shown advancing over the front of his vehicle in his lust for battle.

The final scene in the relief (though not the end of the legend) shows Shiva as a bearded and haloed Yogishvara, Lord of Ascetics, wearing his traditional snake-armlets but with a Buddhist-looking robe replacing the animal skin over his shoulder. He is seated regally on the summit of his mountain home, Kailasa (situated in Tibet, at the northern end of the Manasarovara lake), which is represented in Chinese style, the lower caves on its slopes inhabited by semidivine beings, the higher ones by worshipping ascetics, one of whom Bana himself once was. Beside his throne sits his unwarlike son, the elephant-headed Ganesha, flanked by a parasol-bearer and the guardian of his axe. Shiva, two-armed, holds his symbol, the iron trident, prominently in his right hand, and with his left makes a gesture toward the figure kneeling respectfully before him in the posture of a Thai or Cambodian supplicant. This is none other than Vishnu-Krishna, emerged from battle and listening quietly to the words of Bana's adoptive father. He is still multiheaded and eight-armed, as in the battle scenes, but now holds only three weapons, his other hands displaying a lotus (one of his own emblems) and two other flowers, which are offerings to Shiva. His two empty hands are joined in worshipful greeting, the gesture of one who receives spiritual instruction from a superior. For Brahma had already reminded Shiva of his oneness with Vishnu and on this basis advised him to withdraw from the battle, which he did; now it is for him in turn to remind Vishnu-Krishna, hot from the same battle, of the same teaching. By this means Shiva dissuades Vishnu, who has permanently humbled his adoptive son, from persisting in his intention of killing him. "Let him live," responds Krishna. "Since you have promised him his life, I withhold my discus. For we are not different from one another. What you are, I am also." The two great gods are reconciled, the faults of Bana are exposed and neutralized, and the conflict is resolved to the benefit of all concerned. It remains only for Krishna to tie up the political loose ends resulting from the war in Shonitapura and return to his own city in triumph.

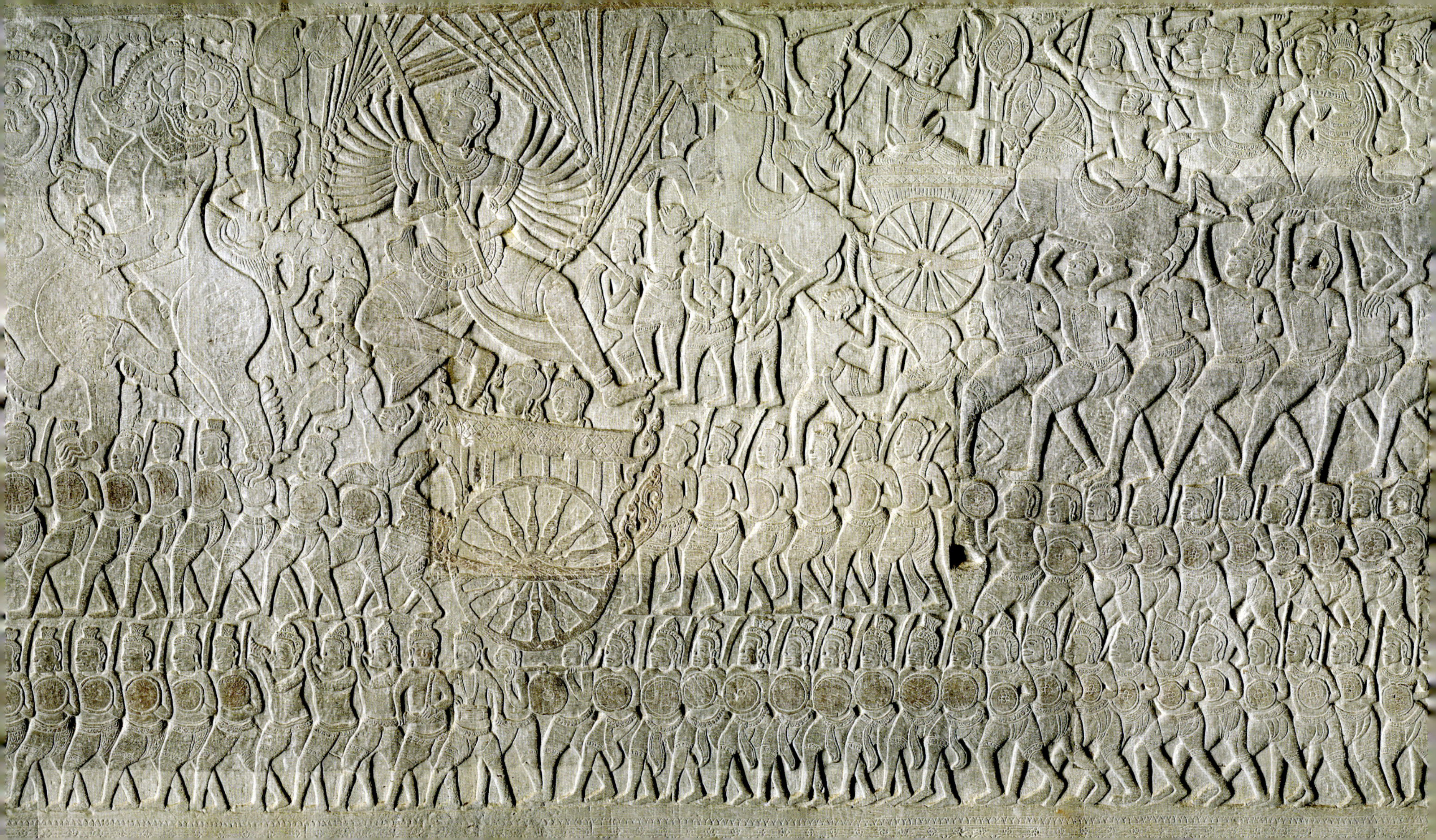

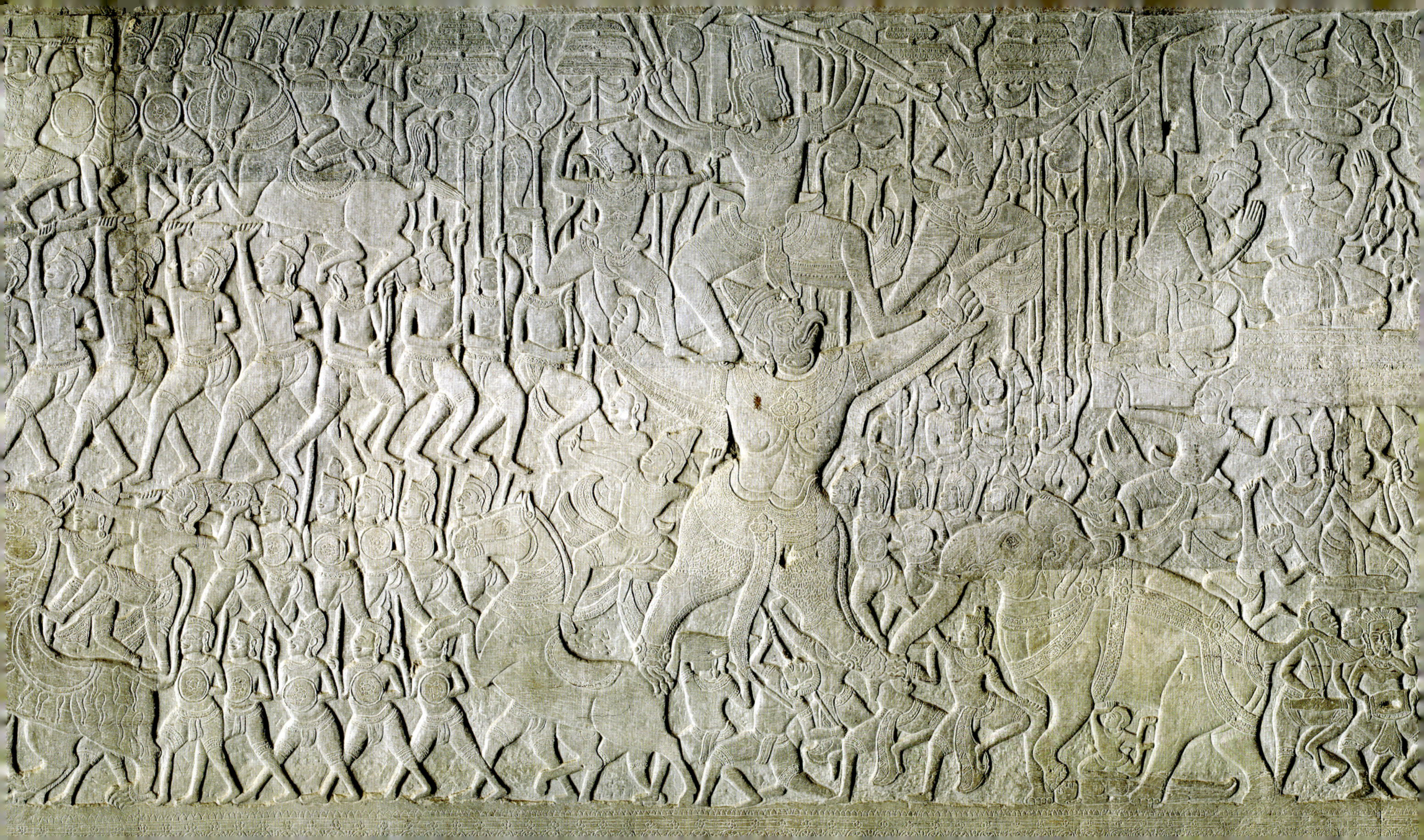

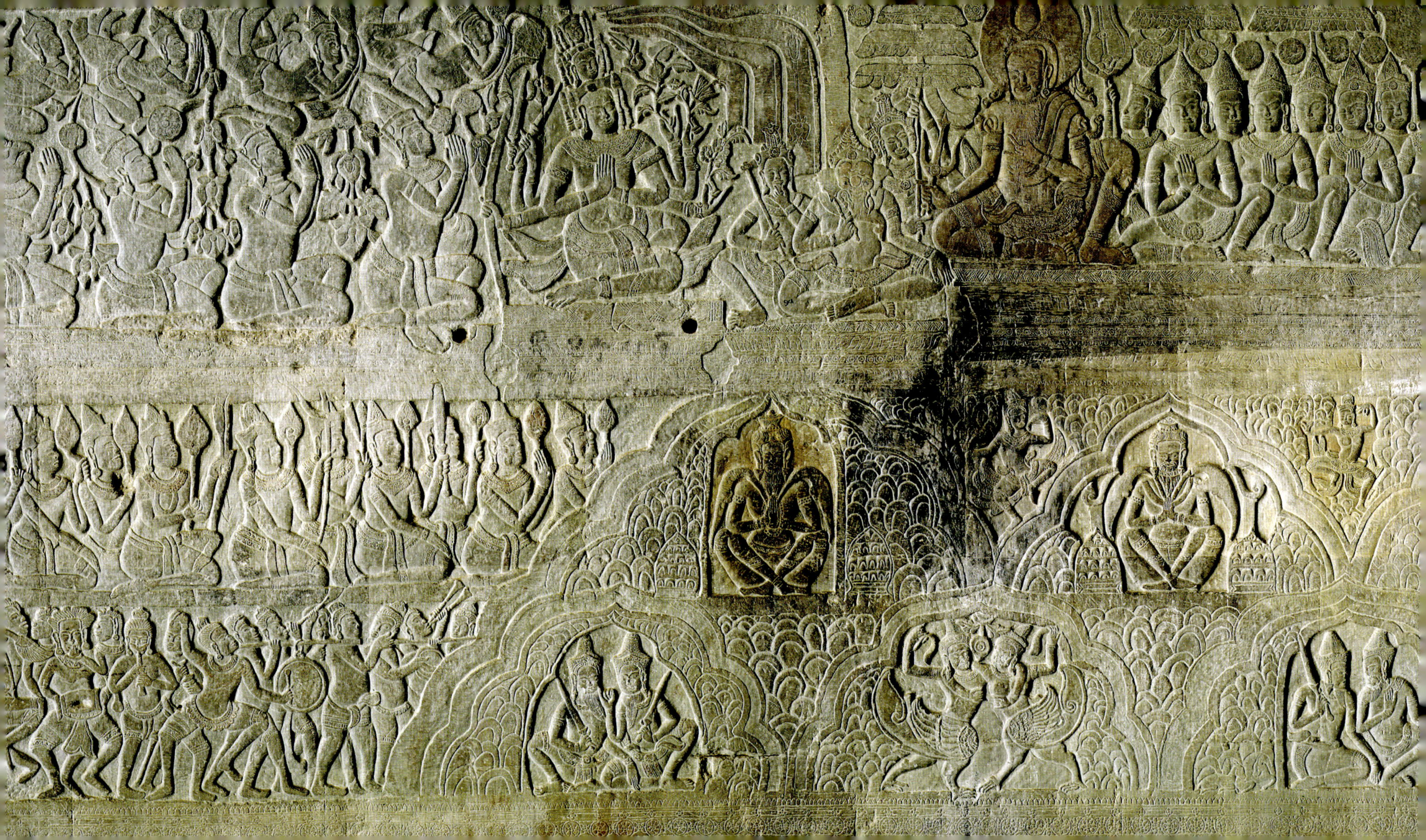

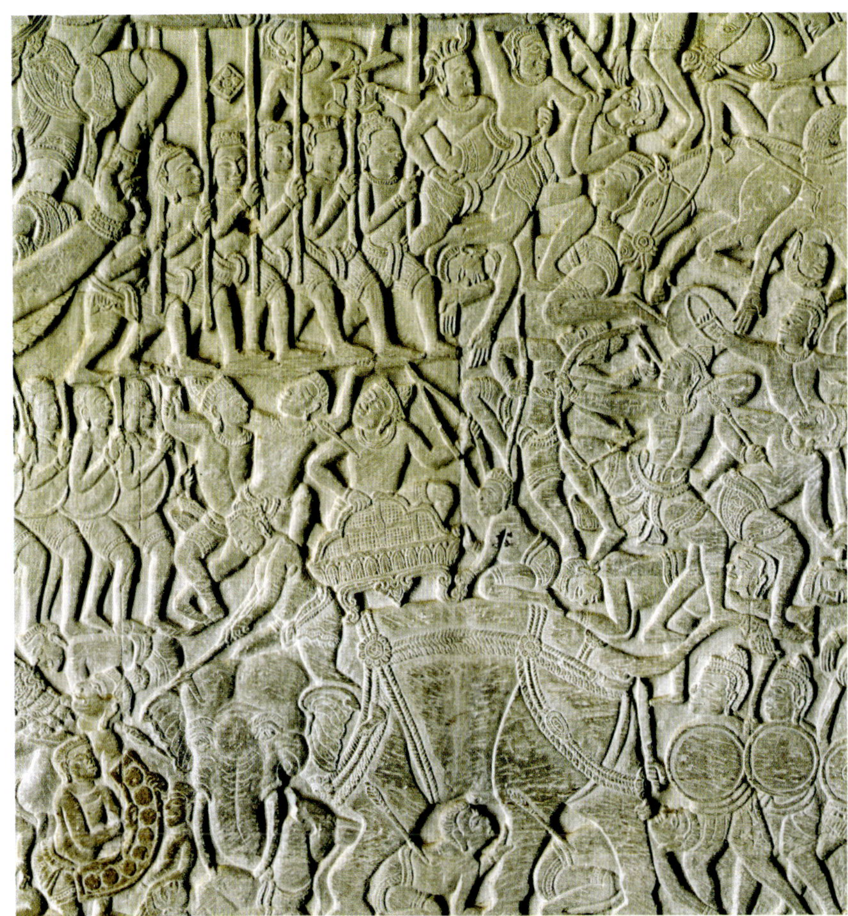

The two north-eastern reliefs of Angkor Wat represent Vishnu-Krishna's campaigns in the north-east of India. Their didactic purpose is to demonstrate the inevitability of his triumph over the forces of evil, either by total military victory or by superior knowledge, or preferably both. The definition of evil is force motivated by inferior knowledge and destabilizing ambition, which is called arrogance or self-referencing *(abhimana)*, and which automatically entails harm to others, resulting in anarchy. The supernatural powers deriving from spiritual discipline can be achieved, however, even by an individual possessed of inferior knowledge and self-centred interest, like Bana. That is where the threat to the stability of the universe lies, and it cannot be resolved by military means alone without generating even greater instability. The final resolution depends on acknowledgement of the unity of the universe (represented here by the impartial Brahma) and on the preservation of this greater unity as the highest priority in handling every local conflict. By identifying the Khmer king with Vishnu-Krishna in these mythological conflicts depicted at Angkor Wat, the political motives of the Cambodian state could be justified as harmonious with the balance of the universe, and their victorious outcome symbolically assured. The literature and beliefs of Theravada Buddhism did not convey such matters with the impact of Hindu legends, which, as these 16th-century reliefs show, had remained alive in memory and relevant to Khmer thinking.

The next relief panel takes us still deeper into the ideology of struggle for the survival of order in the midst of chaos, and returns us to the original vision of the 12th-century artists.

THE TARAKAMAYA WAR:

VISHNU AND THE ASURA KALANEMI

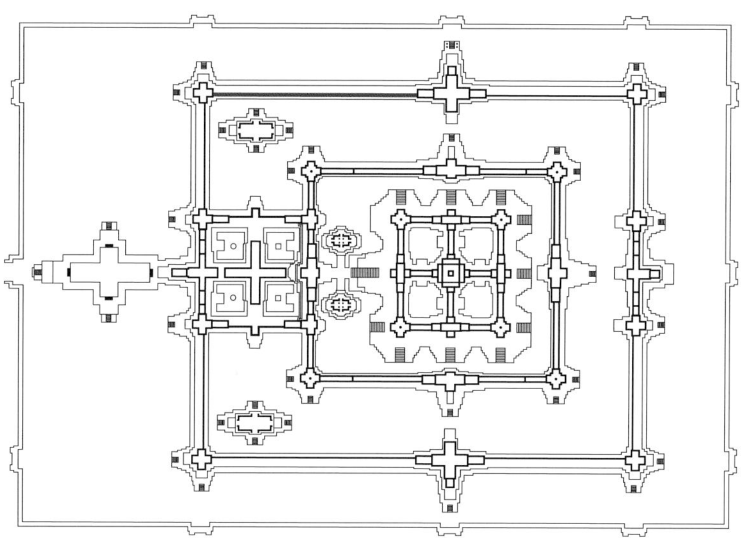

North Gallery, West Wing

THE TARAKAMAYA WAR:

VISHNU AND THE ASURA KALANEMI

Treta Yuga II

After leaving the story of Krishna's wars in Kamarupa and Shonitapura, the north-west corner of the galleries confronts us with further battles.
In the first of these, the long western gallery on the north side shows Vishnu
mounted on Garuda at the centre of a line of Hindu gods, each of whom fights
against a particular demon. These individual duels take place against a background of innumerable life-and-death struggles between the smaller figures of
foot soldiers and charioteers, a panoramic view of the battleground. Although
Vishnu appears in the midst of other gods, we know from the composition of
the previous panels that the central figure is always to be seen as the leader.
We are therefore looking, not at a discontinuous series of separate mythical
war scenes in which Vishnu appears as one god among many equals, but at
an organized army of gods under Vishnu's command. He leads his host of Devas from the east, to clash with the Asuras who oppose them mostly from the
west. In Vaishnava religion, as in Vaishnava iconographical texts, all gods are
regarded as aspects of Vishnu. This is why even Shiva, the other chief Hindu
deity, is not depicted here on a greater scale than the rest of the Devas. Unlike the story behind the previous panel, depicting the battle against Bana, the
concept operating in this relief does not involve the elevated Hindu Triad of
Brahma-Vishnu-Shiva, nor does it seem to illustrate a particular episode from the
Krishna cycle, but represents Vishnu-Krishna as the one supreme god, storming
the demons in the form of a united pantheon. There are many Hindu texts, from
the *Bhagavadgita's* vision of his cosmic form onward, which describe him as

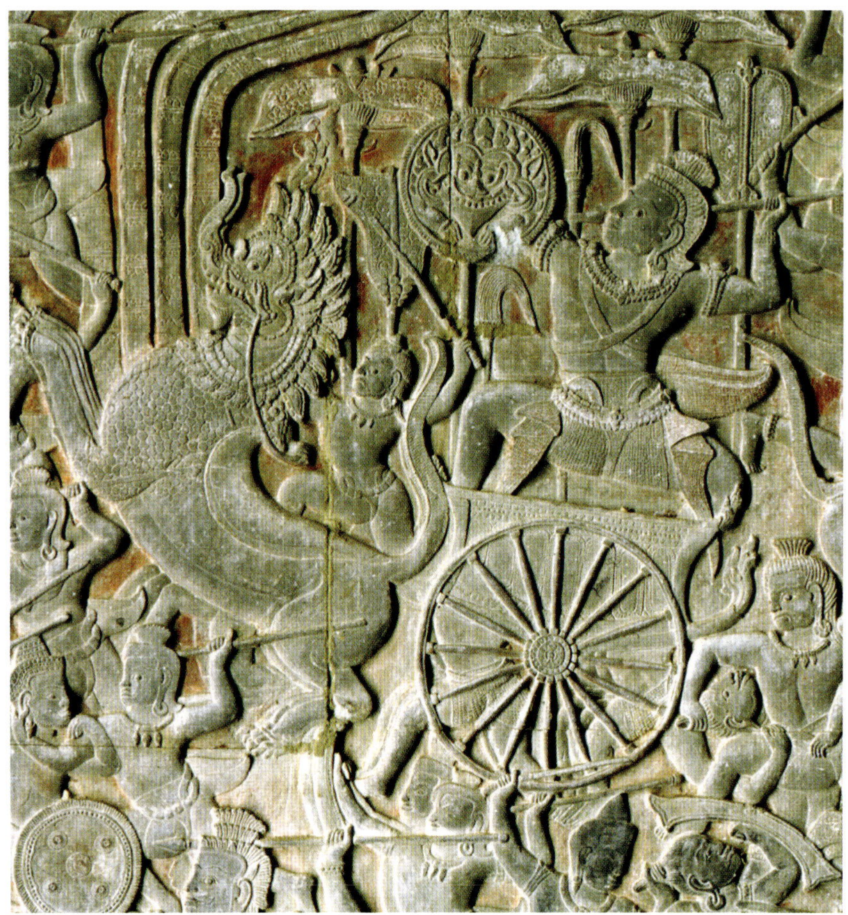

embodying or containing all the gods within himself. It is this universal aspect of his warrior nature that appears to be emphasized in this relief, which thus serves as a reference to his further battles, following on from the local conflicts depicted in the north-eastern reliefs.

George Coedès suggested in 1911 that the Asura opponent confronting Vishnu in the middle of the battle scene is probably to be identified as the demon named Kalanemi, but without stating his reasons, since he could not at that time detect a definite identifying feature in the relief on which to base an argument. Since then, numerous attempts have been made to identify the particular mythological battle to which this relief refers. Coedès' proposal remains by far the most reasonable. The great battle in which Kalanemi played a leading role was the so-called Tarakamaya War. It was so named in the Sanskrit texts because it was waged on account of Tārakā (also known as Tārā; both names mean Star), wife of the profoundly revered sage Brihaspati, who was chief priest and counsellor to the gods. She was abducted by Soma (the Moon), who steadfastly refused to return her to her husband despite the entreaties of the gods. While the Devas continued to support their priest in the dispute over his wife, the Asuras and their priest, Shukra, sided with the abductor. Negotiations having failed, each side drew up its army. Thus the war took place, ostensibly, over possession of the beautiful Taraka; but in a puranic version of the same story, her abduction is seen as the pretext for undertaking the war to end all wars, for the final extermination of the demons.

Hostilities opened with an awesome exchange of deceptive appearances between Vishnu and one of the Asura leaders named Maya, both of whom

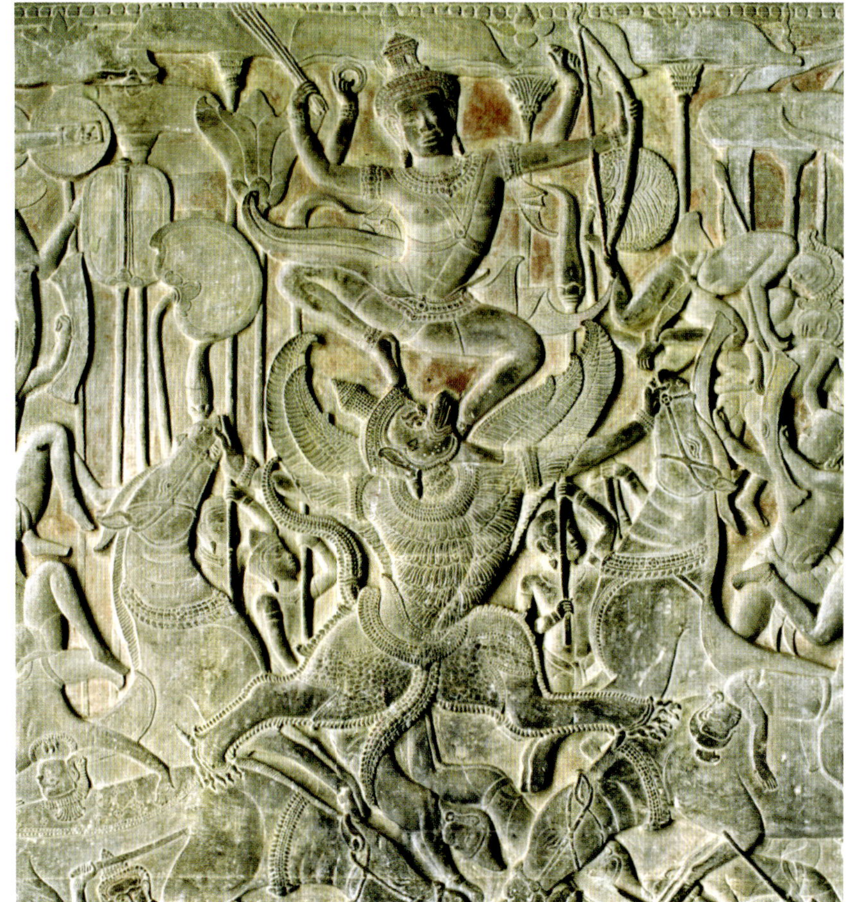

were famed as Lords of Illusion (Mayapati, Mayeshvara). But the decisive phase of the battle, which is the subject of the Angkor Wat relief, began when another leader of the demons, Kalanemi (Rim of the Wheel of Time), commanded the attack on Vishnu. As embodiment of the cutting edge of time (Kala, which also means Death), his strategy was to rob Vishnu of the dimension that he ruled, which was space – Vishnu is Spacemaker (as Trivikrama) and the Pervader of All Space (Sarvadigvyapin) – and then move in to destroy him. This the demon sought to achieve by slaying the Lokapalas, Guardians of the Directions of Space, who were present on the battlefield in the form of gods fighting on Vishnu's side. In the Hindu scheme there are eight such Lokapalas, each of whom rules over one of the four cardinal or intermediate directions, and they are all represented in the army of Vishnu in the Angkor Wat relief. Although interspersed among many other figures, they are identifiable by their iconographical features. From east to west, they are: 1: Kubera, god of wealth and ruler of the north, riding a demonic Yaksha; 2: Agni, god of fire and ruler of the south-east, mounted on a rhinoceros; 3: Indra, leader of the Vedic gods and ruler of the east, on his four-tusked elephant named Airavata; 4: Yama, ruler of the death kingdom in the south, in a chariot drawn by black water-buffaloes; 5: Shiva as Ishana, god of the north-east, his ascetic's topknot dishevelled by battle and his chariot drawn by the humped bull that is both his animal symbol and conveyance; 6: Surya, the sun-god, ruler of the south-west, encircled by the solar disk behind a Garuda-like charioteer, the sun-eagle here replacing Aruna, the red personfication of the rising sun in Indian iconography; 7: Vayu, lord of the winds, ruler of the north-west, also in a horse-drawn chariot; and 8: Varuna, god of the west, lord of waters and shown riding an undulating Naga symbolic of them, which replaces the "water-formed" *makara* (fabulous alligator-like beast) of Indian iconography.

The depiction of these Lokapalas is concentrated mostly in the western half of the panel, beginning with Kubera (the eighth figure) and ending with Varuna (the eighteenth). The central Garuda-mounted Vishnu figure is flanked by Indra and Yama, rulers of the east and south, and they in turn are flanked appropriately by Skanda, god of war, and by his father, Shiva, representing the north-east. This grouping is preceded by Kubera and Agni (north and south-east) and followed by Brahma and Surya (south-west), after which the last of the Lokapalas, Vayu and Varuna (north-west and west, representing the actual location of the relief on the temple), proceed toward the end of the panel at the north-west corner. The chief identification problems concern the first seven Devas and the last two, since they are defined exclusively by Khmer Hindu iconography, which differed in many respects from the better-known Indian conventions. The positioning of the Lokapalas around and in front of Vishnu, however, strongly suggests that it is the Tarakamaya War that is represented by the battle scene in this panel: the Asura leaders attack the Guardians of the Directions who are hedged around their leader, while the planner of this strategy, Kalanemi, breaks through these individual engagements and goes for Vishnu at the centre. It is this critical moment, the point of maximum danger, that is shown in the relief. However, the flaw in Kalanemi's plan is that he, as the Disk of Time, ignores the fact that Vishnu possesses the Disk of Space, the blazing Sudarshana Chakra, representing all the directions in a single weapon. Although the Lokapalas are under attack, Vishnu can therefore still mobilize his command of space. In the sequel (narrated in the texts but not shown in the relief) Vishnu, armed with this all-conquering space symbol, and growing to gigantic size – a form often employed in Vaishnava mythology as a *deus ex machina* device – first overwhelms his attacker and decapitates him, then destroys his Asura forces.

Concerning the nature and personality of Kalanemi there are many stories, and several different genealogies, in the Indian texts. Regarding the sequencing of the Angkor Wat galleries, two significant elements from these divers traditions are that he was the uncle of the demon Ravana; and that Ravana persuaded him to make an attempt on the life of Hanuman – who in the event defeated Kalanemi in grand and humiliating manner, but did not kill him. These and other *Ramayana* themes connect this panel with the following relief on the western side of the north-west corner, as we shall see below. In the present northern scene from the Tarakamaya War, Kalanemi, in a horse-drawn chariot, is depicted with a tower of seven visible heads arranged in two rows of three, one face frontal and two in profile, with one more at the apex. It may well be the case that where three heads in a line are shown in this way, four were intended, as in Indian iconography, the one at the back being concealed; in which case the demon would be nine-headed. In the Sanskrit narratives Kalanemi is said to have a hundred or a thousand heads, for which the uncertain number in the relief is presumably symbolic[6]. With thirty-two arms he wields his weapons in a scything motion very suggestive of his identity – the wheel of time and death advancing like a war-machine on the embattled Vishnu. There appears to be no strict correla-

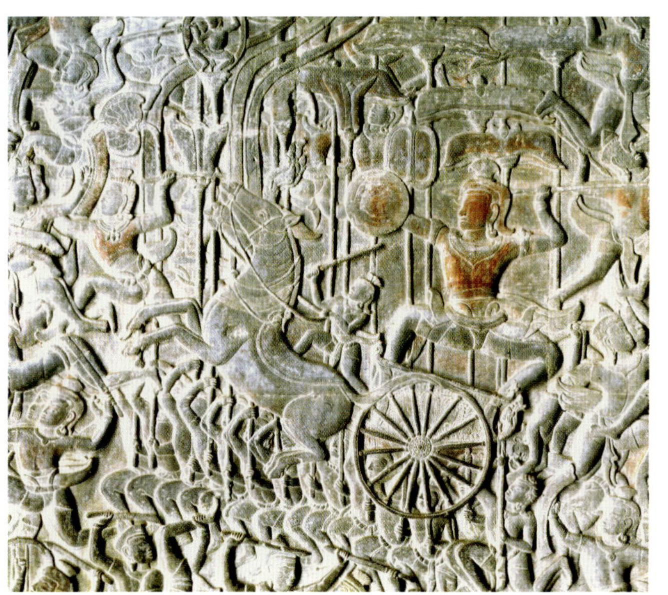

tion between the number of the demon's faces and arms in the relief, leaving one with the impression that these Asuras from Indian mythology had no very specific iconography in Cambodia – where a different spirit world with its own demonology existed alongside the Hinduism of the élite – so that the artists were relatively free to generate their own imagery in keeping with the contextual aesthetic; the striking multiplicity of heads and arms, however, appears to be derived from the conception of wrathful transformation, in gods as well as in demons, as mentioned above in connection with Krishna and Bana at the battle of Shonitapura. Vishnu himself, confronting Kalanemi, appears in his standard single-headed and four-armed form: his multiplicity here consists of the gods under his command, who are emanations of himself.

This Tarakamaya panel represents at once the climax of Vishnu's battles against specific demons, begun on the east side with the Battle of Pragjyotisha, and the transition to his further war against the best-known of all the Asura kings, Ravana of Lanka, on the west. Whereas the first three episodes concern Vishnu fully embodied in King Krishna and as Vishnu King of the Gods, the next shows him changed in nature and in another role – as Rama, the king-to-be, the ideal prince.

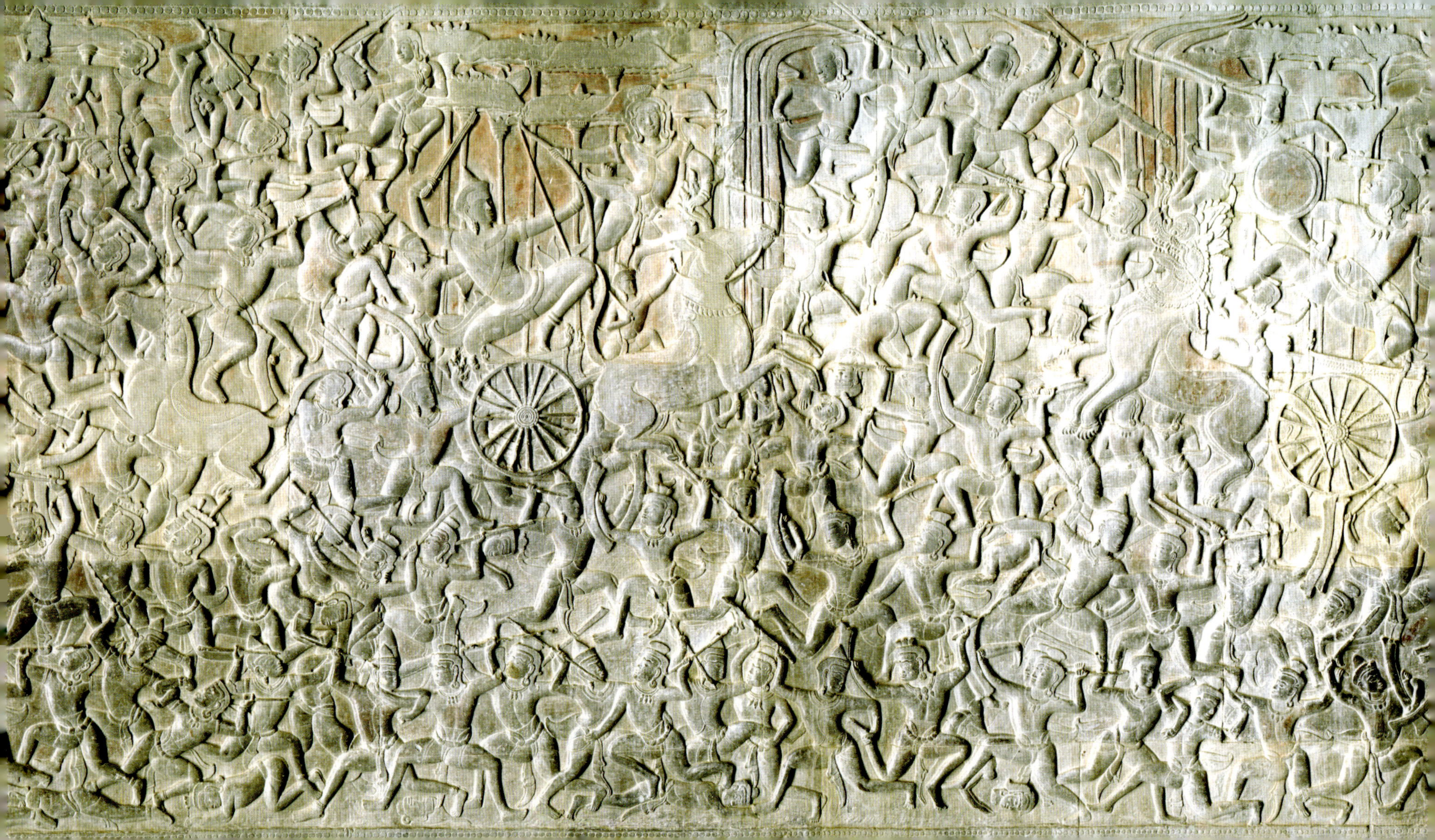

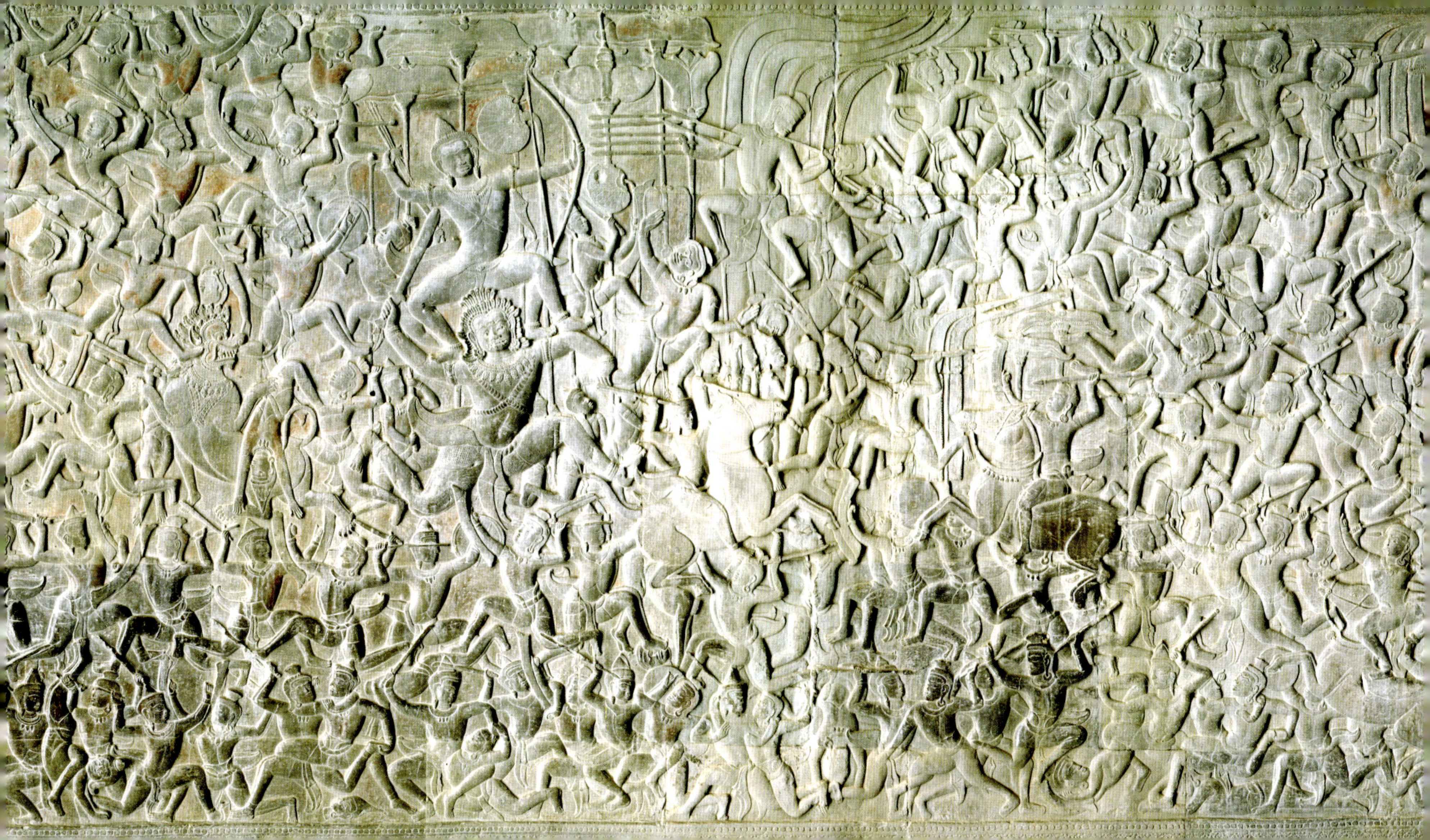

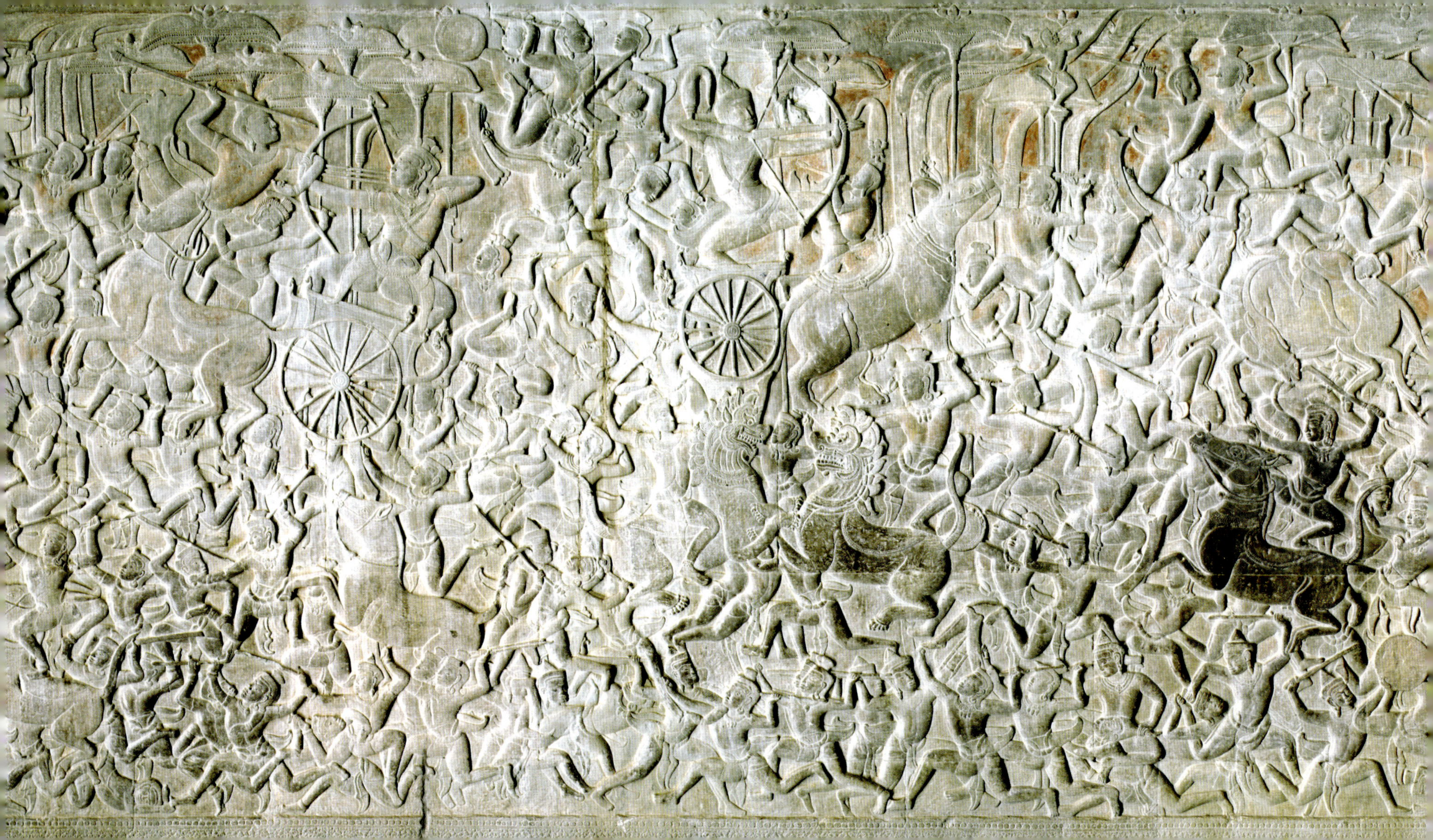

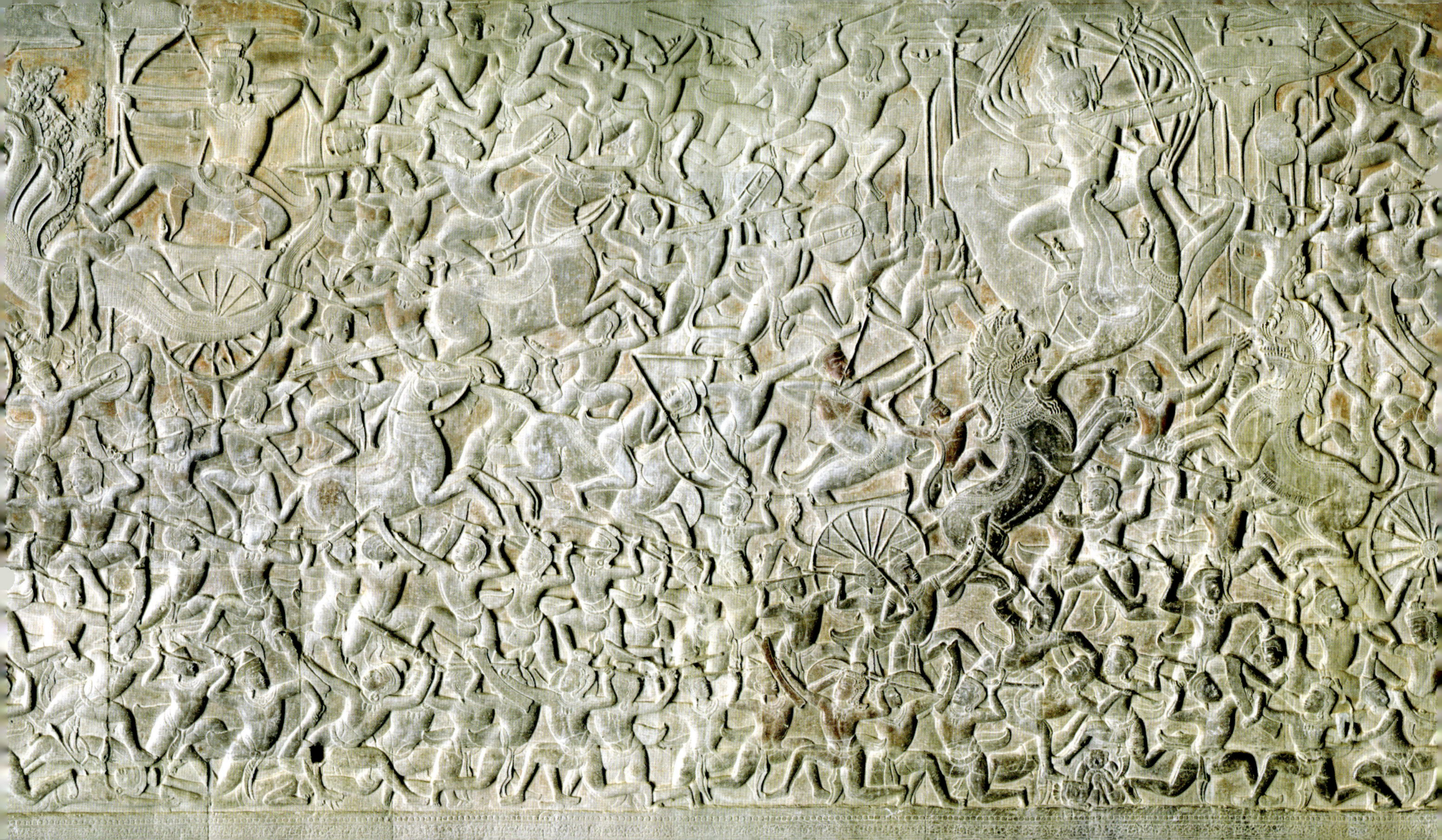

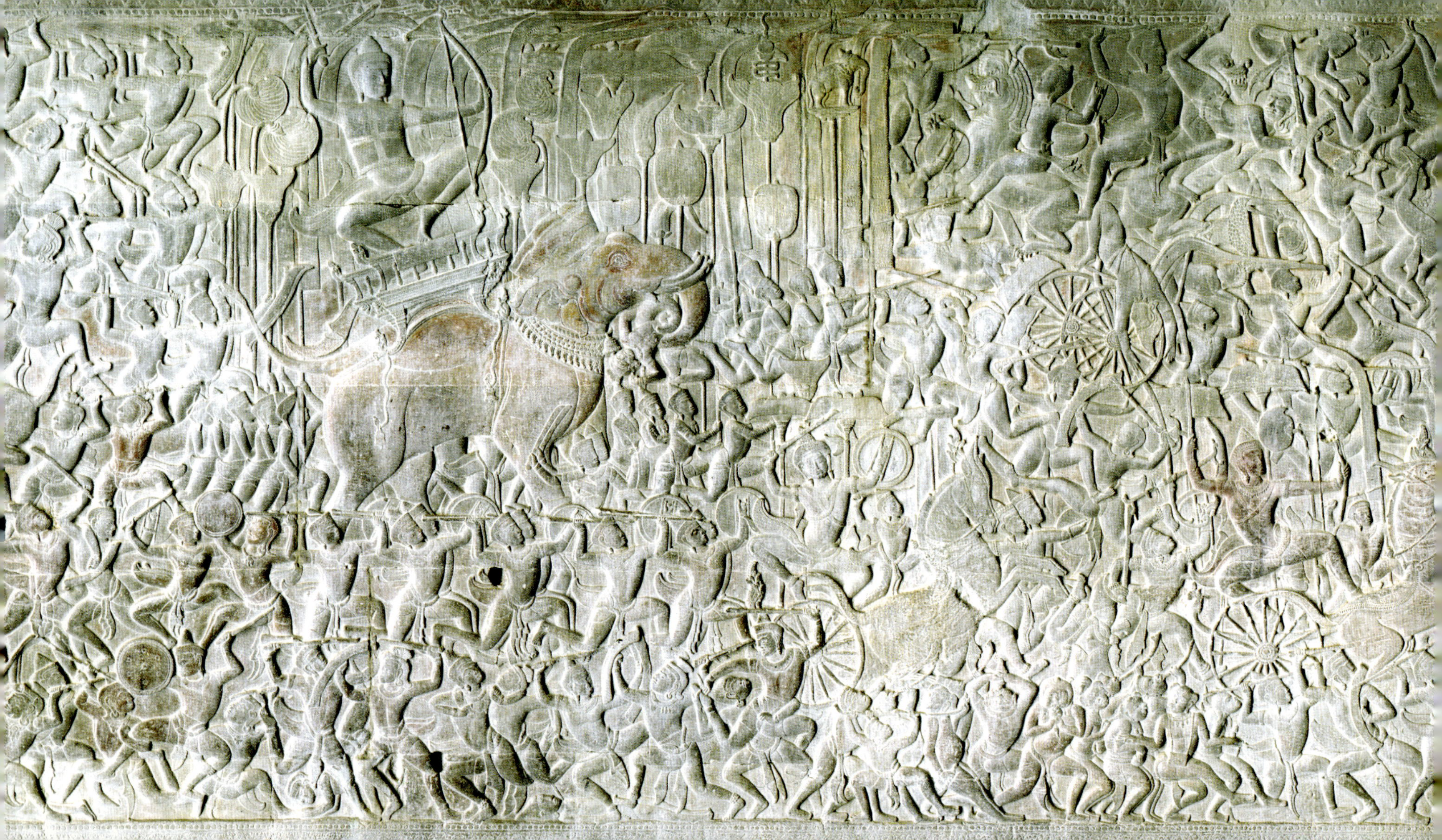

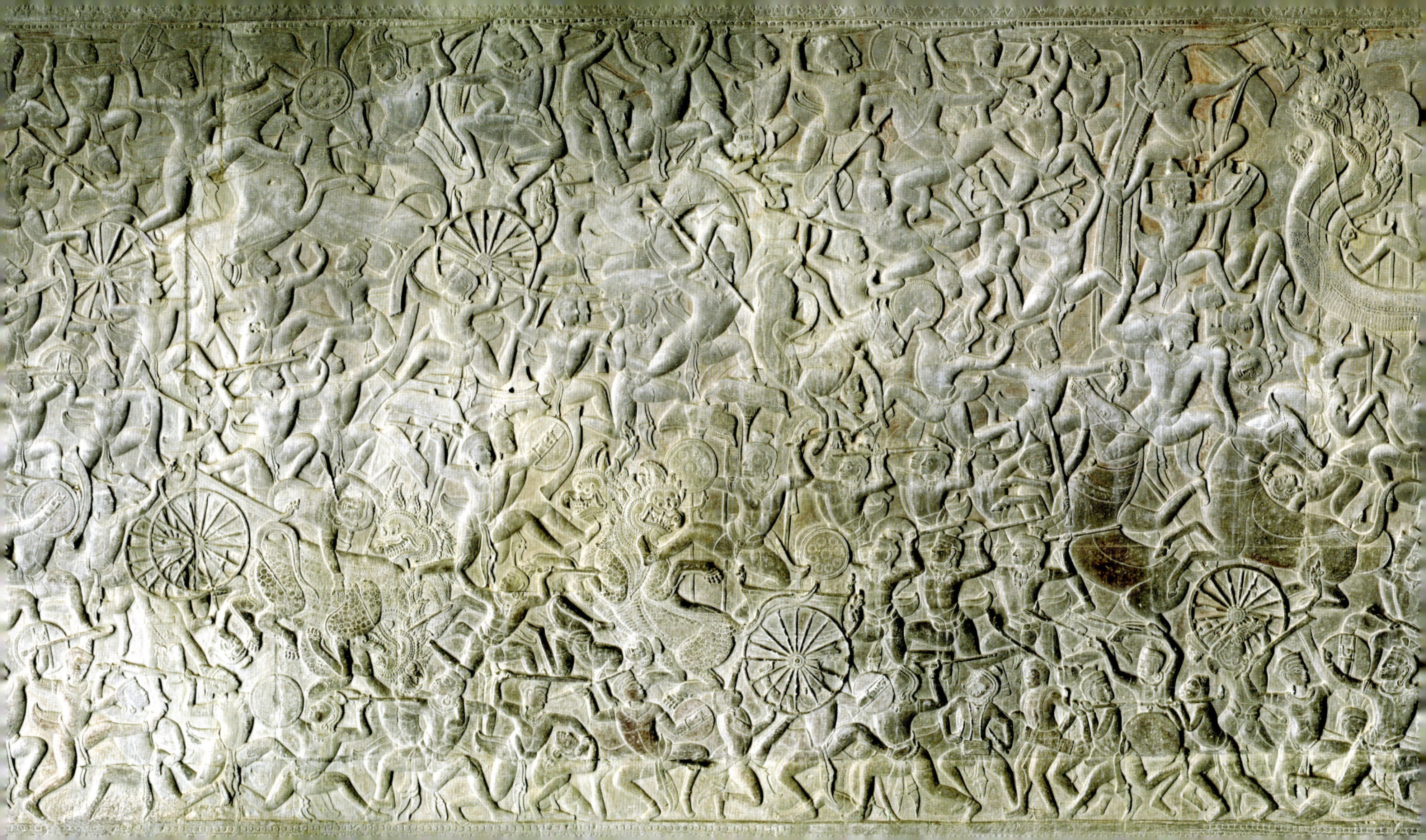

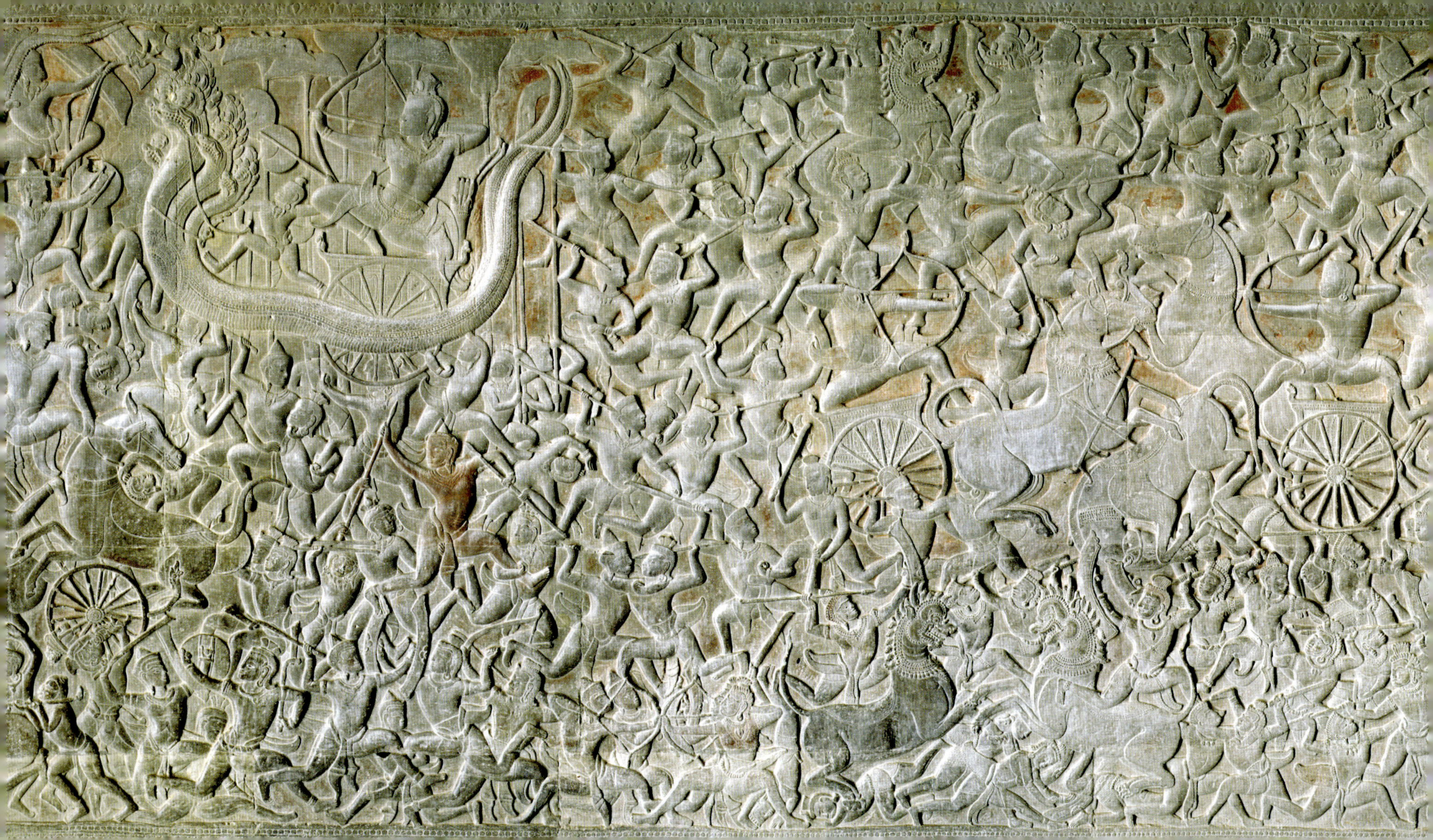

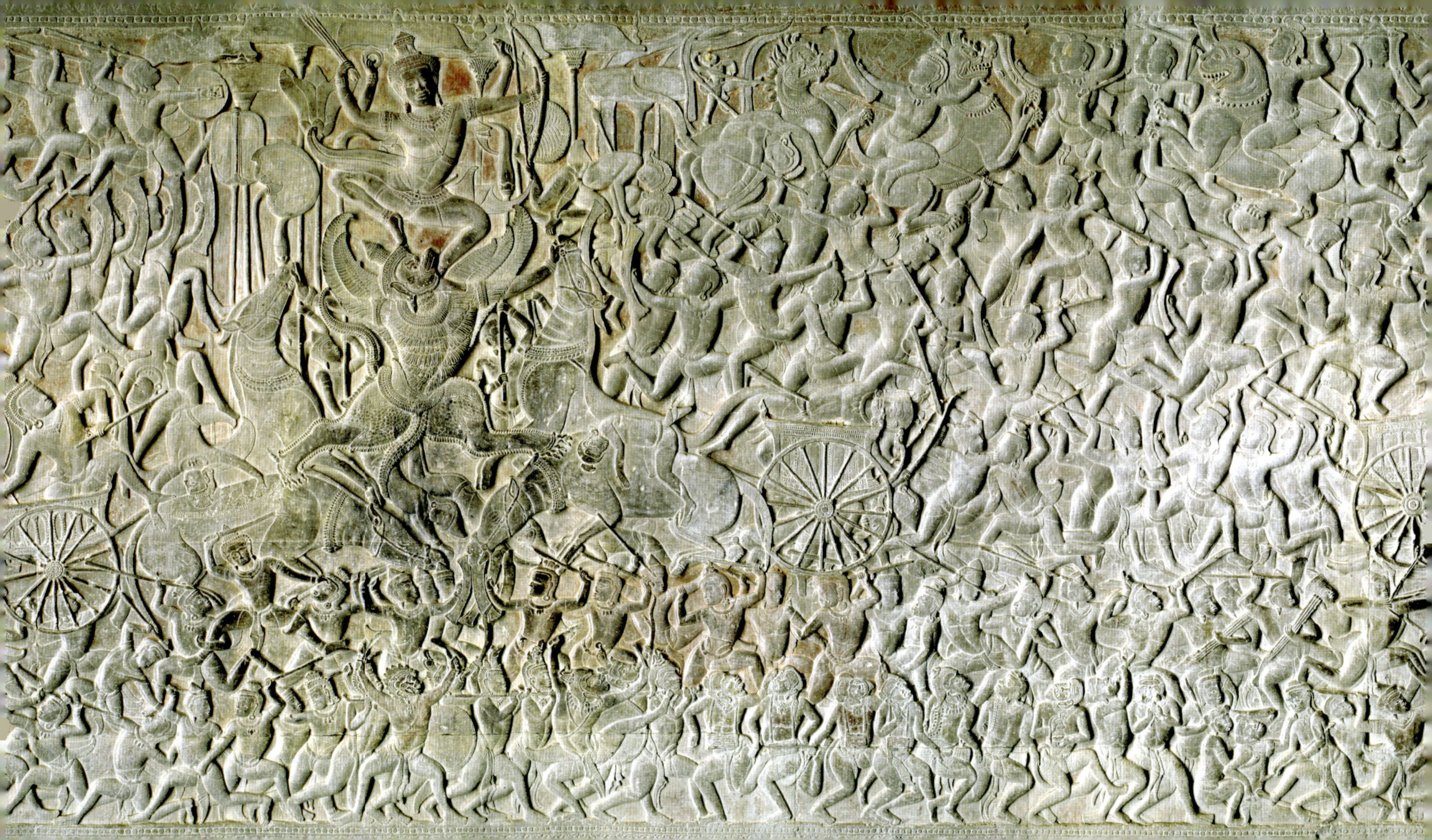

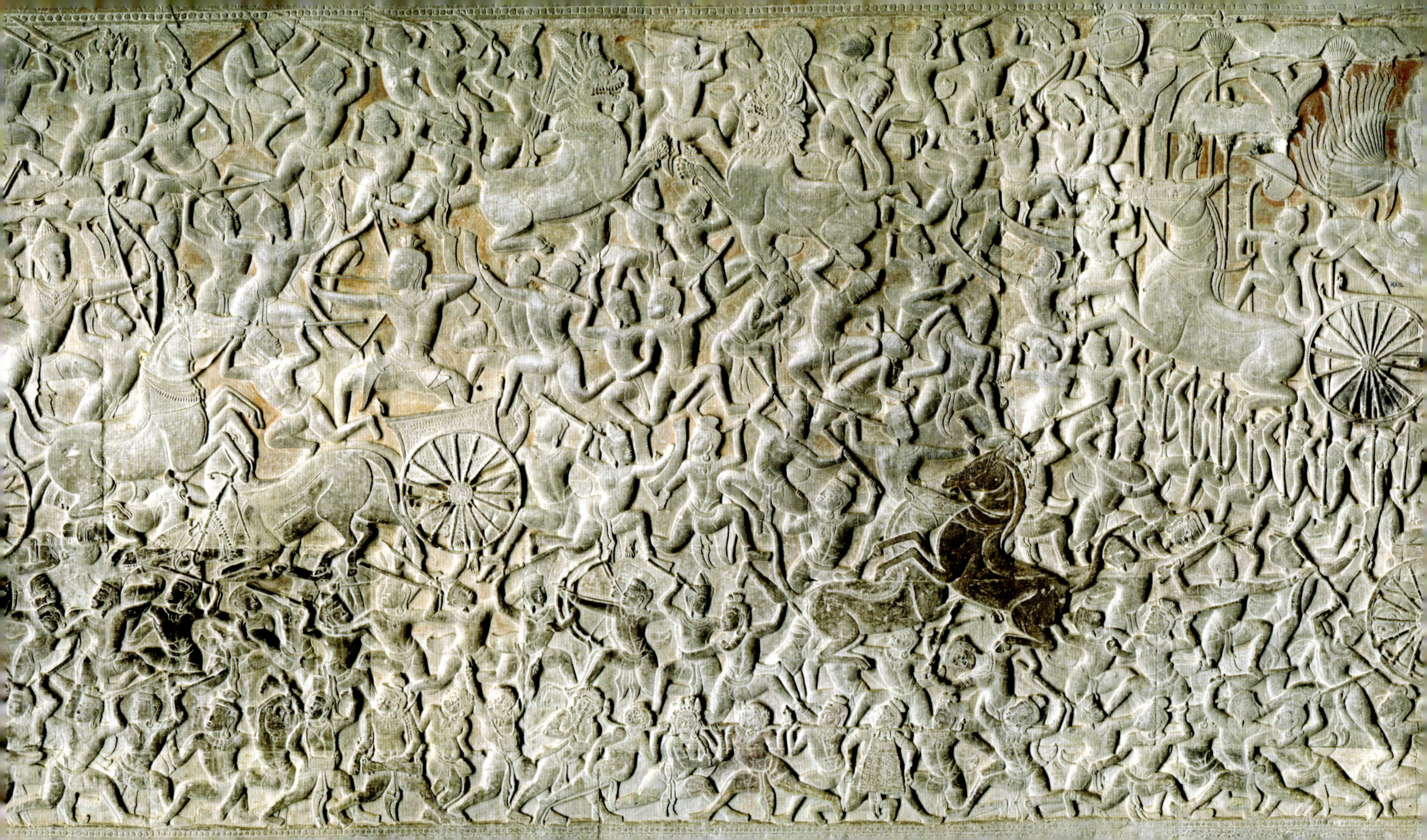

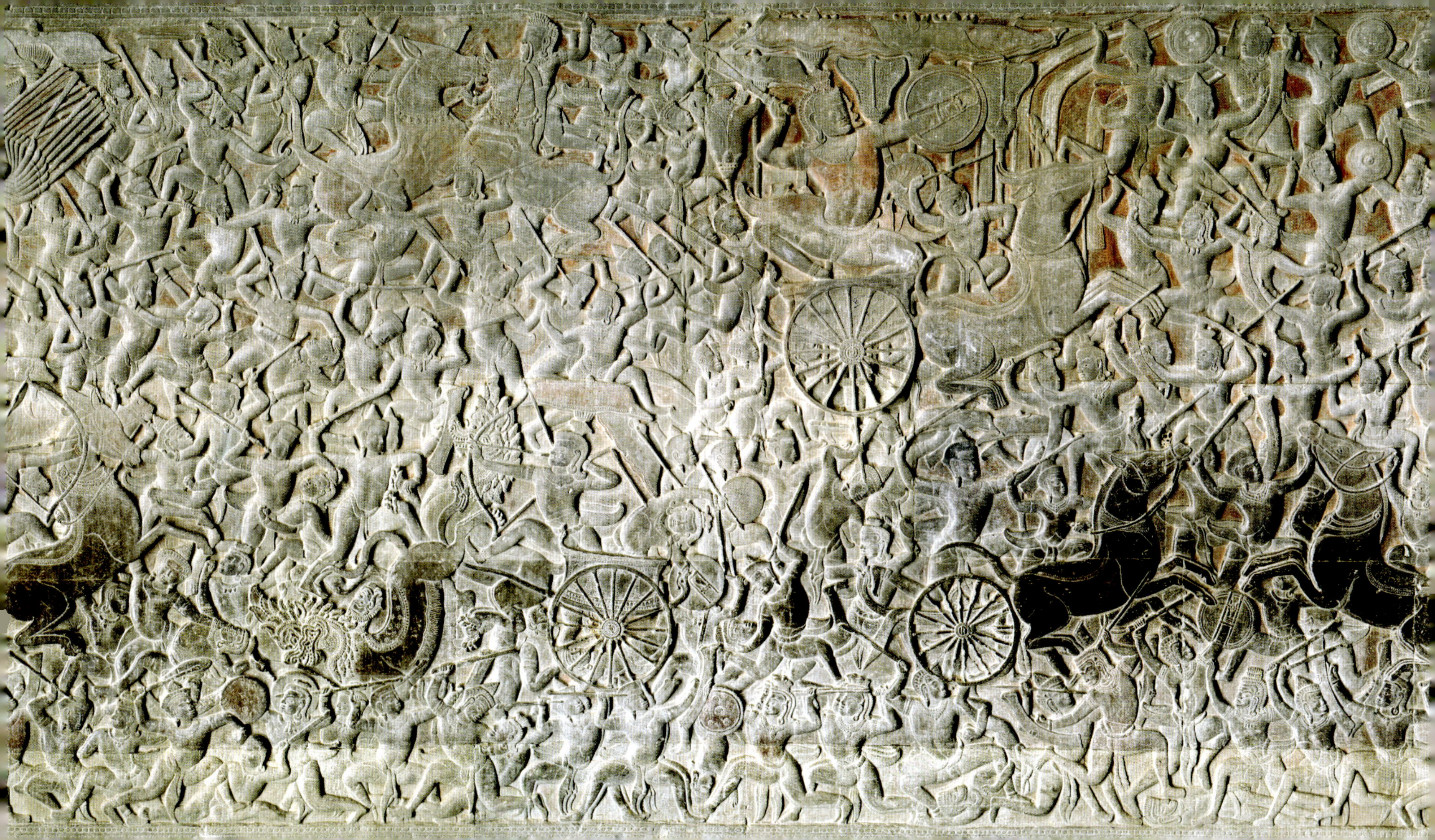

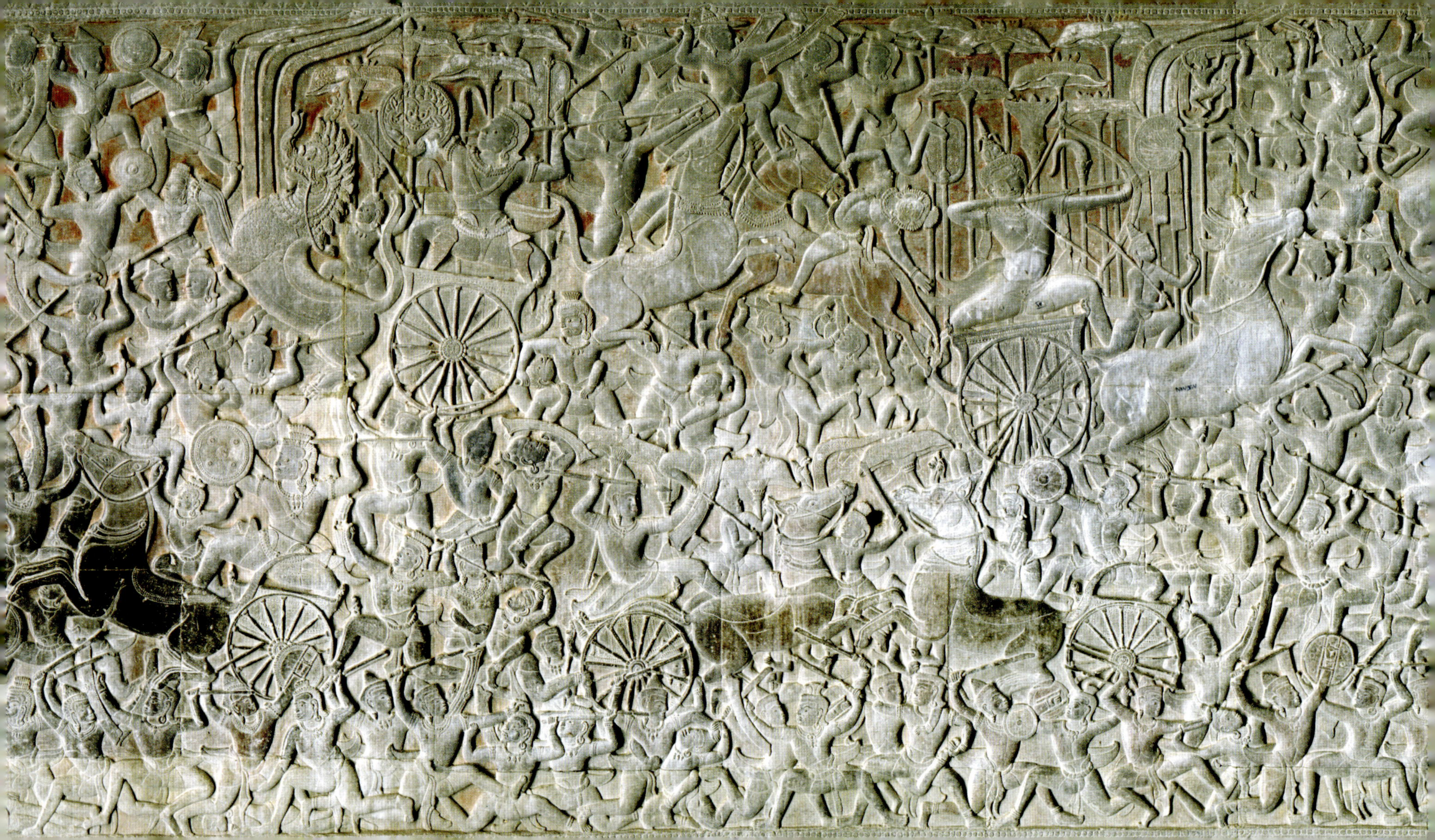

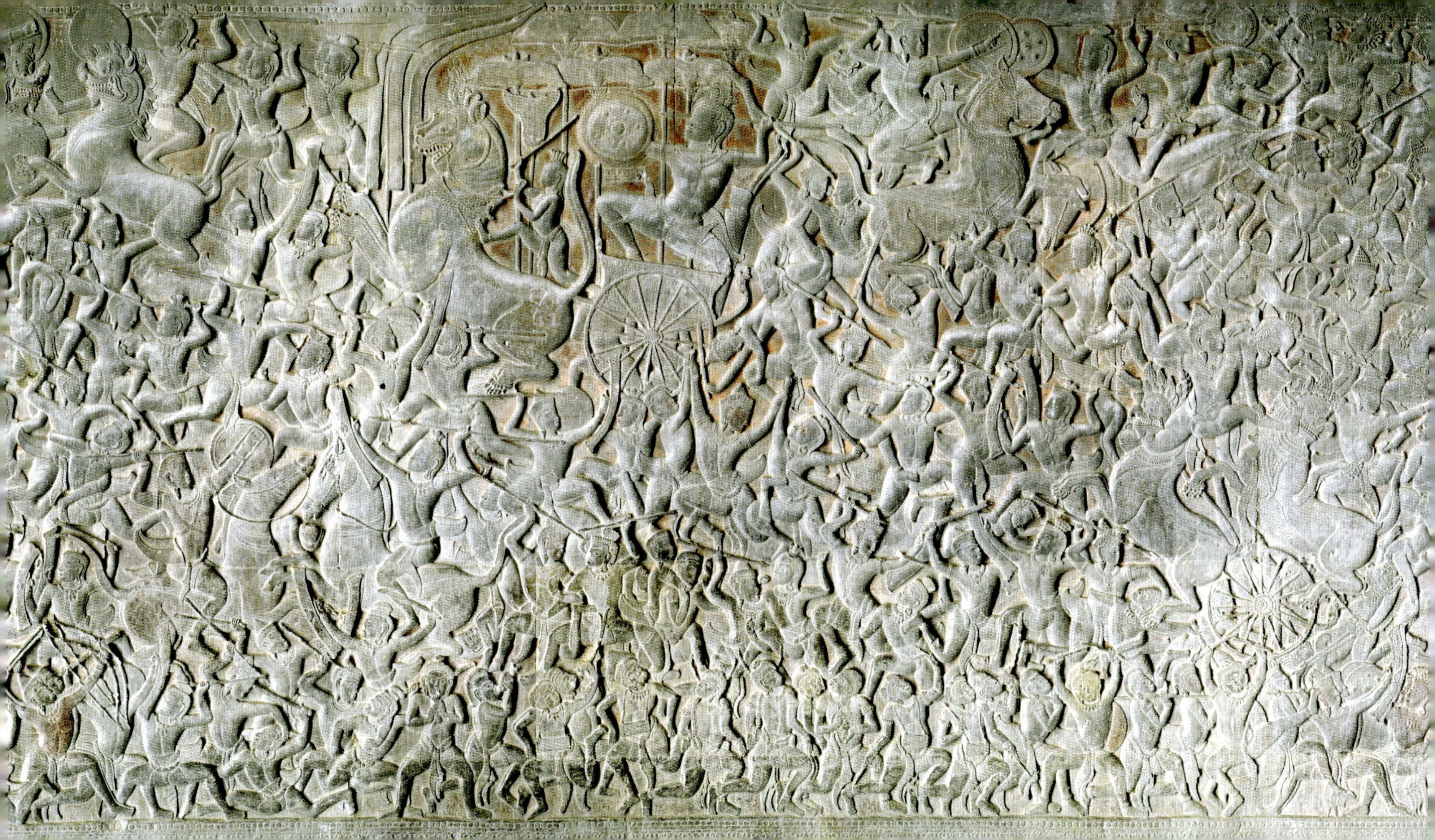

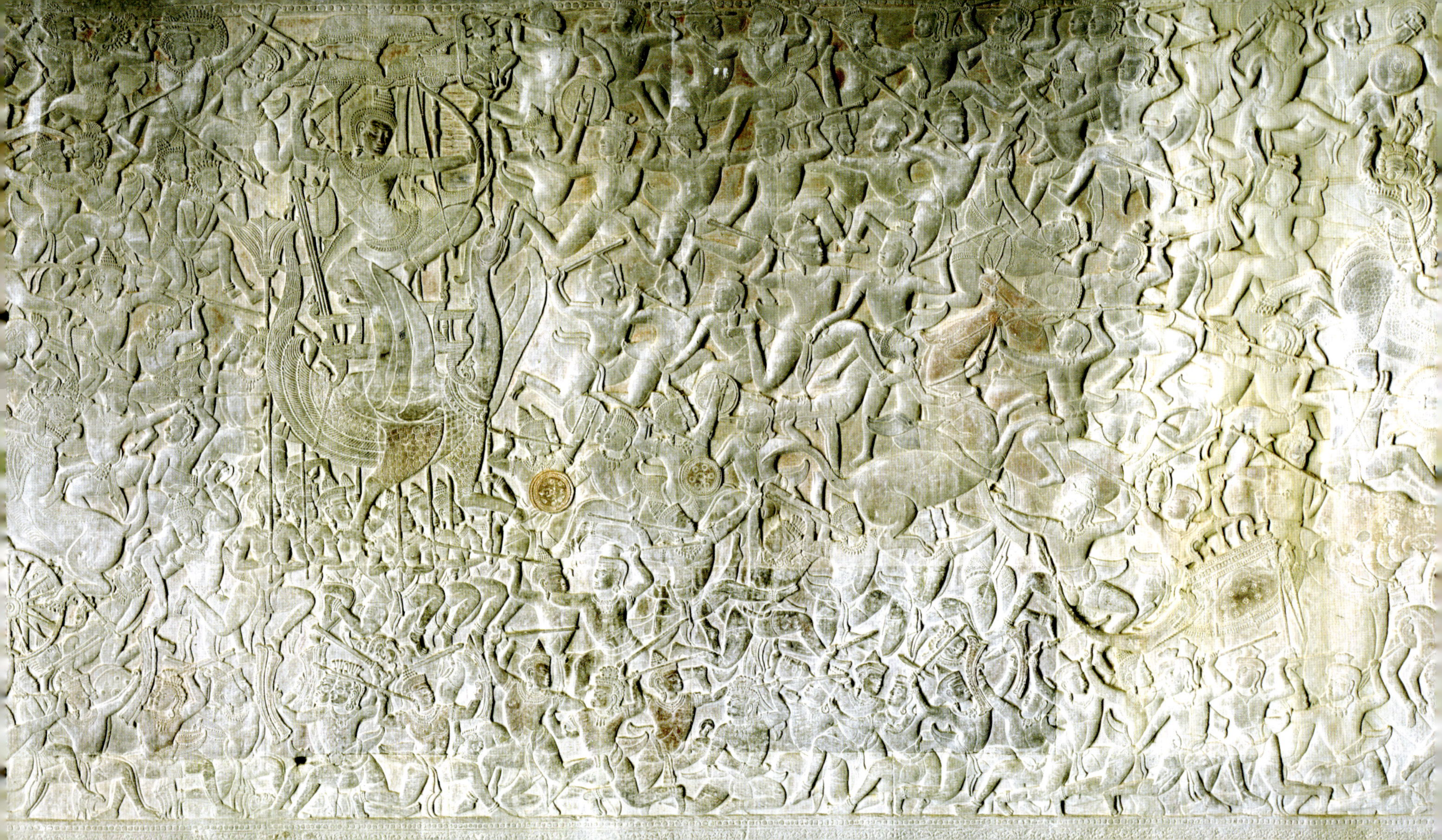

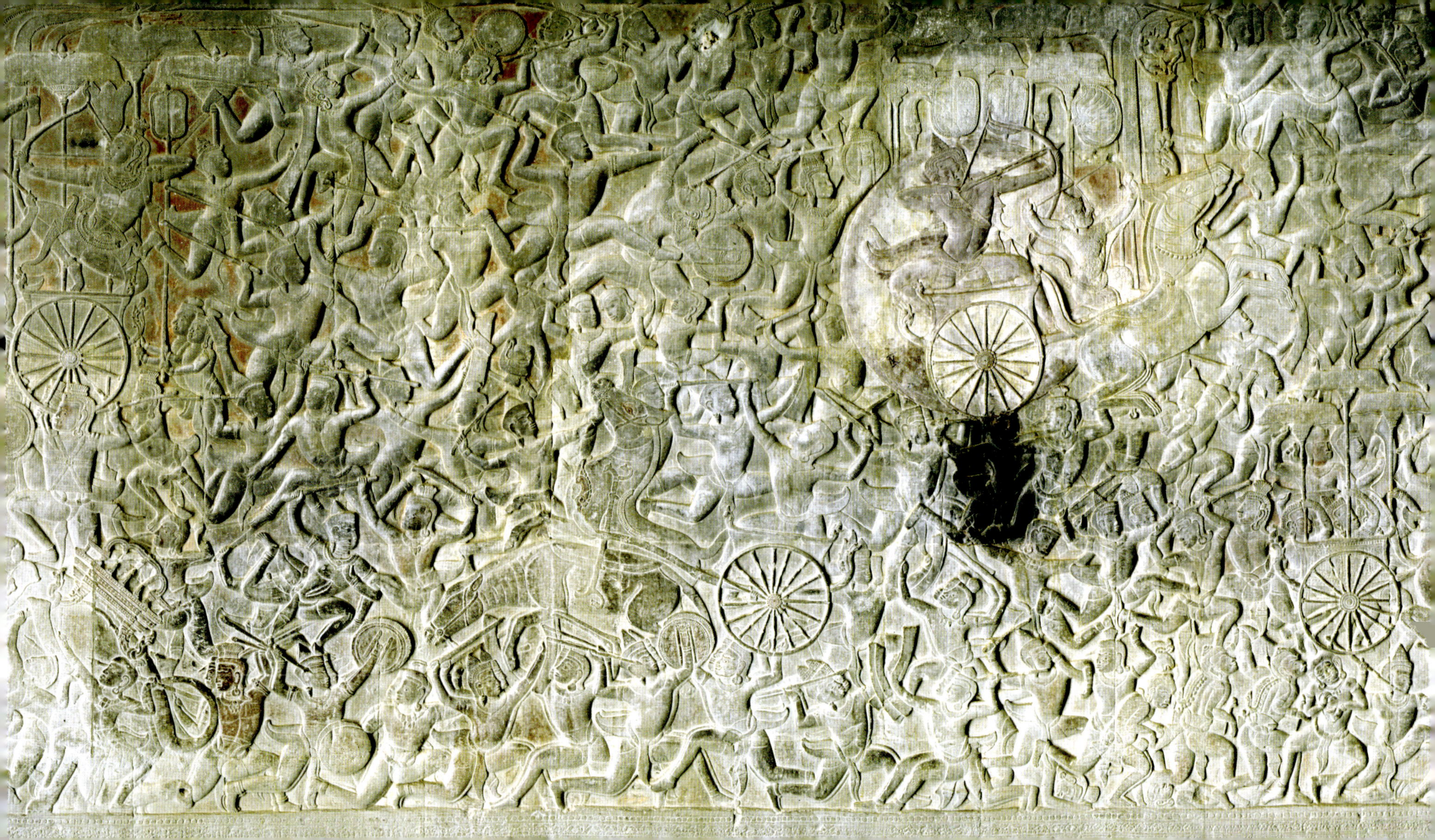

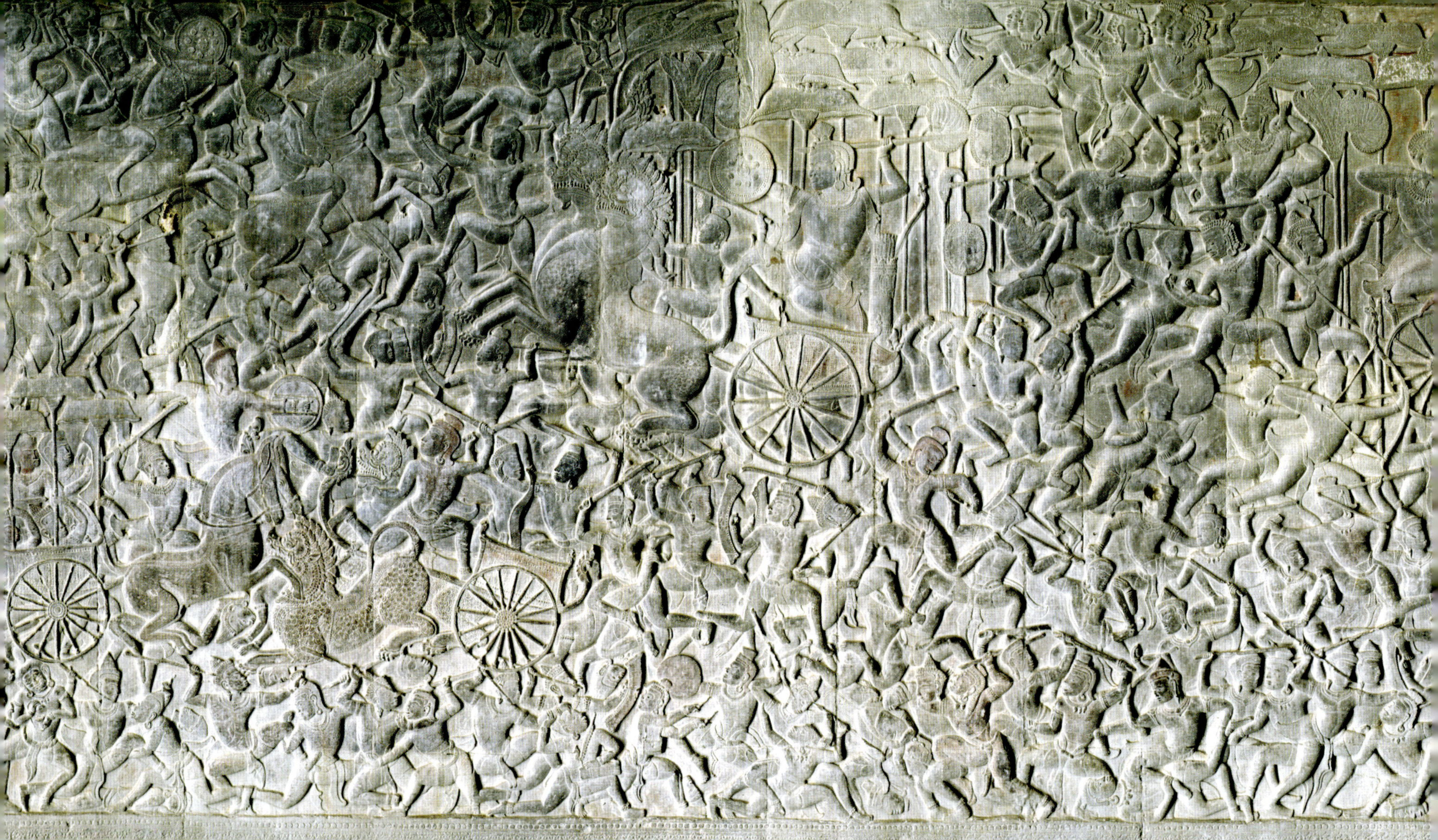

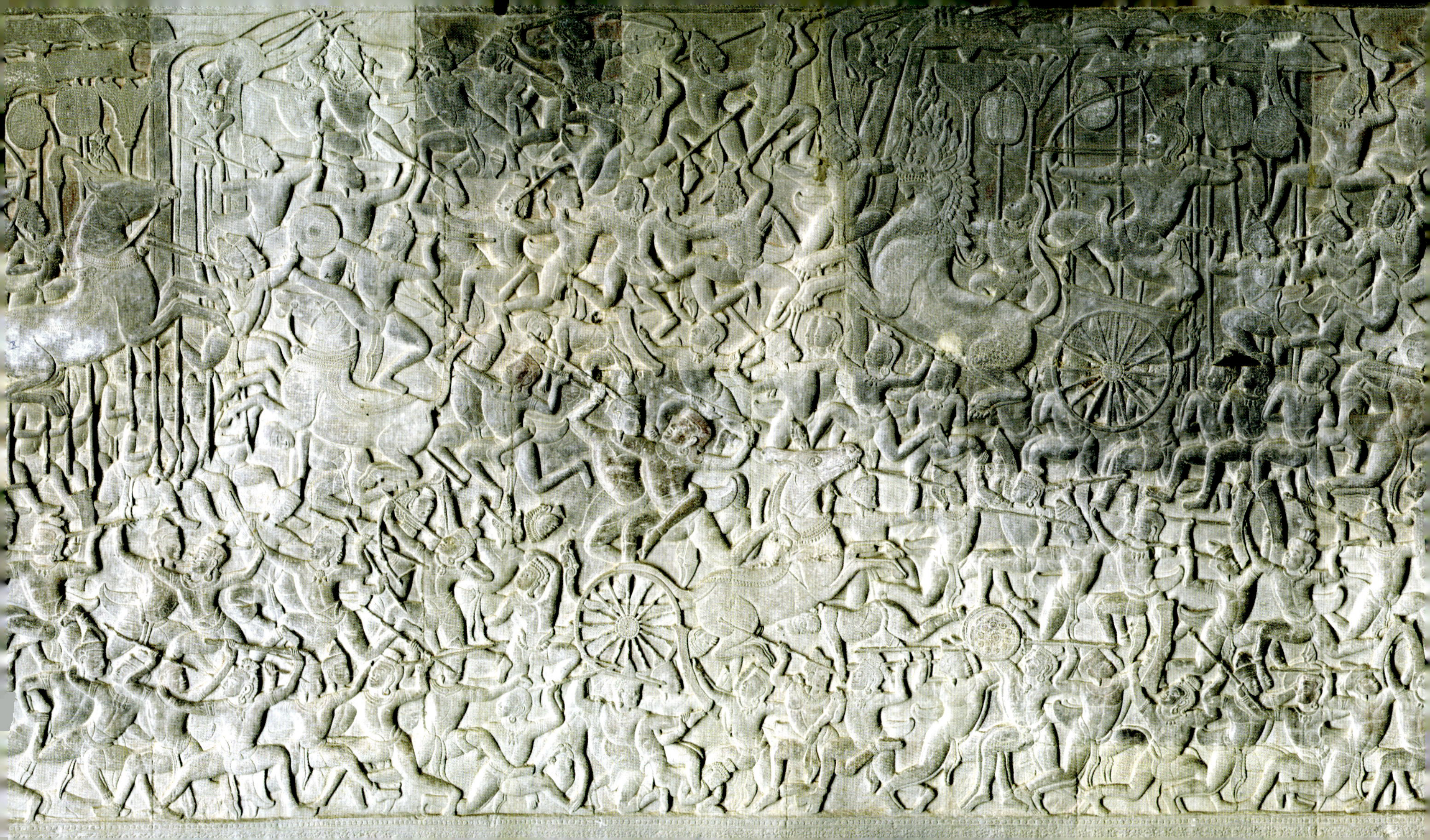

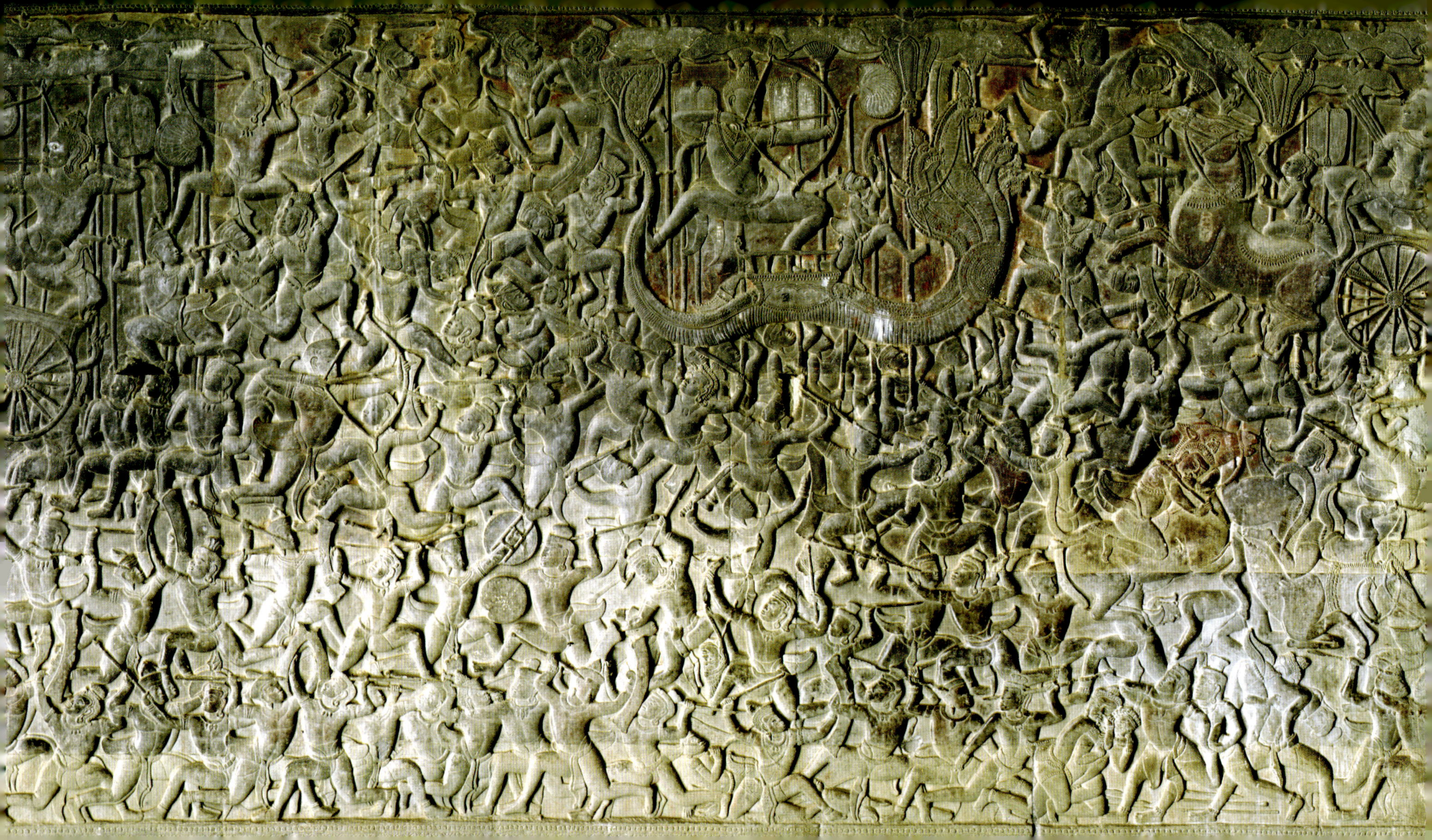

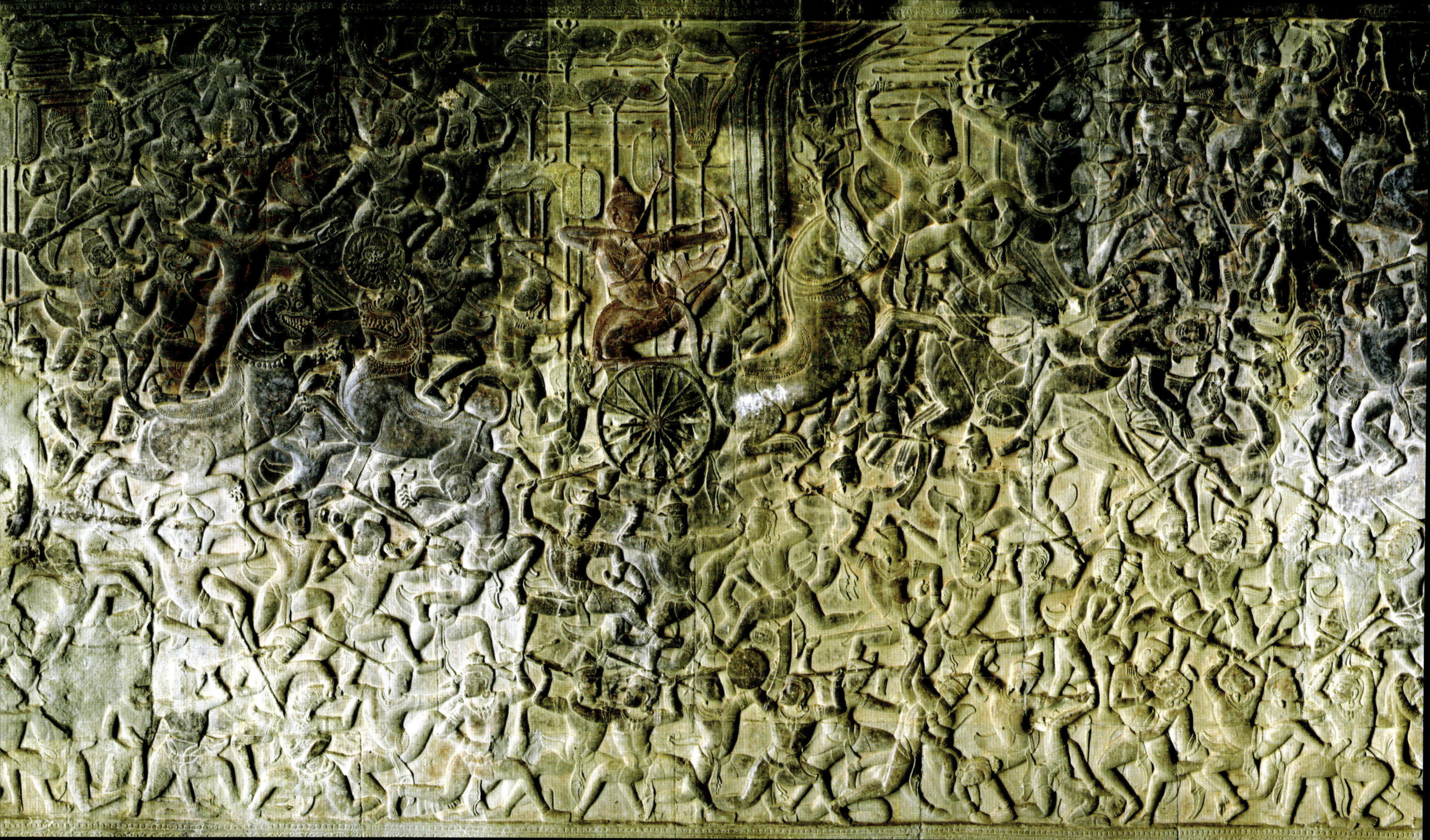

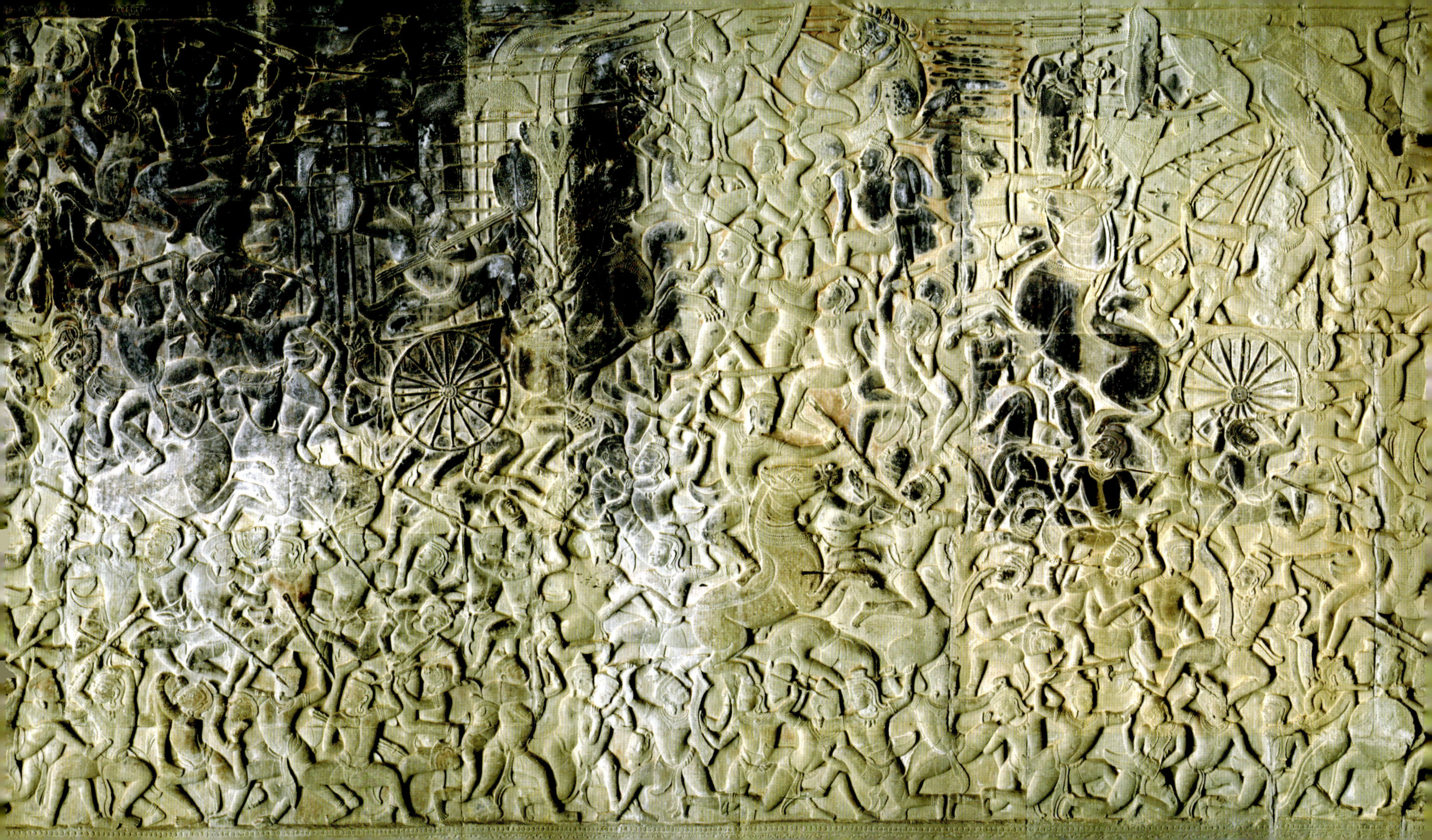

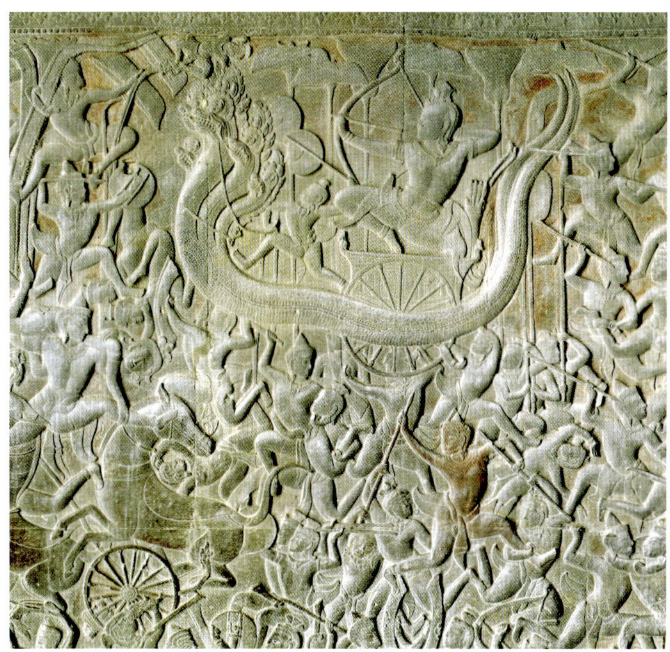

THE BATTLE OF LANKA:

RAMA AND RAVANA

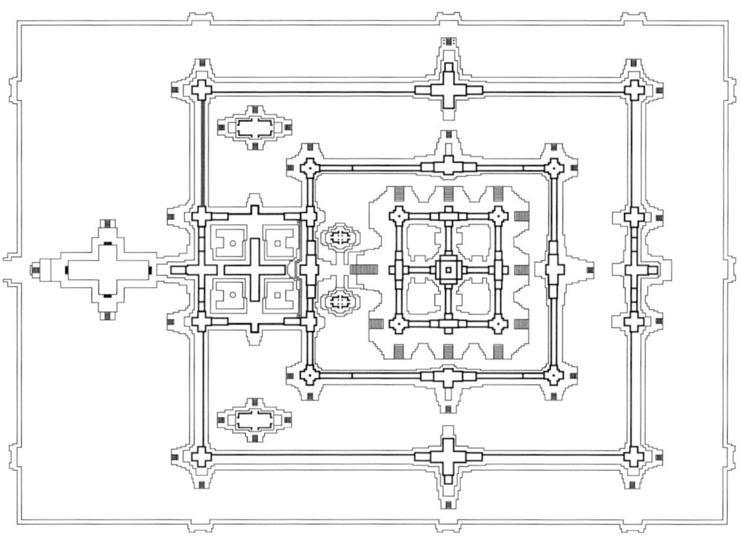

West Gallery, North Wing

RAMA AND RAVANA
End of the Treta, beginning of the Dvapara.

Passing through the north-west corner pavilion to the western side of the enclosure, we enter a new phase in the Hindu conception of time, and a new conceptual realm, one in which the human aspect of Vishnu increasingly informs the eternal struggle of righteousness against disorder, where human nature conflicts with itself and with intimations of its divine origin. It is from this corner of the galleries that the rapid three-stage descent from the world of the immortals to the world of men begins. We are leaving the Treta Yuga and entering the Dvapara which heralds the approach of the present, the Kali-yuga.

The Sanskrit text on which the depiction in this panel was based is not a sacred scripture but an epic story, the famous and profoundly influential *Ramayana* of Valmiki, of which there exist numerous later versions, from India to Burma, Thailand, Cambodia, Laos, China and Japan, in all major religious contexts – Hindu, Buddhist, Jain, and Islamic – and in many languages, including the Old Javanese *Ramayana Kakawin* (10th century), the Malay *Hikayat Sri Rama* (based on oral recitations beginning in the 13th century), the Thai *Ramakien* (the court version composed in the late 18th century), the Burmese *Rama Thagyin* (in its present form also dating from the late 18th century), and the Khmer *Ramakerti,* the earliest known version of which dates to the 16th-17th century, though the Indian *Ramayana* was known in Cambodia probably from the 6th century onward. This widespread fascination with the Rama story began in India itself, during the centuries-long formation of the epic, a process which probably began as far back as the 4th century BC and

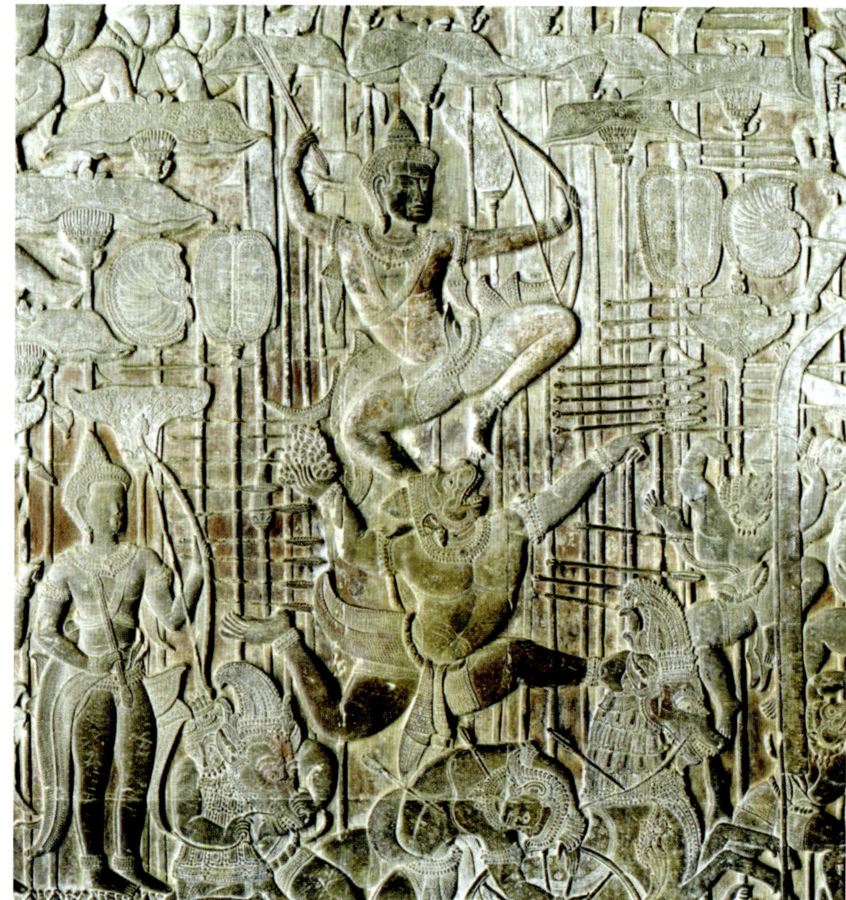

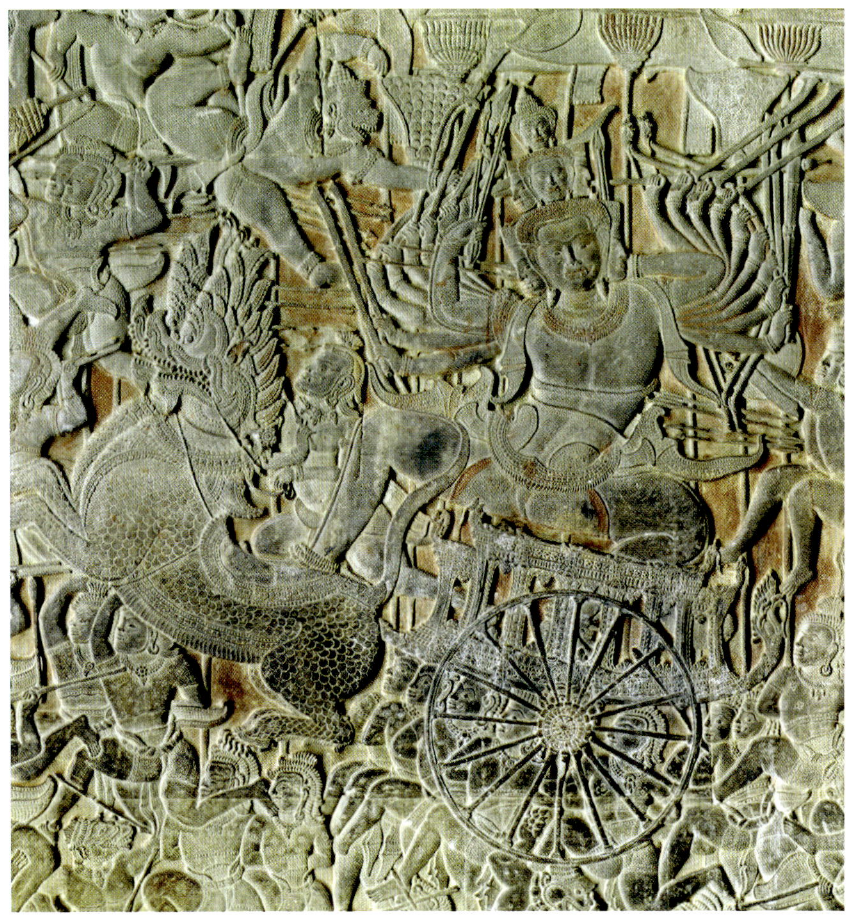

continued into the 3rd century AD. The original Sanskrit version passed through many phases of development before reaching the classic form with which we are now familiar, and the changes wrought at each stage of redaction were reflected in transformations in the nature of the central character, Rama. Changes of this kind occurred frequently in the identities of gods and goddesses of established mythology as older versions of canonical sacred texts were recast to reflect social and political change in India. But in the case of the *Ramayana,* a new and non-sacred epic text, these changes were embodied in a human being.

Throughout the epic, Rama and other characters within the story state clearly that he is mortal – his divine nature is even on occasion explicitly denied. He is compared with several different gods, though mostly with Indra, in the same way that early Hindu kings in India and South East Asia were eulogised in their official inscriptions; but, also like those kings, he is not identified with the gods. This is a vital distinction. Overlaying these assertions of Rama's mortality, however, there are later passages in which he is indeed regarded as a divine figure; and only in the latest parts of the text is he identified with one particular god, Vishnu. As it stands, the resulting story therefore contains numerous paradoxical references to Rama the man, the god-like man, the man who is part-god, and the god in man-like form. The word *avatara,* in the sense of a "descent" or incarnation of a deity, does not occur in the text, either with specific reference to Rama or in other passages: unlike later texts such as the *Puranas,* the *Ramayana* belongs to a period before such formal structures of Vaishnava thought had taken hold, and Rama is therefore seen as an individual operating in a context that is more socially than theologically defined, though his life is determined, like everyone's, by the actions of the gods *(devyakriya)* or, which sometimes amounts to the same thing,

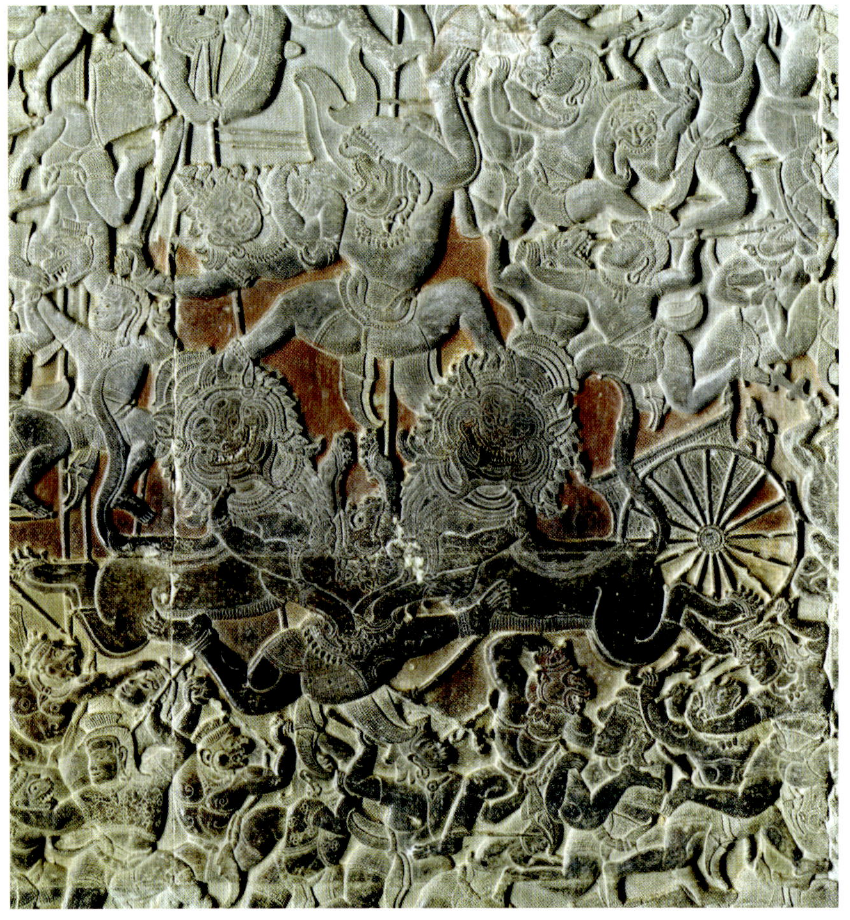

fate *(daiva, niyati)*. In this context it is the human perception of morality or lack of it that governs action, and Rama stands for Dharma in the sense of appropriate moral behaviour and response. It is the paradoxical nature of his humanity, the dilemmas with which he is confronted, his adherence to moral solutions in the face of these problems, the nobility of his character, and his final victory, that account for the vast popularity of this epic. For Asian society, the *Ramayana* in every sense tells the story of a universal hero.

As with the story of the Tarakamaya War, the Battle of Lanka, climax of the *Ramayana,* also revolves around the abduction of a woman, in this case Sita, wife of Rama. But whereas Tara was the wife of a revered priest, Sita is the betrothed of a warrior, noble and devout, and she is carried off by a demon–king whose kingdom, Lanka, lies beyond the sea, a location symbolic of the ultimate in distance, strangeness and impurity, where she is held captive. A concatenation of evil events, set in train by female jealousy and sustained by male literal–mind-edness, are represented as responsible for this situation. The links in the chain, essential to an understanding of the battle, are these.

Long ago in Ayodhya in northern India, the old childless king, Dasa-ratha, resorts to sacrifices in order to father children and preserve his line. He then has four sons – Rama, Bharata, Lakshmana, and Satrughna – of whom Rama marries the beautiful Sita. While Rama is still a teenager, his father appoints him crown prince *(yuvaraja)*. But a woman named Manthara (Crooked), servant to Kaikeyi, one of Dasaratha's wives and mother of Bharata, persuades her mistress to insist that her son be given the kingdom instead. Thus motivated, Kaikeyi reminds Dasaratha that he had made her certain promises, and finally with a heavy heart Dasaratha agrees to send Rama into exile and name Bharata crown prince in his place. This causes the old king such anguish that he dies. Rama, however, accepts his father's reversed decision with equanimity and leaves the city, together with Sita and his brother Lakshmana, for exile in the wilds. The new crown prince, Bharata, who was absent during these events, now returns to the city and, horrified at what has happened, sets out to catch up with Rama and bring him back. Rama still insists on carrying out his dead father's command to the letter, however, and Bharata goes back to Ayodhya to govern alone – but not to rule: he intends to function as regent until Rama shall return, and as token of this he takes with him a pair of Rama's sandals as symbol of the true king he serves.

In the great Dandaka forest, Rama, Sita and Lakshmana spend ten years among the hermits who live there practising religious austerities. But what starts out as an idyllic life in tune with nature and spiritual values soon degenerates into a battleground as another tortured female enters the story. This is Surpanakha (Fingernails like Winnowing Fans), a hideous demoness who, having hilariously failed to seduce Rama and Lakshmana, vents her embittered fury on the laughing Sita, threatening to devour her. As punishment for this attack Lakshmana cuts off her nose and ears, thus further disfiguring the already ugly demoness. Her rage heightened by these accumulating humiliations, Surpanakha turns to her brother, Khara, but his revenge in the shape of demon hordes is stopped in its tracks by the warrior brothers. The demoness then seeks vengeance through another of her brothers – and this is where the plot thickens, for he is none other than ten-headed Ravana, nephew of Kalanemi and demon ruler of the island kingdom of Lanka. Surpanakha excites his lust for Sita, and the die is cast. Ravana accomplishes the abduction of Sita through two deceptions. He orders his brother to assume the

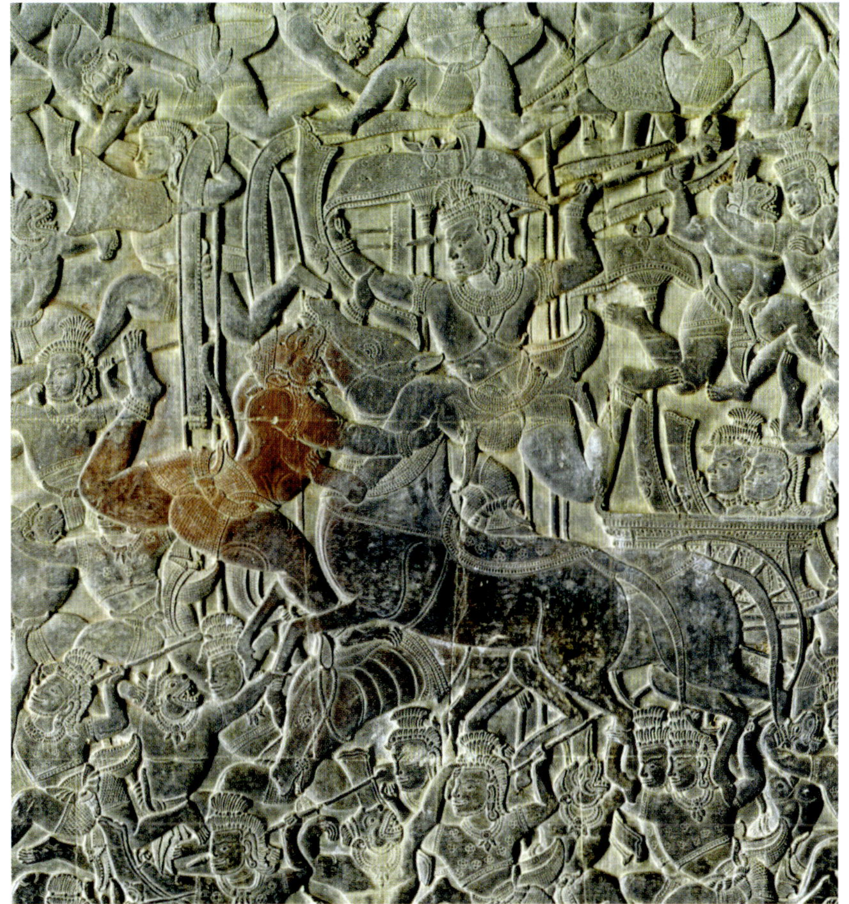

shape of a golden deer and to appear in this form to Rama and Lakshmana deep in the forest. The brothers, encouraged by Sita herself, go in pursuit of the fabulous animal. Unprotected, Sita is now easy game for the wily Ravana, who approaches her in the guise of a harmless religious mendicant. He seizes her and transports her to his palace in Lanka. There follows the story of the two brothers' desperate search for Sita, eventually aided by a vast army of jungle-dwellers represented as Vanaras (monkeys) led by their king, Sugriva, and his minister, Hanuman, who leaps the strait to Lanka, reconnoitres the island, finds Sita and talks with her. He is later captured and mistreated, but escapes with his tail on fire and causes havoc by setting the demon's capital ablaze, then leaps back across the strait to the mainland, where he reports to Rama. A causeway is then built across the sea, the vast monkey army crosses, and the great battle ensues.

This is the fantastical scene presented by the relief: a densely animated field of action, in which demons are pitted against monkeys, forms the background, resembling a tapestry of complicated design, effectively conveying the concept of close-quarter jungle warfare in which the monkey warriors gain the upper hand, fighting as they are in their natural element and using ferocious fang-and-claw tactics. In the foreground, a long series of formal duels - the high points of the long drawn-out battle as described in the *Ramayana* - form the more rational narrative of the main phases of the action. The climax of this sequence is presented as the second confrontation between Rama and Ravana, the struggle between whom takes place in two stages. In the first, Rama overcomes the demon king but spares his life. When his son Indrajit is slain by Rama's brother Lakshmana, however, Ravana re-enters the battle to fight a second arduous struggle with Rama, and it is the beginning of this decisive duel that the relief illustrates. Though Rama has already

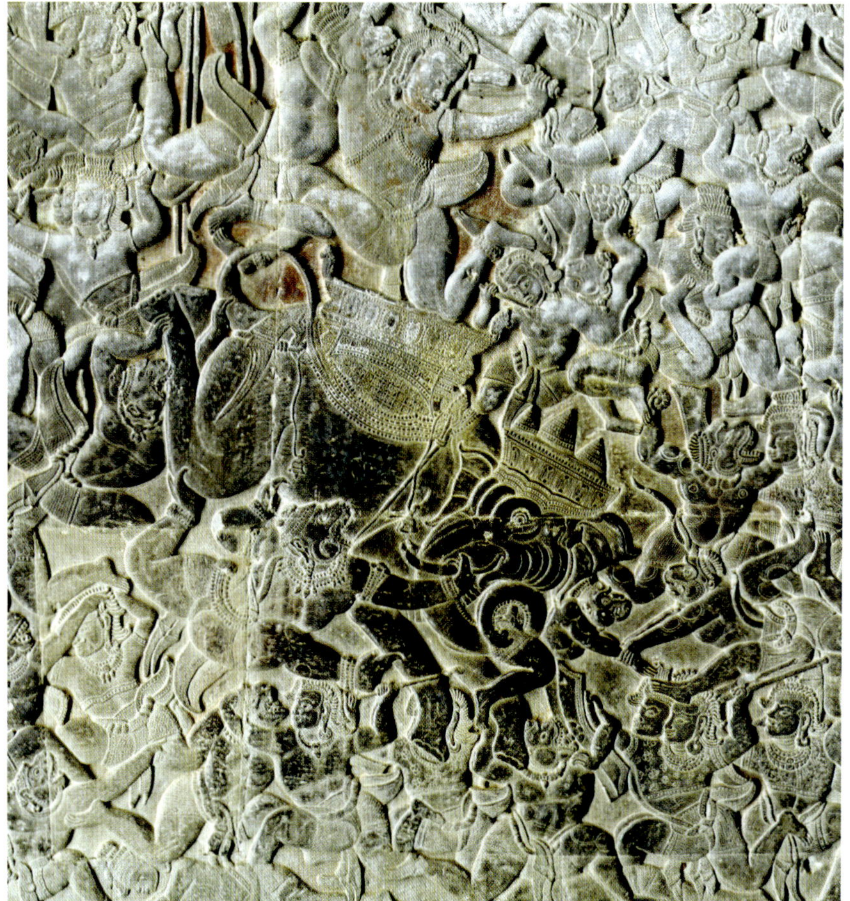

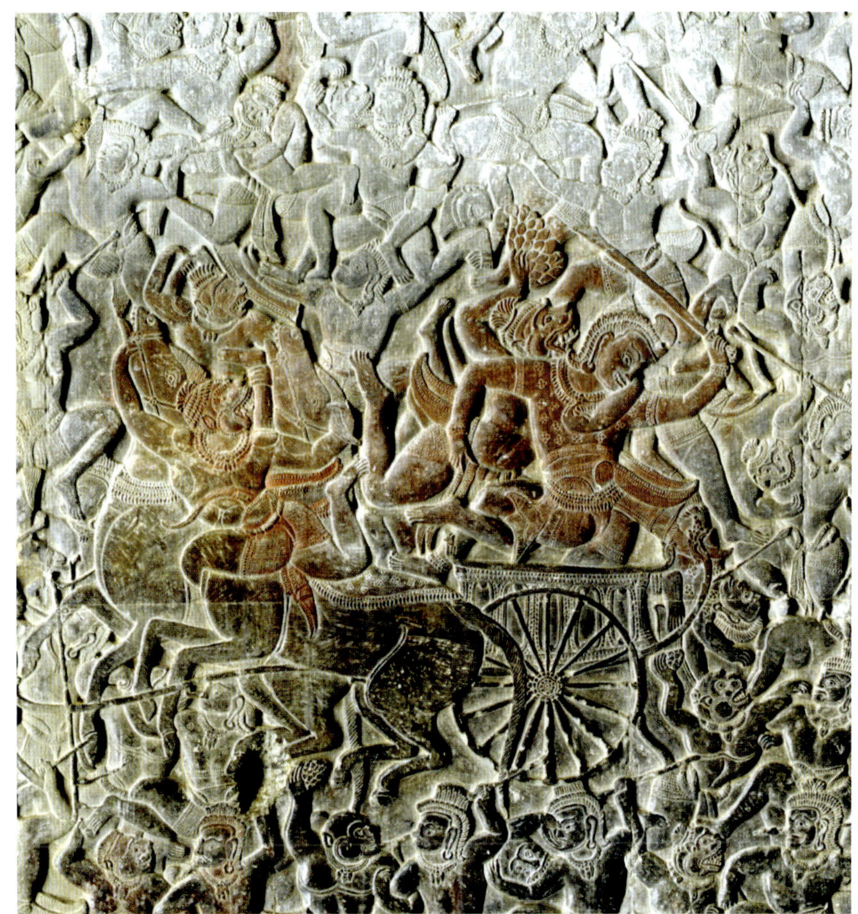

worsted the demon once, and despite having right on his side, the result is by no means a foregone conclusion. What we are witnessing – in the *Ramayana* text itself but also in the greater continuum so clearly provided by the Angkor Wat reliefs – is once again the ancient struggle between the gods and demons, now translated into the terms of a human and animal conflict. Man, instrumentalising his own animal nature in the form of the monkey army, launches an assault on immorality and the abuse of power in the monstrous shape of Ravana. This is brilliantly and power-fully conveyed at the centre of the relief by showing Rama riding the great monkey Hanuman into battle against the ten-headed demon. The ancient wars of the Treta Yuga, depicted on the eastern and northern reliefs, are now at the north-western corner transposed into the Dvapara Yuga, at the moment when Dharma loses half its force and the conflict descends from the realms of the gods to be fought out by men in this world. This is the cause of Rama's inner conflict, of which his outward battle is symbolic, between his human self with his godly or righteous principles, on the one hand, and the intervention in his life of the old evil consisting of envy and jealousy, epitomised by Ravana, on the other. In slaying Ravana, he finally defeats the amoral element in his own nature and allies himself with the gods: victory in this last struggle with the demon-king is accomplished only with the help of Indra himself, who sends his war-chariot to convey Rama in the last battle.

In the sequel Sita is rescued, Rama returns to rule his kingdom, and righteousness has temporarily prevailed in the human world. But the descent from the divine struggle to the human conflict has begun, and will sink yet further as the falling-off of Dharma accelerates. This is explained in the next relief, in which the last of the mythological and legendary episodes is depicted, before we enter the "real time" of human history.

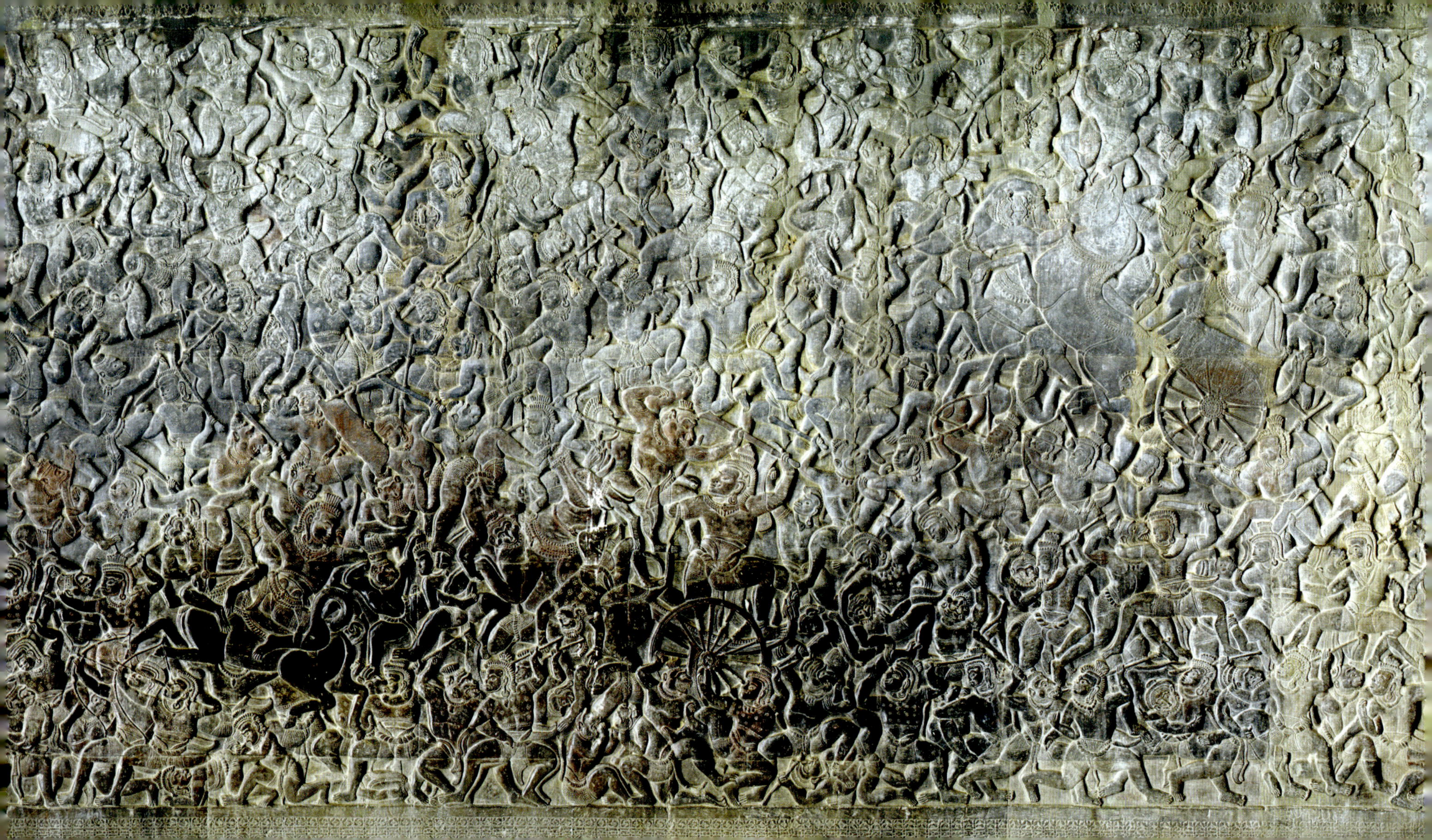

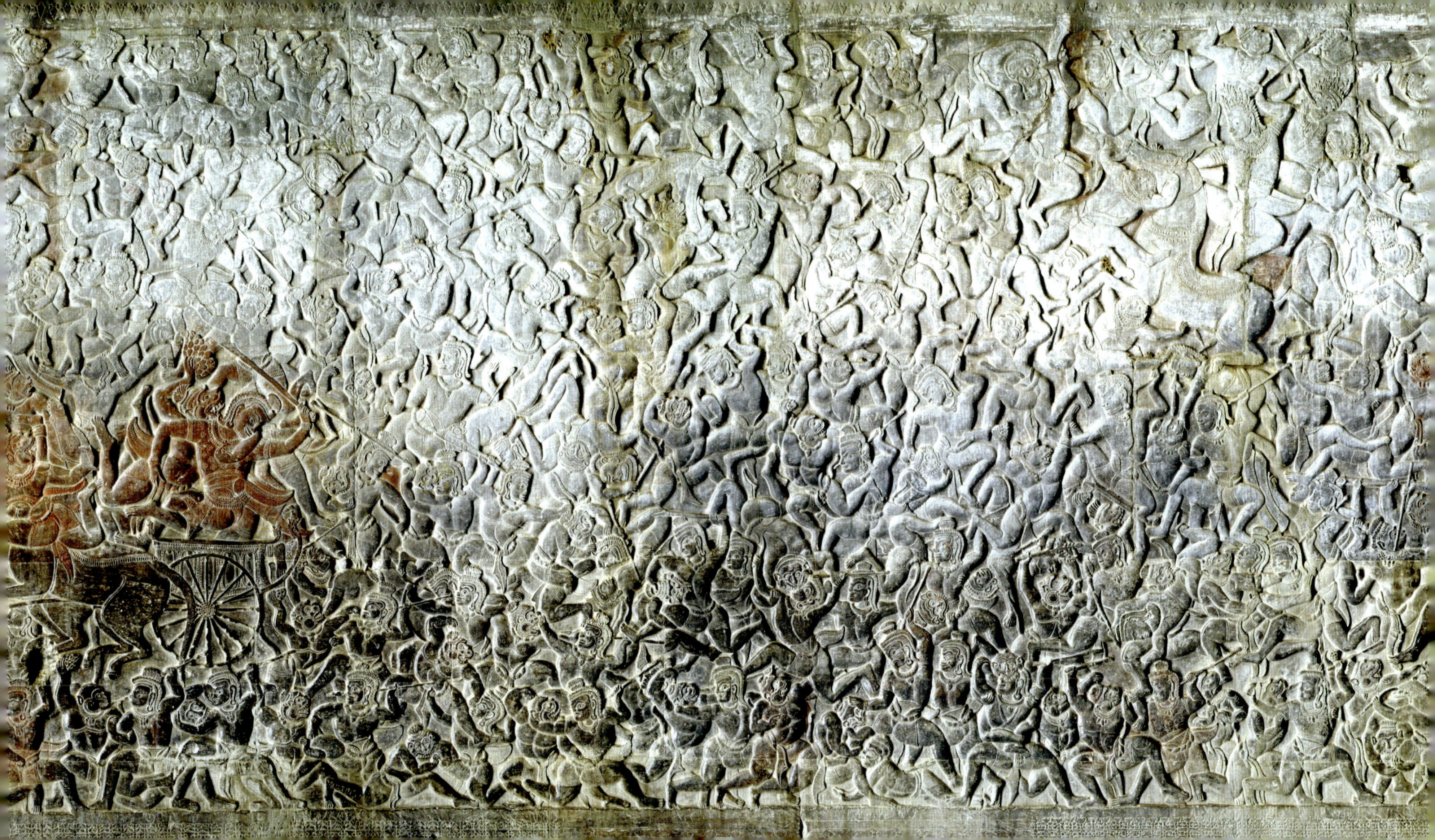

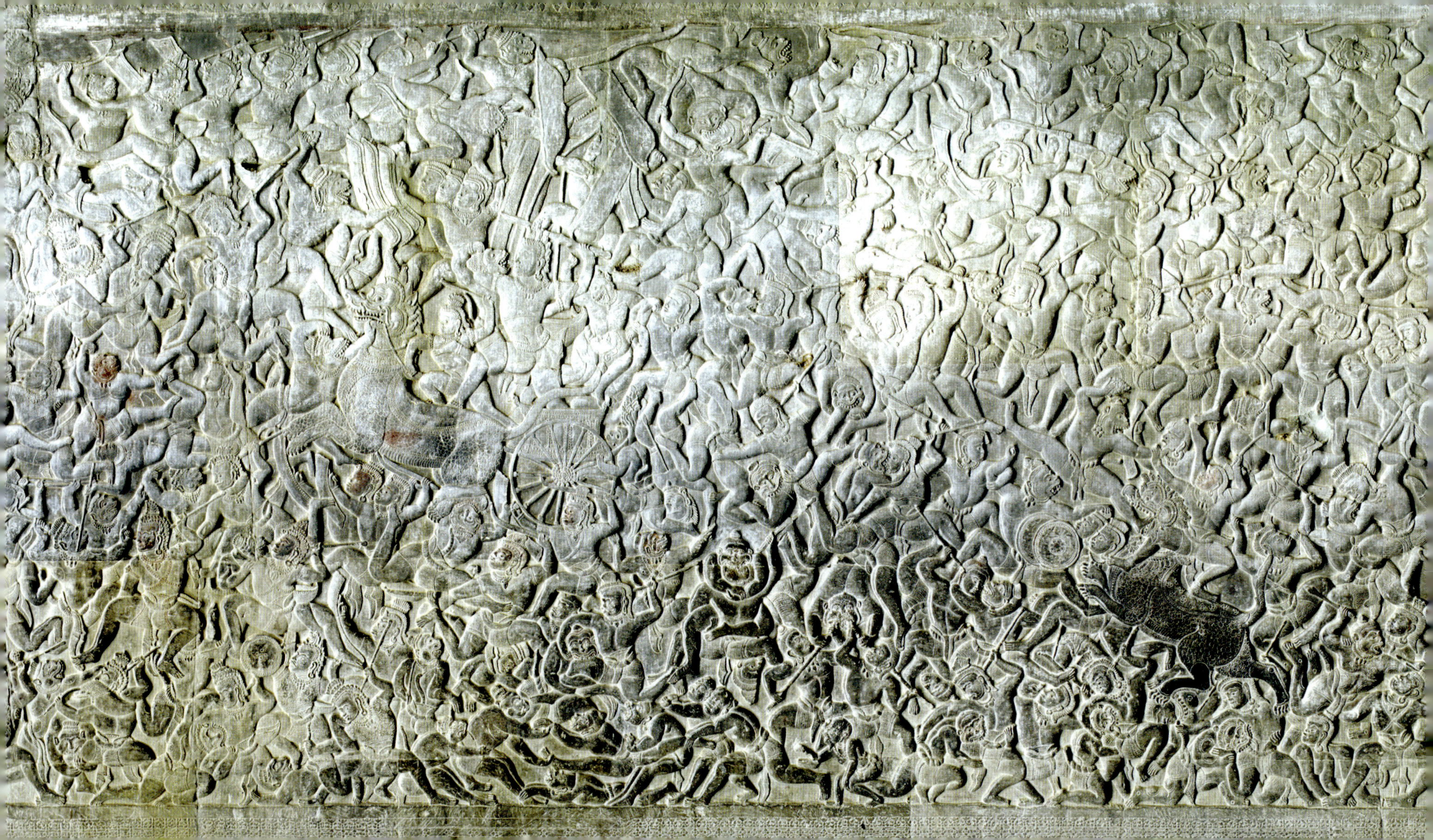

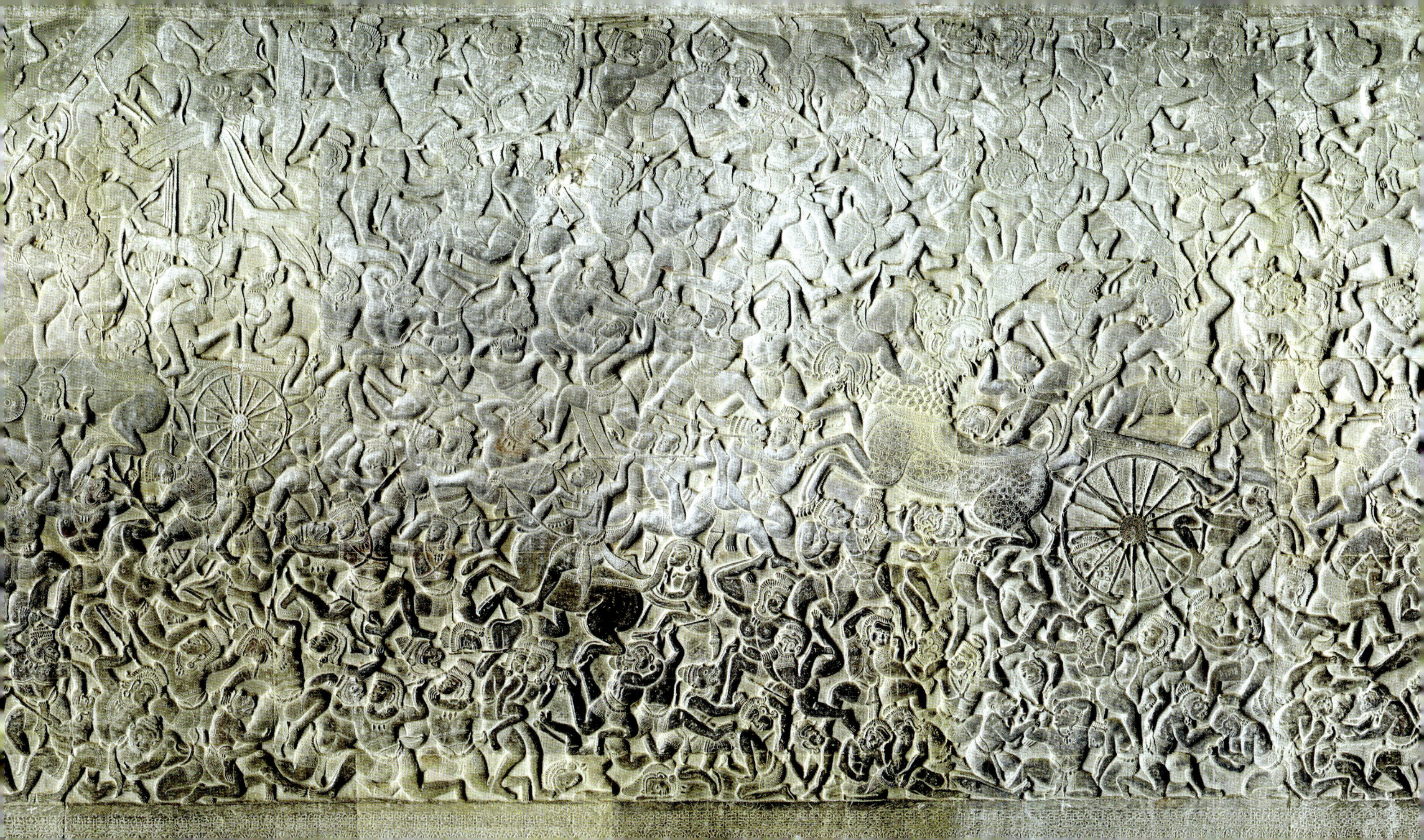

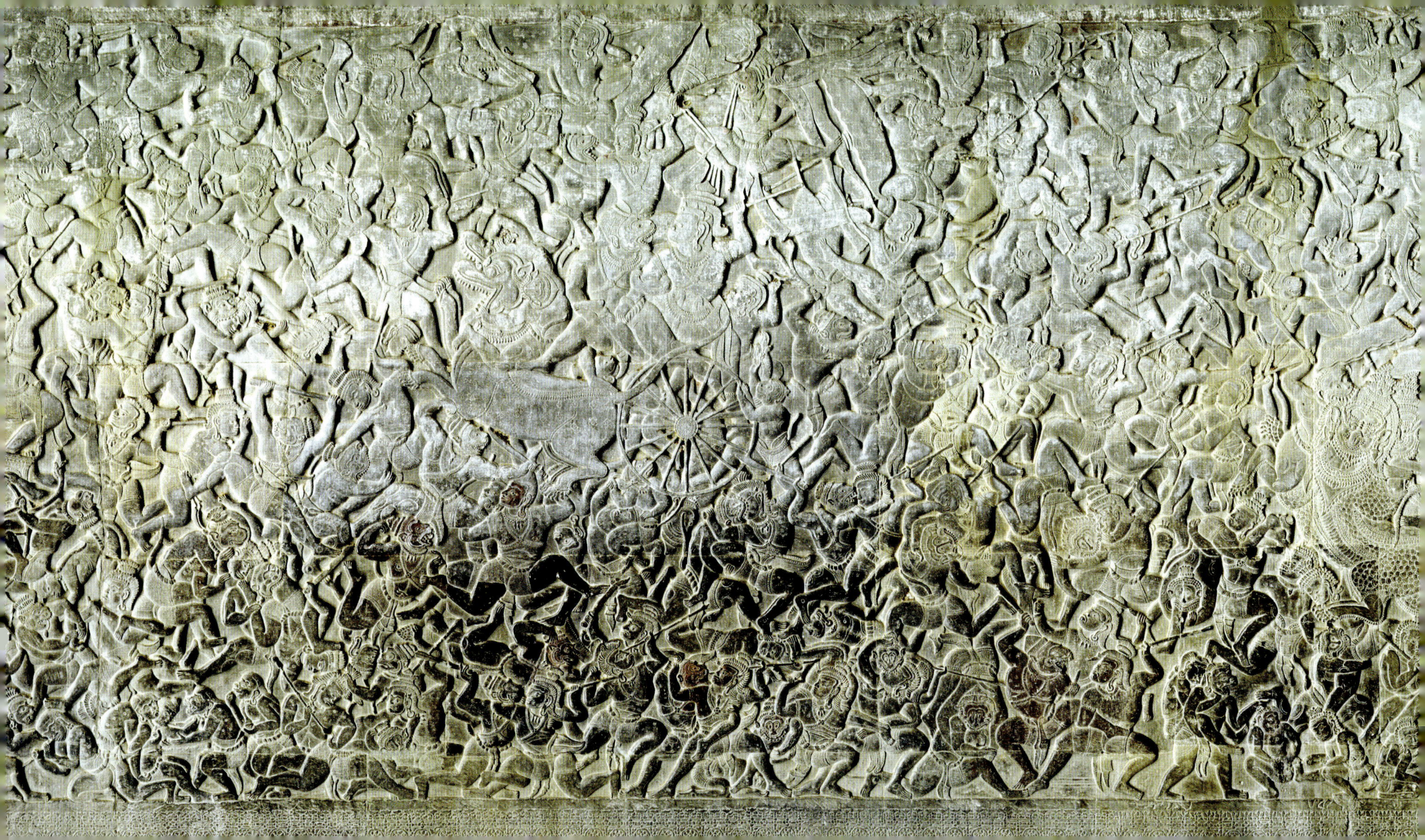

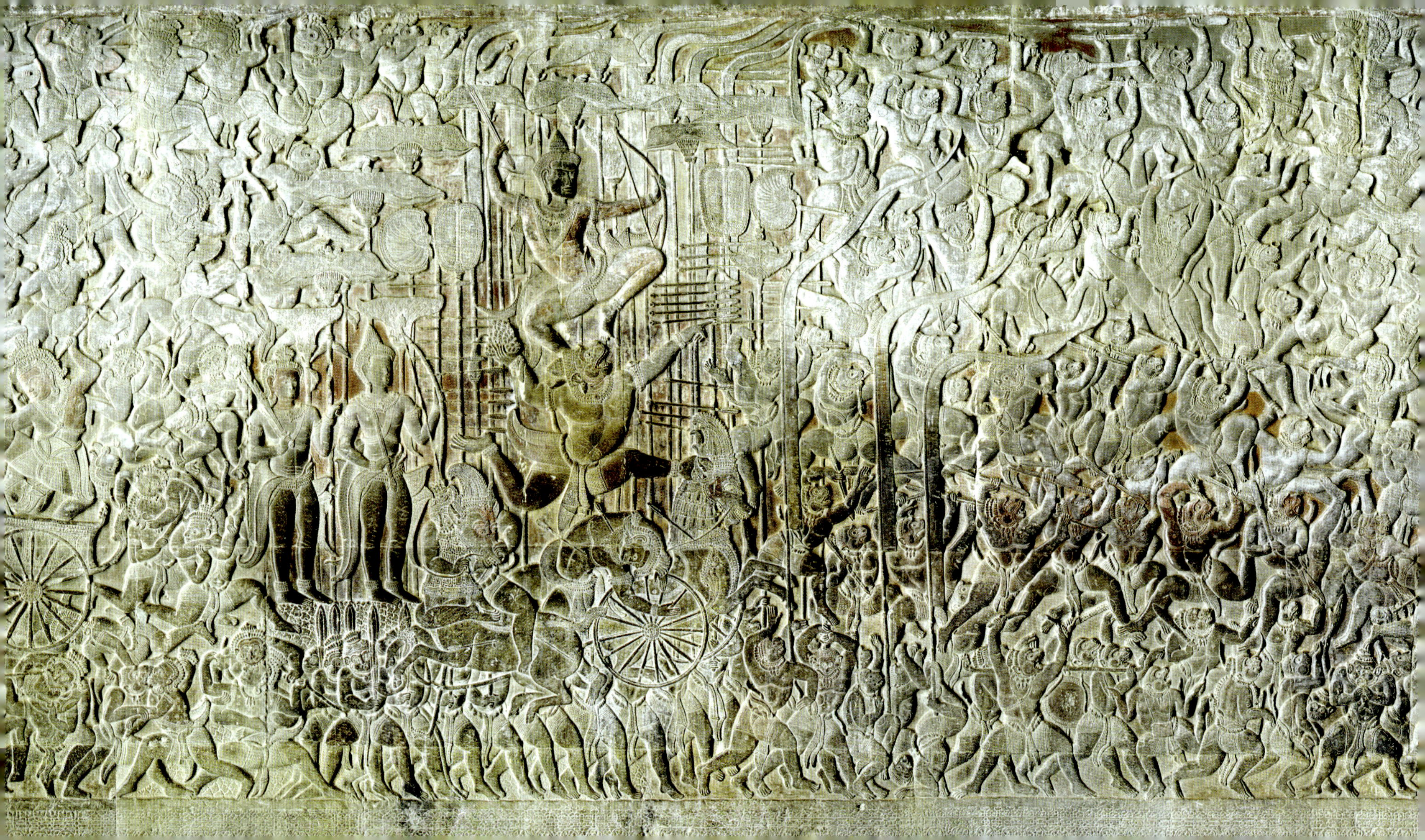

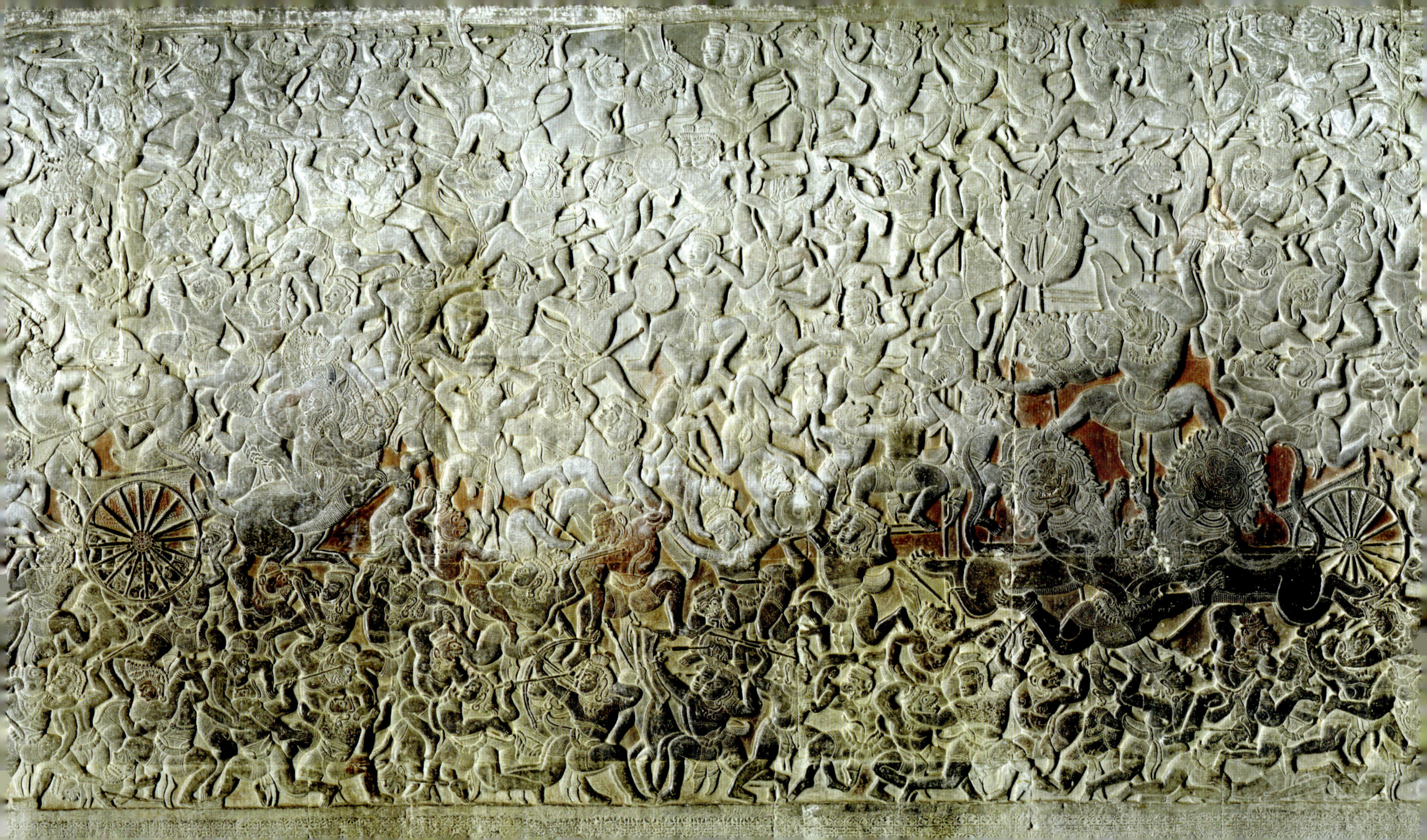

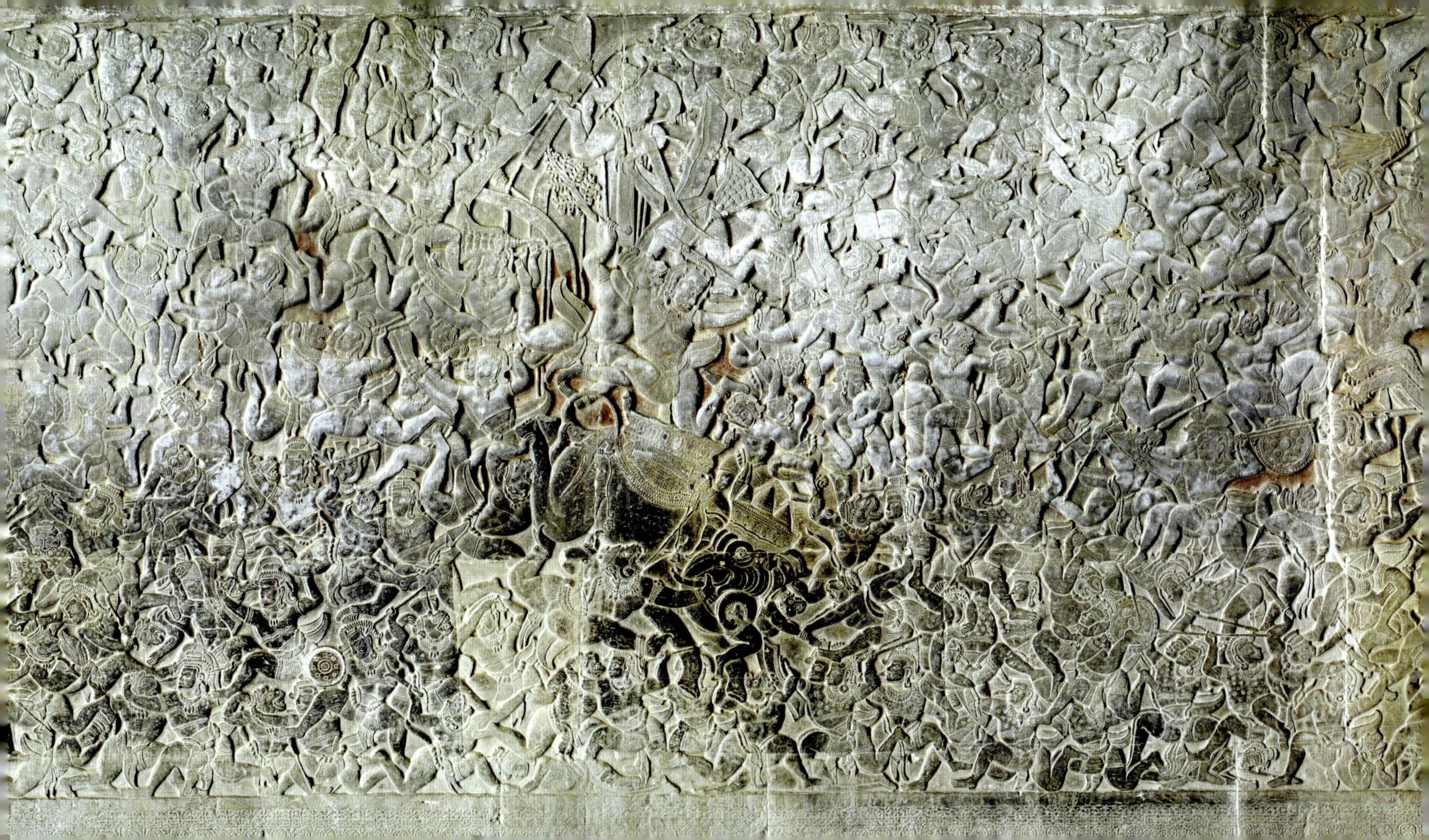

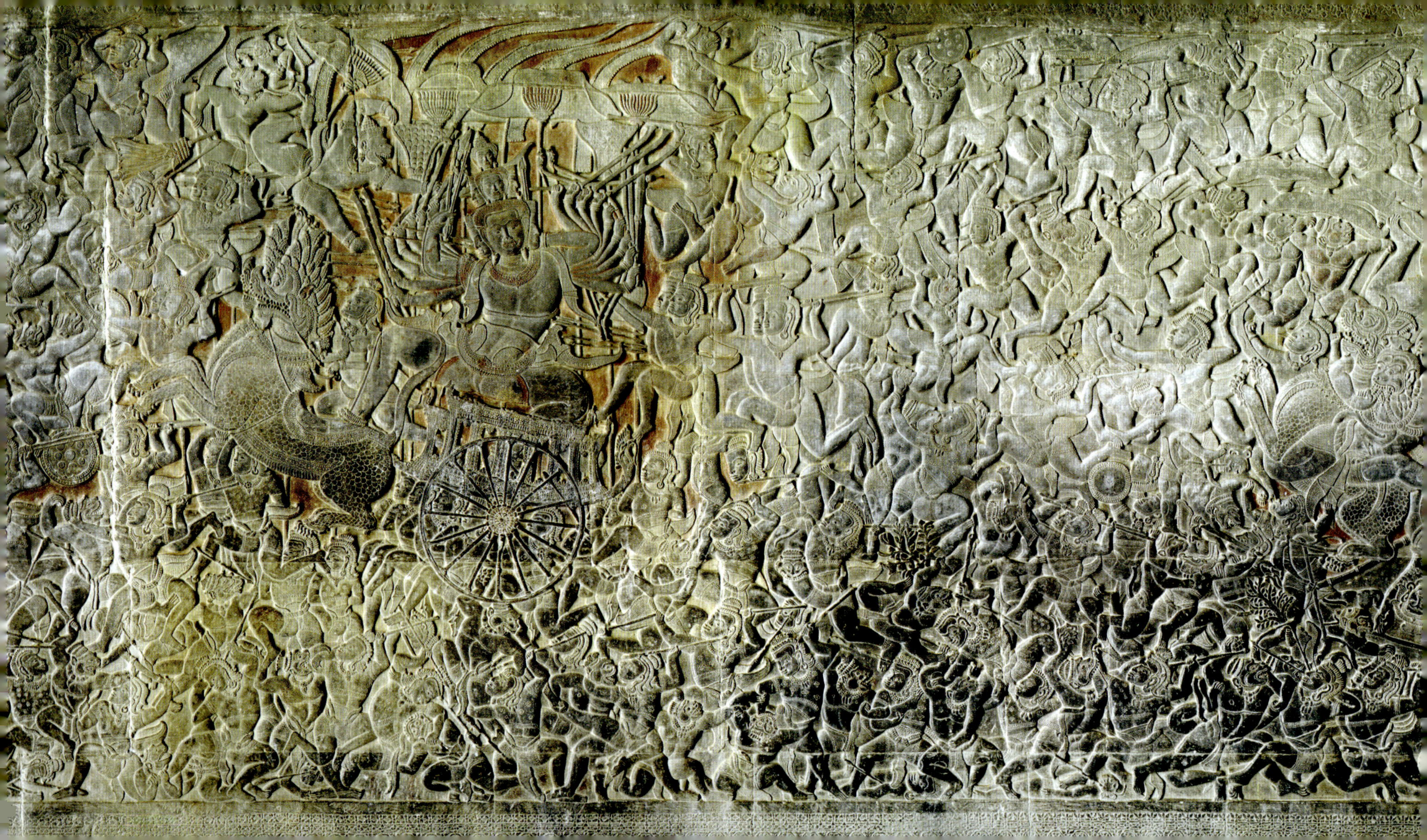

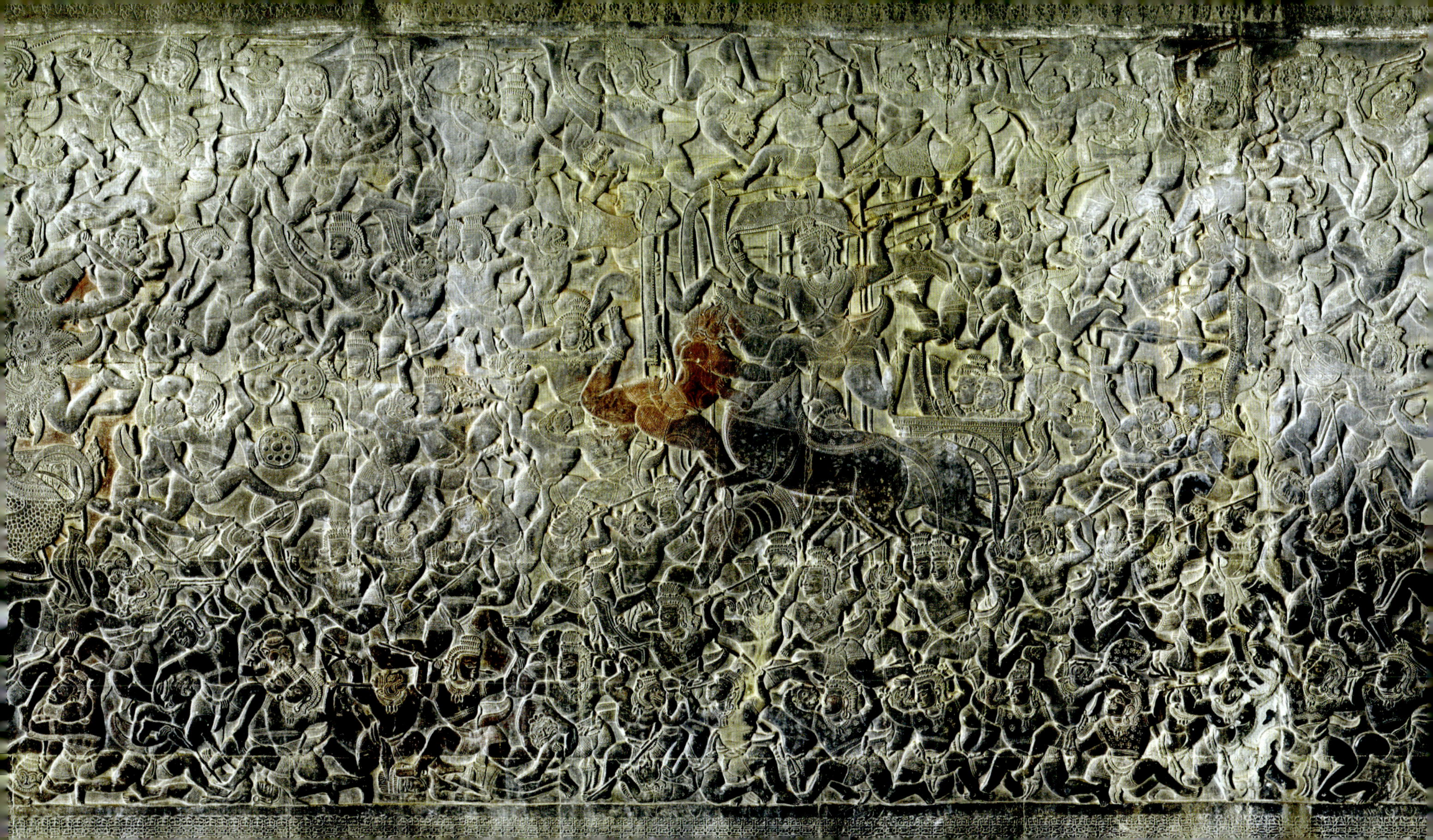

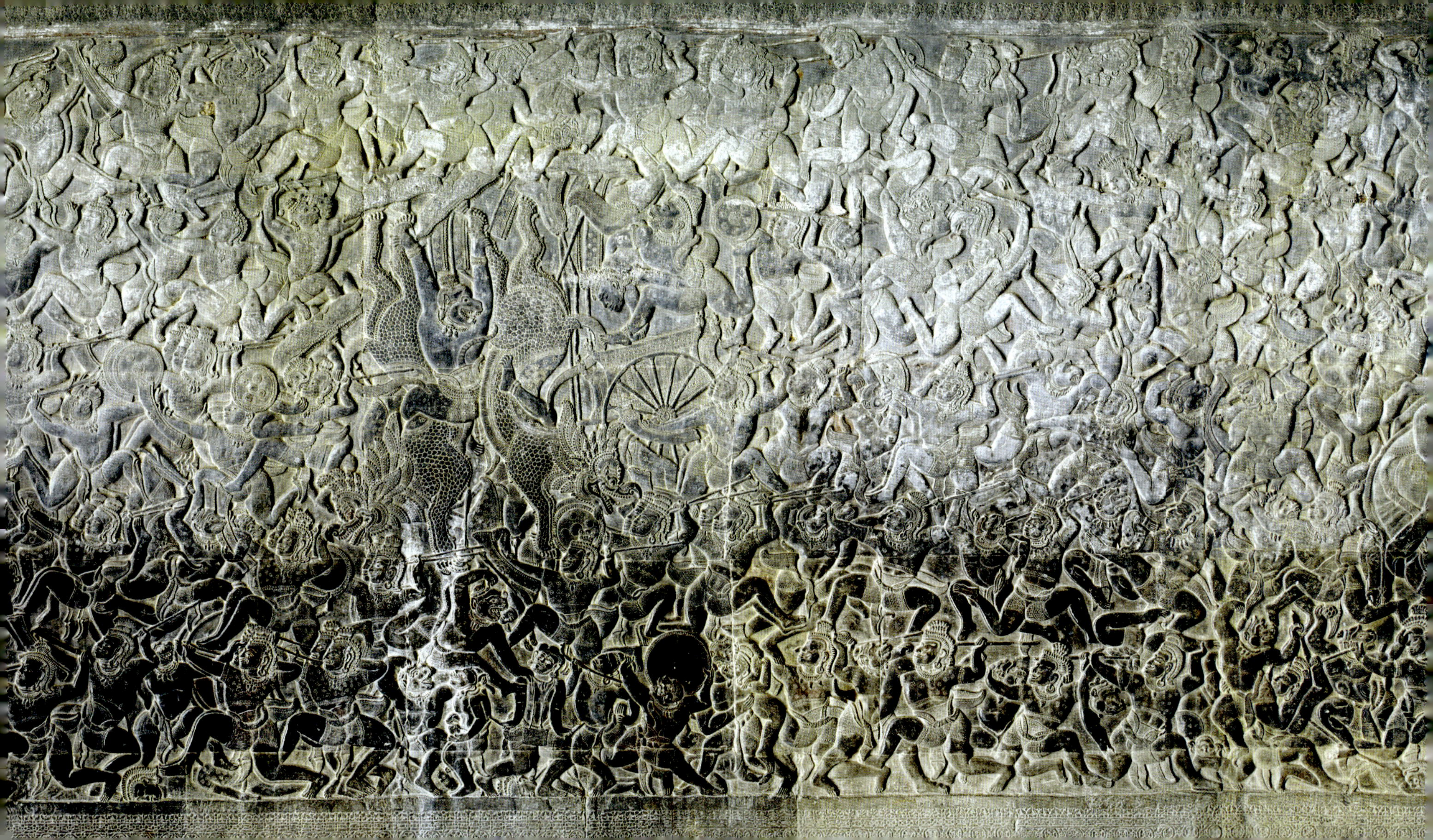

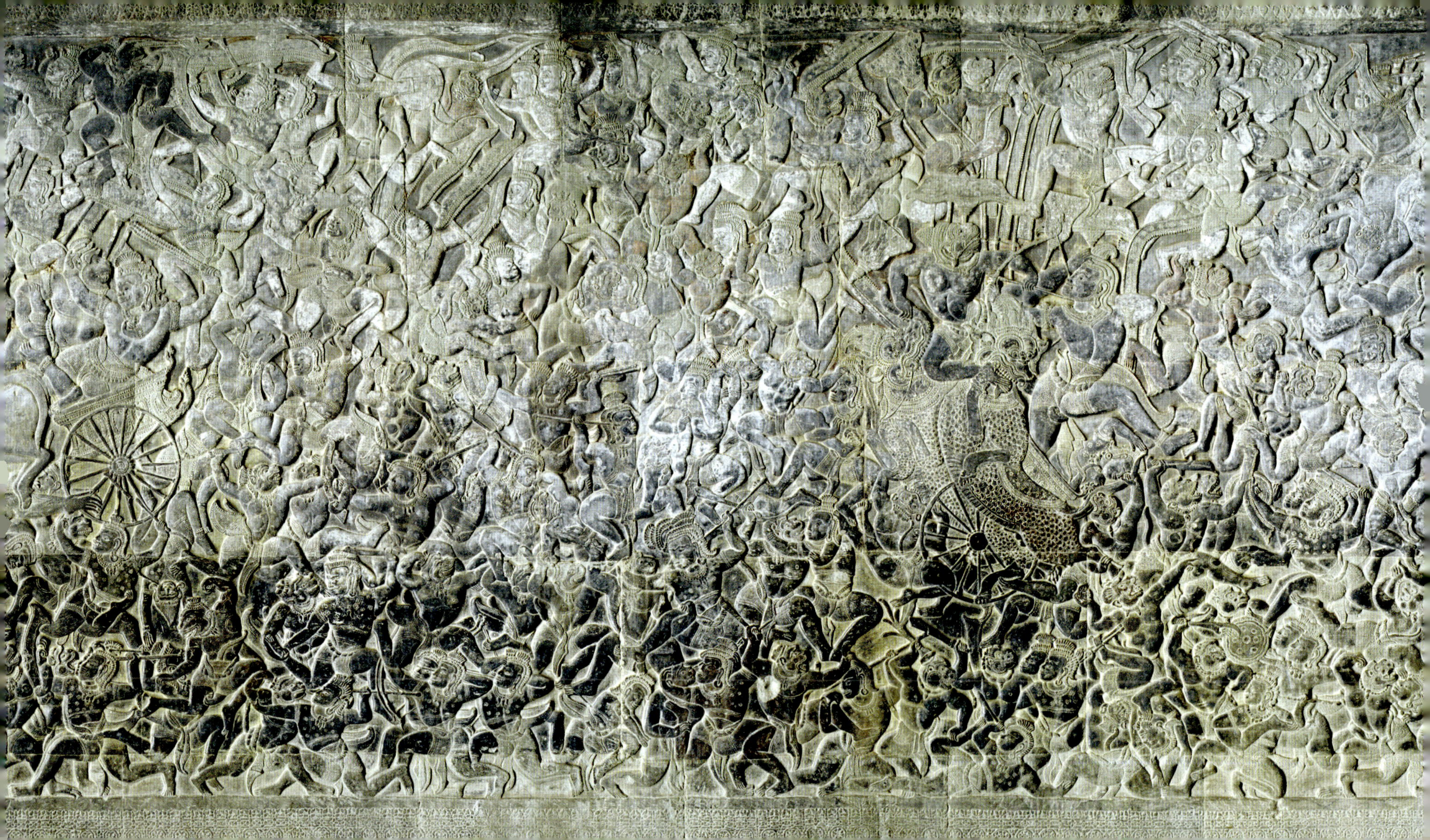

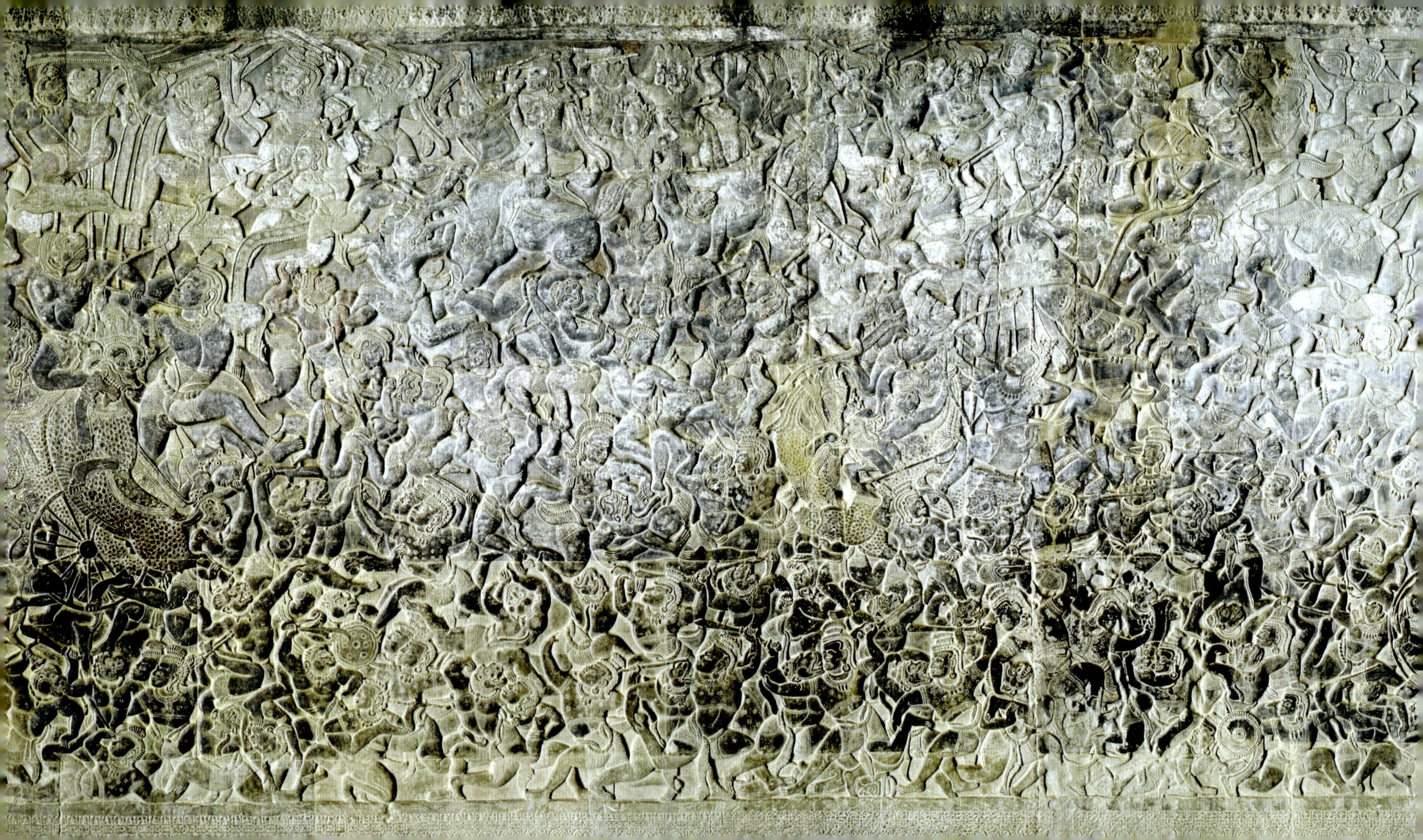

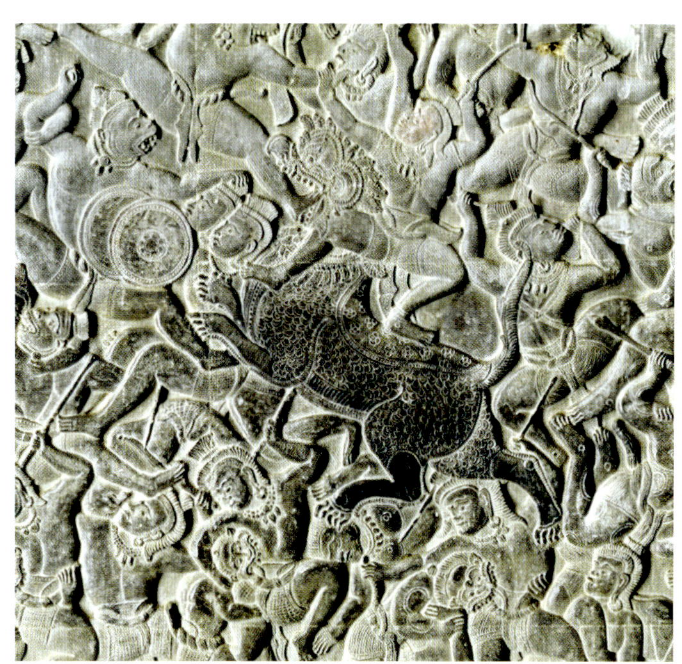

THE BATTLE OF KURUKSHETRA:

YUDHISHTHIRA AND SALYA

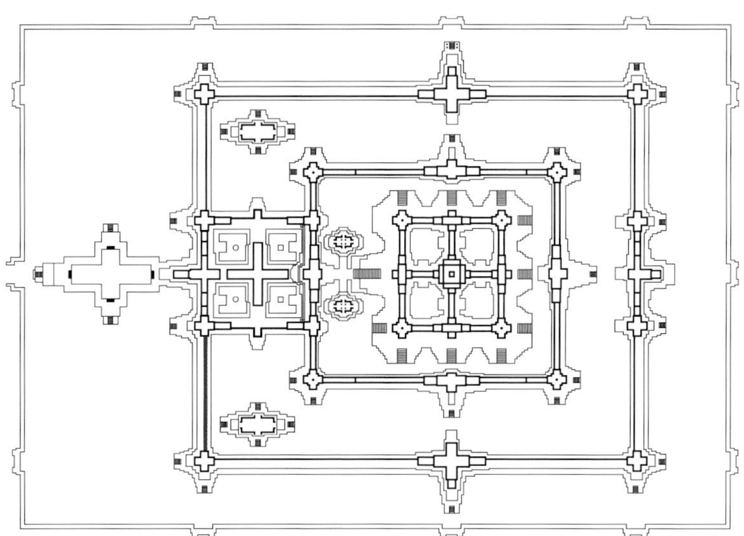

West Gallery, South Wing

THE BATTLE OF KURUKSHETRA:
YUDHISHTHIRA AND SALYA
End of the Dvapara, beginning of the Kali

At the south-west corner of the galleries we make the transition from the Dvapara to the Kali Yuga: the southern wing on the western side depicts part of the Mahabharata War fought at Kurukshetra, Field of the Kurus. The cause of conflict this time is not abduction, nor are the enemy demons, but jealousy and humiliation once again play a critical motivating role. The Battle of Kurukshetra is part of a war of succession, and it is fought between kinsmen. The essential background is this. The princes Dhritarashtra and Pandu are brothers. Dhritarashtra was born blind and is therefore disqualified from inheriting the kingdom, but he has a hundred sons by his wife Gandhari; these sons are known as the Kauravas.

His brother Pandu, on the other hand, has two wives, named Madri and Kunti, but has been cursed to die if he has sexual intercourse with them. Under these circumstances his wife Kunti has five heroic sons by a succession of gods: by the god Dharma, Yudhishthira; by Vayu, Bhima; by Indra, Arjuna; and by the twin Asvins, Nakula and Sahadeva. The five brothers are all married jointly to Draupadi. Pandu eventually has intercourse with his other wife, Madri, and thereupon dies in accordance with the curse. The widowed Madri burns herself to death in his funeral pyre, leaving Kunti to raise the five brothers – the Pandavas, whose name means simply Sons of Pandu – alone. Yudhishthira, son of Dharma, is named crown prince, but until he comes of age his uncle, Dhritarashtra, rules as regent. He and the other four semi-divine Pandavas exhibit exceptional talent and skill, which causes growing envy on the part of the Kauravas. Dhritarashtra gives half the kingdom to the Pandava brothers, but rather than heading off trouble, this temporary

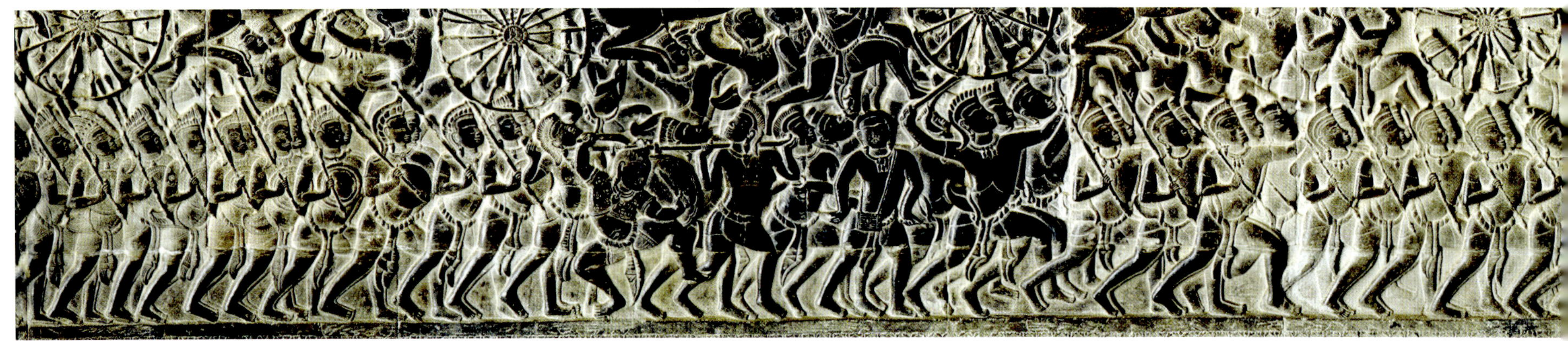

measure only deepens the divide between the two groups. Drawn into a game of dice by Duryodhana, one of the Kauravas, Yudhishthira gambles everything on a final throw – his wife Draupadi and all claims to his share of the kingdom, for a period of thirteen years, twelve of which are to be spent in exile, and the final year incognito – and loses. Draupadi, wife of the losers, is basely humiliated in front of the whole assembled court. But, like Rama obeying his father's unwilling command, Yudhishthira and his closest kin, bound by the fall of the dice, must now withdraw from all political pretensions for the duration agreed upon.

At the end of that time, despite many discussions and proposals in favour of reconciliation, war becomes unavoidable, and the story now focusses on the comportment and actions of warriors on both sides during the battle. The most famous scene, described in the *Bhagavad-Gita,* involves Arjuna, son of Indra, and his charioteer, who is none other than Krishna (Vishnu incarnate), who has opted to take the side of the Pandavas, but as a non-combatant. In ancient Indian warfare, the charioteer *(sarathi)* was a man of very high status, the essential fighting partner for any leading warrior. Upon his understanding of the rules of war, his knowledge of and skill with horses, and his ability in balancing and equipping the chariot itself, depended the success or failure of his master on the battlefield. When he assumes this vital role for Arjuna, therefore, Krishna is placed in the ideal position to advise and guide the prince in battle, while at the same time leaving the deadly business of war entirely to the mortal actors in the drama. Arjuna, positioned on the battlefield facing the Kauravas and seeing hosts of his kinsmen ranged against him, undergoes a crisis of conscience and slumps down in the chariot, letting his bow fall from his hand, declaring that he cannot fight against his own people. First as his charioteer, then as Vishnu,

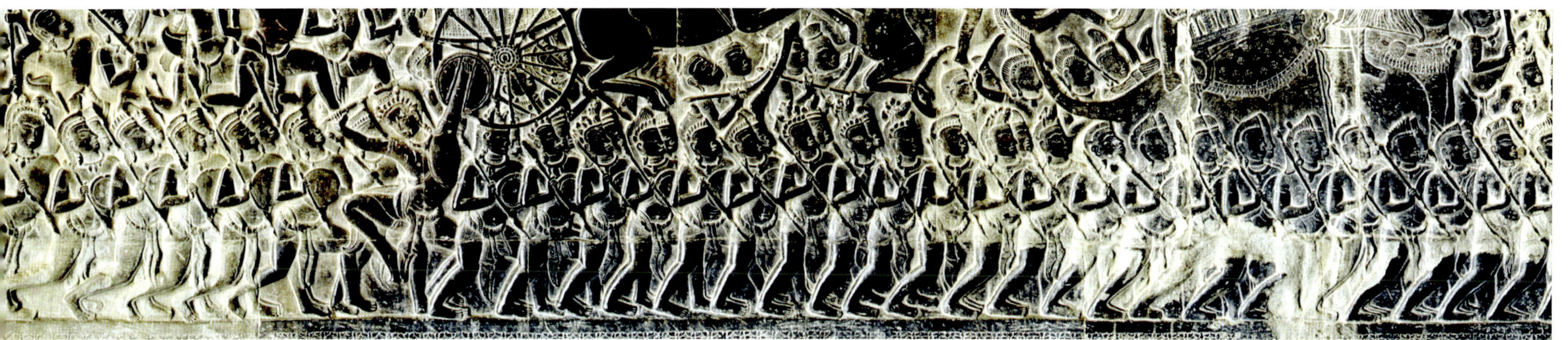

Krishna now teaches the reluctant warrior the new Vaishnava doctrine and demonstrates in these terms that he must fight – in order to discharge his highest social duty as a *kshatriya* and thereby to conform to the divine plan, and also to accept the will of God, since he, Krishna as Vishnu the All-God, has already slain the warriors of both sides before the battle commences. To Arjuna alone he then manifests a horrific vision of himself in which he appears with towers of devouring bloodstained faces, eating alive those very warriors whom a moment before Arjuna was identifying as his kin. Despite the fact that this revelatory form of the god makes such a powerful impact in the *Bhagavad-Gita* – and subsequently became one of the great themes of classical Hindu iconography in northern India between the 5th and the 13th centuries – it is not depicted in the Khmer Kurukshetra relief; nor do Krishna and Arjuna in their chariot, after Arjuna has been convinced that he must fight, appear as the centrepiece of the panel, as one might expect, but are located well to the right of centre in the upper register. The reasons for this will become clear as we consider two other key elements in this representation of the battle.

To the far left of the relief – that is, near the beginning of its narrative – a dying warrior is shown lying on his back, his body bristling with arrows.

This is the great Bhishma, son of a king named Santanu and the river goddess Ganga, who led the Kauravas in the first ten days of the battle and fought in

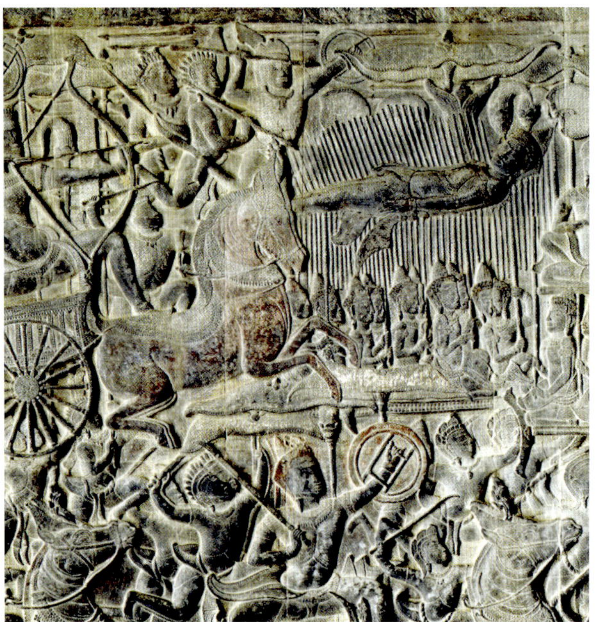

four encounters with Arjuna, fighting on despite his wounds. He is finally put out of action, however, by the clusters of arrows shot at him with deadly accuracy by Arjuna. It is by his own choice that Bhishma does not die where he falls: he has been granted the power of choosing the moment of his own death, a moment which he now wishes to postpone until Krishna personally permits him to leave his body. He is provided with a headrest and water, and as he lies on his bed of arrows he is visited with deep respect by the kings of both warring parties, who are shown in the relief seated facing each other before him, listening to his dying words. He is advising them for the last time to cease hostilities, just as he had counselled against the war from the beginning. To his right sit the five Pandava brothers, whose leader, Yudhishthira, is listening to his discourse concerning Dharma. This is a significant moment for several reasons. It is only the first of Yudhishthira's appearances in this relief, as we shall see; and, as we have already seen above, he is the son of Dharma as a god, and is therefore known throughout the *Mahabharata* text as Dharmaraja (King of Dharma, or Righteous King), a most important concept that also makes the first of its several appearances at this point. In this war at the end of the Dvapara Yuga, Yudhishthira is the physical incarnation of Dharma, just as Arjuna is the incarnation of Indra, and Krishna of Vishnu. What we are witnessing is therefore a clash of old and new ideas, a war of change and supersession in the moral, political and theological fields, and the battle narrative both flows from and symbolises this critical struggle. The dying Bhishma is depicted at the beginning of the relief in order to provide the spectator with a temporal reference point in the phases of this battle – he is mortally wounded on the tenth day, therefore the chief incidents shown to the right of him take place within the remaining eight days. After delivering many lengthy discourses giving his parting advice, Bhishma dies – but the battle inevitably recommences under new leadership, for the Dvapara Yuga must run its course and the Kali must supervene.

In the poetic sense, the pathetic figure of Bhishma, shot full of arrows yet still preaching the doctrine of right conduct, is the symbol of the growing impotence of human beings to control their cosmic destiny as time inevitably sweeps away their capacity for understanding it. In the text narrative, as in this relief, his dying heralds the last battle in which the old values are still, like him, partly alive: Kurukshetra, the Field of the Kurus, is also called Dharmakshetra, the Field of Dharma, the battlefield on

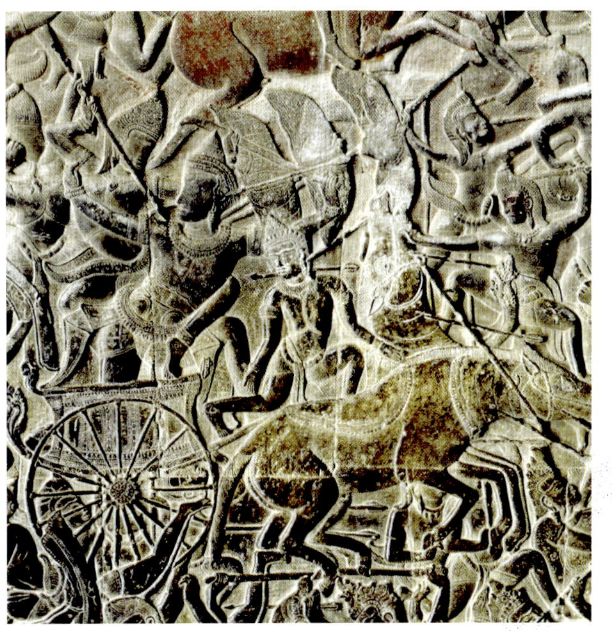

which the survival of the moral code is decided. The profound pessimistic realism behind this view of inevitable decay, and the corresponding forward-looking belief in cosmic renewal inherent in a cyclical conception of time, is perfectly engineered in the structuring of the *Mahabharata,* and miraculously reinvoked in the reliefs of Angkor Wat. Such lucid grasp of the epic text, conveyed visually on such a magnificent scale, is to be seen nowhere else in the art of the Asian world.

We might well ask why, after this death scene, the centre and climax of the panel is occupied merely by a struggle between two unidentified warriors, while Krishna and Arjuna are placed further to the right in a relatively subsidiary position. The answer is to be found in the over-all concept expressed by the sequencing of these reliefs. It is not the function of this particular scene to focus yet again on the divine heroics of Vishnu–Krishna; that purpose has already been fulfilled in the panels that we have seen on the east and north sides. Those cosmic events of the Krita and Treta Yugas are behind us, as is the first major weakening of Dharma in the transition to the Dvapara Yuga, and we are now on the western flank of the south-west corner, in the outgoing Dvapara, poised to enter the ill-starred Kali Yuga. At this advanced stage in the decline of Dharma, the men and partly-divine agents of Vishnu who try to sustain it are far more the victims of their human nature than Rama had been; to ensure the progression of the ages, Krishna himself is now reduced to amorality in guiding the affairs of men.

As we have seen, the representative of Dharma at this transitional moment is Yudhishthira, whose name means Firm in Battle, the Dharmaraja. On the eighteenth and final day of the battle of Kurukshetra, it is he who leads the Pandava forces. His face transformed with rage, he advances in his chariot drawn by ivory-white horses to confront Salya, his maternal uncle, who is fighting on the Kaurava side. Following the usual practice, the chariot of each warrior is protected by four others, called *chakrarakshas*, two on the flanks and one ahead and behind. The chariot at Yudhishthira's rear is that manned by the deadly fighting team of Arjuna and Krishna. Yudhishthira strikes down Salya's two chariot guards and his charioteer, shoots down the device at the top of his standard, and kills his horses. But a number of Kaurava chariots hedge around Salya, blocking the attack and enabling him to be rescued by another warrior and mount a new chariot. In the renewed fight, it is Yudhishthira's horses and charioteer that are killed. There now follows the final struggle, and it is this that is depicted at the centre of the Kurukshetra relief, in the space between the two armies.

In the text, the word *sakti* is used for the magical weapon that Yudhishthira uses to slay Salya. This word has several meanings, including "effective female power" – and indeed, the text makes full use of this sense to personify the weapon as Kalaratri, goddess of death – but in both epics, *sakti* is also one of the most frequently used terms for "spear" and it was clearly one of the most common words for this kind of weapon in the late centuries BC. However the wider range of Sanskrit terms for spears (there are at least eight different words, in addition to *sakti,* in the *Mahabharata,* and twelve in the *Ramayana*) indicates that chariots were equipped with an array of different spear-types from which the warrior selected, depending on the nature of the combat. The most basic distinction was presumably between stabbing and throwing spears or javelins, but the texts do not pause to explain such differences. In the *Mahabharata* description of the combat with Salya, Yudhishthira is clearly said to throw the fateful spear – albeit from close range, since the chariots of both warriors were at this point disabled – but the artists of Angkor Wat chose to depict him using it as a stabbing spear, thus concentrating the moment of Salya's death into an intimate deathly embrace, intensifying the drama and focussing the observer's attention on the physical act of killing. This is a far cry from the bows and arrows more conventionally employed from a distance by the heraldically represented warriors in the rest of the panel. The need to represent mortality and the human aspect of conflict in the western reliefs reaches its climax here.

The presence of the supernatural in this mortal struggle lies in the spear itself, which is the central point of the entire composition and an object of repeated attention in the text, for in reality it is far more than a spear: "Yudhishthira seized the golden-hued spear with its shaft of gold and gems and, his blazing eyes violently convulsed, glared with wrath at Salya the Madra king. Then swiftly and with great force he threw it at Salya, its shining dreadful shaft ablaze and bristling with gems. All the assembled Kauravas watched it descending swiftly, blazing and sparkling with mighty power, like the great fire that falls from the sky at the end of the Yuga. Yudhishthira hurled it and it was like Kalaratri, the Mother of Death, hideous in appearance and holding a noose, unerring, the image of

Brahma's curse. The image of the world-destroying fire, like the ferocious magic of sorcerers, it (she) was zealously worshipped by the Pandavas with food and drink, with a high pedestal, and with garlands and incense. Consuming the lives of enemies, able to annihilate demons on land, in water, and in the air, it had been made by Tvashtri (the gods' weapon maker) at the behest of Shiva Ishana. Tvashtri had created it with care and according to precept, with diamonds, gem-stones, flags and bells, its shaft made of gold purified by fire, the colour of beryl; it was unerring, deadly, and hostile to the true faith. This was the swift spear that Yudhishthira hurled with all his strength, intoning terrible mantras, to kill Salya at that moment. "Now you are slain!," roared Yudhishthira, who seemed to dance with rage as he drew back his powerful arm. As the sacrificial fire roars to seize the ritually offered stream of ghee, so Salya roared to receive that spear of irresistible power thrown by Yudhishthira. The spear penetrated his broad chest and armour as water flows unimpeded into the ground, tearing asunder his vital organs and burning up his great renown" (*Mahabharata* 9.16.40-49)[7].

In the relief we are shown Salya, his horses struck by arrows and collapsing, his charioteer shot through the neck, his honorific parasols toppling, spreading his arms in desperation and attempting to clamber out of his immobilised chariot. But he is held back by the grim-faced Yudhishthira, who has climbed up behind him, grasped his swordblade in his bare hand, and hooked his leg around his enemy's body, holding him fast to receive the descending spear-point through his heart. The Khmer artists thus made Yudhishthira's lower body assume the same posture as that of Vishnu when he supports Mount Mandara at the centre of the Churning of the Ocean panel – and indeed the *Mahabharata* text twice compares the stricken Salya to a mountain: "His limbs soaked in the blood that flowed from his wounds and sprang from his nose, eyes, ears, and mouth, he resembled the great Mount Krauncha when struck by the war-god; he stretched out his arms and fell from his chariot, his armour cleft by Yudhishthira, like a mountain peak struck by a bolt of lightning; stretching out his arms, Salya toppled to the ground in front of Yudhishthira like Indra's lofty banner" (*Mahabharata* 9.16.50-52)[8]. The two literary symbols of Salya's defeat – the shattering mountain and the falling banner - and his physical gesture of despair, are all finely interpreted in the Khmer relief. The fateful goddess of the spear is not shown: the weapon in Yudhishthira's hand looks like many others wielded by the Pandava infantry in the battle raging all around him, and one has to know the text to see why it is this weapon that is significantly located at the centre of the whole relief: as we have seen, it is Kalaratri herself, called into being by the ritualised fury of the Pandavas. Once turned loose, she - the force of destruction embodied in the spear and inherent in the Kali Yuga which begins here - is unstoppable and indiscriminate: in a Kaurava night raid after the battle, the *Mahabharata* informs us, the victorious warriors of the Pandava army (with the exception of the famous Five Pandavas, who had left for the capital) were slaughtered as they slept. After the mass cremation of the dead, the Pandava brothers walk into the Himalayas and disappear from the earth, leaving the world to the mercies of lesser kings who come after them.

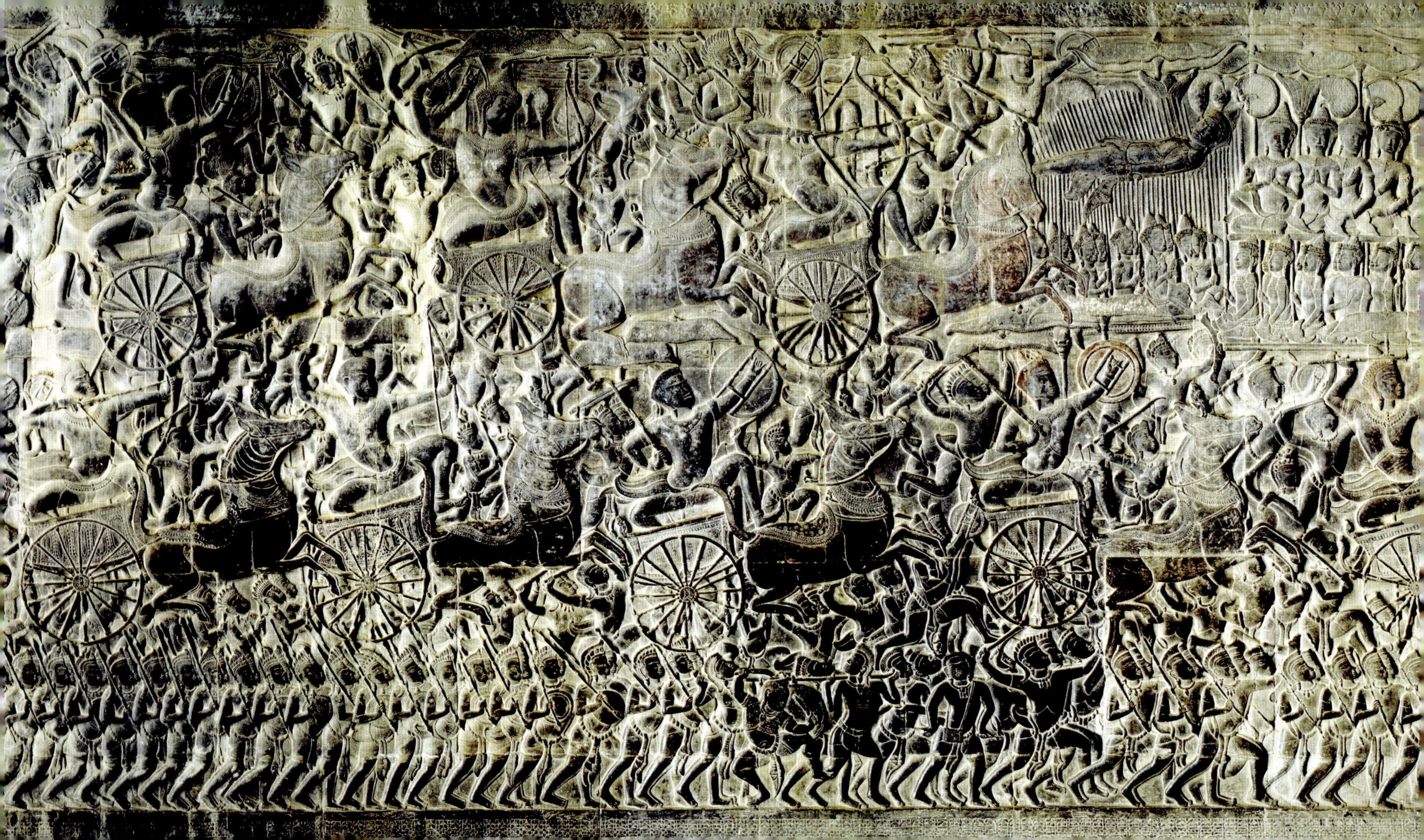

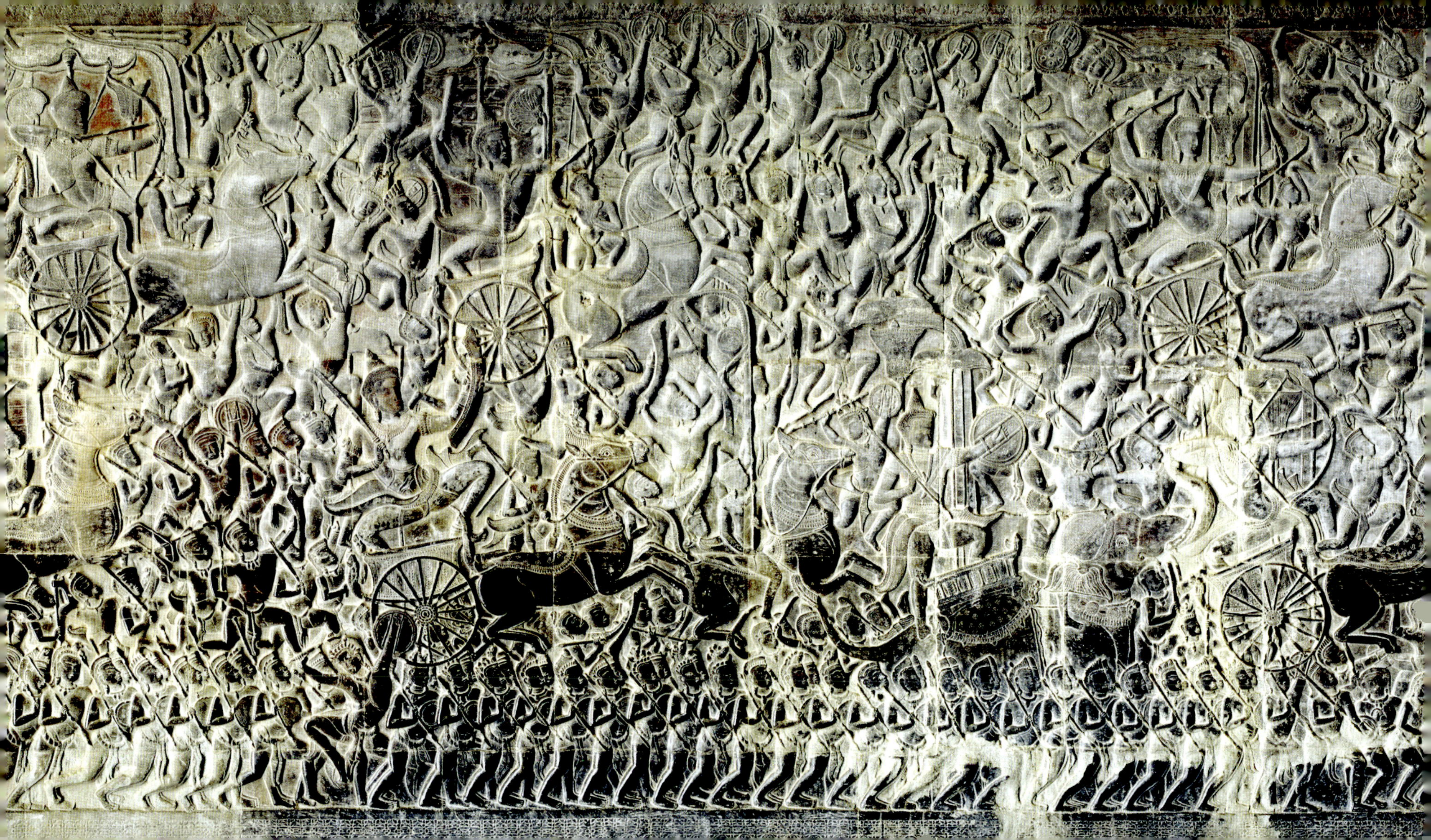

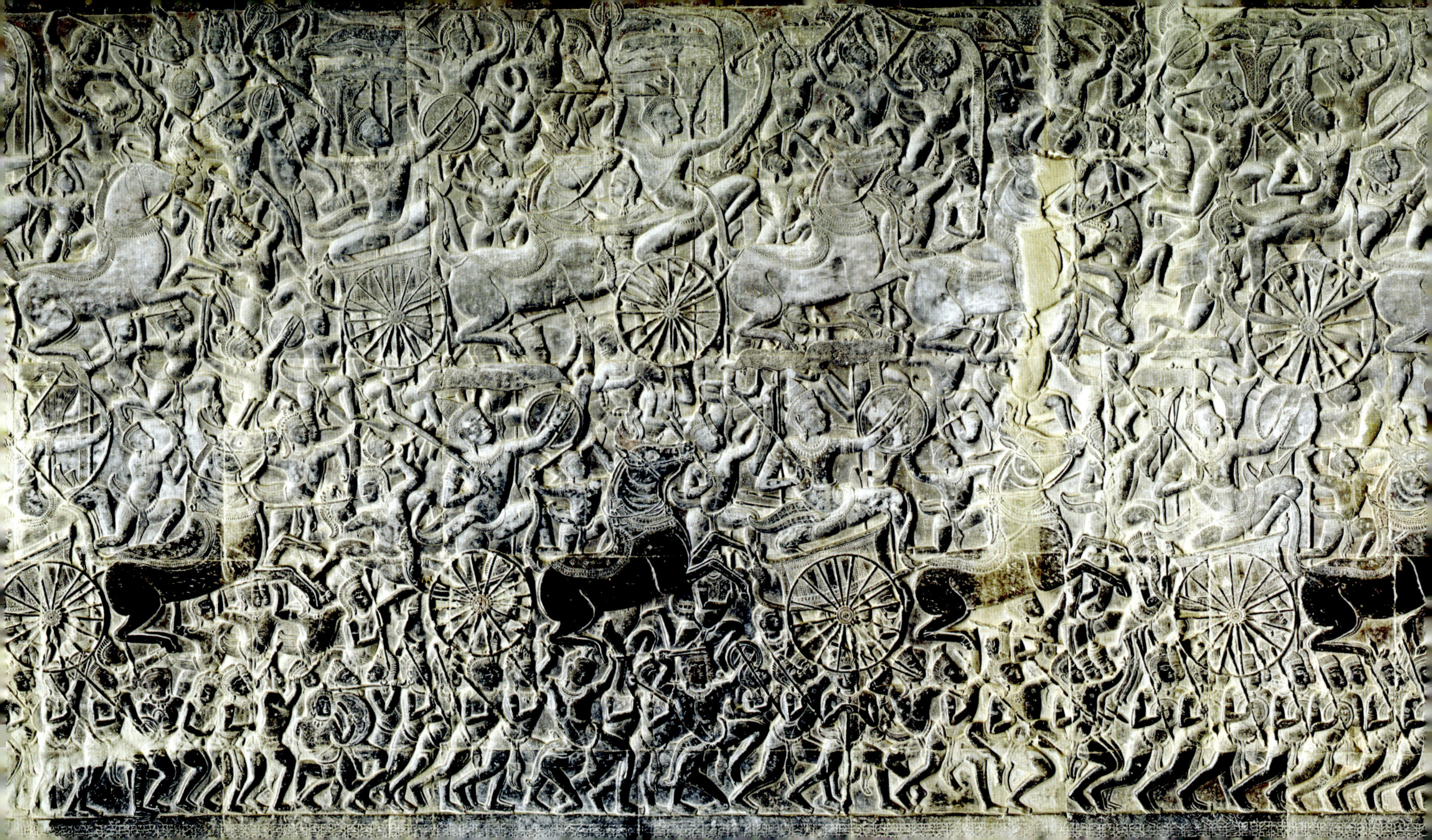

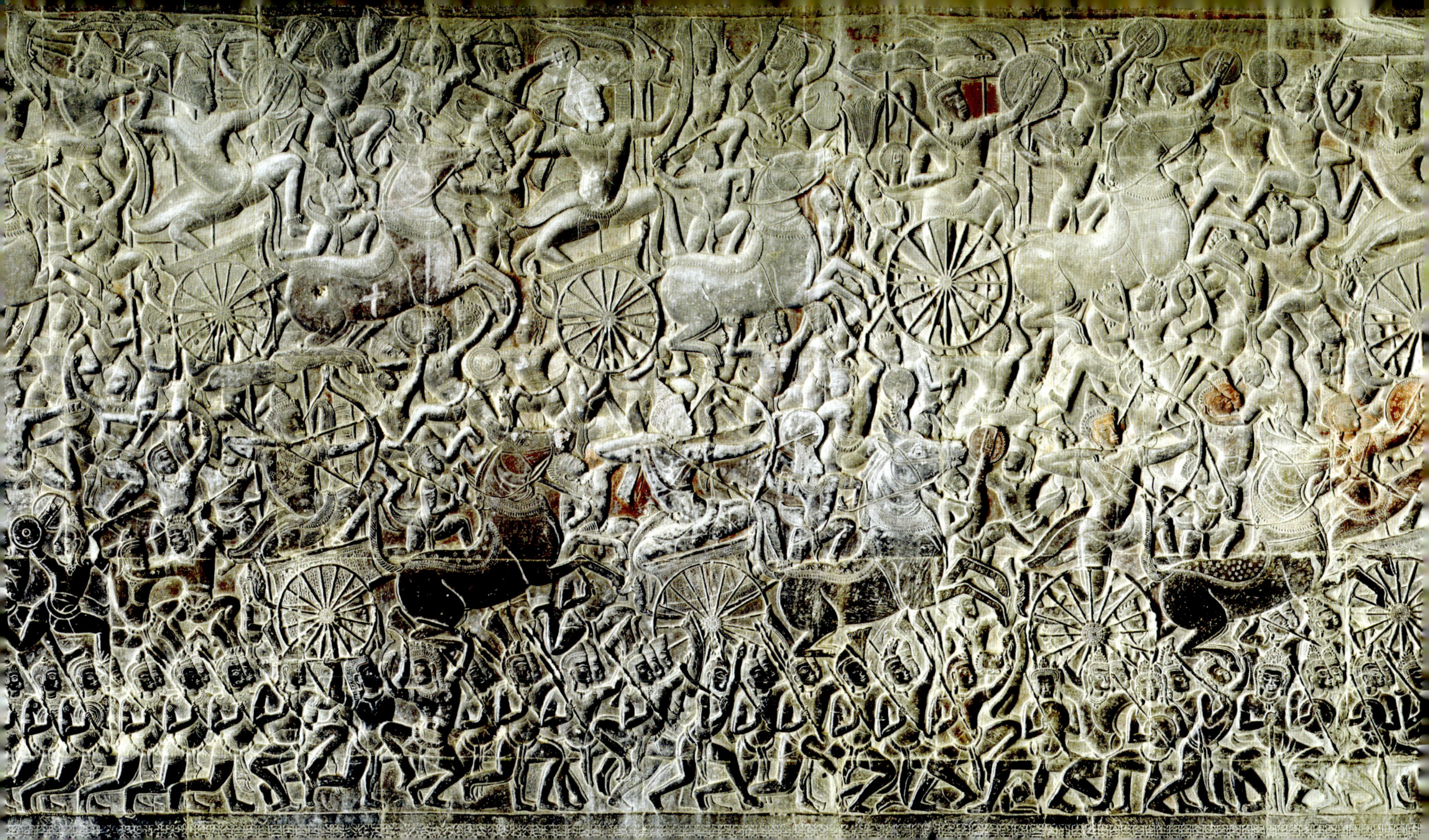

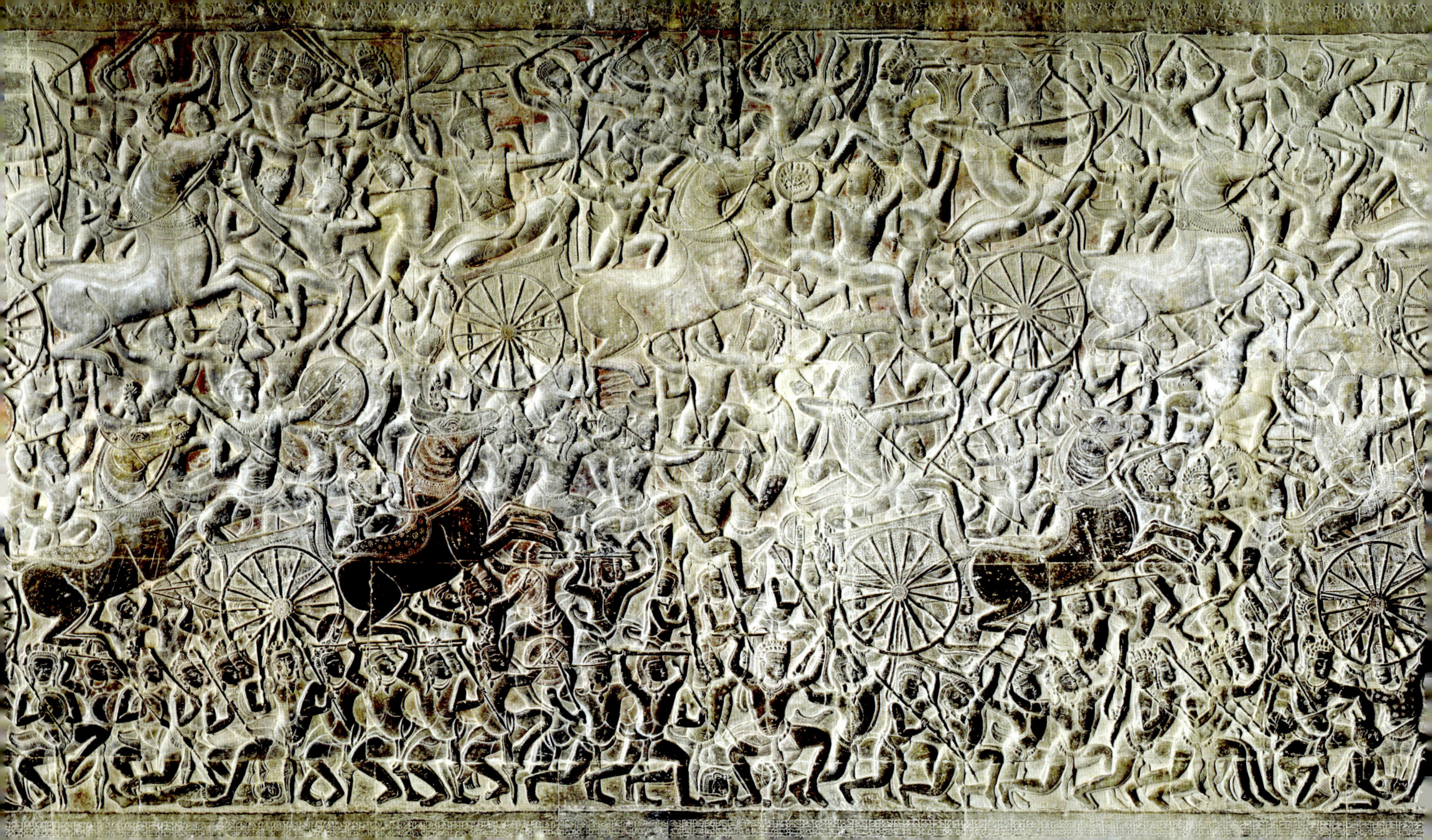

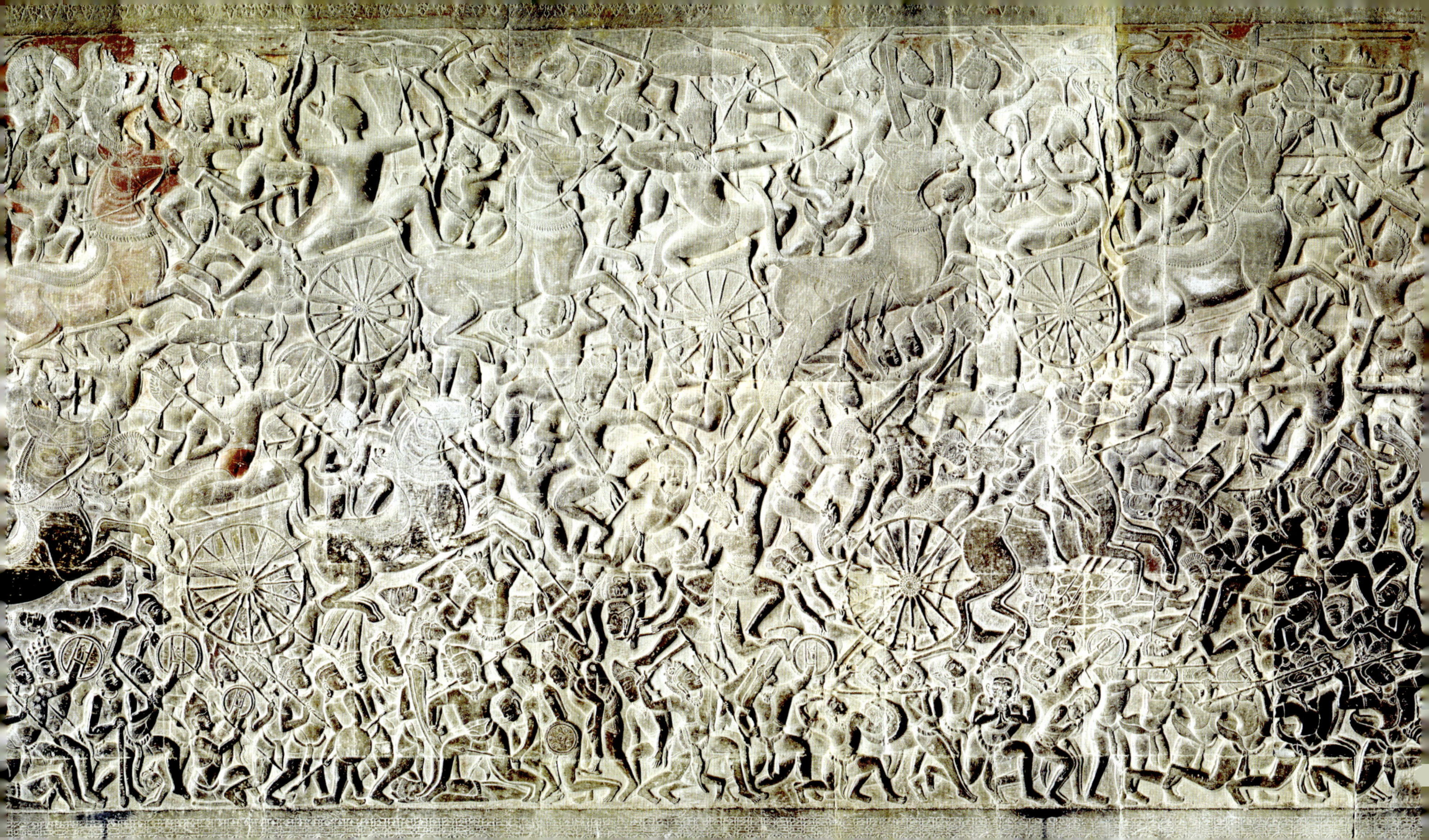

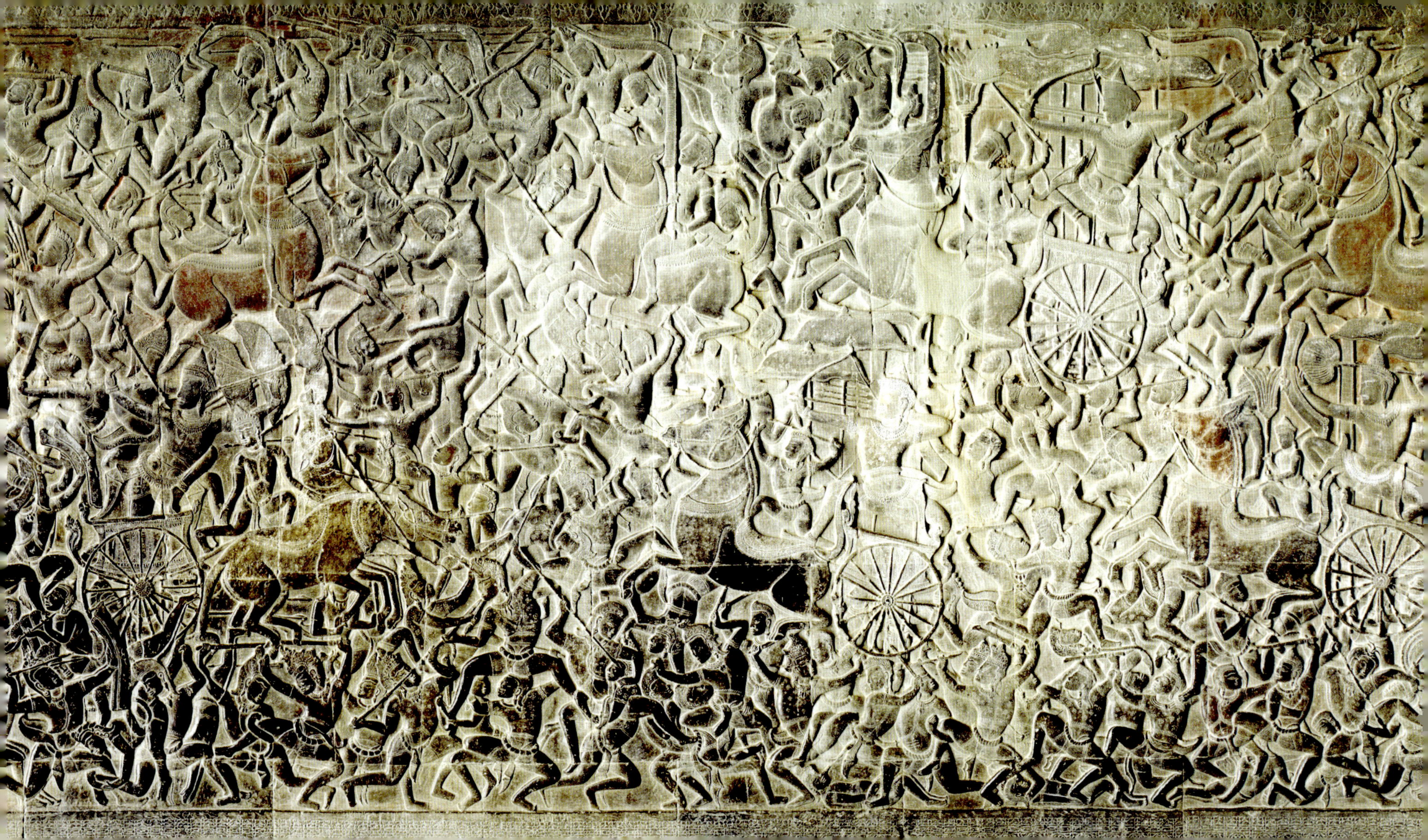

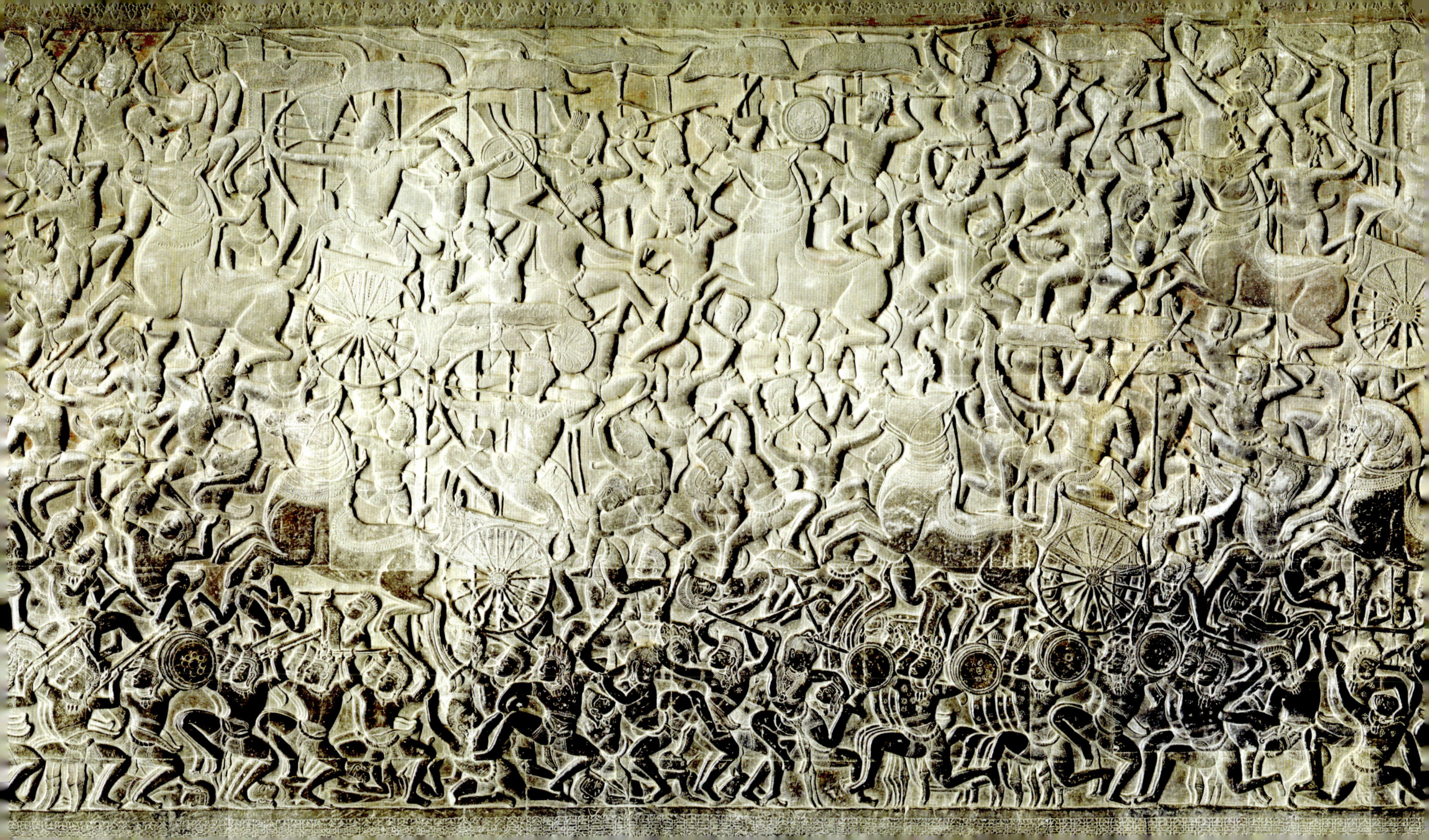

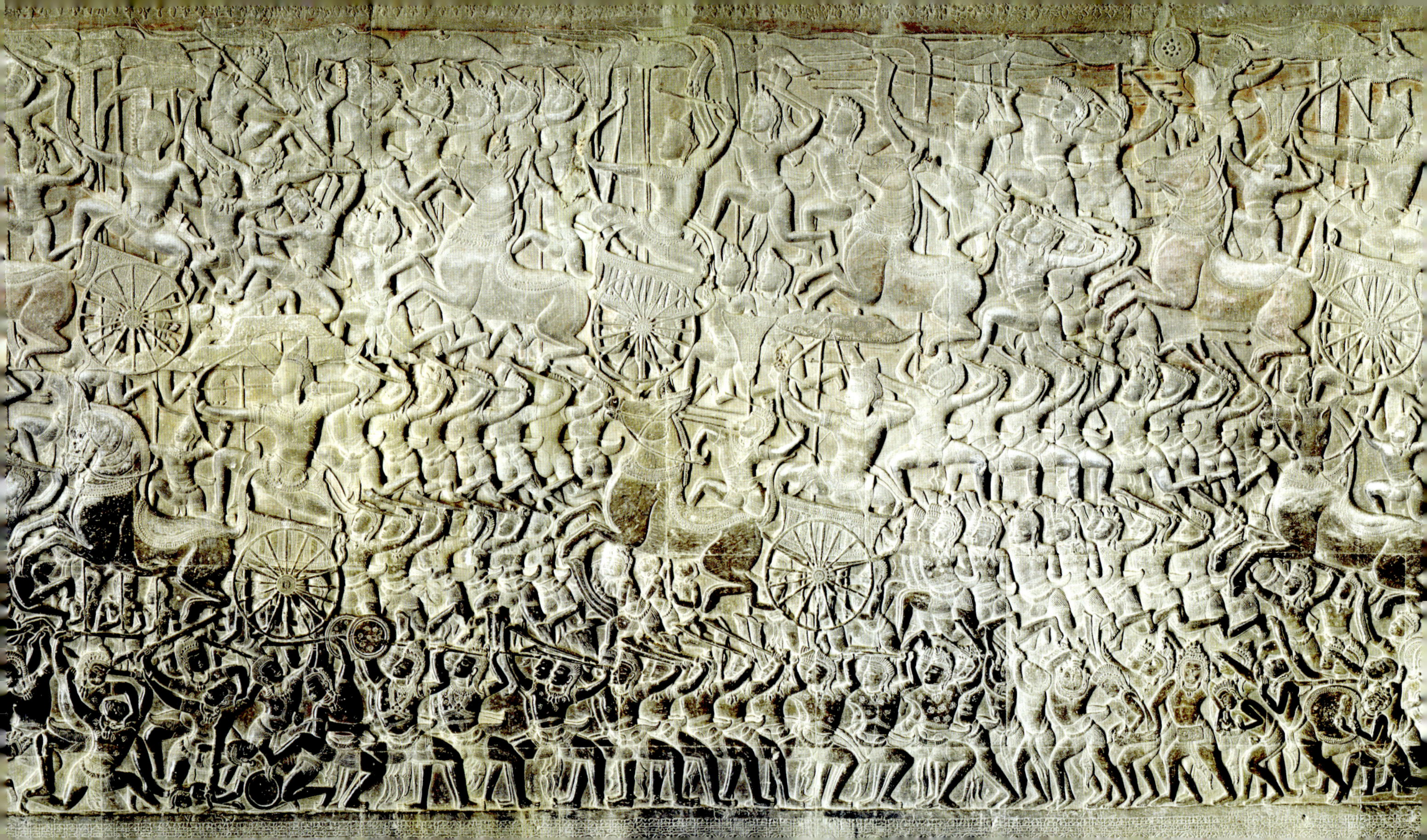

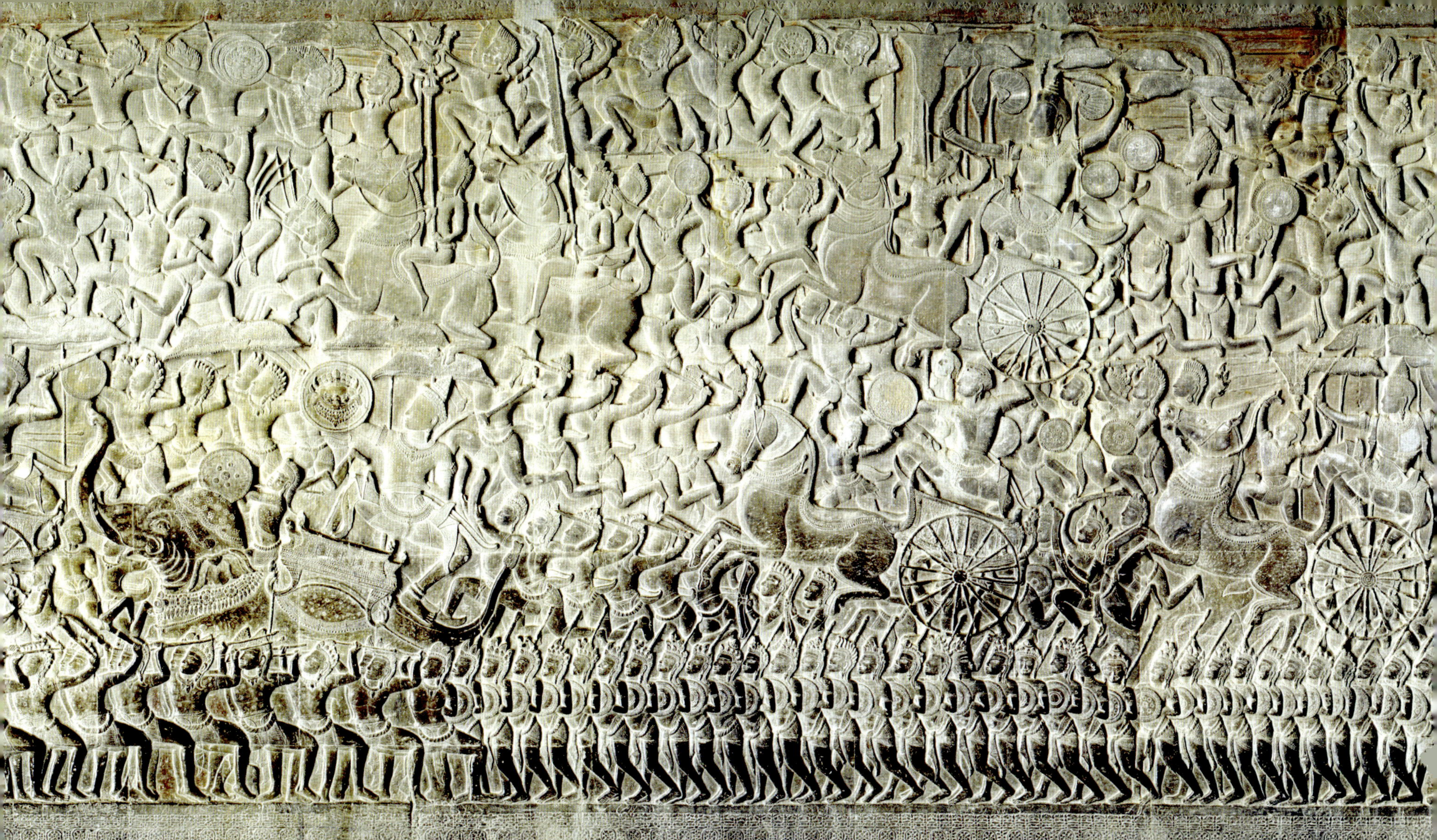

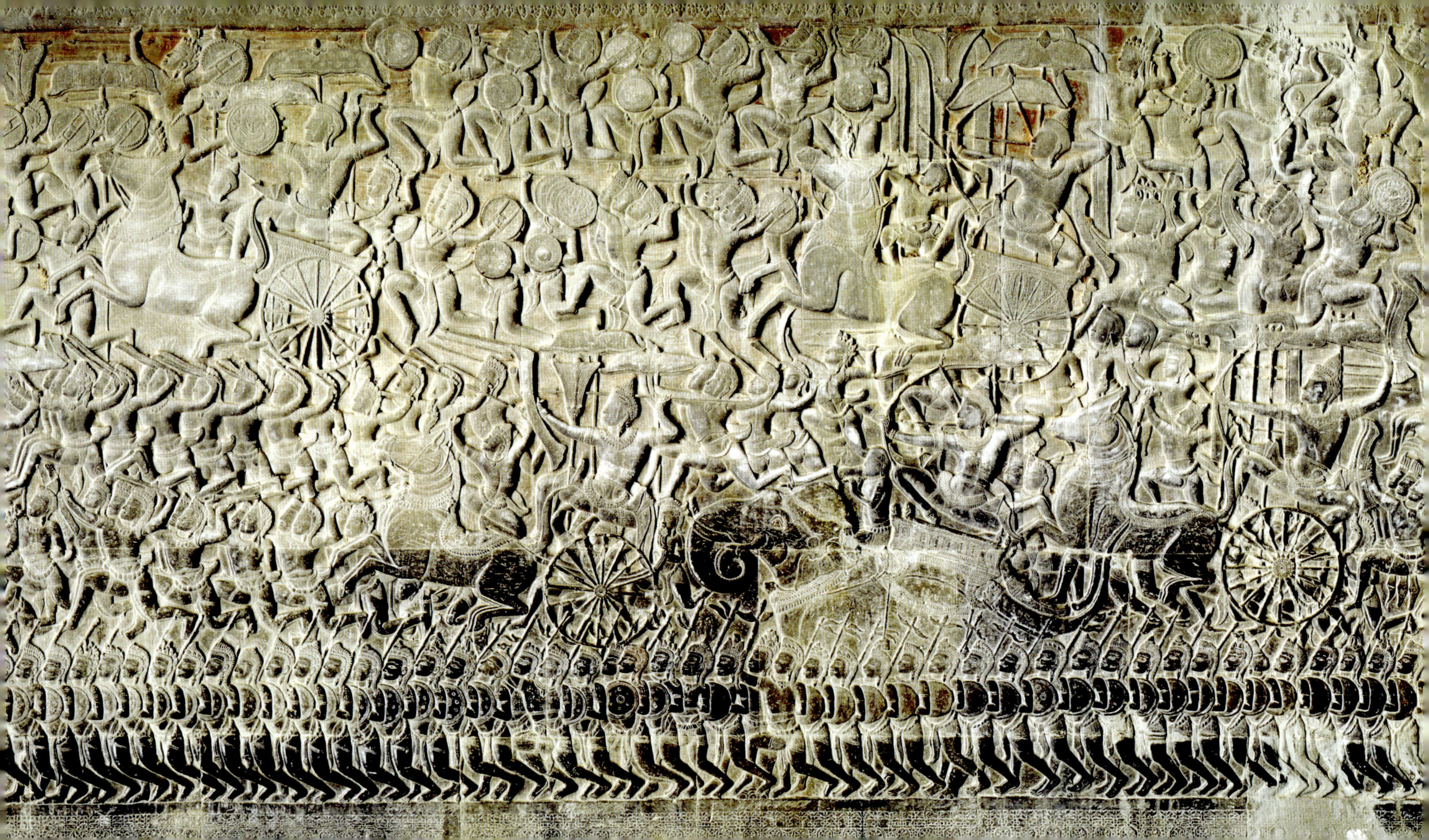

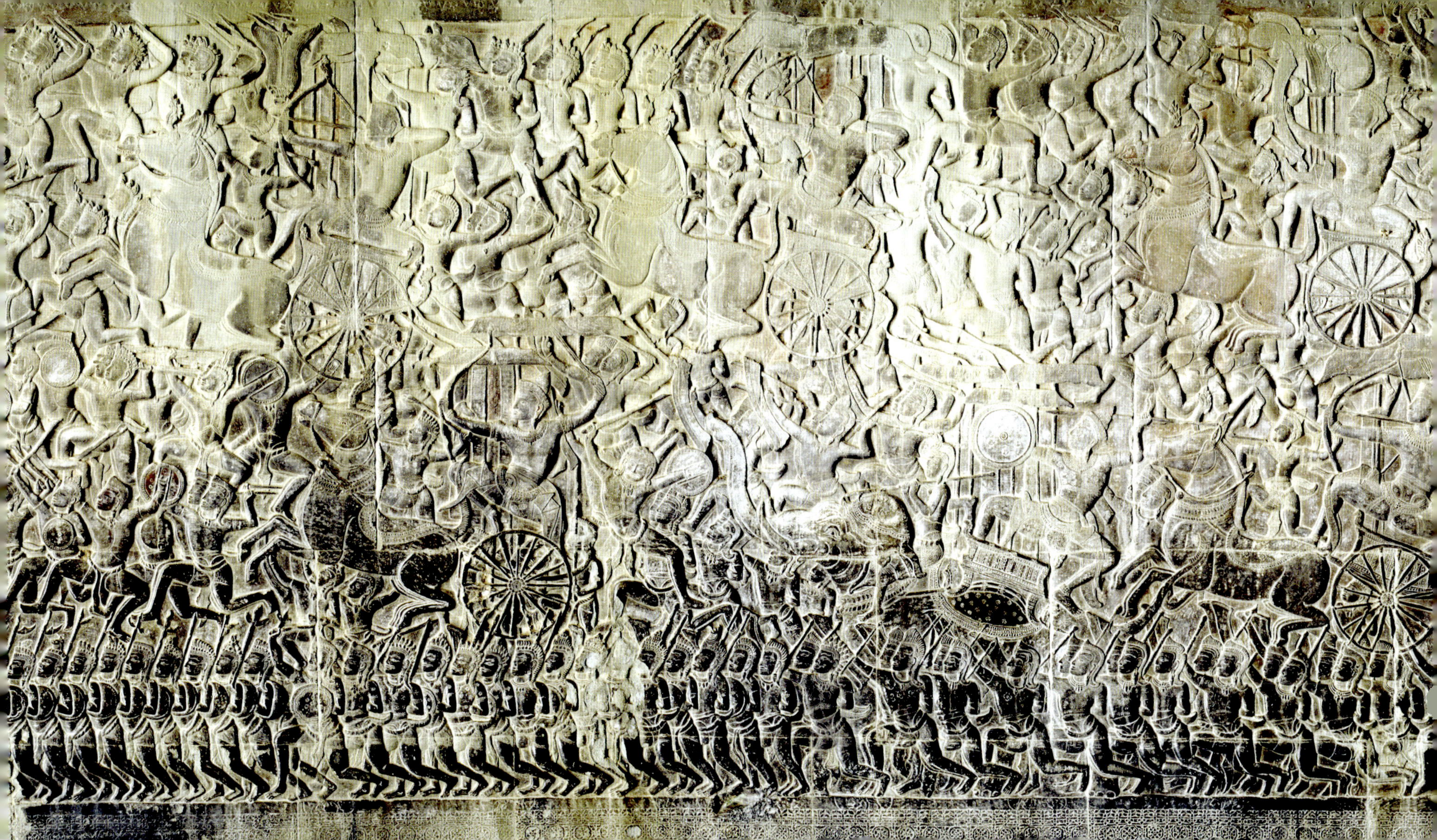

KING PARAMAVISHNULOKA AND THE APPARATUS
OF STATE

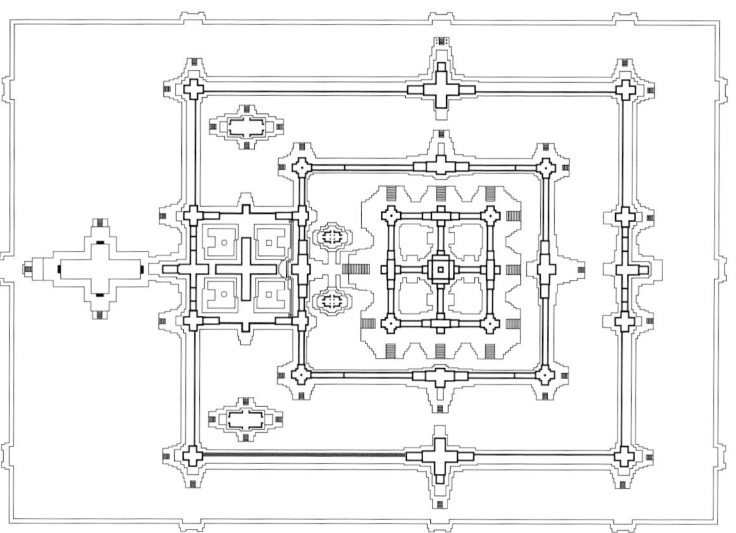

South Gallery, West Wing

KING PAPRAMAVISHNULOKA AND THE APPARATUS OF STATE
Kali Yuga I

Turning the south-west corner of the galleries to the southern side, we emerge from the realm of legend and enter the world of the here and now. This is the Kali Yuga, the age when Dharma, now in its final decline, is represented by two further Dharmarajas, the earthly Khmer king at Angkor, named Paramavishnuloka, and the god Yama, King of the Dead. Their images, identified by inscription[9], stand at opposite ends of the whole sweep of the southern galleries, the king sending people forth, the god receiving them. The essential difference between the Dharmaraja Yudhishthira in the previous panel, and these two Dharma Kings of the Kali Yuga, is that the roles of the latter strictly concern only control over the life and death of human beings, not their spiritual welfare. Between them they define the limits of the mortal condition. Unlike Yudhishthira, they are no semi-divine Sons of Dharma, but representatives and executives of Dharma in the sense of legal and karmic justice. All the panels that have gone before, from the Churning of the Ocean to the Battle of Kurukshetra, provide the cosmic background and justification for their temporal power. Vishnu is no longer to be seen, being only nominally present in the title of the ruler, He Who is Destined for the Highest World of Vishnu, which defines this king (presumably Suryavarman II) as a mortal, not a god. The god Yama merely extends the role of the king into the afterlife; he is not an object of worship in the same sense that Vishnu is. Indeed, except for the king, none of the mortals depicted in this relief is destined after death for anything more than a temporary sojourn, earned through actions performed in life, in a particular heaven or hell unconnected with

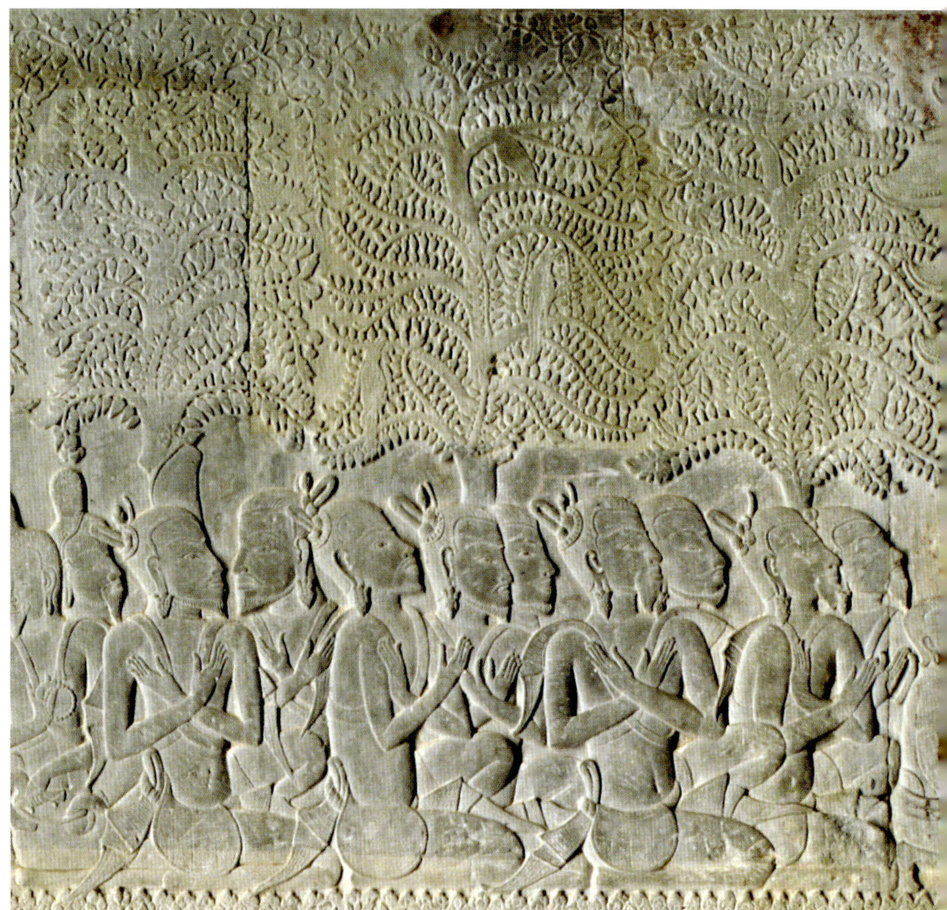

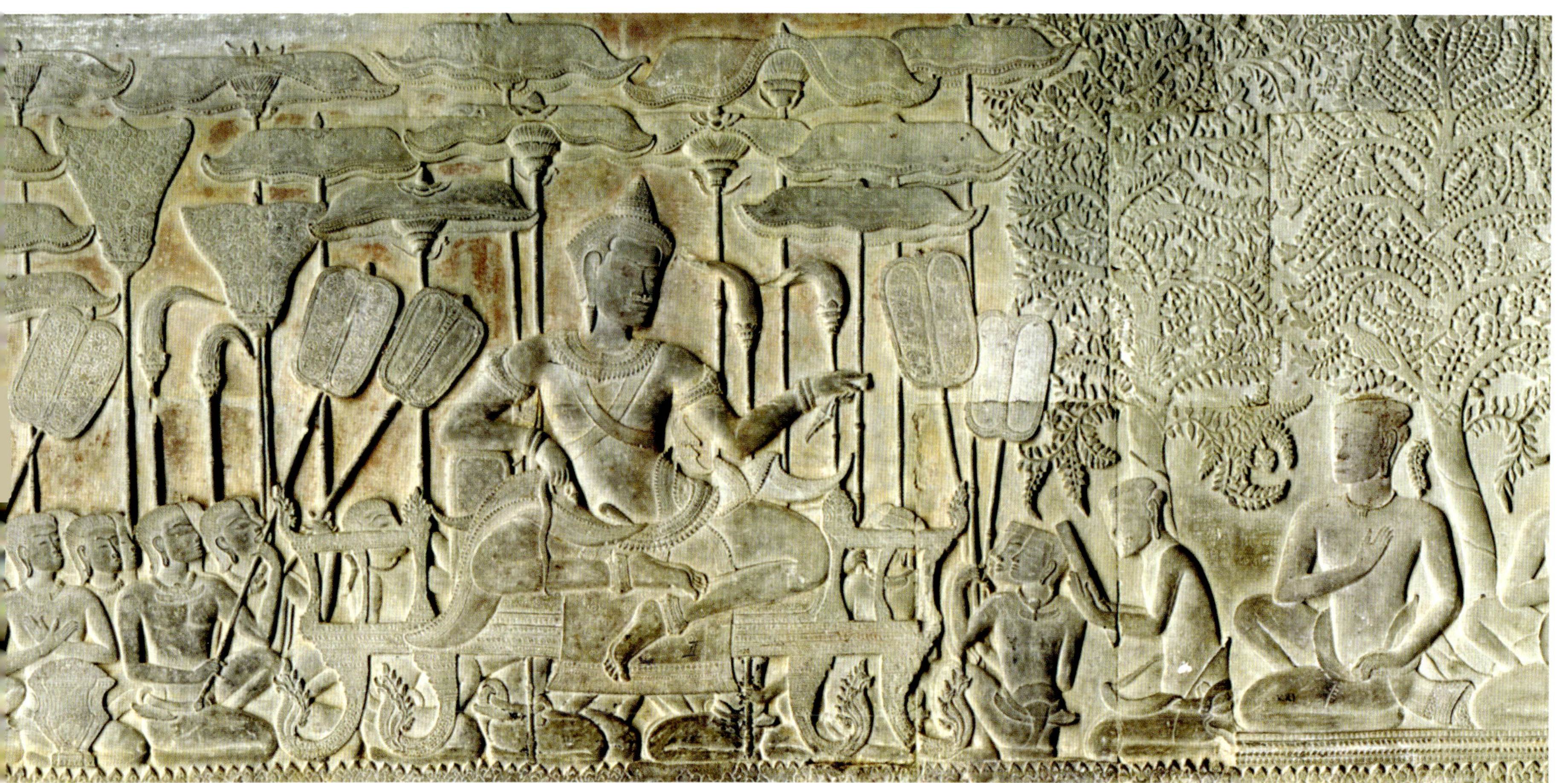

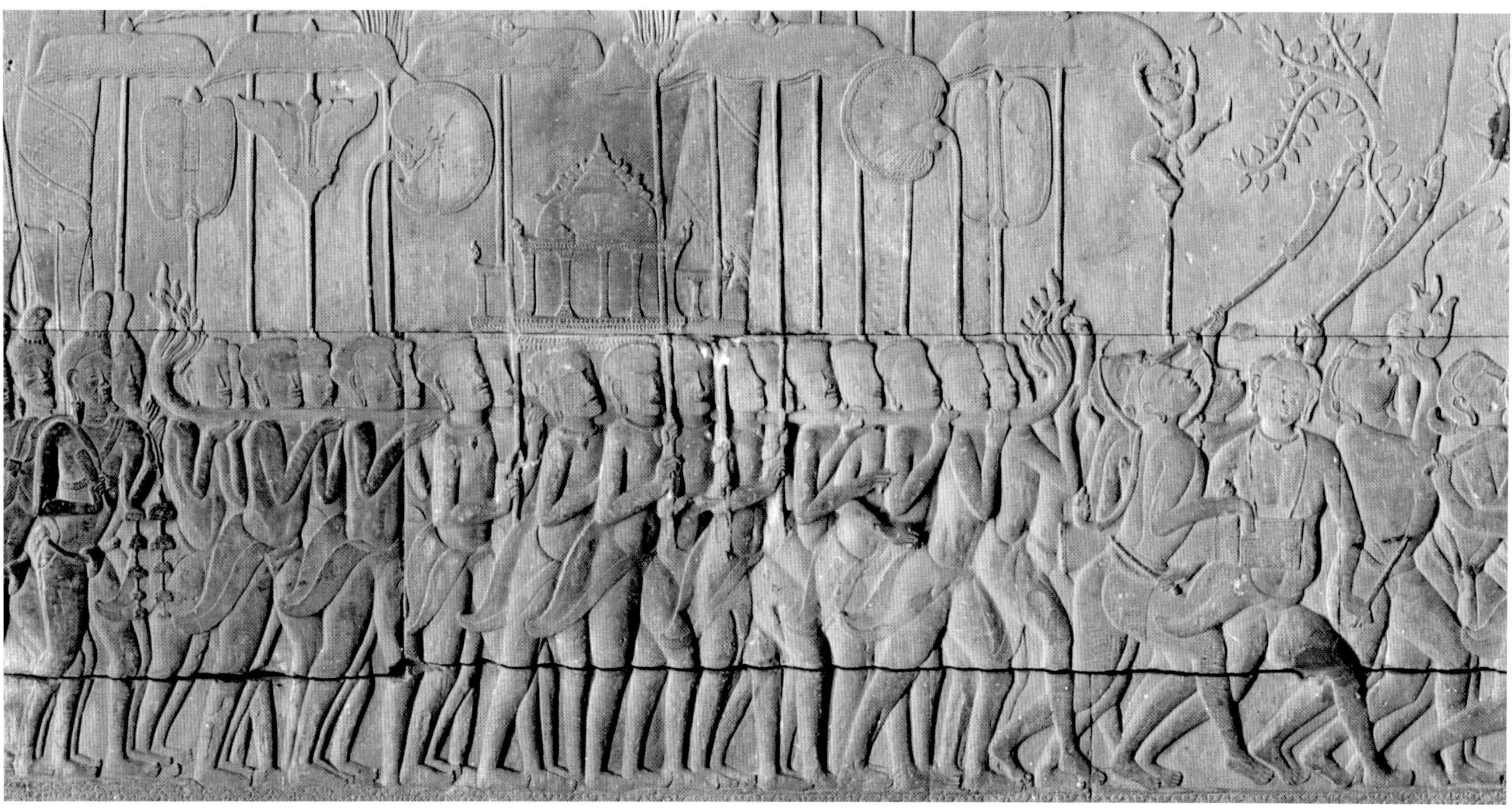

spiritual advancement through any particular deity. The heavens are represented as godless luxury apartments, the hells as crude torture scenes. What the individual can expect from life and death is here presented as the linear pursuit of reward or punishment. Powers higher than king, death and karma do not exist in the ideology of the present portrayed in these southern reliefs.

The eastern wing houses the relief which immediately follows on from the Battle of Kurukshetra, the centrepiece of which depicted two kings locked in mortal combat. Here on the south side we are also shown two kings, the first of whom is the Khmer ruler in person. He is seated at ease on a capacious throne, surrounded by attentive holy men of differing schools, ministers and army generals. A pandit is shown offering him something, while on his other side an aide reads from a document. It is a businesslike scene centred on the chief executive of the kingdom. With his left arm outstretched, the king addresses his ministers and directs his generals to proceed to the east. The inscription above him reads, in the translation of George Coedès, "His Majesty King Paramavishnuloka at the time he was residing on Mount Sivapada to send down the army." And indeed, a long column of warriors is shown following the direction of the imperious left arm, scrambling down the steep forested mountainside and then forming into marching order on the plain below. This river of humanity set in motion by the king extends the whole length of the relief. Most of the people depicted are warriors grouped into regiments from various parts of the empire under the command of their local lords and followed separately by their wives. The leaders are depicted on a larger scale and identified, by name and title and region, in accompanying inscriptions; each is further distinguished by symbols of rank and status carried by his servants. The king appears a second time near the centre of this column, now as field commander of the army on the move, preceded by his chief priest *(rajahota),* the sacred fire, priestly ascetics, and a military orchestra, and still accompanied by two of his high-ranking ministers (named Dhananjaya and Varddhana) from the mountaintop council. The fire *(vrah vleng),* a soldier's god carried by soldiers and followed by Hindu ascetics wielding the vajra-bells used in conjuration ritual, is housed in a portable shrine in the form of a small pillared pavilion. This concentration of religious-political power around the king forms the nucleus of the long procession extending far to the rear and casting far ahead. Unlike the previous panels, this relief is not a battle scene but a demonstration of the combined political, religious, and military machinery of the Khmer state, first as a centralised hierarchy, then as a highly organised mobile force. Kings were required as a matter of course to discharge their duties while travelling, during administrative tours and military campaigns, and the apparatus of state necessarily travelled with them; this depiction of the Khmer court assembled in the open air on a mountaintop and marching in formation across the forested Angkor plain therefore conforms to the active realities of life surrounding the ruler. The panoramic scale of the army represented here nevertheless indicates a specific major campaign, and the welding of numerous regiments into a single force for the purpose is no doubt intentionally symbolic of the political unity of the empire. The army commanders hail from far-flung provinces with such picturesque names as Ldau, Chok Vakula, Chanlattai, Travang Svay, Lvo, or Jeng Jhala. From this last province, the name of which may indicate a border (Jeng) region, comes a tribal regiment known as Syam Kuk commanded by one Paman (Hunter) who has entered the king's service. They present a marked contrast to the Khmer officers and soldiery in both appearance and bearing. The first difference one notices is that they walk in ragged file and do not move their arms in

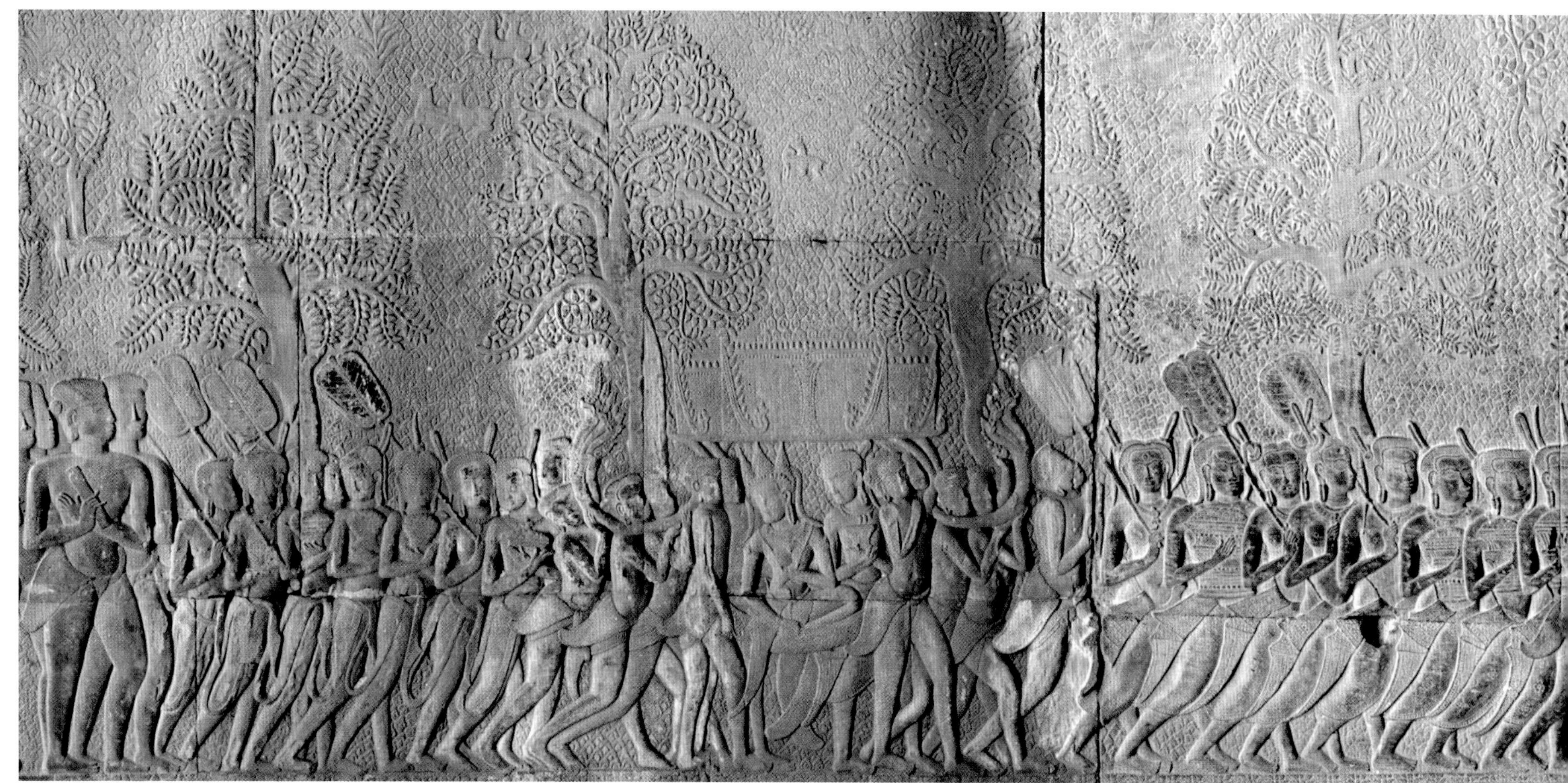

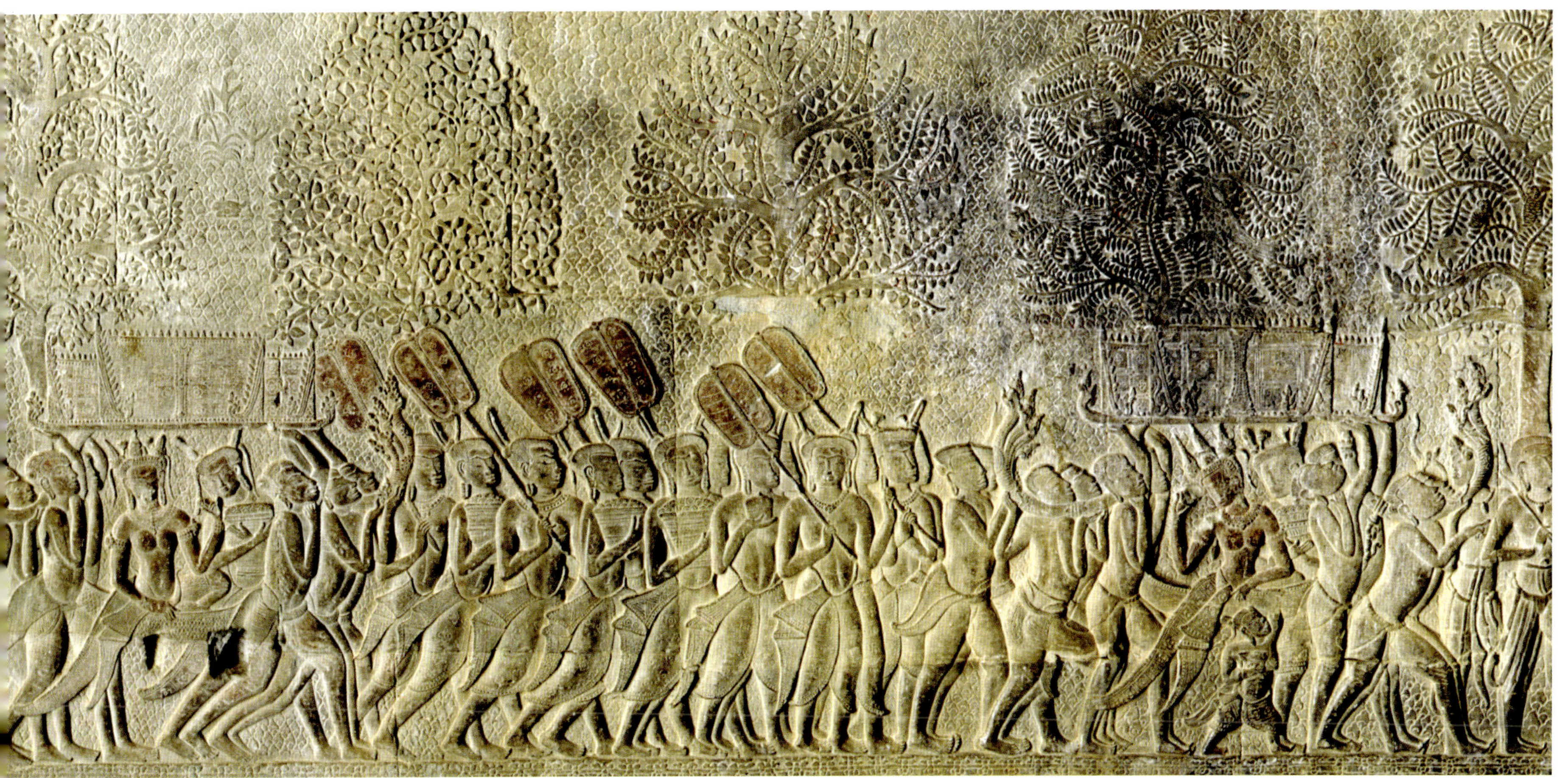

unison, unlike the Khmers who march solidly in step. Dressed in long skirts with tassled aprons, wearing shoulder-length hair surmounted by dishevelled-looking plumes, and carrying tufted spears and tall shields covering the whole body, they also have smaller heads and rounder faces than the square-jawed Khmer troops. Their leader, Paman, stands on his howdah in less heroic posture than the Khmer generals, and he notches an arrow into a short hunter's bow of less sophisticated design than the ornamented bows of the Khmer. Like his own troops, and again unlike the Khmer, his attention does not follow the line of the march but is directed watchfully into the trees around him. The Syam Kuk have been assigned to the head of the column, clearly in order to scout the route ahead, reinforcing the impression that the column is passing through an unexplored jungle region represented by the dense background of trees and creepers. Indeed, the formal regiment immediately behind them, also without a battle standard and consisting of troops from Lvo or Lavo (Lopburi), is stated expressly in the inscription to be led by Lord Jayasimhavarman "in the forest."

The emblems of rank carried beside or in front of the leading Khmer figures consist of honorific parasols, long-handled fans, banners, and battle standards: these flamboyant emblems constitute the basic vocabulary of power symbolism. Each individual leader has at least six parasols except the king's fire-priest *(rajahota)*, who has none. The sacred fire *(vrah vleng)* and its priest are, on the other hand, accorded six and thirteen fans respectively as symbols of religious standing. The fire, however, conceived on the Indian model as the god of the east (Agni) who burns all before him and leads the army forward, is further distinguished by ten parasols – the same number as those carried by the minister Dhananjaya and indicative of very high social position – and a Hanuman

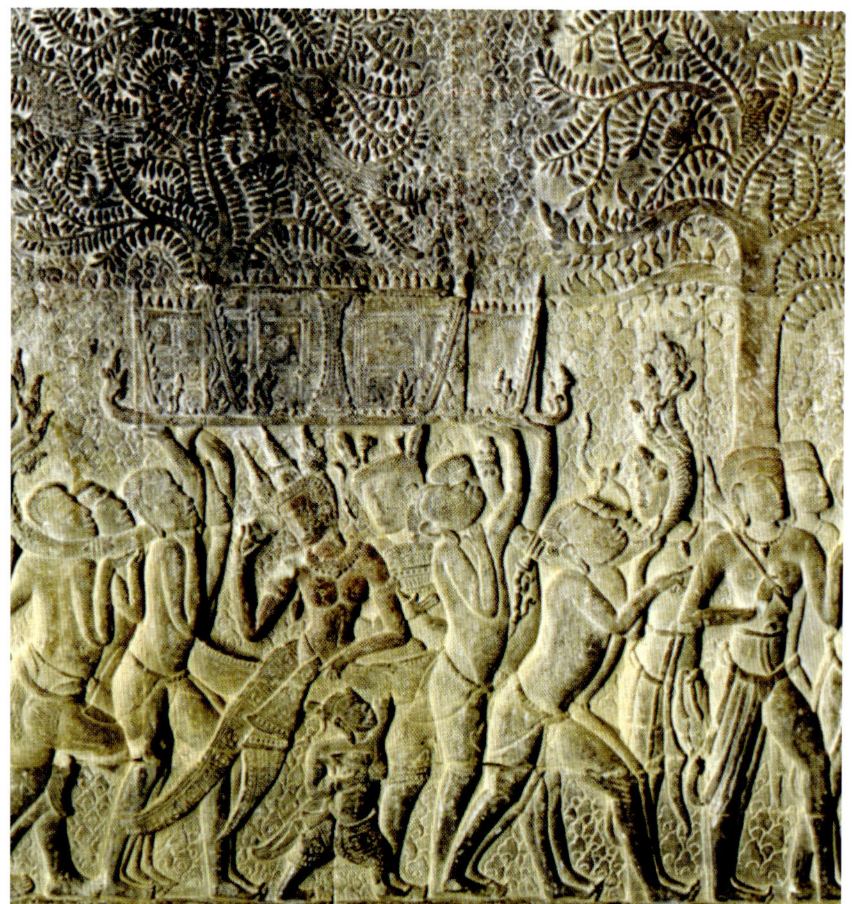

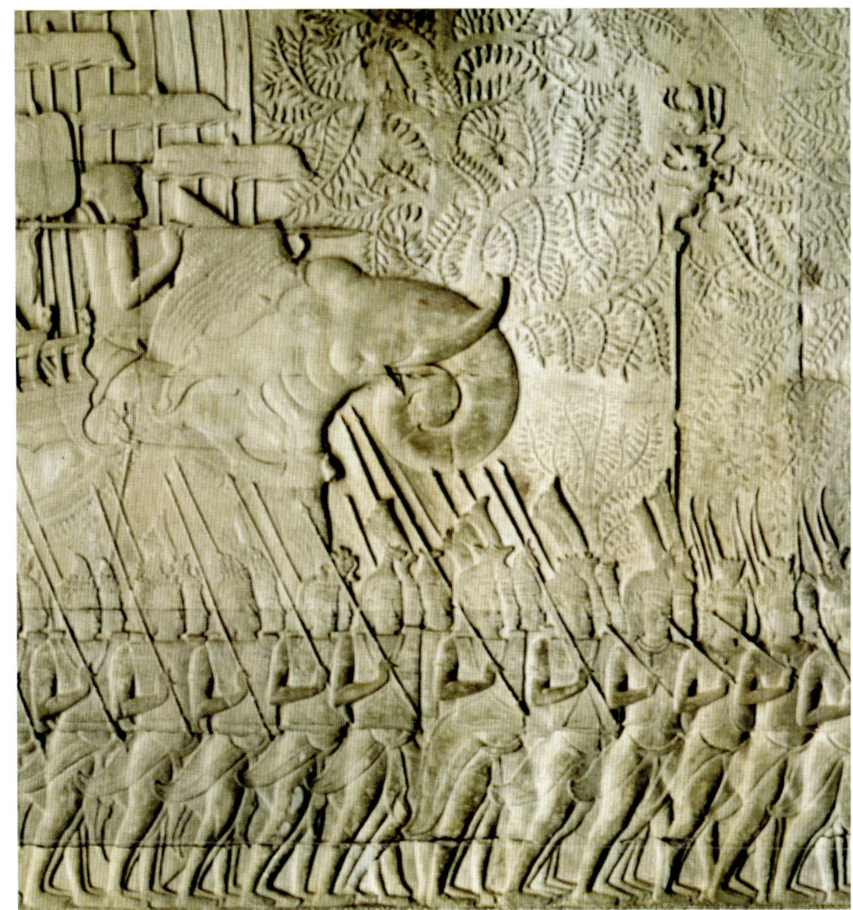

standard, which means that the fire-god was given a definite military rank, exactly as if he were one of the army commanders, a rank which he held in addition to his religious function signified by the six fans and his entourage of ascetics. It is exceedingly difficult to grasp the whole of the system by which the Khmers calculated nuances of status in terms of such symbols. What is clear is that these were serious matters involving a complex scale of values operating within a hierarchical power structure that was far more sophisticated than modern army ranking systems. The sophistication arose, not because of technological developments in weaponry and a corresponding need for more military specialists, but because of the multiple social roles and symbolic cultural functions required of a leader in an intricate traditional society. Of the twenty-one leaders in this relief (including the king and the sacred fire, but excluding the fire-priest, whom the artist obviously regarded as a mere appendage of the fire itself), nine are distinguished by a Hanuman standard and two by a standard crowned with the device of Garuda, the sun-eagle of Vishnu; only the king appears under the aegis of Vishnu himself mounted on Garuda, a distinction that clearly relates to his after-death destiny in the realm of Vishnu and hence to his identity as Paramavishnuloka.

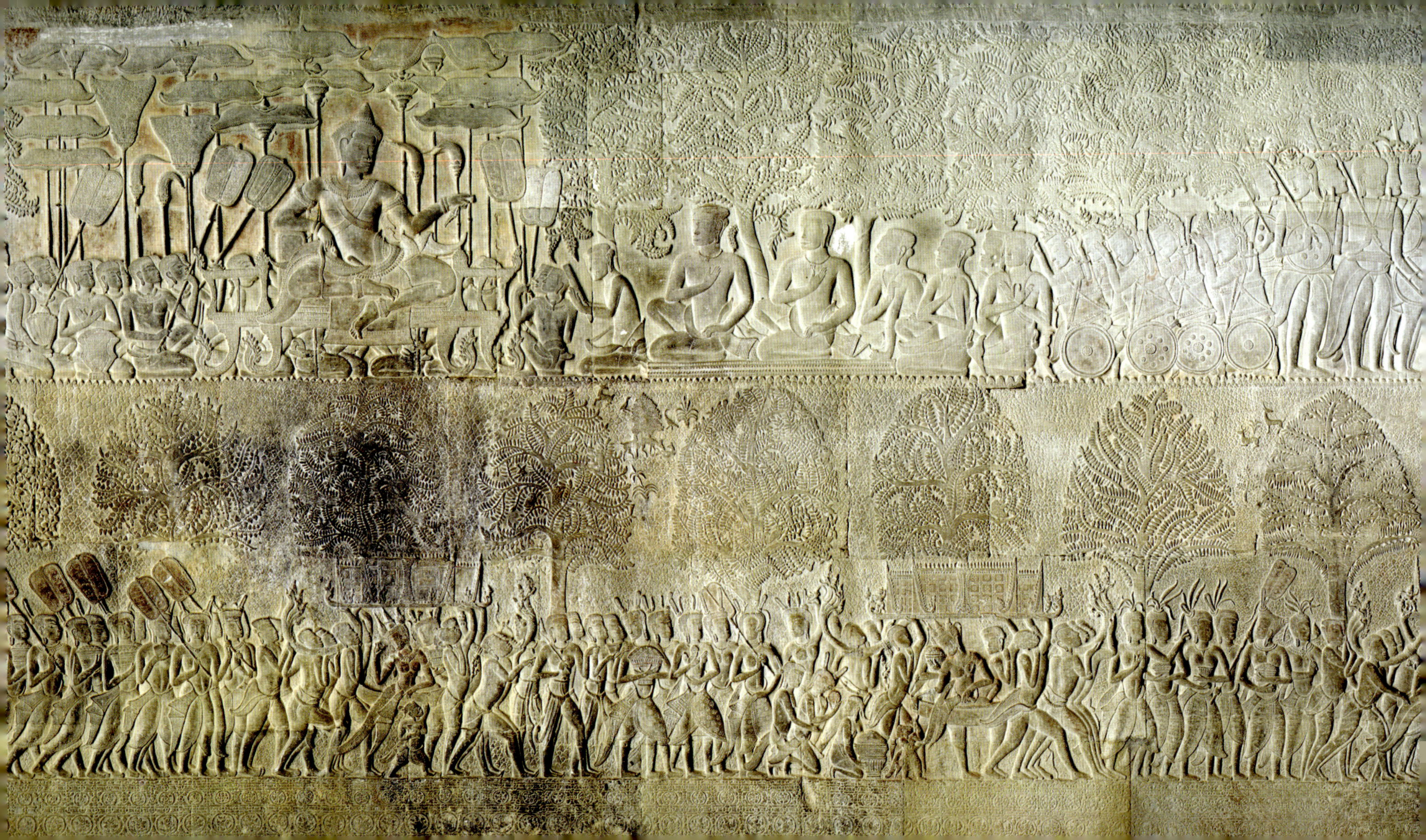

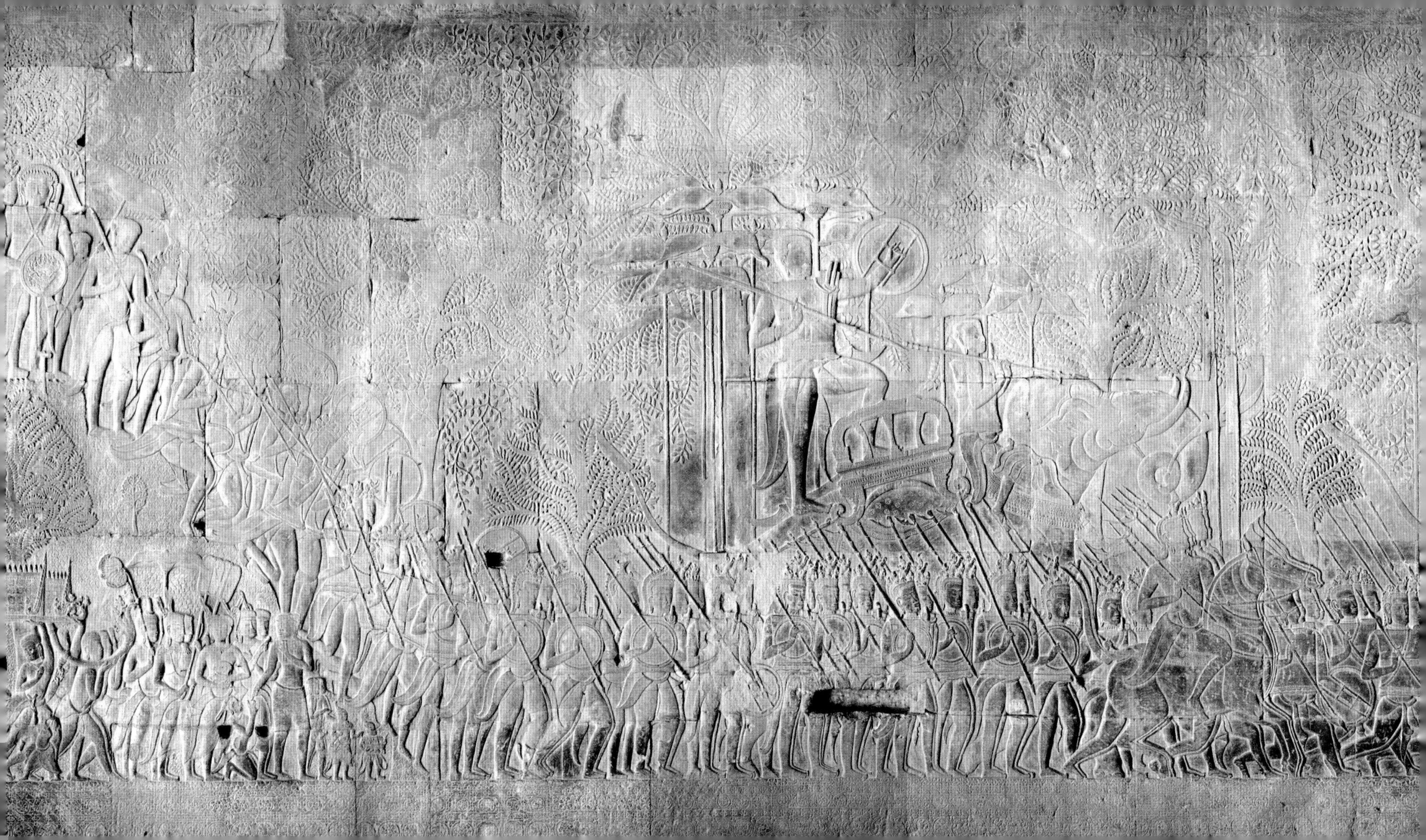

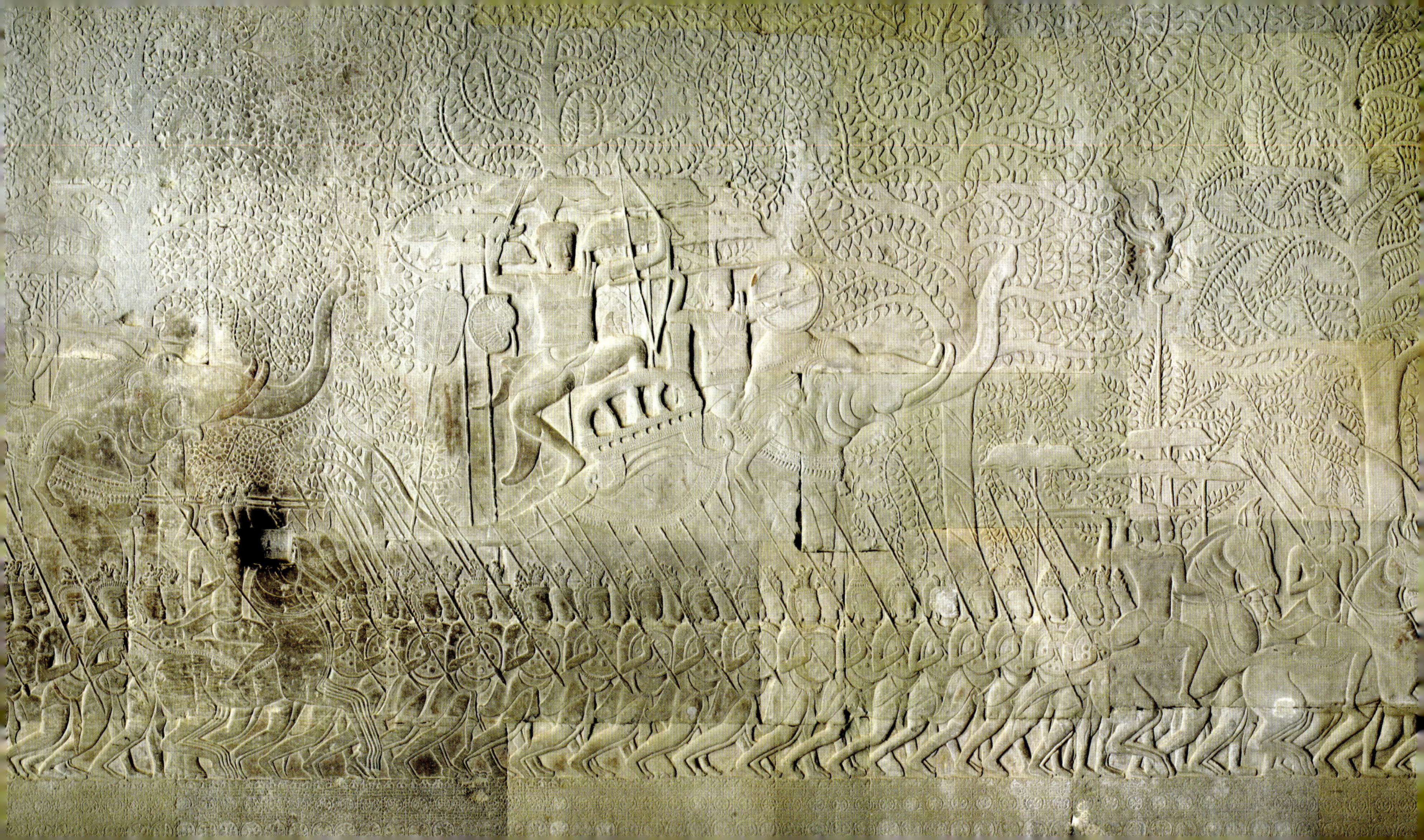

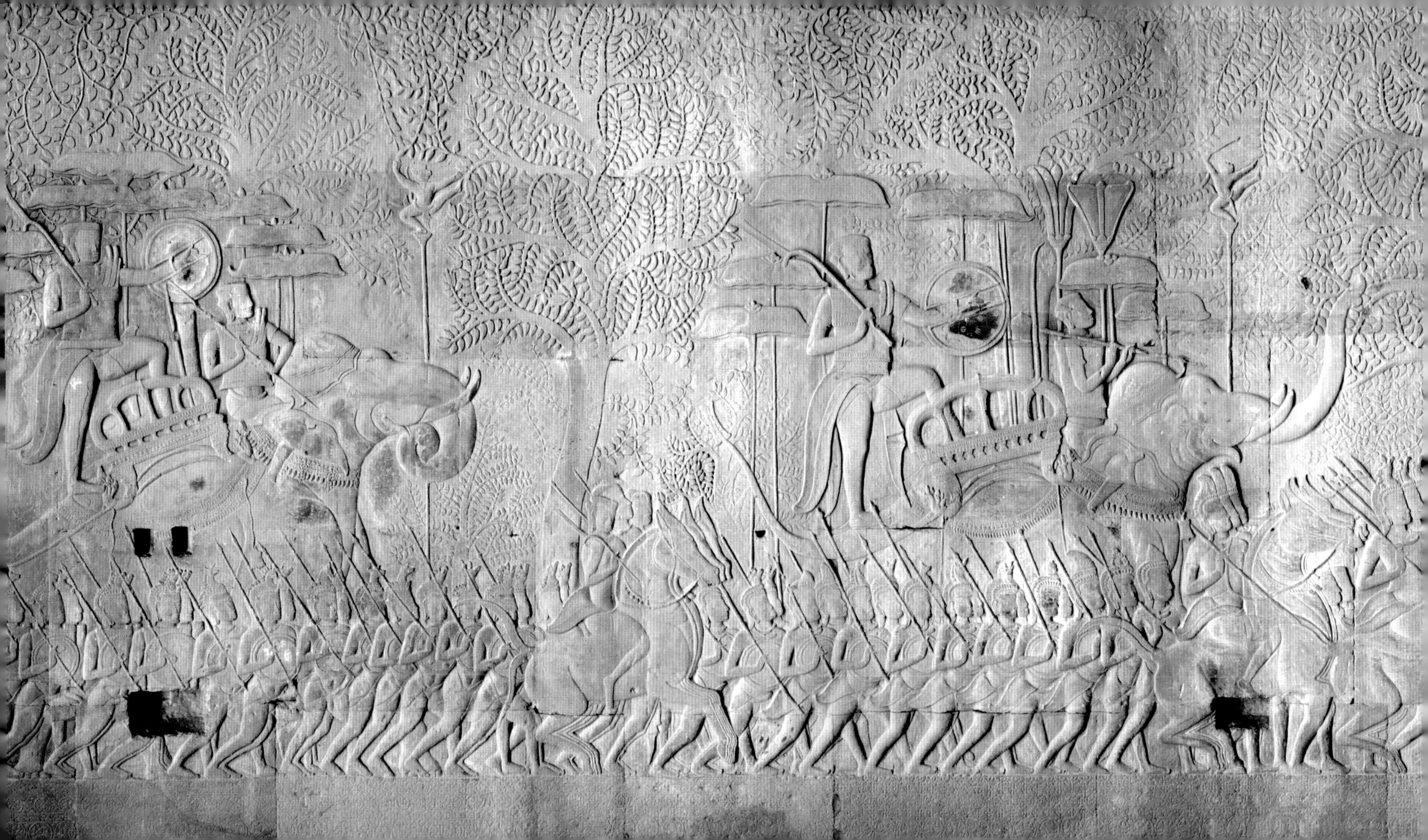

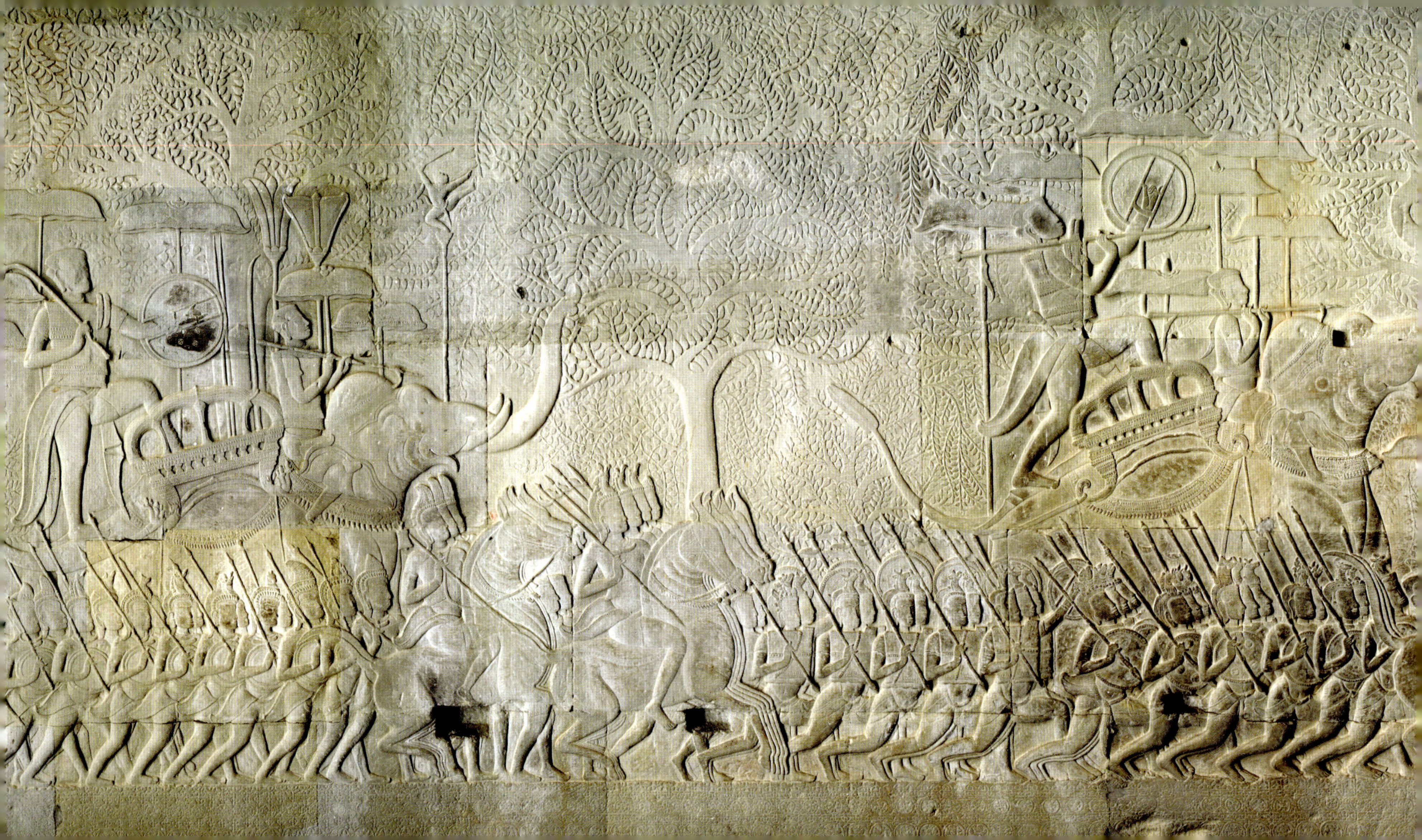

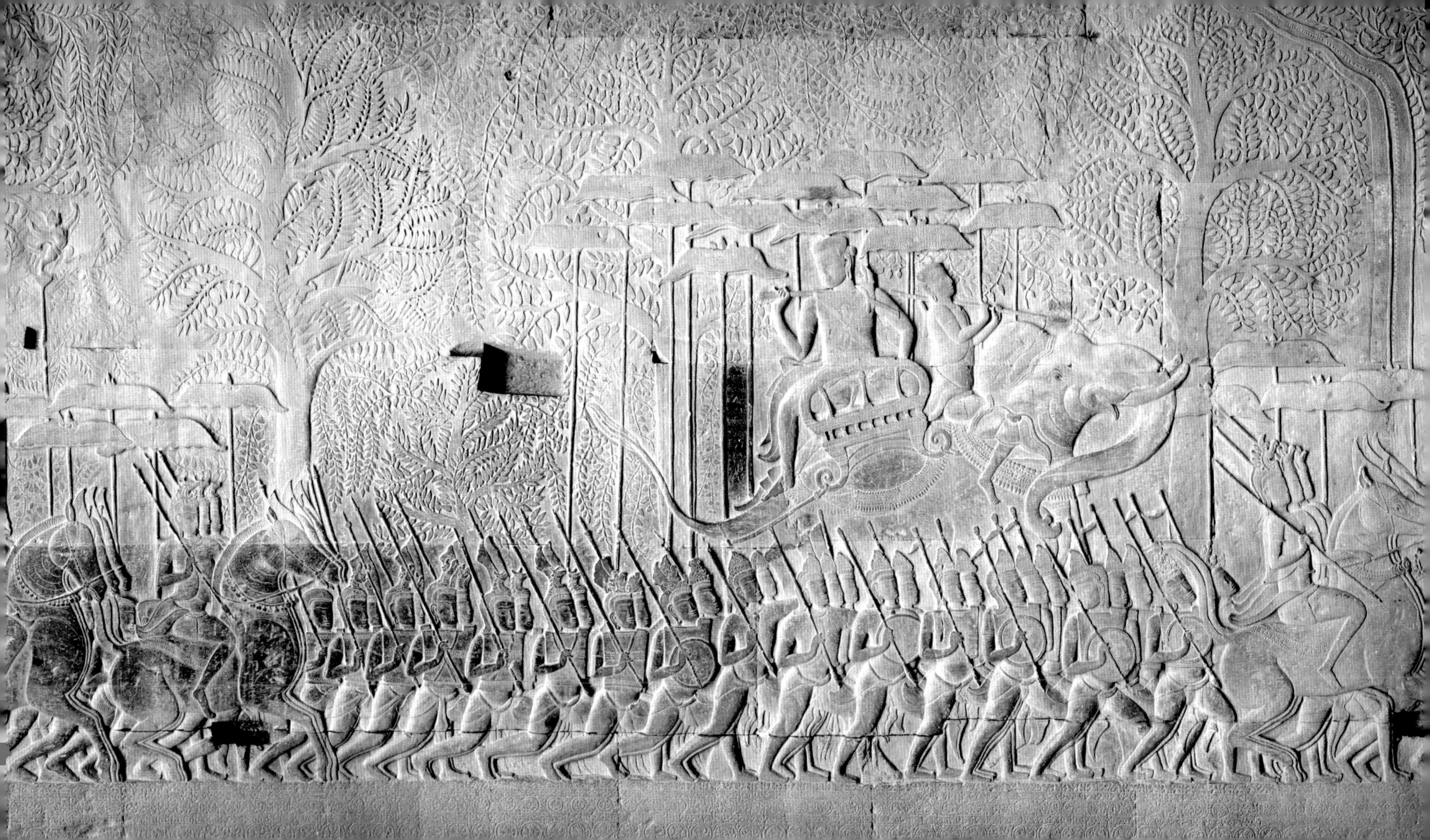

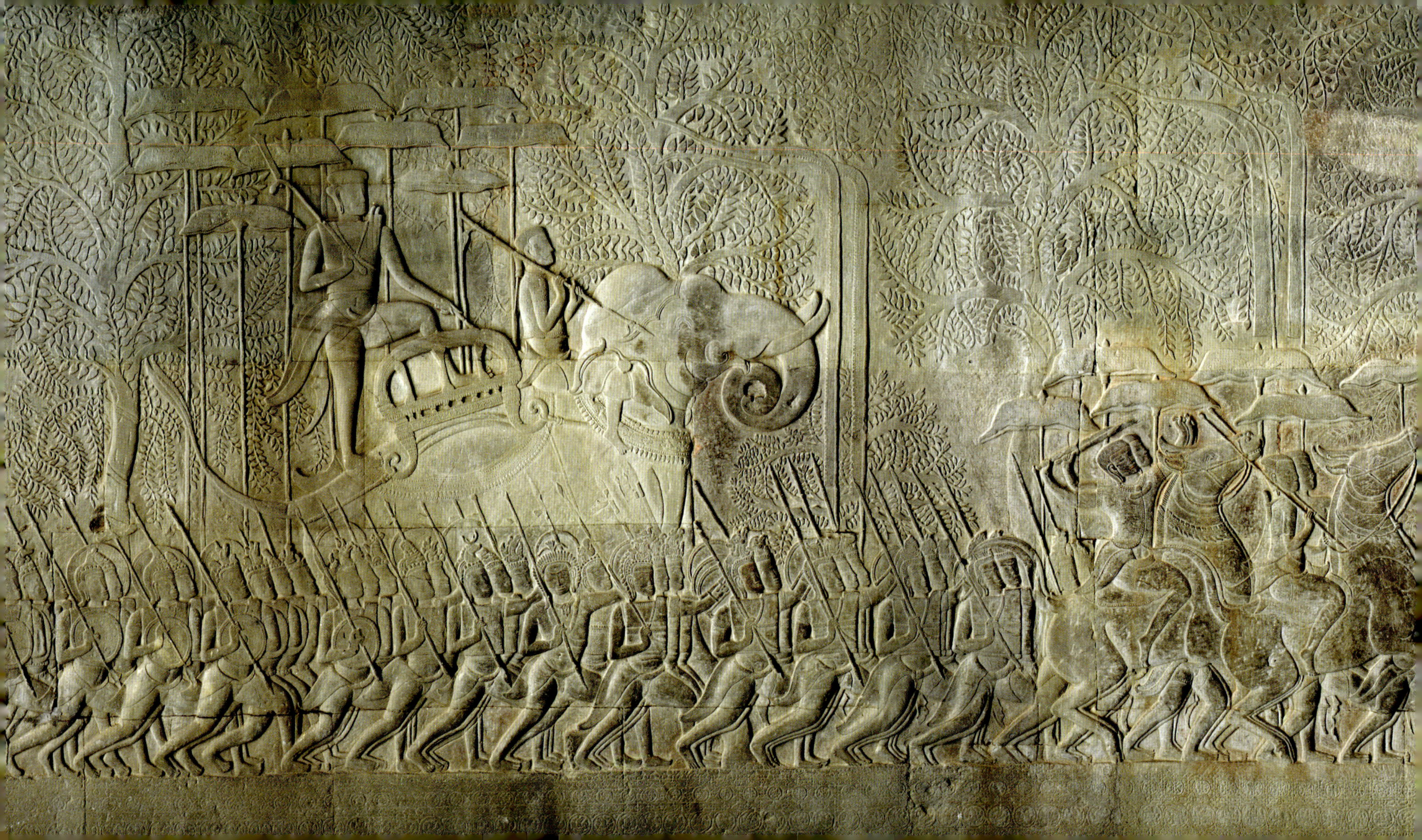

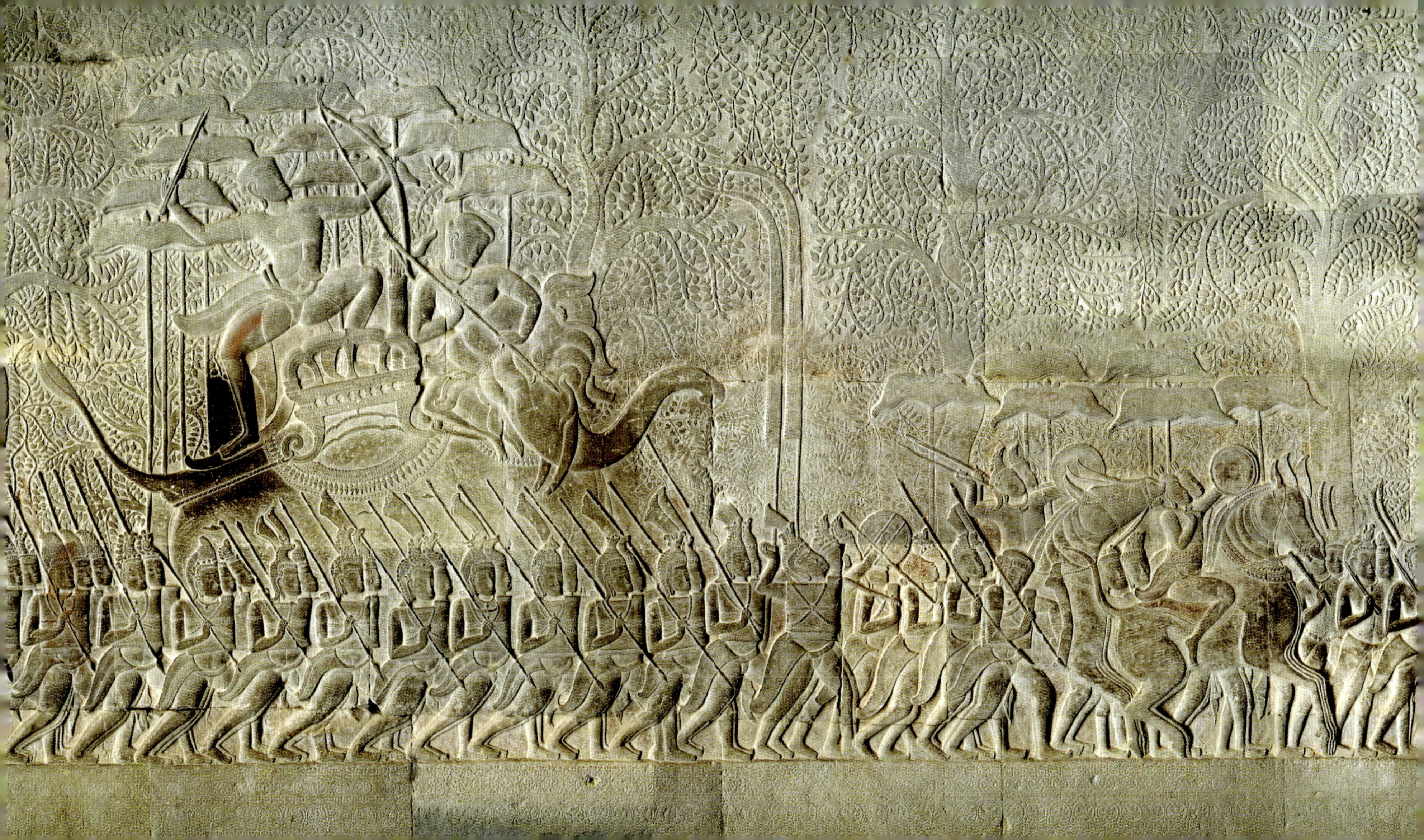

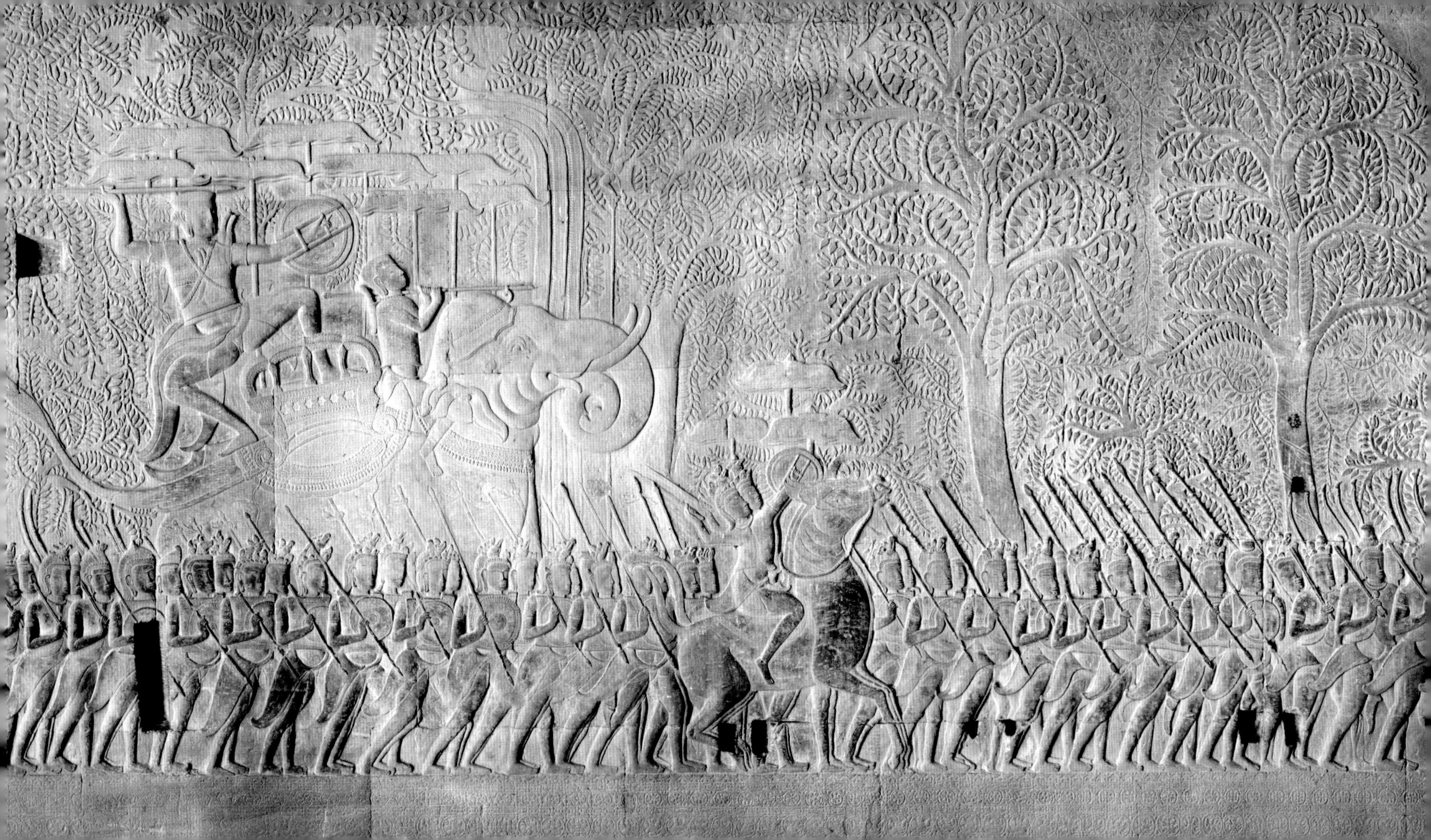

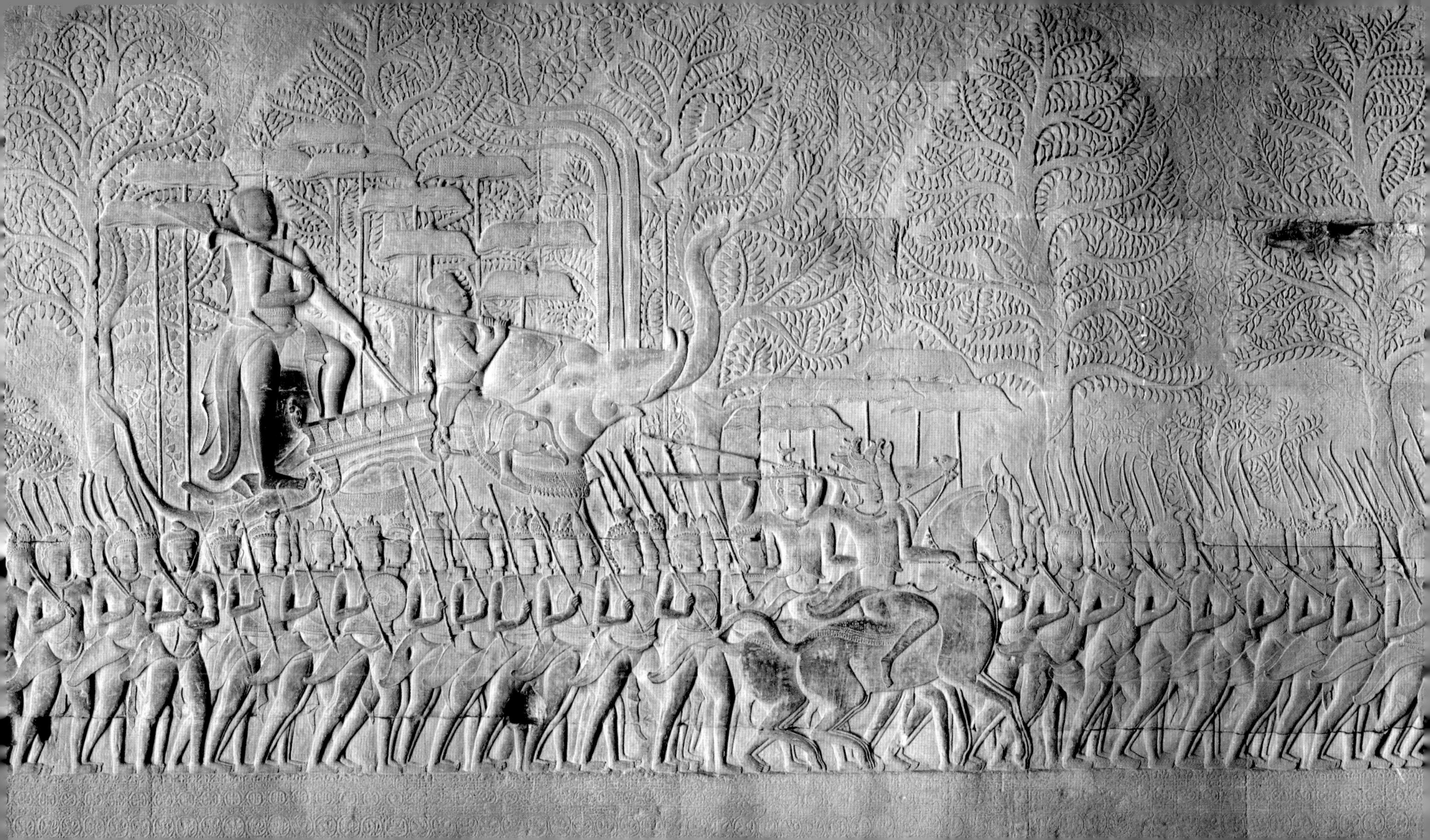

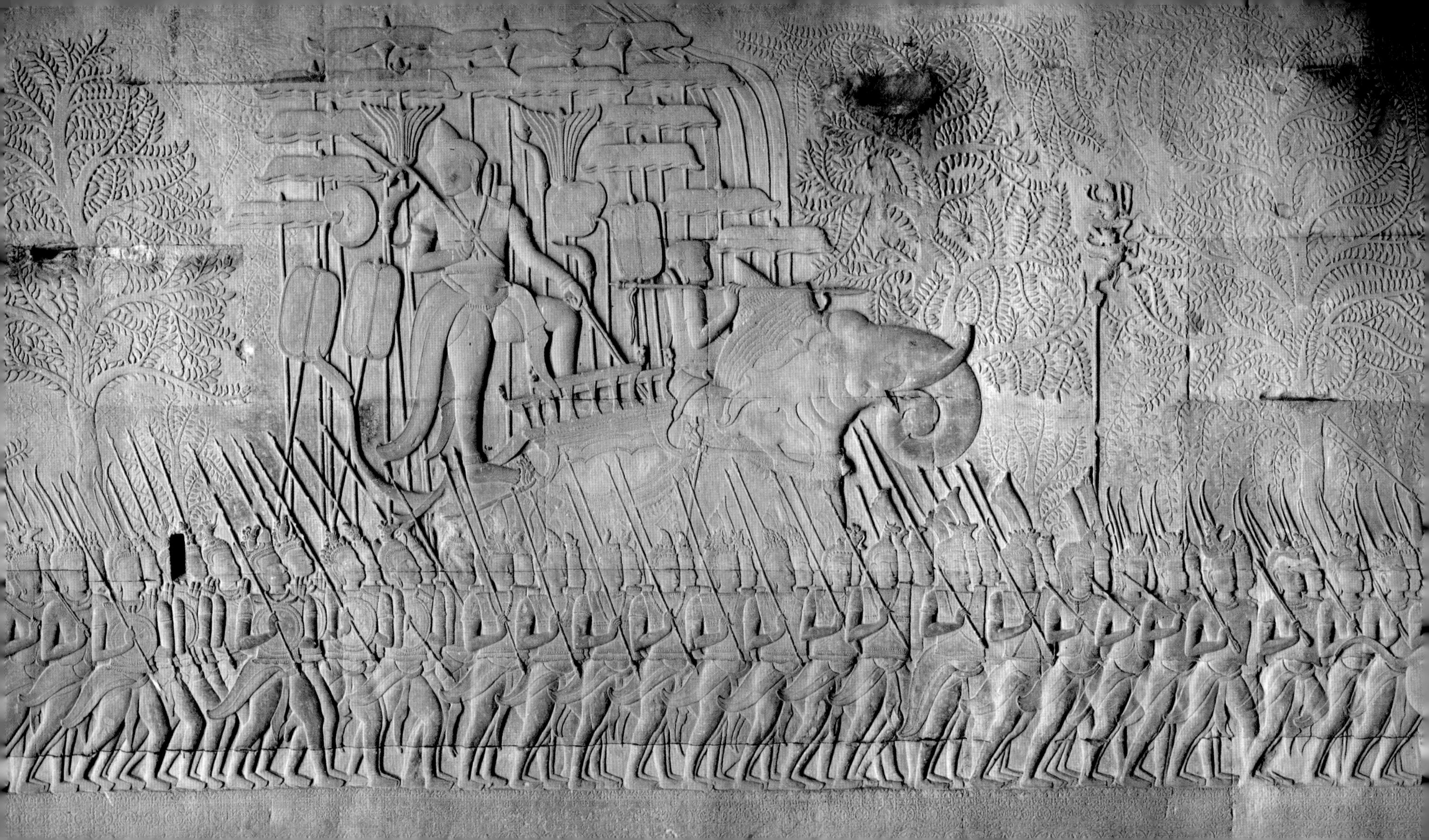

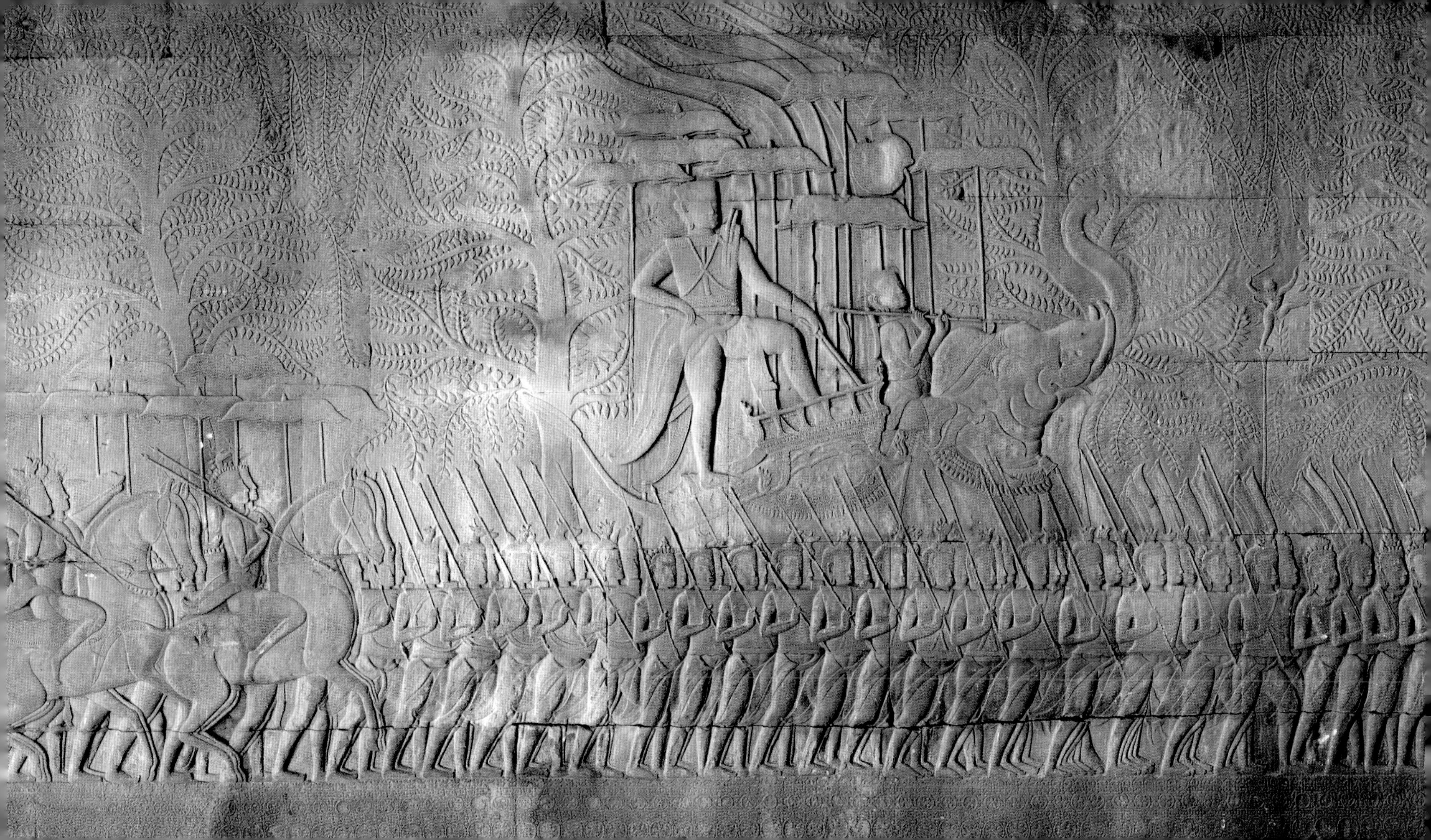

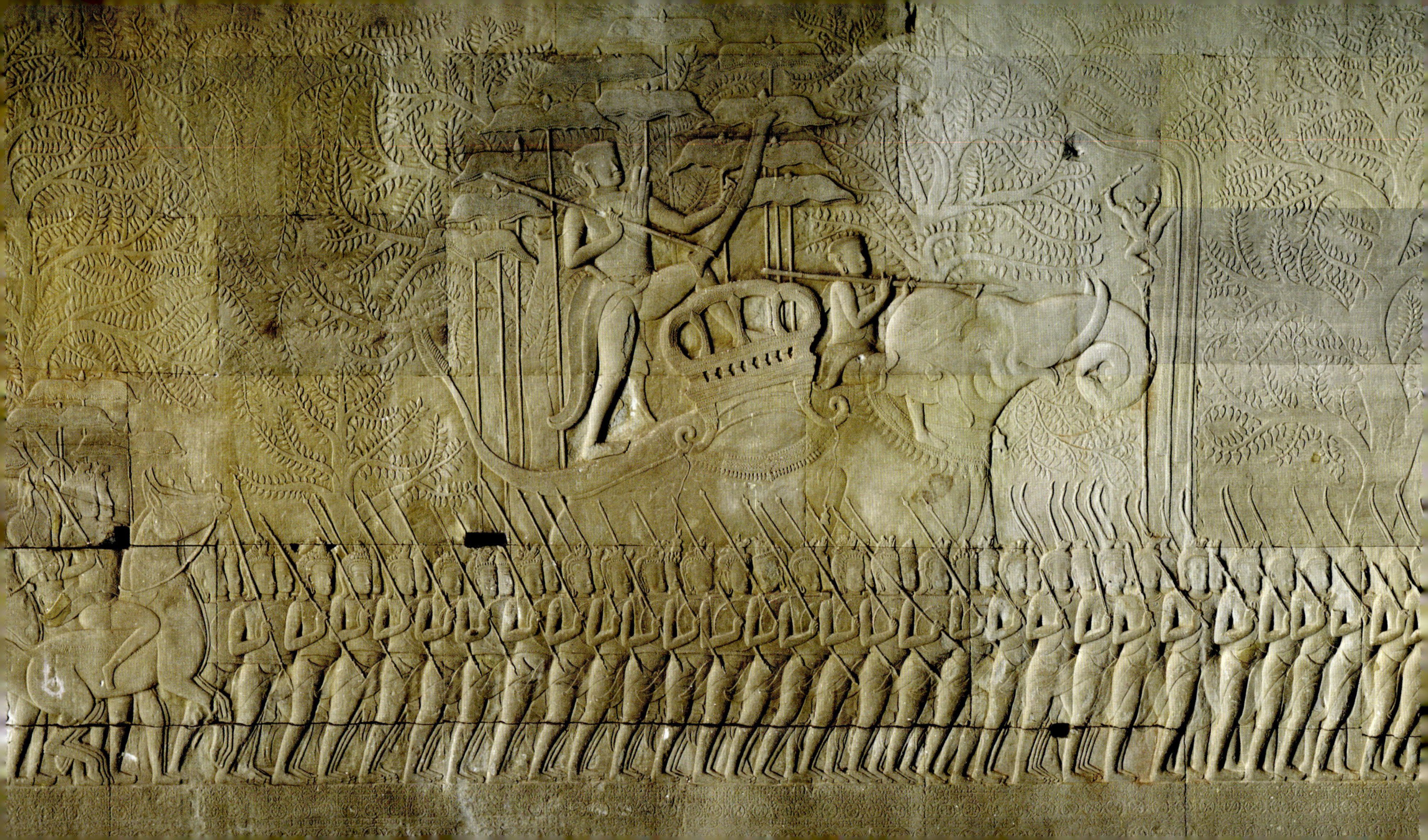

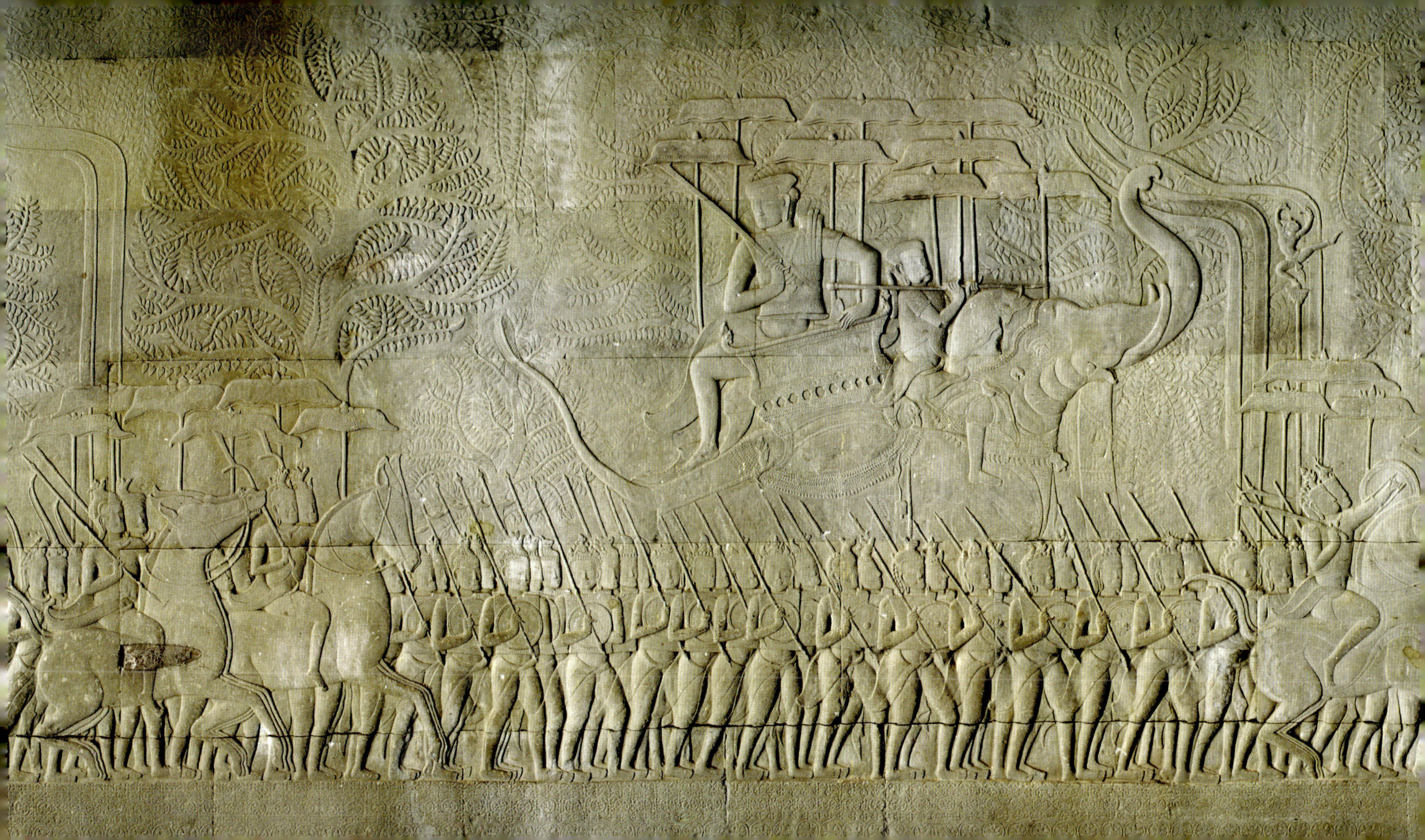

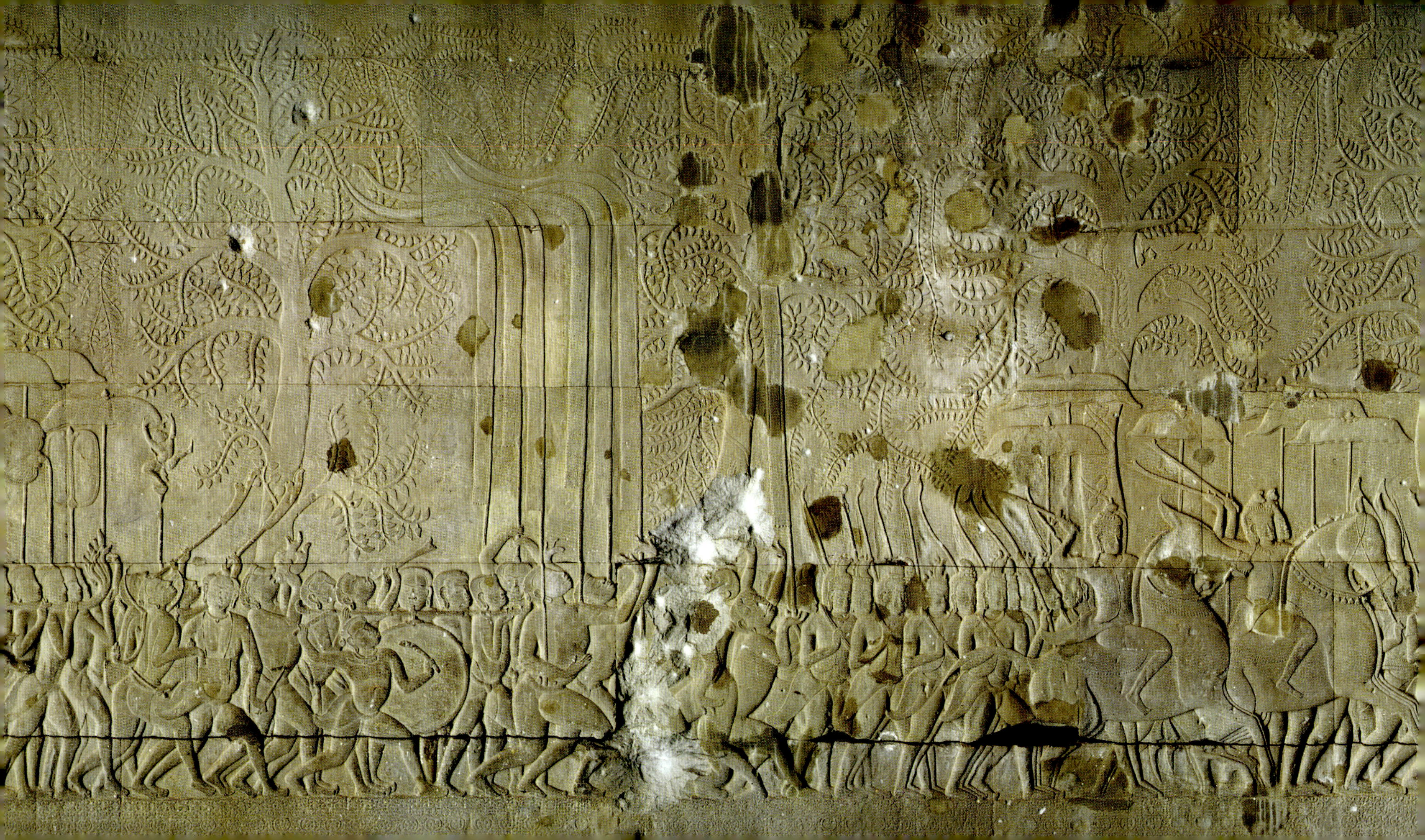

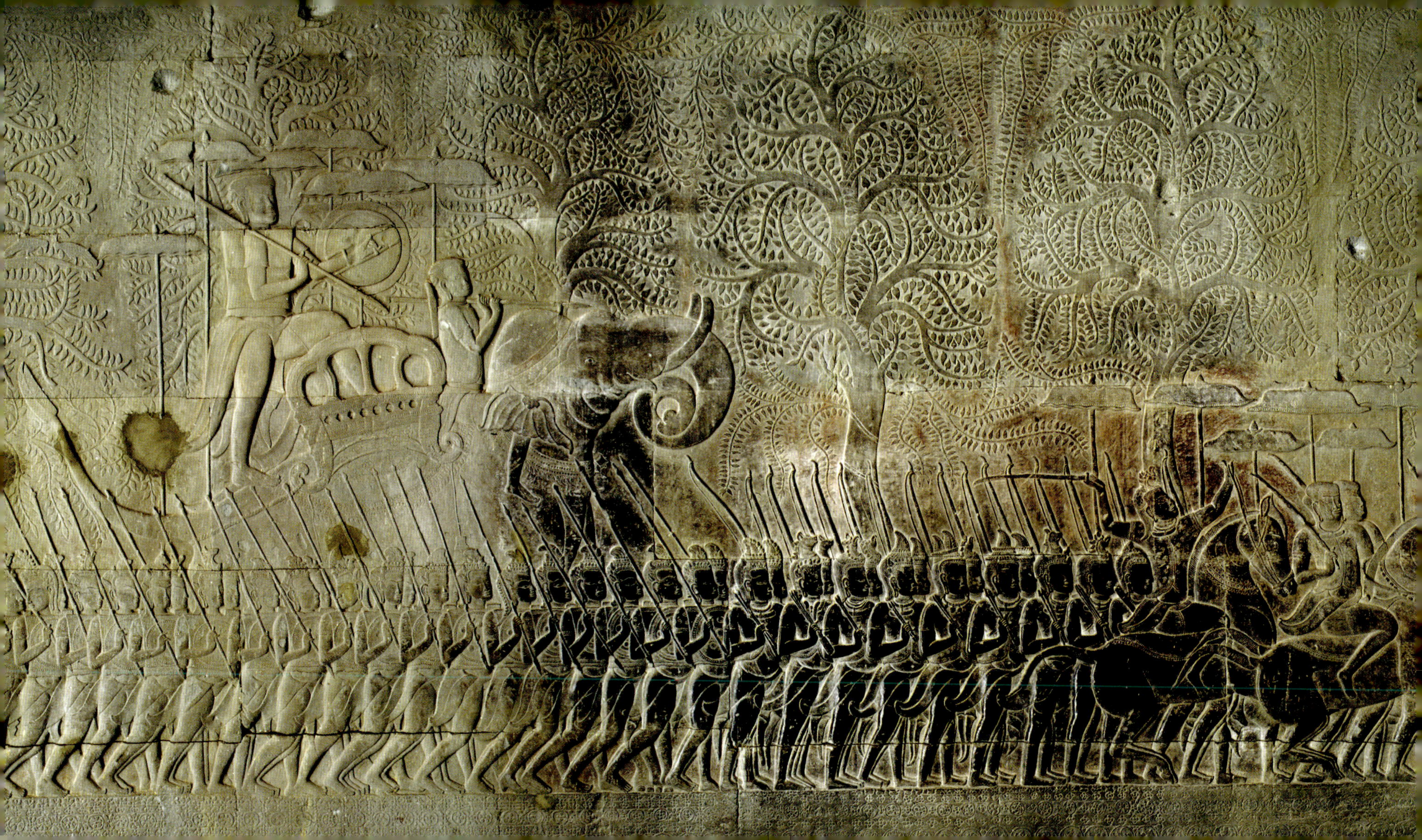

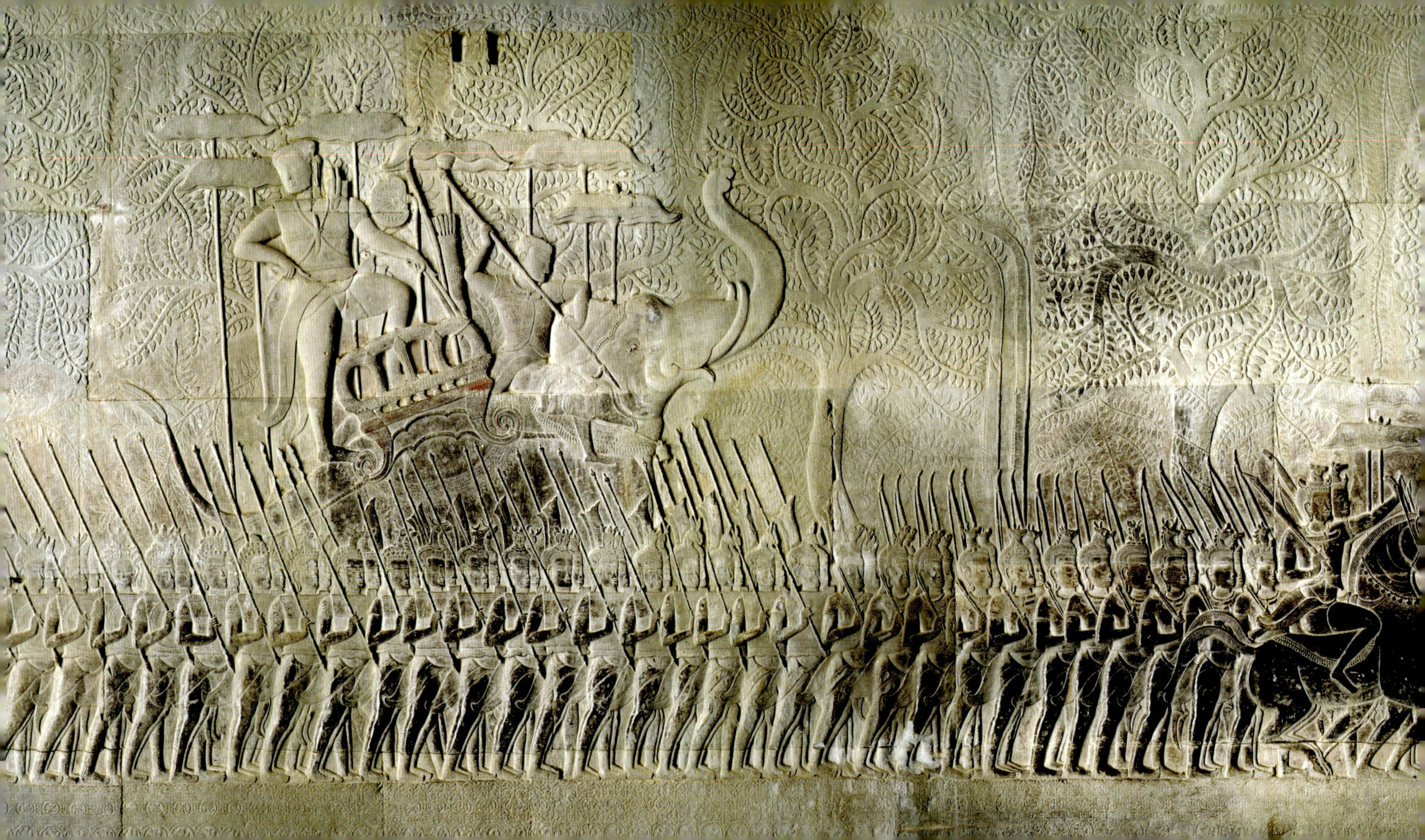

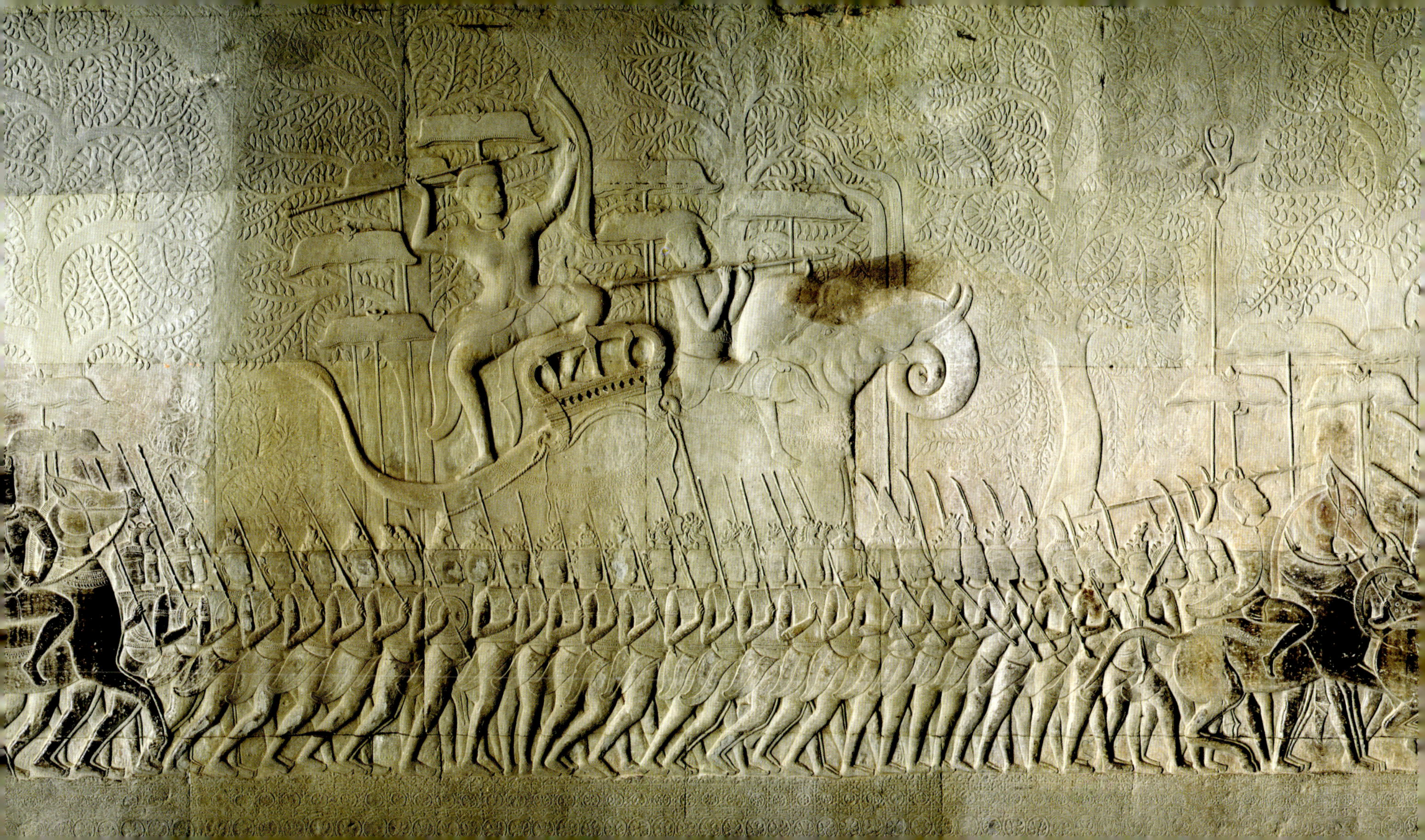

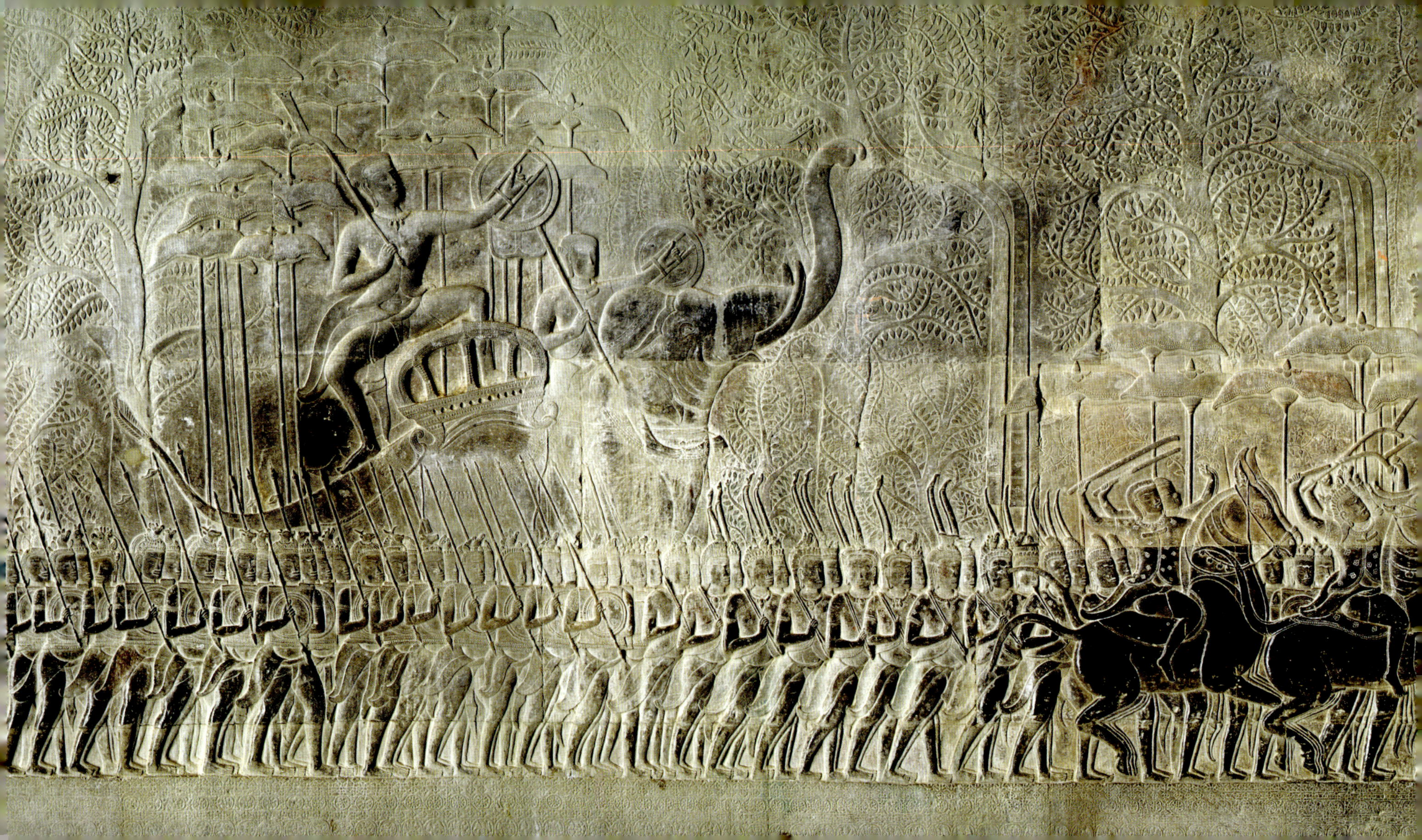

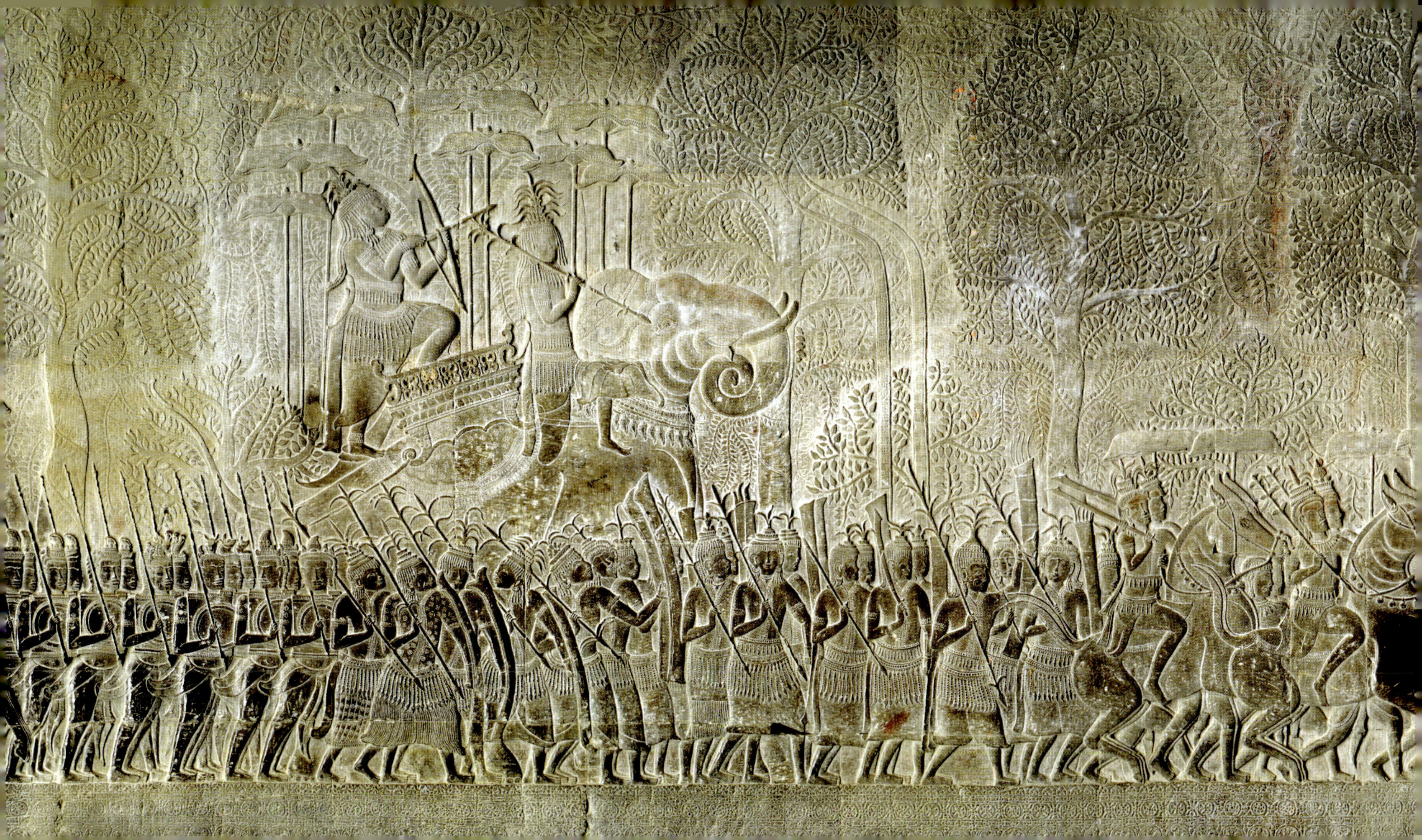

KING YAMA AND THE APPARATUS OF DEATH

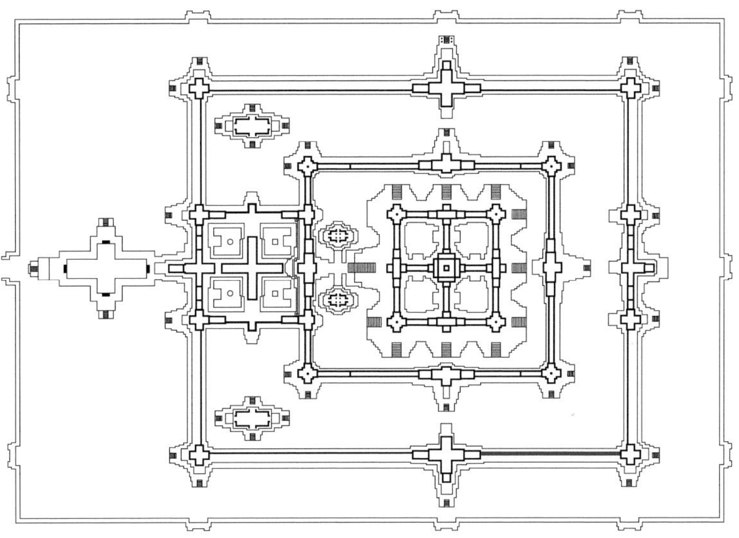

South Gallery, East Wing

KING YAMA AND THE APPARATUS OF DEATH
Kali Yuga II

Not everyone could look forward to an afterlife in the world of Vishnu. The river of humanity, bereft now of all political purpose, continues in the next and final relief, where it confronts Yama, Ruler of the Death Kingdom. Just as the earthly king commands the individual in life, so Yama dispenses justice at the threshold of the world to come. For everyone except the king, this is the moment of truth, the mirror of personal human destiny. Yama sits in royal posture on a lotus seat placed on the back of his black water-buffalo, encircled by sixteen yamadandas, his rods of justice, with one of which he orders the dead into hell to his left, having singled them out individually with the index finger of his right hand. With his host of parasols and fans, Yama is very much the likeness of the earthly king, iconographically translated into the image of death – a passing frisson for the modern observer, but certain reality for Khmers of the 12th century. What the king has set in motion in life, leads in a straight line from the jungles of Kambuja to the forest of death.

But it is no longer a single line: beyond the moment of death there is an abrupt upward deflection and the line divides into three. The lowest line is a direct continuation of the march in the jungle, the screen of trees arbouring now the torments of hell where in life the army advanced in all its pomp and power. But mounting on the backs of the damned as on a ramp – the counterpart of the mountainside from which all descended in life – those not summoned by Yama ascend into a two-tiered void whence they are conveyed to their individual heavens

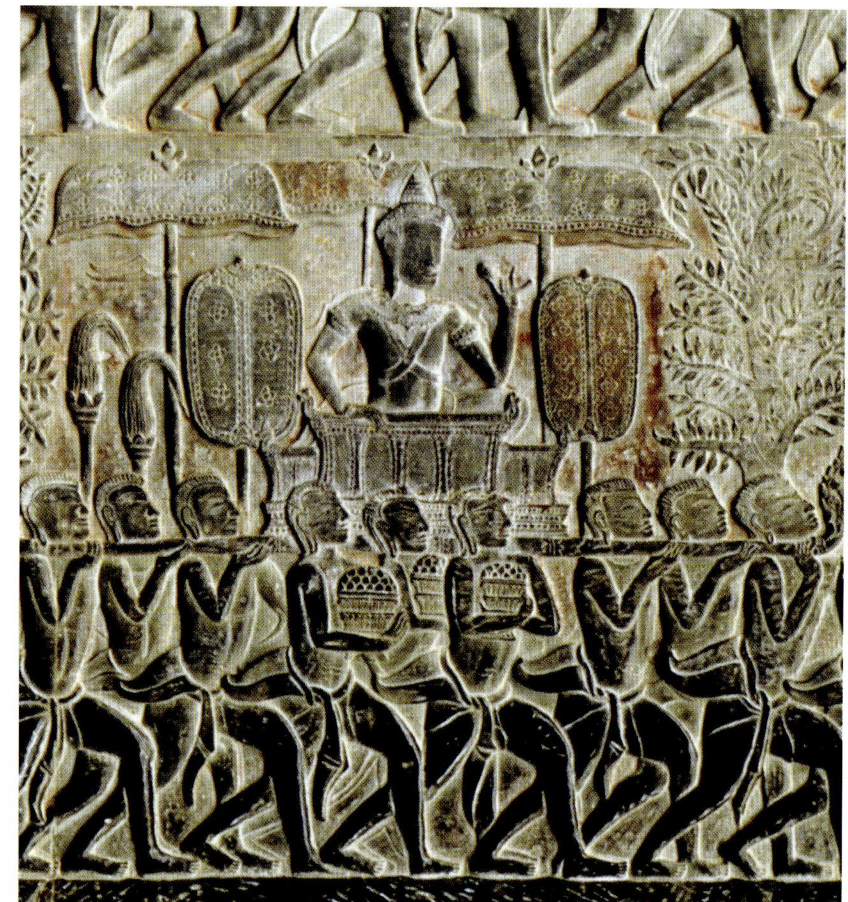

on elaborate palanquins, accompanied still by the fans and parasols of rank. The heavens, described by most commentators as rather boring, consist of a succession of grand pavilions with doubled barrel roofs and curtained interiors, a place where attentive bejewelled servants sit in neighbouring rooms ministering loyally to the vanities of the occupants in the central apartments. What is boring about these scenes is not the repetitiousness of paradise but its triviality: men strike princely poses, women sit and primp, all in an atmosphere of refined vacuousness. But in the Kali Yuga, the relief is telling us, such dreams of aimless luxury beyond the grave substitute for the spiritual values of earlier ages when gods incarnated in men and Dharma was something to be fought for. The only transcendent force operating in the Kali as represented here is the mechanical law of karma – policed and adjudicated by Yama – which constrains all mortals to live out the consequences of their actions in the heaven or hell of their own making. No gods of salvation are present because no such gods are called for, and in such an age none will come. Those who occupy the compartments of heaven, however, are seated on lotus seats like the figure of Yama on his buffalo, signifying that they are themselves now to be understood as deities.

The hells, as mentioned above, are situated in a forest, apparently the continuation of the jungle through which the king and his army were shown marching in life. But it is rather a transformation of that jungle, just as Yama is a transformation of the king, for with the shift of scene strange growths appear in this other forest. They resemble some form of cactus covered in thorns, and in nine out of the thirty-four hells depicted these plants are put to use for torturing the damned, for example as a gallows from which the dead are suspended, or as a means of lacerating their flesh. Other natural phenomena of the forest can also be

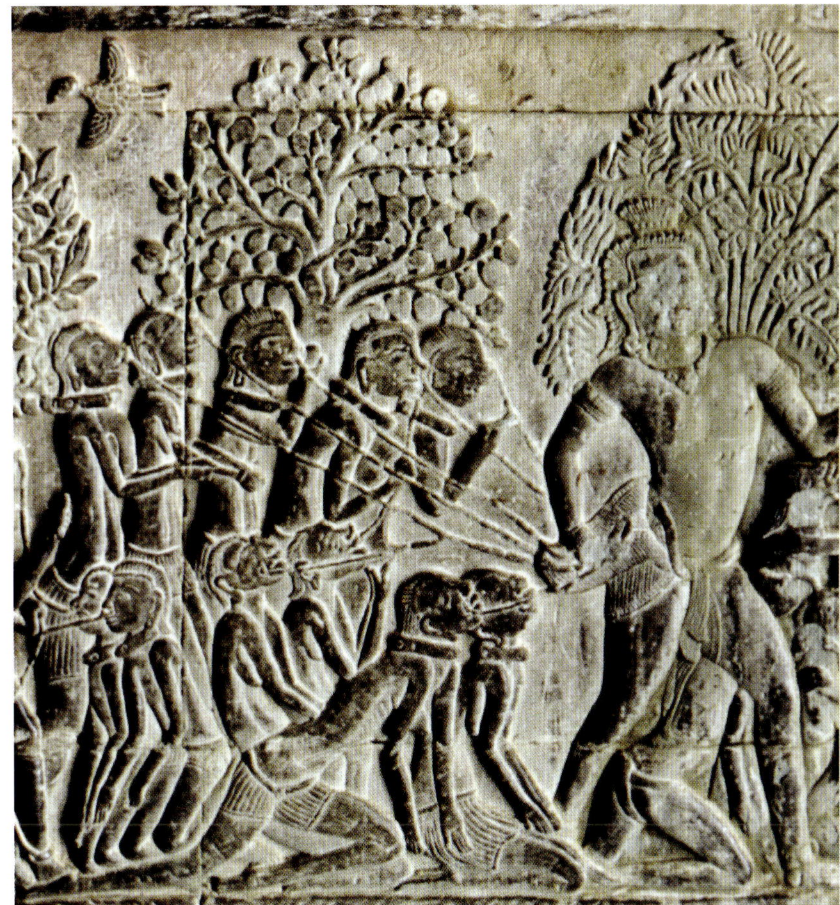

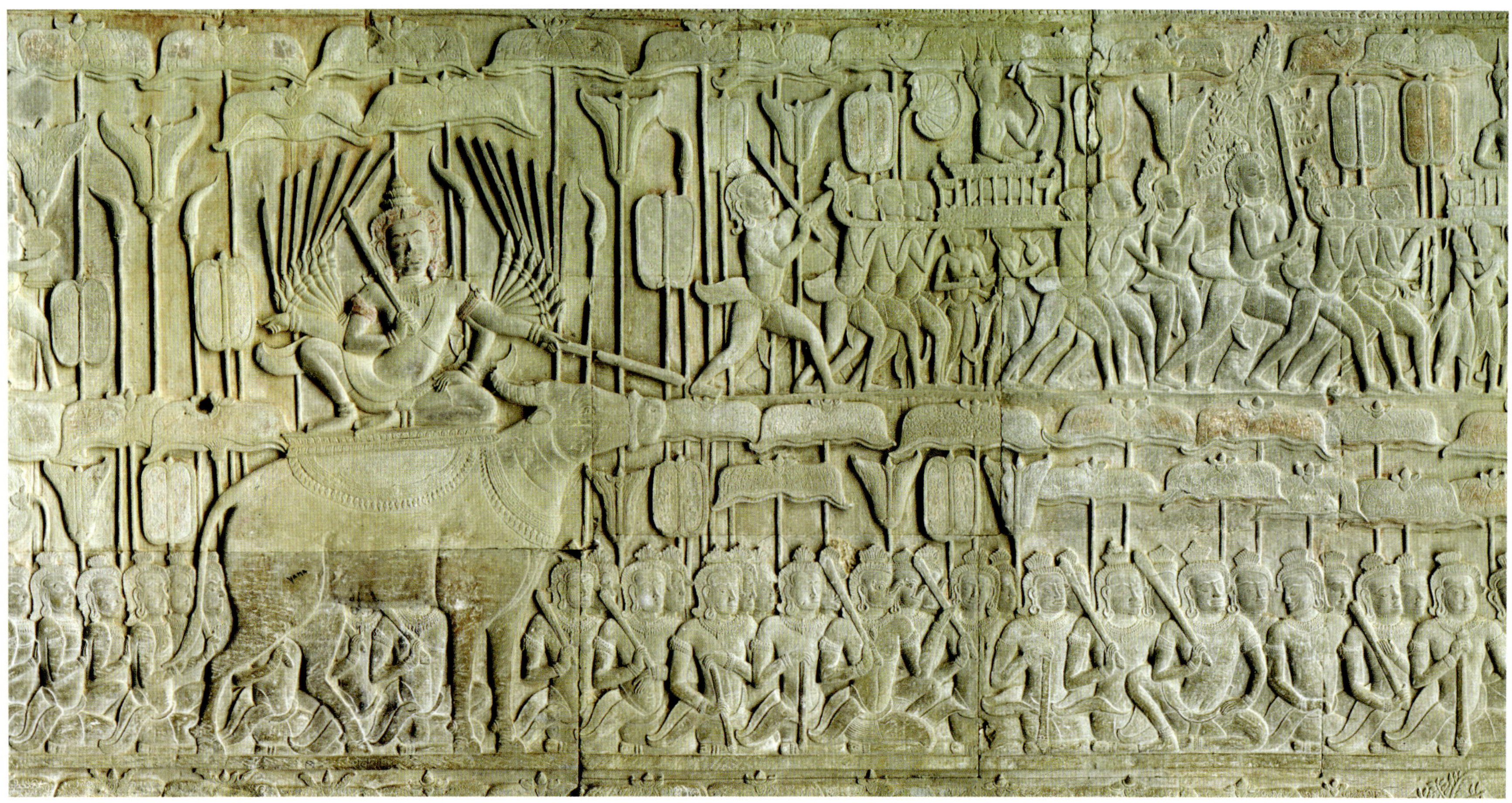

put to sadistic purpose, for example the terrible Clashing Mountains, Yugmaparvata, between which the dead can be crushed two at a time, or the six ponds, lakes and rivers filled not with water but with blood, pus, mucous, or molten lead, not to mention the nine terrible uses of fire. Then there are the worms, dogs, and birds of prey, and all the devilish machineries and tools of torture devised by man, such as tongs for the extraction of tongues, vices for crushing the jaw or neck, awls for blinding, special maces for smashing flesh and crushing bone, knives for hacking, nails for hammering into limbs and heads, and of course gallows constructed for various means of hanging. If the landscape of hell begins to sound like an all too familiar reality, this is because the Khmers, like European artists and poets, were only presenting a visualisation of the side of real life we prefer to override and forget if we can, and warning that what survives of the human personality after death will have no further defence against it. Hell therefore is death, the other side of life, just as this relief panel is the negative version of the previous one.

The Dharmaraja aspect of Yama is projected and separately personified amid the hells in this relief; his inscription names him Vrah Dharma. Here we see the ultimate transformation of the Dharma itself as it appears in the Kali Yuga, shorn of all its religious dimension, reduced to the role of a mere functionary, the representative of karmic justice without mercy. He sits like a petty king on a narrow lotus seat as Yama himself does, holding a single *yamadanda* with which he prods his next terrified victim in the chest in accordance with the karmic assessment of the precise bureaucrat Chitragupta, recorder of each individual's transgressions in life, seated next to him. And thus the pedantic, indifferent machinery of karma would grind on until every last mortal soul had been accounted for and run its course in the heavens or hells of the afterlife, were it not for the cataclysmic Fire of Time, Kalagni, which intervenes to dissolve everything at the end of all the Yugas.

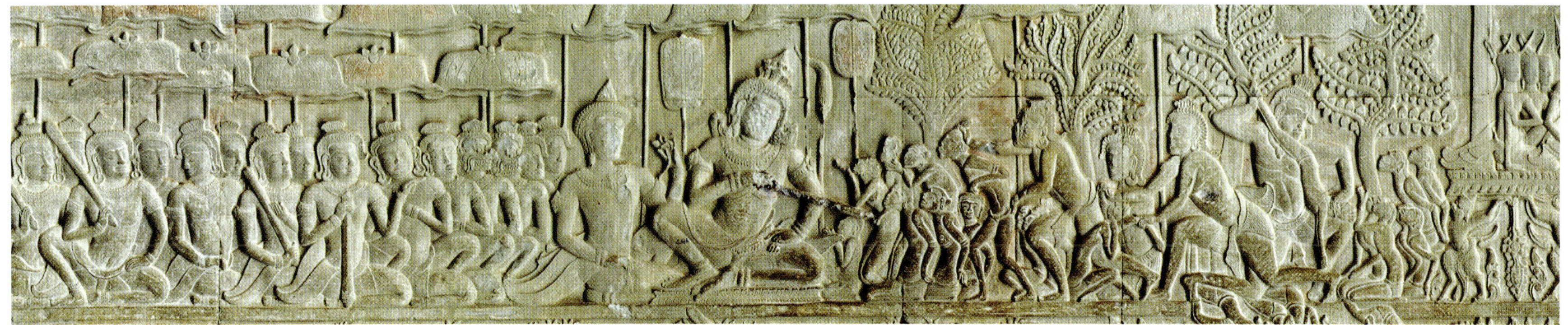

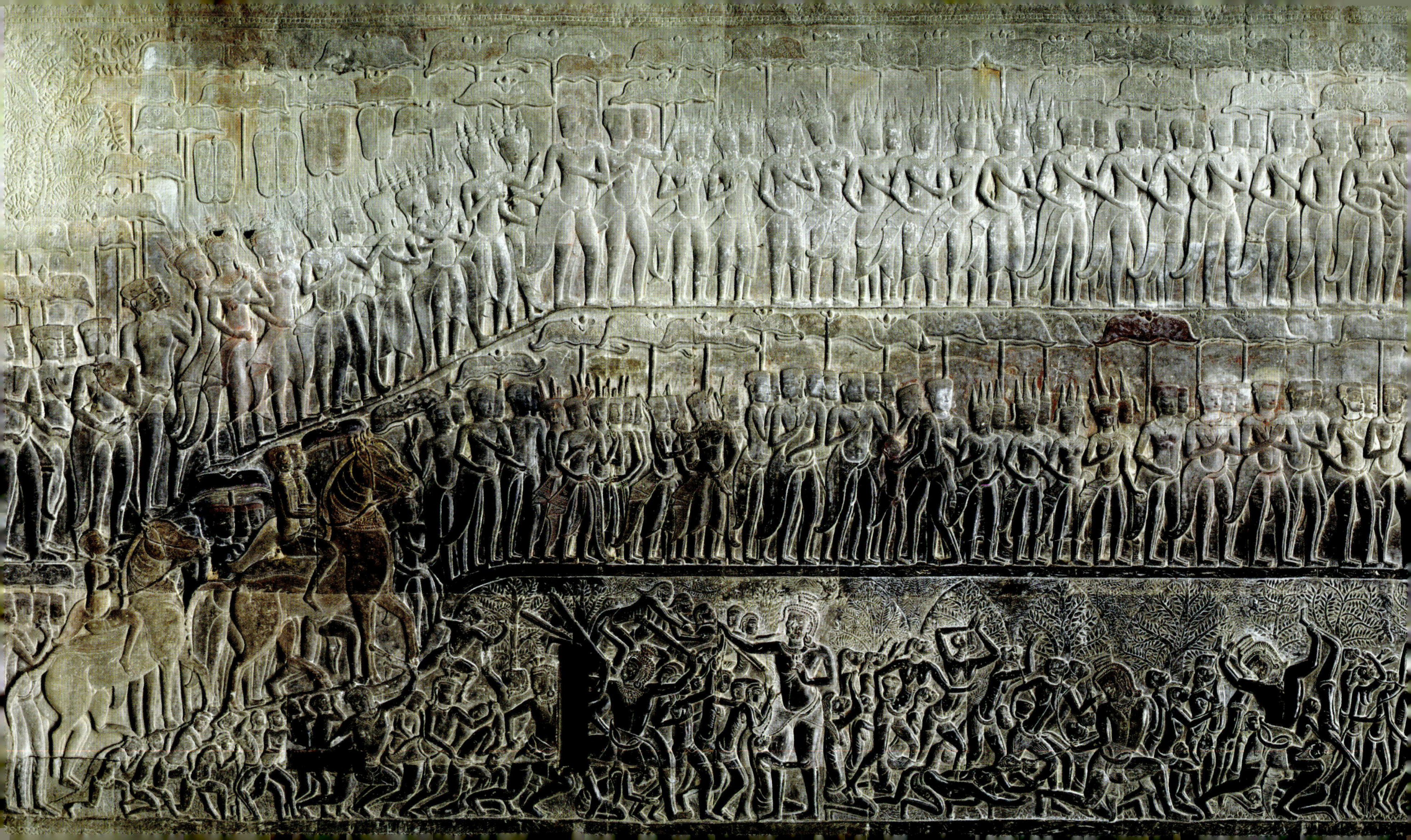

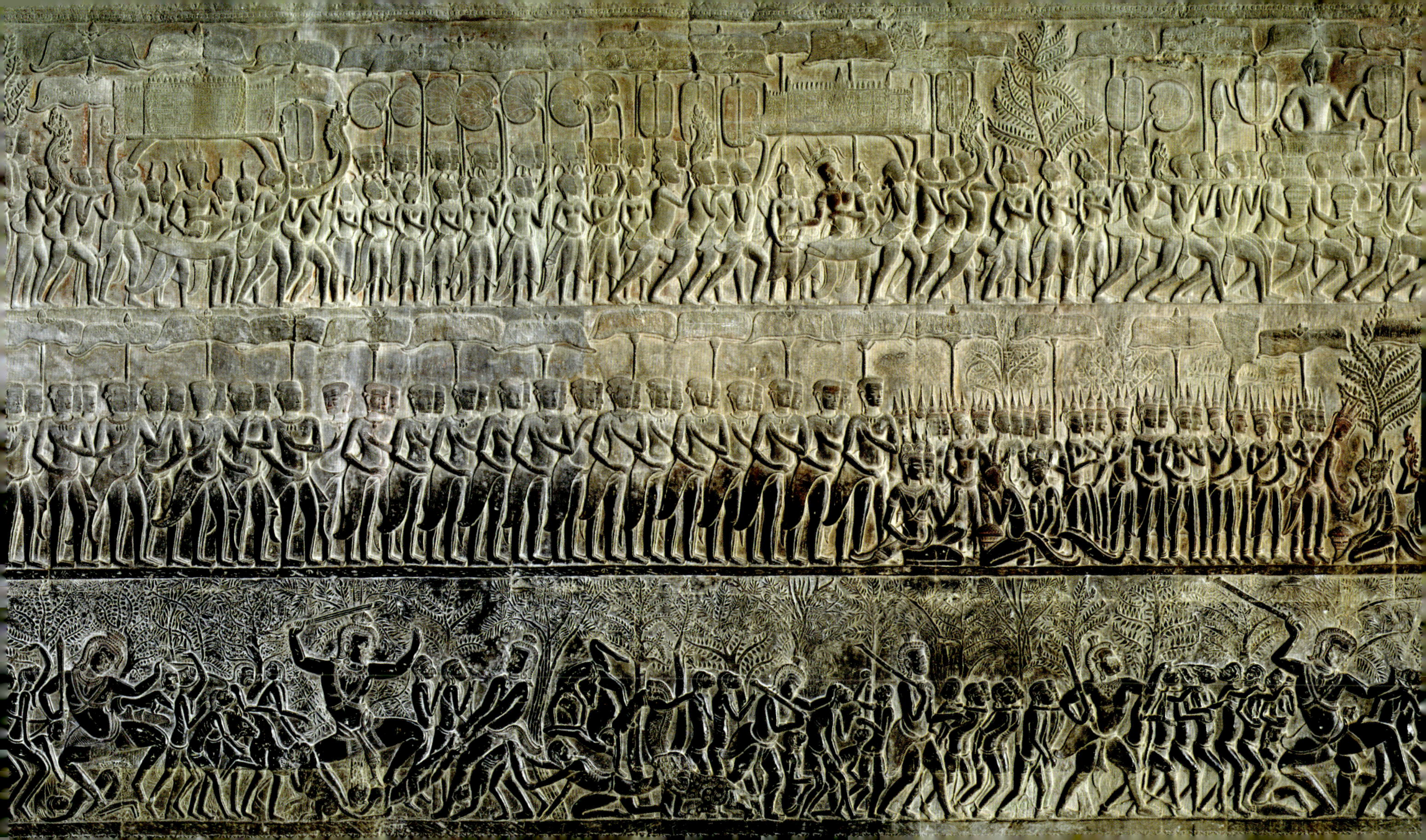

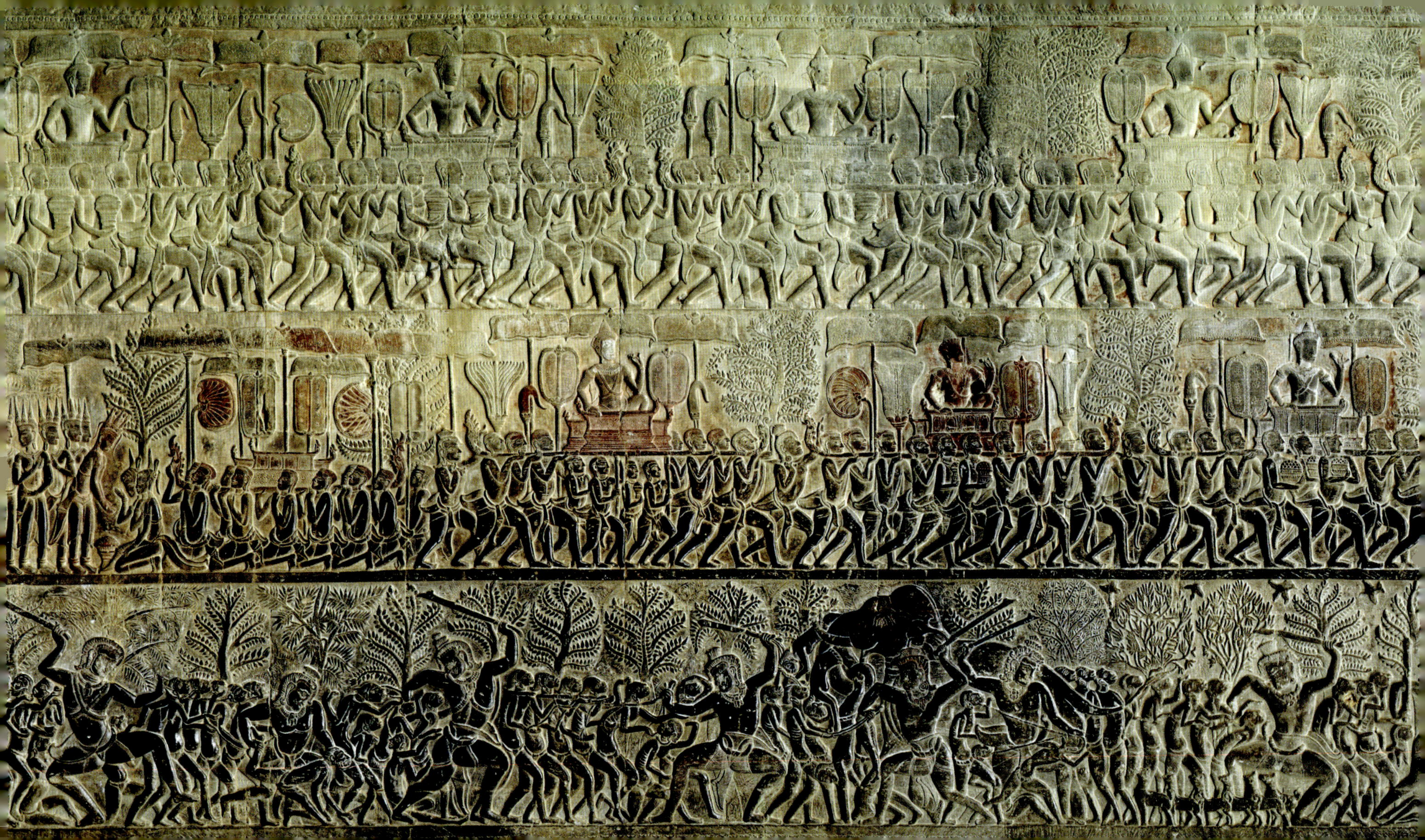

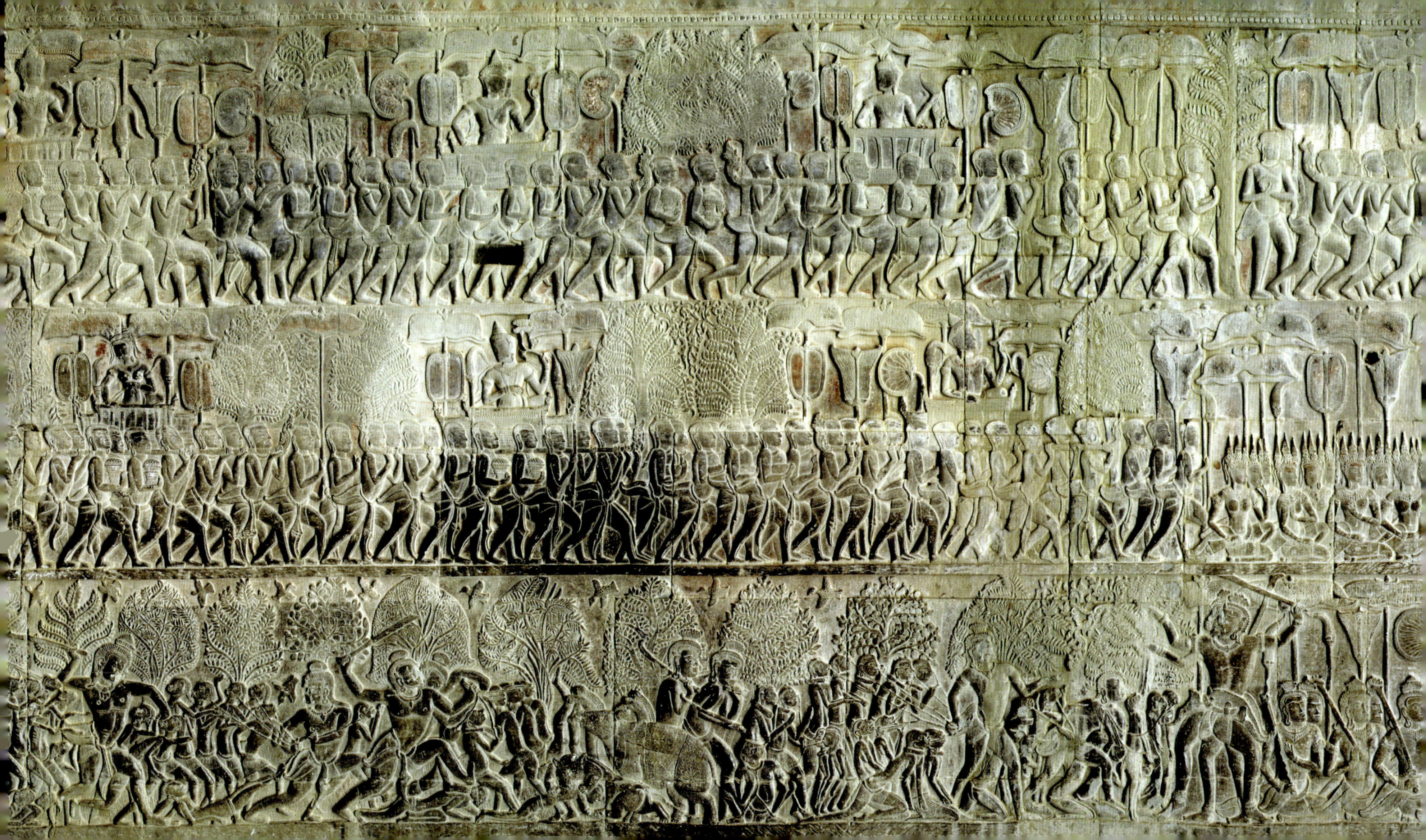

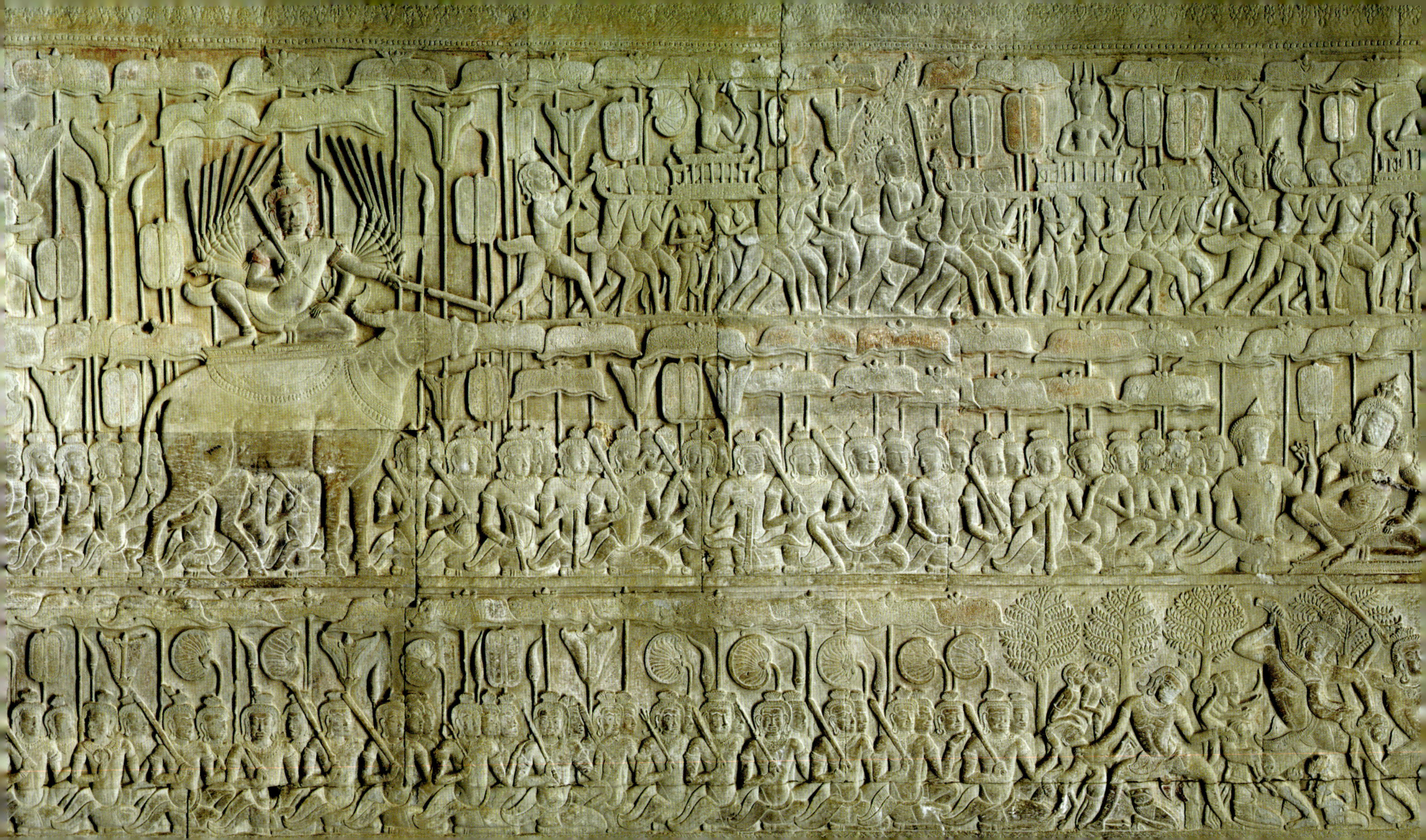

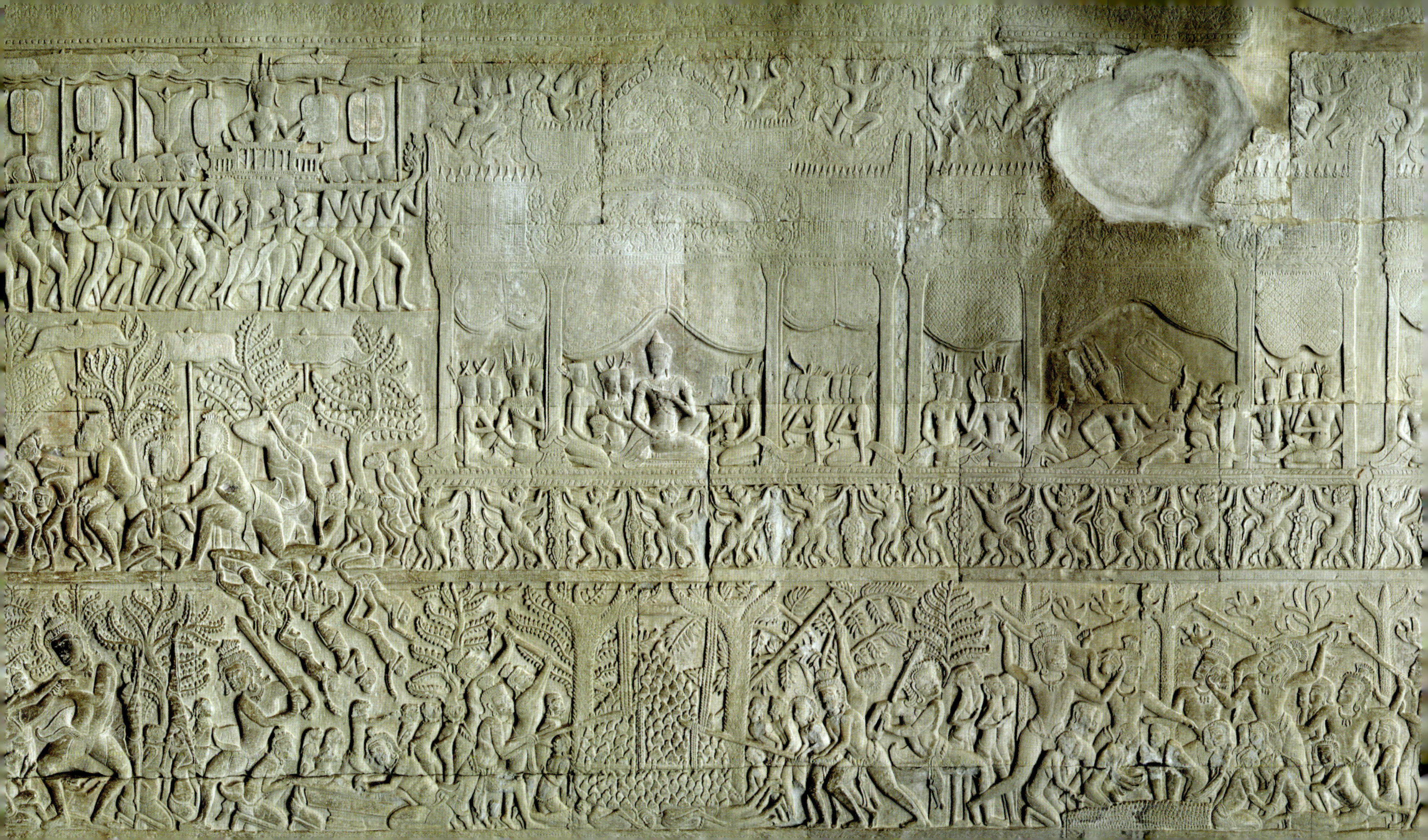

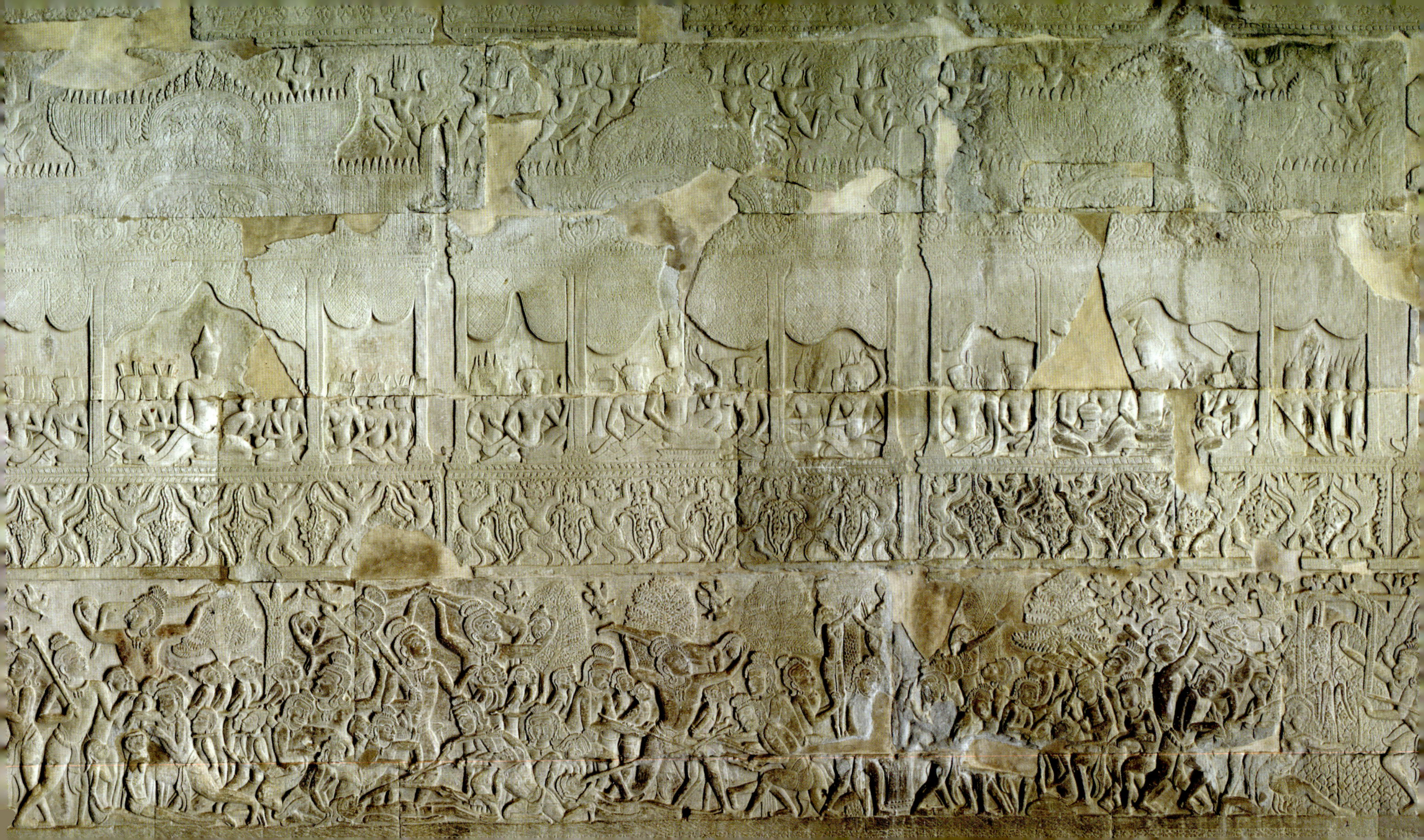

THE FOUR SIDES

The cosmic cycle

A new universe then arises, passing through the same cycle of four Yugas, recommencing at our point of departure, the Churning of the Ocean. In performing a counterclockwise circumambulation of the temple from the east at the dawn of a new day, as we have just done, the individual worshipper – or a procession of priests and devotees – thus experienced and ritually enacted a new creation, from the beginnings of cosmic evolution to the end-phase of the present. The theme within this evolution upon which the reliefs focus, does not concern the equations of matter, energy and time, but the dynamics of the universe perceived as a moral process, and the relationship of this process to the human condition. Morality understood as a code of human beliefs, behaviour and actions that conform to the workings and destiny of the universe as a whole is defined as Dharma, and it is therefore the dharmic history of the cosmos that is presented in these reliefs on the outer walls which spatially define the ritual enclosure of the temple. In this history, time is equated with phases in the ageing and devolution of Dharma, a process which is measured in Yugas. Evolution and devolution therefore run in parallel at two different levels. The critical turning-points in the devolutionary process, the transitions from one Yuga to the next, in each of which Dharma declines by one fourth of its ideal mass, are represented by the four corners of the enclosure, the junctures between the relief sequences, known in the Sanskrit texts as *sandhyas* or twilights, which are represented architecturally at Angkor Wat by the darker corner-pavilions. These junctures are the weak points in the continuum of dharmic time, the moments of maximum threat to the survival of Dharma, and

hence the preferred instants of divine incarnation in the physical universe. If any specific rituals were performed in the course of the circumambulation of the reliefs, they would therefore have been performed in these corner-pavilions, to ensure the unbroken continuity of time and hence to preserve the communication between the present and the mythological past which explains it. Having secured the continuous flow of time by these ritual means, a circumambulation in the opposite, clockwise direction would then lead the worshipper back in time to its origins in which Dharma first arose. The regular and repeated act of circumambulation along these reliefs would in itself have symbolically kept this channel of communication open, establishing the present in the past, the past in the present, and so locating the temple of Vishnu inside these walls within a cosmic-moral time scale meaningful to both gods and men. These Angkor Wat reliefs are not decoration, they are working parts of a huge ritual apparatus whose function it was to establish the dharmic rule of Vishnu in Kambuja through the concept of the righteous king, the Dharmaraja, in all his manifestations.

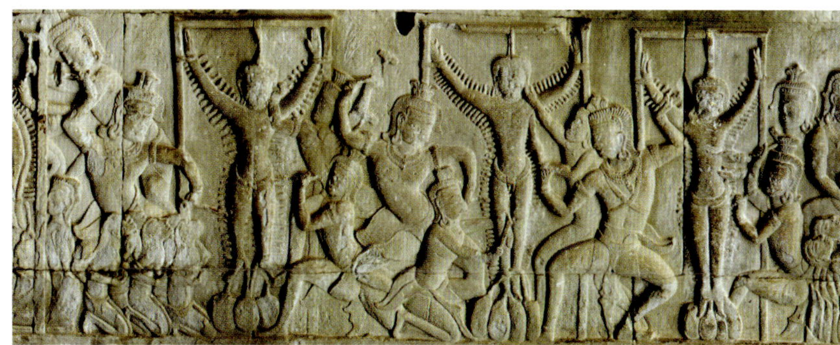

APPENDIX 1:

SLIT–SCAN–TECHNIK AT ANGKOR

Jaroslav Poncar

For the very first time, a photographic documentation of the bas-reliefs at Angkor Vat and the Bayon has made use of "slit–scan photography." Now, what exactly is that? Well, in principle, it is nothing entirely new. Panorama cameras with rotating lenses were invented 150 years ago, and their principle of operation has always been a progressive "scan through a slit." While the photograph is taken, a slit, which is firmly mounted on the rotating lens, moves along the film, which is arched on a cylinder inside the body of the camera. Once angles of more than 210 degrees are desired, the whole camera has to rotate. Introduced 100 years ago, the American Cirkut panorama camera turned this technique into a commercial application. The speed of the film's transport past the slit has to be exactly synchronous with the rotation of the camera, since the image must not move while the film is being exposed to light, if it is to be in focus. For the film's movement, the traditional panorama cameras used a drive that was mechanically synchronized with the rotation of the camera by means of a shaft. The innovation of precise stepper motors and appropriate electronic control systems renders a mechanical connection of camera and film movement obsolete. This opens new possibilities for the slit–scan–technique. Inside the Roundshot Super Camera, one stepper motor powers the movement of the camera and another one transports the film along the slit. The motor that used to turn the camera during a panorama shot now can be separated from the camera's body and – given the adequate programming for the controls of the stepper motors – may be used for something else: it can be turned – for instance – into an engine for a dolly on

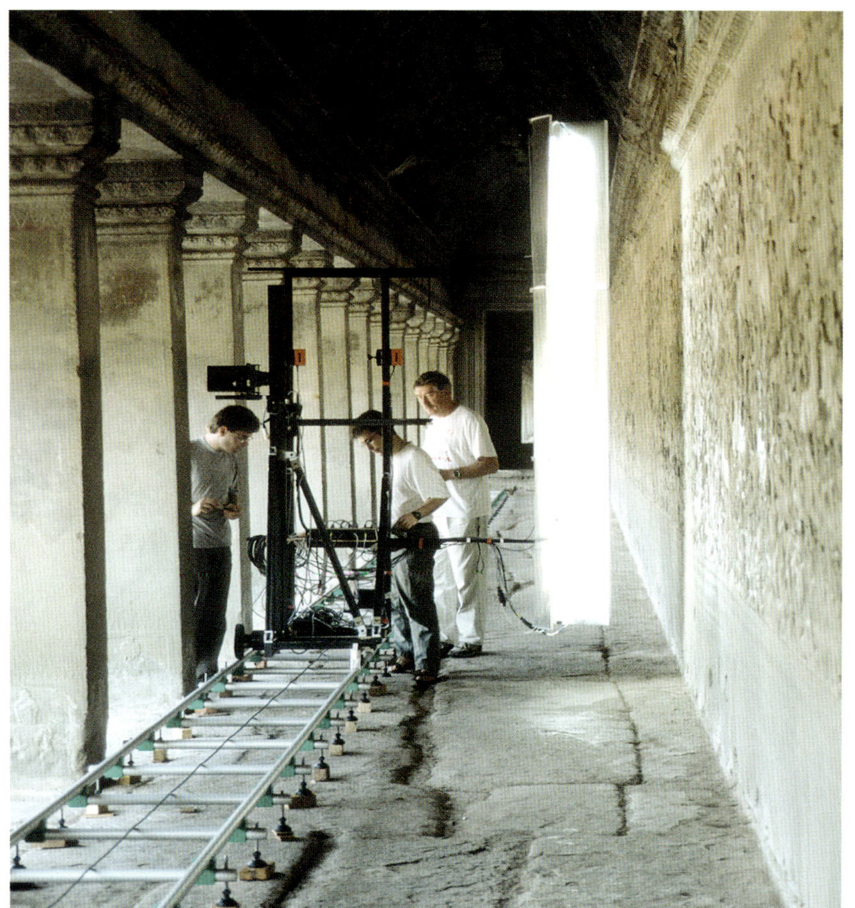

tracks that transports a mounted camera along a bas-relief. This camera dolly can also carry the source of lighting. There is no need for consistent lighting in the direction of the camera's forward movement, as long as the light remains steady in the 90-degree angle relative to the forward direction.

The bas-reliefs in the gallery of Angkor Vat were a supreme challenge for this technique: 2 m in height, more than 500 m in overall length, divided into eight scenes, 2 to 3 cm deep on average, the distance between lens and relief up to 2 m. To make these reliefs visible in an appropriate way, a kind of lighting is needed that illuminates its object from the side in a low angle. There is one single scene of the reliefs that is 2.40 m in height (p. 49) and the adjustment of the whole technical apparatus had to use this as a point of reference. The close distance between the pillars of the gallery and the relief necessitated an extreme wide-angle lens. This kind of lens always suffers a considerable loss of light sensitivity at its edges. In the studio of the Department for Photo Engineering at the University of Applied Sciences at Cologne, the conditions for photographing at Angkor were simulated. One wall was painted in an even grey colour to discern even the smallest decrease in light sensitivity on a test film. After a series of failures, we found the solution to the problem: a reflector of 3.5 m in height, containing 2.5 m long daylight fluorescent tubes. This piece of equipment is produced for the film industry in the USA. The transport of tubes this length to Cambodia proved to be the source of the most pressing anxieties for the team: they broke twice already on their way from Munich to Cologne.

The tests at the University of Applied Sciences also demonstrated, that the levelling of the tracks for the camera dolly demanded very special at-tention. Smallest amounts of unevenness set the whole setup vibrating, which may detract from the resolution of the photographs. The necessary precision was achieved by using a laser level device. Our colleagues from the Department for Civil Engineering instructed us in the use of this device.

Team and equipment were subjected to a test of endurance at Angkor. Everything we had practised at Cologne now had to be performed under conditions of tropical heat. To avoid the distraction of natural light, photographs had to be taken at night. To expose a scene of 94 m in length takes 35 minutes. The documentation was shot on black and white as well as colour film. As a safety measure, the takes of each scene were repeated for both kinds of film material. This was to make sure, that mishaps during the developing of the more than 2 m long film negatives would not render our efforts obsolete. In the afternoon, we laid the tracks and once the sun had set, we started with the exposure of a test film. Before dinner, this film had been developed in the darkroom of the Conservation D'Angkor. At 2:30 a.m., we started to expose the real thing. The team cleared the site at sunrise. After lunch, we moved to the next site and started to prepare the next scene. The outer walls of the Bayon included, thus more than 800 m of reliefs were photographed every night. All added up, the camera covered a distance of roughly seven kilometres in the process.

This is the place to thank the members of the student's team of the University of Applied Sciences at Cologne (Markus Hitzler, Martin Strehle, Stefan Reiser, Markus Kreisel, Andreas Kotulek, Michael Wagener) for their co-operation. Their commitment and creativity were essential for the success of this project.

APPENDIX 2:

ASIAN NAMES AND TERMS

Thomas S. Maxwell

For technical and editorial reasons the diacritical marks conventionally used for accurately transliterating Sanskrit and Old Khmer texts do not appear in this book. Instead, approximately equivalent English spellings have been used. In this Appendix, Asian proper names and terms, plus a few brief quotations, are given in the first column as they are printed in the main text. In the second column, the same words are shown as they are written with standard diacritics, where the transliteration differs from the anglicized spelling. The language concerned is indicated by the abbreviations (S.) = Sanskrit, (K.) = Old Khmer, or (K.–S.) = Old Khmer and Sanskrit; it should be noted that Old Khmer incorporated many Sanskrit names and terms, and that such words are locally adapted forms of the Sanskrit. The sequence of the entries is alphabetical based on the anglicized versions found in the book.

A	abhimana	abhimāna (S.)
	Airavata	Airāvata (S.)
	Akupara	Akūpāra (S.)
	amrita	amṛta (S.)
	Aruna	Aruṇa (S.)
	Asvin	Aśvin (S.)
	avatara	avatāra (S.)
	Ayodhya	Ayodhyā (S.)
B	Balarama	Balarāma (S.)
	Bana	Bāṇa (S.)
	Bhagavadgita	Bhagavadgītā (S.)
	Bhima	Bhīma (S.)
	Bhishma	Bhīṣma (S.)
	Brah Bishnulok	Braḥ Biṣṇulok (K., from S. Viṣṇuloka)
	Brah Mahidhara	Braḥ Mahīdhara (K.– S.)
	Brahma	Brahmā (S.)
	Brihaspati	Bṛhaspati (S.)
C	chakra	cakra (S.)
	chakraraksha	cakrarakṣa (S.)
	Chanlattai	Canlattai (K.)
	Chitragupta	Citragupta (S.)
D	Dandaka	Daṇḍaka (S.)
	Dasaratha	Daśaratha (S.)
	Dasavatara	Daśāvatāra (S.)
	Deogarh	Devagaḍh (Hindi)
	Deori	Devrī (Hindi)
	Dhananjaya	Dhanañjaya (S.)
	Dharmakshetra	Dharmakṣetra (S.)
	Dharmaraja	Dharmarāja (S.)
	Dhritarashtra	Dhṛtarāṣṭra (S.)
	divyakriya	divyakriyā (S.)
	Draupadi	Draupadī (S.)
	Dvapara–yuga	dvāparayuga (S.)
	Dvaraka	Dvārakā (S.)

174

G	Gandhari	Gāndhārī (S.)
	gandharvavivaha	gandharvavivāha (S.)
	Ganesha	Gaṇeśa (S.)
	Ganga	Gaṅgā (S.)
	Garuda	Garuḍa (S.)
H	Hanuman	Hanumat, Hanumān (S.)
	Harivamsa	Harivaṃśa (S.)
	Hayagriva	Hayagrīva (S.)
	Hikayat Sri Rama	Ḥikāyat Srī Rāma (Malay)
	Himalaya	Himālaya (S.)
I	isana	īśāna (S.)
	ishtadevata	iṣṭadevatā (S.)
J	Jayasimhavarman	Jayasiṃhavarman (S.)
	Jeng Jhala	Jeṅ Jhāla (K.)
K	Kaikeyi	Kaikeyī (S.)
	Kailasa	Kailāsa (S.)
	Kala	Kāla (S.)
	Kalagni	Kālāgni (S.)
	Kalanemi	Kālanemi (S.)
	Kalaratri	Kālarātri, Kālarātrī (S.)
	Kalika-Purana	Kālikāpurāṇa (S.)
	Kamakhya	Kāmākhyā (S.)
	Kamarupa	Kāmarūpa (S.)
	khadga, khadgin	khaḍga, khaḍgin (S.)
	Krishna	Kṛṣṇa (S.)
	Krita (-yuga)	kṛtayuga (S.)

	kshatriya	kṣatriya (S.)
	Kunti	Kuntī (S.)
	Kurukshetra	Kurukṣetra (S.)
	kuti	kuṭi (S.)
L	Lakshmana	Lakṣmaṇa (S.)
	Lakshmi	Lakṣmī (S.)
	Lanka	Laṅkā (S.)
	Lokapala	Lokapāla (S.)
M	Madra	Mādra (S.)
	Madri	Mādrī (S.)
	Mahabharata	Mahābhārata (S.)
	Mahavishnuloka	Mahāviṣṇuloka (S.)
	Manasarovara	Mānasarovara (S.)
	mandala	maṇḍala (S.)
	Manthara	Mantharā (S.)
	matsyanyaya	matsyanyāya (S.)
	Marhia	Maḍhiyā (Hindi)
	Mayapati	Māyāpati (S.)
N	Naga	Nāga (S.)
O	... oy chlak niyay	... oy chlāk niyāy (K.)
	Pancanada	Pañcanada (S.)
	Pandava	Pāṇḍava (S.)
	pandit	paṇḍita (S.)
	Pandu	Pāṇḍu (S.)
	Paramavishnuloka	Paramaviṣṇuloka (S.)
	Parvati	Pārvatī (S.)

	pascima	paścima (S.)
	Phalguna	Phālguna (S.)
	phdan byar	phdāṅ byar (K.)
	pradakshina	pradakṣiṇā (S.)
	Pragjyotisha	Prāgjyotiṣa (S.)
	Prithivi	Pṛthivī (S.)
	...punah chlak phen niyay	...punaḥ chlak phen niyāy (K.)
	Purana	Purāṇa (S.)
	purva	pūrva (S.)
R	Rahu	Rāhu (S.)
	rajahota	rājahotā (K., from S. rājahotṛ, rājahotā)
	rajasilpi	rājasilpi / –śilpi (K., from S.rājaśilpin,rājaśilpī)
	Rama	Rāma (S.)
	Ramakerti	Rāmakerti (K.)
	Ramakien	Rāmakien (Thai)
	Ramayana	Rāmāyaṇa (S.)
	Ravana	Rāvaṇa (S.)
	rishi	ṛṣi (S.)
S	Saka	Śaka (S.)
	sakti	śakti (S.)
	Salya	Śalya (S.)
	samrac	saṃrac (K.)
	sandhya	sandhyā (S.)
	sarathi	sārathi (S.)

	Sarvadigvyapin	Sarvadigvyāpin (S.)
	Satrughna	Śatrughna (S.)
	Shesha	Śeṣa (S.)
	Shiva	Śiva
	Shonitapura	Śoṇitapura (S.)
	Shukra	Śukra (S.)
	Sita	Sītā (S.)
	Sivapada	Śivapāda (S.)
	Sthanu	Sthāṇu (S.)
	Sudarshana	Sudarśana (S.)
	Sugriva	Sugrīva (S.)
	Sura	Surā (S.)
	Surpanakha	Śūrpaṇakhā (S.)
	Suryavarman	Sūryavarman (S.)
	Syam Kuk	Syāṃ Kuk (K.)
T	Tara	Tārā (S.)
	Taraka	Tārakā (S.)
	Tarakamaya	Tārakāmaya (S.)
	Travang Svay	Travāṅ Svāy (K.)
	Treta-yuga	tretāyuga (S.)
	Tvashtri	Tvaṣṭṛ (S.)
U	Uccaihsravas	Ucchaiḥśravas (S.)
	Usha	Uṣā (S.)
V	Vaishnava	Vaiṣṇava (S.)
	Valmiki	Vālmīki (S.)
	Vamana	Vāmana (S.)

	Vanara	Vānara (S.)
	Varaha	Varāha (S.)
	Varuna	Varuṇa (S.)
	Vayu	Vāyu (S.)
	Vishnu	Viṣṇu (S.)
	Vishnuloka	Viṣṇuloka (S.)
	Vishnu–Purana	Viṣṇupurāṇa (S.)
	Vrah Dharma	Vraḥ Dharma (K.–S.)
	vrah kuti uttaravayavyapaschima	vraḥ kuṭi uttaravāyavyapaścima (K.–S.)
	vrah kuti uttaresanapaschima	vraḥ kuṭi uttareśānapaścima (K.–S.)
	vrah vleng	vraḥ vleṅ (K.)
Y	Yaksha	Yakṣa (S.)
	yamadanda	yamadaṇḍa (S.)
	Yogishvara	Yogīśvara (S.)
	Yudhishthira	Yudhiṣṭhira (S.)
	yuvaraja	yuvarāja (S.)

Note: The Sanskrit word *apsaras* has the *s*-ending in its basic undeclined form and can occur both as *apsarās* and *apsarā* in the nominative singular; its plural nominative form is *apsarasaḥ*. To avoid artificial use of these terminations in an English context, and to suppress the anglicized plural "*apsarases*", the basic form of the word is used in this book for both singular and plural.

APPENDIX 3

SANSKRIT AND OLD KHMER SOURCES
Thomas S. Maxwell

Inscriptions and text extracts which are translated or cited in the book are transliterated here in full to provide context. Note that in inscriptions, the spelling of certain words varies and may be different from dictionary spellings. The language concerned is indicated in square brackets. Translations are mine unless otherwise indicated.

3.1: [Sanskrit] *Mahābhārata* (Text as Constituted in the Critical Edition), *Ādiparvan*, 1.16.10-11, Churning of the Ocean, Indra and the Summit of the Mountain :
ūcuś ca kūrmarājānam akūpāraṃ surāsurāḥ / girer adhiṣṭhānam asya bhavān bhavitum arhati // 10 // kūrmeṇa tu tathety uktvā pṛṣṭham asya samarpitam / tasya śailasya cāgraṃ vai yantreṇendro 'bhyapīḍayat // 11 //

3.2(1): [Khmer] Angkor Wat, east gallery, north wing:
Inscription on the Battle of Prāgjyotiṣa relief:
brah pāda mahāviṣṇuloka thve bvuṃ dān srac nau phen byar luh thleṅ rāja brah pāda stac brah rājaoṅkāra parmmarājādhirāja rāmādhipati parmmacakrabartt[i]rāja pre brah mahīdhara nā rājasilpi punaḥ chlak phen niyāy anu . . . kuṃluṅ aṣṭasaka maminakṣatra buddhabāra purṇṇami bhadrapadda

3.2(2): [Khmer] Angkor Wat, north gallery, east wing:
Inscription on the Battle of Śoṇitapura relief:

vrah pāda mahāviṣṇuloka thve bvuṃ dān samrac nau phdāṅ byar thleṅ rāja vrah pāda samtec vrah rājaoṅkāra parmmarājādhirāja ta parmmapavitra oy chlāk niyāy osā samrac nā luh ekacatvaraaṣṭapañcasaka kurnakṣatra pūrnnamī phalguna ādityabāra samrac nu rppyaṅ bhnāk tai byar mum ru vreṅ

3.3(1): [Khmer] Bayon, Angkor, Inscription 5 (K), Location of deities in the temple:

1. *° vrah kuṭi uttaravāyavyapaścima vrah vuddha kamrateṅ añ ratnatraya viṃndhya*
2. *parvvata ° kamrateṅ jagat śrītribhuvanadeva ° kamrateṅ jagat śrībhaiṣajya*
3. *guruvaidūryyaprabharāja anle noḥ ° kamrateṅ jagat chluy maleṅ ° ka*
4. *mrateṅ jagat śrībhaiṣajyaguruvaidūryyaprabharāja maleṅ ° kamrateṅ*
5. *jagat śrībhaiṣajyaguruvaidūryyaprabharāja jraiṇan ° kamrateṅ jagat*
6. *vrah pāda samvok ° kamrateṅ jagat lyoṅ ° kamrateṅ jagat ta śakti*
7. *samvok ° kamrateṅ jagat śrībhaiṣajyaguruvaidūryyaprabharāja [a]nl[e] noḥ*

"In the shrine (*vrah kuṭi*) in the north-west square of the north-west quadrant, [ten statues]:

1. The holy Buddha Lord Ratnatraya of Vindhyaparvata.
2. The God Tribhuvanadeva.
3. The God Bhaiṣajyaguruvaidūryaprabharāja of that place (Vindhyaparvata).
4. The God of Chluy Maleṅ.
5. The God Bhaiṣajyaguruvaidūryaprabharāja of Maleṅ.
6. The God Bhaiṣajyaguruvaidūryaprabharāja of Jraiṇan.
7. The God of His Majesty (vrah pāda) of Saṃvok.

8. The God of Lyoṅ.

9. The Goddess Śakti of Saṃvok.

10. The God Bhaiṣajyaguruvaidūryaprabharāja of that place (Saṃvok)."

3.3(2): [Khmer] Bayon, Angkor, Inscription 7 (M), Location of deities in the temple:

1.   °vrah kuṭi uttareśānapaścima ° kanloṅ kamrateṅ añ śrī

2.   jayamaṅgalārthacūḍāmaṇi kṣaca ° kamrateṅ jagat śrītri[bhu]

3.   vanadeva ° kamrateṅ jagat śrīśākyasiṃha tralyaṅ ° ka

4.   mrateṅ jagat śrībhaiṣajyaguruvaidūryyaprabharāja ...

5.   gara catvāri ° kamrateṅ jagat śrīmadhurendreśvara stuk thkū ° [ka]

6.   mrateṅ jagat śrītribhuvanamaheśvara stuk thkū °kamra[teṅ]

7.   jagat ... ° kamrateṅ jagat snāṃ dyoṅ ° kamrateṅ [ja]

8.   gat ja ... ° kamrateṅ jagat saṅga ° kamrateṅ jagat mā ...

9.   ra ° phsaṃ [anle] tāp mvay °

"In the shrine (vrah kuṭi) in the north-west square of the north-east quadrant, eleven places [for statues]:

1. The deceased Lady Jayamaṅgalārtha-Cūḍāmani.

2. The God Tribhuvanadeva.

3. The God Śākyasiṃha of Tralyaṅ.

4. The God Bhaiṣajyaguruvaidūryaprabharāja of Gara Catvāri.

5. The God Madhurendreśvara of Stuk Thkū.

6. The God Tribhuvanamaheśvara of Stuk Thkū.

7. The God .... (illegible).

8. The God of Snāṃ Dyoṅ.

9. The God of Ja....(illegible).

10. The God of Saṅga.

11. The God of Mā...ra."

3.4: [Sanskrit] *Harivaṃśa* (*Mahābhārata,* Text as Constituted in the Critical Edition), 91.18-21 and 9.43-52, The Battle before Prāgjyotiṣa:

yaṃ mahī suṣuve devī yasya prāgjyotiṣaṃ puram / tasyāntapālāś catvāras
tasyāsan yuddhadurmadāḥ // 18 // hayagrīvo nisundaś ca vīraḥ pañcajanas tathā
/ muruḥ putrasahasraiś ca varadatto mahāsuraḥ // 19 // ādevayānam āvṛtya
panthānaṃ samavasthitaḥ / vitrāsanaḥ sukṛtināṃ virūpai rākṣasaiḥ saha // 20
// tadvadhārtham mahābāhuḥ śaṅkhacakragadāsibhṛt / jāto vṛṣṇiṣu devakyāṃ
vasudevāj janārdanaḥ // 21 //

samādhāyetikartavyaṃ vāsavo vibudhādhipaḥ / svam eva bhavanaṃ prāyāt kṛṣṇaḥ
prāgjyotiṣaṃ yayau // 43 // so 'gryān rakṣogaṇān hatvā narakasya mahābalān
/ kṣurāntān mauravān pāśān ṣaṭsahasrān dadarśa ha // 44 // saṃchidya pāśān
sarvāṃs tān muraṃ hatvā sahānvayam / śilāsaṃghān atikramya nisundam avapoth-
ayat / yaḥ sahasrasamās tv ekaḥ sarvān devān apothayat // 45 // tathā devāsuraṃ
yuddham abhavad bharatarṣabha / nānāpraharaṇākīrṇam tathā ghoram avartata //
46 // tataḥ śārṅgavinirmuktair nānāvarṇair mahāśaraiḥ / garuḍastho mahābāhur
nijaghāna mahāsurān // 47 // mahālāṅgalanirbhinnāḥ śarakhaḍganipātitāḥ / vineśur
dānavās tatra samāsādya janārdanam // 48 // kecic cakrāgrinirdagdhā dānavāḥ
petur ambarāt / saṃnikarṣagatāḥ kecid gatāsuvikṛtānanāḥ // 49 // taṃ jaghāna
mahāghoraṃ hayagrīvaṃ mahāsuram / apāratejo durdharṣaḥ sarvayādavanandanaḥ
// 50 // madhye lohitagaṅgasya bhagavān devakīsutaḥ / alakāyāṃ virūpākṣaṃ

pāpmānaṃ puruṣottamaḥ // 51 // aṣṭau śatasahasrāṇi dānavānāṃ paraṃtapaḥ / nihatya puruṣavyāghraḥ prāgjyotiṣam upādravat / taṃ ca pañcajanaṃ ghoraṃ narakasya mahāsuram // 52 // tataḥ prāgjyotiṣaṃ nāma dīpyamānam iva śriyā / puram āsādayām āsa tatra yuddham abhūn mahat // 53 //

"He (Naraka), who was born of the Earth Goddess, and whose city was Prāgjyotiṣa, had four outpost guards crazed with battle-lust: Hayagrīva, the brave Nisunda, Pañcajana, and Muru. This great demon with his thousand sons, terrifying to the virtuous, had blocked the way to the gods and occupied it along with deformed Rākṣasas. To kill him, Janārdana (Viṣṇu as Kṛṣṇa) was born to Devakī and Vasudeva among the Vṛṣṇis, strong of arm and wielding the conch, disk, mace and sword."

"The king of the gods, Vāsava (Indra), having decided what was to be done, Kṛṣṇa set out from his abode and went to Prāgjyotiṣa. Having slain Naraka's leading companies of mighty Rākṣasas, he then beheld the six thousand barbed snares of Muru. Having cut through all the snares, and killed Mura (= Muru) and his retinue, he crossed over clusters of rocks and overthrew Nisunda. Then, my lord, a terrible battle ensued between the gods and demons with all kinds of weapons. With multicoloured arrows shot from his bow, the strong-armed [Kṛṣṇa], mounted on Garuḍa, slew the great demons. Lacerated by the great ploughshare, felled by his arrows and sword, the Dānavas perished there as they advanced toward him - some, burned by the edge of his disk, fell from the sky, while the faces of others contorted in death as they came near him. Joy of all the Yādavas, boundless in glory, invincible, [Kṛṣṇa] slew the terrible demon Hayagrīva; between the Ganges and the Lohita, on the Alakā, he, the Lord, Son of Devakī, the Highest Spirit, [slew] the evil one with deformed eyes (Virūpākṣa). Having slain eight hundred thousand Dānavas and Naraka's terrible demon Pañcajana, he, the great scourge (Paraṃtapa), a tiger in human form, [then] attacked Prāgjyotiṣa."

3.5: [Sanskrit] *Harivaṃśa* (*Mahābhārata,* Text as Constituted in the Critical Edition), 109. 4-19, Kṛṣṇa's transformation and Garuḍa's encounter with the Fire of Śoṇitapura:

athāṣṭabāhuḥ kṛṣṇas tu parvatākārasaṃnibhaḥ / vibabhau puṇḍarīkākṣo vikāṅkṣan bāṇasaṃkṣayam // 4 // asicakragadābāṇā dakṣiṇam pārśvam āsthitāḥ / carma śārṅgam tathā cāpaṃ śaṅkhaṃ caivāsya vāmataḥ // 5 // śīrṣāṇāṃ vai sahasraṃ tu vihitaṃ śārṅgadhanvanā / sahasraṃ caiva kāyānāṃ vahan saṃkarṣaṇas tadā // 6 // śvetapraharaṇo 'dhṛṣyaḥ kailāsa iva śṛṅgavān / āsthito garuḍaṃ rāma udyann iva niśākaraḥ // 7 // sanatkumārasya vapuḥ prādurāsīn mahātmanaḥ / pradyumnasya mahābāhoḥ saṃgrāme vikramiṣyata // 8 // sa pakṣabalavikṣepair vidhunvan parvatān bahūn / jagāma mārgam balavān vātasya pratiṣedhayan // 9 // ati vāyor atha gatim āsthāya garuḍas tadā / siddhacāraṇasaṃghānāṃ śubhaṃ mārgam avātarat // 10 // atha rāmo 'bravīd vākyaṃ kṛṣṇam apratimaṃ raṇe / svābhiḥ prabhābhir hīnāḥ smaḥ kṛṣṇa kasmād apūrvavat // 11 // sarve kanakavarṇābhāḥ saṃvṛttāḥ sma na saṃśayaḥ / kim idaṃ brūhi nas tattvaṃ kim meroḥ pārśvagā vayam // 12 // [Kṛṣṇa:] agner āhavanīyasya prabhayā sma samāhatāḥ / tena no varṇavairūpyam idaṃ jātaṃ halāyudha // 13 // [Balarāma:] yadi sma saṃnikarṣasthā yadi niṣprabhatāṃ gatāḥ /tad vidhatsva svayam buddhyā yad atrānantaraṃ hitam // 14 // [Kṛṣṇa:] kuruṣva vainateya tvaṃ yan naḥ kāryam anantaram / tvayā vidhāne vihite kariṣyāmy aham uttaram // 15 // etac chrutvā tadā vākyaṃ keśavasya mahātmanaḥ / gaṅgām apāgamat tūrṇaṃ vainateyas tato balī // 16 // gṛhītvā salilaṃ tatra tam agnim abhiṣecayat / agnir āhavanīyas tu tataḥ śāntim upāgamat // 17 //

"Kṛṣṇa the Lotus-Eyed, desiring the death of Bāṇa, taking form like a mountain, became eight-armed - on his right side were the sword, the disk, the mace, and the arrow, and on his left the shield, the bow of horn, and the conch. Armed with the bow of horn, he assumed a thousand heads and a thousand bodies. Then the invincible Saṃkarṣaṇa, (Bala-)Rāma, white-weaponed like Kailāsa with its many peaks, mounted Garuḍa like the rising moon. The form of great-souled Sanatkumāra, the strong-armed Pradyumna desiring conquest, appeared in the conflict. The mighty (Garuḍa), shaking many mountains with the powerful movements of his wings, rose into the path of the wind. After mounting the path of the wind, Garuḍa descended to the bright path of the saints and celestial singers. Then [Bala-]Rāma spoke to the incomparable Kṛṣṇa in the conflict: 'We have lost our (godly) lustre, which has never happened before. Kṛṣṇa, why is this? There is no doubt that all our golden radiance is eclipsed. What is happening? Tell us the truth. Have we come to the (brilliant golden) slopes of Mount Meru?' [Kṛṣṇa replied:] 'We are caught in the brilliance of Agni Āhavanīya, the sacrificial fire. That is why our own radiance has faded.' [Balarāma said:] 'If we are so close to it and losing our lustre, you must plan our rescue here and now with your own intelligence.' [Kṛṣṇa said:] 'Garuḍa, you must execute the task we give you immediately. When you have completed this plan, I will do the rest.' Having listened to noble Kṛṣṇa's words, mighty Garuḍa sped to the Ganges. Taking water from there, he sprinkled it on the fire. Then the sacrificial fire was quenched."

3.6: [Sanskrit] *Harivaṃśa* (*Mahābhārata,* Text as Constituted in the Critical Edition), 36. 47-60, The Appearance of Kālanemi:
kālanemir iti khyāto dānavaḥ pratyadṛśyata // 47 // bhāskarākāramukuṭaḥ śiñjitābharaṇāṅgadaḥ / mandarotkīrṇasaṃkāśo mahārajatasaṃvṛtaḥ // 48 //

śatapraharaṇodagraḥ śatabāhuḥ śatānanaḥ / śataśīrṣaḥ sthitaḥ śrīmāñ śataśṛṅga ivācalaḥ / kakṣe mahati saṃvṛddho nidāgha iva pāpakaḥ // 49 // dhūmrakeśo hariśmaśrur daṃṣṭrālauṣṭhapuṭānanaḥ / trailokyāntaravistāri dhārayan vipulaṃ vapuḥ // 50 // bāhubhis tulayan vyoma kṣipan padbhyāṃ mahīdharān / īrayan mukhaniḥśvāsair vṛṣṭimanto balāhakān // 51 // tiryag āyataraktākṣaṃ mandarodagravakṣasam / didhakṣantam ivāyāntaṃ sarvān devagaṇān mṛdhe // 52 // tarjayantaṃ suragaṇāṃś chādayantaṃ diśo daśa / saṃvartakāle tṛṣitaṃ dṛptaṃ mṛtyum ivotthitam // 53 // sutalenocchrayavatā vipulāṅguliparvaṇā / lambābharaṇapūrṇenaa kiṃcic calitavarmaṇā // 54 // ucchritenāgrahastena dakṣiṇena vapuṣmatā / dānavān devanihatān uttiṣṭhata iti bruvan // 55 // taṃ kālanemiṃ samare dviṣatāṃ kālasammitam / vīkṣanti sma surāḥ sarve bhayavitrastalocanāḥ // 56 // taṃ sma vīkṣanti bhūtāni kramantaṃ kālaneminam / trivikrame vikramantaṃ nārāyaṇam ivāparam // 57 // socchrayan prathamaṃ pādaṃ mārutāghurṇitāmbaram / prākrāmad asuro yuddhe trāsayan sarvadevatāḥ // 58 // sa mayenāsurendreṇa pariṣvaktaḥ kraman raṇe / kālanemir babhau daityaḥ saviṣṇur iva mandaraḥ // 59 // atha pravivyathur devāḥ sarve śakrapurogamāḥ / dṛṣṭvā kālam ivāyāntaṃ kālanemiṃ bhayāvaham // 60 //

"The demon known as Kālanemi became visible. With his crown like the sun, and with ornaments jingling on his arms and body, covered in great quantities of silver, he seemed like the risen mountain Mandara. Hundred-armed, hundred-mouthed, hundred-headed, he stood with a hundred weapons raised, like glorious Śataśṛṅga, the hundred-peaked mountain, and evil waxed upon his mighty flanks like summer heat. His vast body extended throughout the threefold universe, with smoke-dark hair and tawny beard, his parted lips revealing fangs, balancing the sky with his arms, kicking down mountains with his feet, his outbreaths issuing as thunderclouds. His chest thrown out like Mandara, his long oblique eyes reddened, he approached as if longing to burn up the hosts of gods in battle. Covering the ten directions of space, threatening all the gods like thirsting, raging Death rising from hell at the end of the world, he stood fully embodied, his armour covered with pendant ornaments trembling as he raised fingers of his right hand with their huge knuckles, lifting up the demons slain by the gods. All the gods, their eyes trembling with fear, saw Kālanemi as certain death to (them,) his enemies, and mortal creatures saw the approaching Kālanemi as another Nārāyaṇa (Viṣṇu) striding through (the universe) as Trivikrama. Taking his first step, his clothing swirling around his raised leg in wind, the demon strode into battle, terrifying all the gods. Into battle strode Kālanemi with Maya, the demon leader, like Mount Mandara with Viṣṇu (at the Churning of the Ocean). Then all the gods led by Indra trembled on seeing Kālanemi approaching like Death, bringing fear with him."

3.7: [Sanskrit] *Mahābhārata* (Text as Constituted in the Critical Edition), *Śalyaparvan*, 9.16.40-49, Yudhiṣṭhira and the Kālarātrī Spear:
tatas tu śaktiṃ rucirogradaṇḍām maṇipravālojjvalitām pradīptām / cikṣepa vegāt subhṛśaṃ mahātmā madrādhipāya pravaraḥ kurūṇām // 40 // dīptām athainām mahatā balena savisphuliṅgām sahasā patantīm / praikṣanta sarve kuravaḥ sametā yathā yugānte mahatīm ivolkām // 41 // tāṃ kālarātrīm iva pāśahastām yamasya dhātrīm iva cograrūpām /sabrahmadaṇḍapratimām amoghām sasarja yatto yudhi dharmarājaḥ // 42 // gandhasragagryāsanapānabhojanair abhyarcitām pāṇḍusutaiḥ prayatnāt / samvartakāgnipratimām jvalantīm kṛtyām atharvāṅgirasīm ivogrām // 43 // īśānahetoḥ pratinirmitām tām tvaṣṭrā ripūṇām asudehabhakṣām / bhūmyantarikṣādijalāśayāni prasahya bhūtāni nihantum īśām // 44 // ghaṇ ṭāpatākāmaṇivajrabhājam vaidūryacitrām tapanīyadaṇḍām / tvaṣṭrā prayatnān

of men in life are directed by one king, their private fate in the afterlife is in the hands of another. Both kings are named by the inscriptions, the king of the Khmers as Paramavishnuloka, whose dispensations are known, the king of the afterlife as Yama, whose decisions cannot be known. George Coedès commented in 1911 that "in its entirety, this tableau … was probably intended to edify the faithful." And indeed the composition of the reliefs and the placement of their inscriptions speak less to the formal religious faith of the observer than to his individual conscience.

(1) The Apparatus of State

There are twenty-eight short inscriptions in Old Khmer engraved in very small characters on the southern relief showing the king and the Khmer army. They are evidently contemporaneous with the reliefs themselves, and most of them identify by name and title the elephant-mounted commanders shown leading the troops; others identify the king, prominent ministers, priests or scholars, and the portable shrine of the sacred fire. The personal identifications indicate clearly the complexity of the ranks and titles accorded to leading individuals in the power structure of 12th-century Cambodia. The texts, numbered from left to right, are given below along with tentative translations.

The aristocratic Khmer title *kamraten añ* has been translated here as "Lord", and *vraḥ kamraten añ* as "Honorable Lord". The God-title, *kamraten jagat*, is nowhere used in the Kali Yuga inscriptions. The rank of *anak sañjak* originated as a military title for powerful allies or bodyguards of the king, but it could in later times be awarded to both men and women of high standing. An *anak sañjak*, like a *kamraten añ*, could be identified both by personal name and official title, as well as by place of origin, which sometimes substitutes for the personal name in the inscriptions. In the case of non-sanskritised Khmer appellations, it can be difficult or impossible to distinguish a personal name from a toponym; such cases are indicated by a question-mark. The honorific Sanskrit prefix *śrī* is attached to most titles, but there are exceptions, including the posthumous title of the king himself, who is named (Paramavishnuloka) in inscriptions 2 and 17 with the conventional mode of reference to royalty *vraḥ pāda* ("sacred feet", translated here as "His Majesty") in addition to *kamraten añ*. The diacritical marks used in the transliterations are omitted from the translations, in which the spellings have been anglicised.

1. *tanvāy kamraten añ paṇḍita*
   "Gift of the Lord Pandit."

2. *saṃtac vraḥ pāda kamraten añ paramaviṣṇuloka nā stac nau vnaṃ śivapāda pi pañcuḥ vala*
   "His Supreme Majesty, Lord Paramavishnuloka, staying on Mount Sivapada and commanding the army to descend."

3/1. *vraḥ kamraten añ śrī-vīrasinhavarmma*
   "Honorable Lord Sri-Virasinghavarman."

3/2. *kamraten añ ta mūla śrī-varddha*
   "First Lord Sri-Vardha."

4. *kamraten añ dhanañjaya*
   "Lord Dhananjaya."

5. *vraḥ kamrateṅ añ guṇadoṣa ta pvana*
   "The Honorable Lord [Inspector of] Faults and Qualities, the Fourth."

6. *vraḥ kamrateṅ añ śrī-jayendravarmma ldau*
   "Honorable Lord Sri-Jayendravarman from Ldau."

7. *vraḥ kamrateṅ añ śrī-vīrendrādhipativarmma chok vakula*
   "Honorable Lord Sri-Virendradhipativarman from Chok Vakula."

8. *anak sañjak kañcas pryak ti hau vraḥ kamrateṅ añ śrī-vīrāyudhavarmma*
   "The Anak Sanjak [named] Kanchas Pryak, called [by title] Honorable Lord
   Sri-Virayudhavarman."

9. *anak sañjak mat gnaṅ ti hau vraḥ kamrateṅ añ śrī-jayāyudhavarmma*
   "The Anak Sanjak from Mat Gnang, called [by title] Honorable Lord
   Sri-Jayayudhavarman."

10. *vraḥ kamrateṅ añ śrī-mahīpatīndravarmma canlattai*
    "Honorable Lord Sri-Mahipatindravarman from Chanlattai."

11. *anak sañjak vidyāśrama ti hau vraḥ kamrateṅ añ śrī-raṇavīravarmma*
    "The Anak Sanjak [named] Vidyasrama, called [by title] Honorable Lord
    Sri-Ranaviravarman."

12. *anak sañjak vīrajaya ti hau vraḥ kamrateṅ añ śrī-rājasiṅhavarmma*
    "The Anak Sanjak [named] Virajaya, called [by title] Honorable Lord
    Sri-Rajasinhavarman."

13. *anak sañjak aso vṅya phlāṅ ti hau vraḥ kamrateṅ añ
    vīrendrādhipativarmma*
    "The Anak Sanjak [named?] Vnya Phlang, called [by title] Honorable Lord
    Virendradhipativarman."

14. *anak sañjak anak ciḥ ti hau vraḥ kamrateṅ añ śrī-narapatīndravarmma*
    "The Anak Sanjak [named] Chih, called [by title] Honorable Lord
    Sri-Narapatindravarman."

15. *anak sañjak vnī satra ti hau vraḥ kamrateṅ añ śrī-śūrādhipativarmma*
    "The Anak Sanjak [named?] Vni Satra, called [by title] Honorable Lord
    Sri-Suradhipativarman."

16. *kamrateṅ añ dhanañjaya*
    "Lord Dhananjaya."

17. *vraḥ pāda kamrateṅ añ paramaviṣṇuloka*
    'His Majesty Lord Paramavishnuloka."

18. *anak sañjak trailokyapura (?)*
    "The Anak Sanjak from Trailokyapura."

19. *kamrateṅ añ ta mūla śrī-varddhana*
    "The First Lord, Sri-Vardhana."

20. *anak sañjak aso lṅgis ti hau vraḥ kamrateṅ añ śrī-rājendravarmma*
"The Anak Sanjak [named] Aso from Lṅgis, called [by title] Honorable Lord Sri-Rajendravarman."

21. *rājahotā*
"The king's priest."

22. *vraḥ vleṅ*
"The sacred fire."

23. *anak sañjak travāṅ svāy ti hau vraḥ kamrateṅ añ śrī-pṛthivīnarendra*
"The Anak Sanjak from Travang Svay, called [by title] Honorable Lord Sri-Prthvinarendra."

24. *anak sañjak kavīśvara ti hau vraḥ kamrateṅ añ mahāsenāpati śrī-vīrendravarmma*
"The Anak Sanjak [named] Kavisvara, called [by title] Honorable Lord General Sri-Virendravarman."

25. *vraḥ kamrateṅ añ śrī-siṅhavīravarmma*
"Honorable Lord Sri-Singhavarman"

26. *vraḥ kamrateṅ añ śrī jayasiṅhavarmma kaṃluṅ vrai nāṃ vala lvo*
"Honorable Lord Jayasinghavarman inside the forest, leading the troops of Lvo."

27. *neḥ syāṃ kuk*
"These are the Syam Kuk."

28. *anak rājakāryyabhāga pamañ jeṅ jhāla ta nāṃ syāṃ kuk*
"The participant in the king's service [named] Paman (Hunter) from Jeng Jhala, leading the Syam Kuk."

(2) The Apparatus of Death

The second southern relief represents the continuation of the procession sent forth by the king, as it enters the afterlife. It is literally a depiction of heaven and hell, the ultimate destination and reflex of the pageant of life, and it is the last of the reliefs in the Yuga sequence at Angkor Vat. Thirty-seven heavens *(svarga)* are depicted, and thirty-two hells. Very small, terse inscriptions were engraved on this relief, naming in Sanskrit the three gods of the death kingdom – prefixed with the Khmer term *vraḥ*, without further titles – and all the thirty-two hells (collectively named *naraka*) that they ruled. Lists of thirty-two hells are known in other Cambodian inscriptions dating from the 9th or 10th century onward, and these were clearly adopted from more ancient Indian lists contained in Buddhist as well as Hindu texts. I have translated the names of the hells literally, to facilitate comparison with the relevant crimes and with the punishments depicted in the reliefs. After naming a hell in Sanskrit, the inscriptions specify, in Khmer, which particular evil deeds *(pāpakarma)* are punished in it. Although the names of the hells originated in traditional Sanskrit lists, the crimes are described in the vernacular and appear to reflect moral attitudes that were current in Cambodia at the time of the Angkor Vat reliefs. They mostly concern major offences such as murder, destruction and theft of property, disturbance of social equilibrium;

but they also condemn such antisocial tendencies as greed, exploitativeness, disrespect, deception, hypocrisy and, once, religious intolerance (inscription 6 – those who despise the devotees of Śiva are cast into the hell of worms). Others have a more spontaneous and immediate quality, sometimes betraying irritability and perhaps, to a modern reader, appearing trivial. The theft of parasols and sandals – which in temples are laid aside during worship – for example, seems scarcely to warrant the agonies of being burnt alive in the Santāpana hell (inscription 25 and, conversely, number 33). But the crime described is that of causing affliction – which is equated with heat – to others, and doing so with contempt; the theft of sandals and parasols, which not only protect from the heat but are also status symbols, is merely an illustration of such a crime. The heavens were apparently not inscribed.

The texts of the thirty-six inscriptions and tentative translations are given below. Readers should also consult Saveros Pou 2001: 156-163. Diacritical marks used in the transliterations are omitted from the translations, in which the spellings have been anglicised to make them generally readable. A question mark signifies an unconfirmed reading or uncertain translation. Dotted lines indicate illegible parts of the inscriptions and untranslatable portions of text. The inscriptions are numbered from left to right, commencing with the division of the dead into those taking the upward paths to heaven, and those consigned to the lower regions of hell. It might be noted that in the relief Yama is depicted on his buffalo above the hells, his figure extending upwards through the two levels of heaven, which is indeed the location of his abode in the *Mahābhārata*; his proxy, Dharma, and the latter's assistant, Chitragupta, are seated lower down, in immediate proximity to the hells.

1. *neḥ ti karoma phlū naraka*
   "These are on the lower (*karoma*) path to hell."

2. *neḥ ta vyara ti le phlū svargga*
   "These are on the two higher (*le*) paths to heaven."

3. *vraḥ yama*
   "Lord Yama."

4. *vraḥ dharmma vraḥ citragupta*
   "Lord Dharma, Lord Chitragupta."

5. *avīcī ⁰ anak ta mān saṅvey pi syaṅ aras nu pāpakarmma nau*
   "[The hell named] Avichi (Waveless, Joyless): people who possess good fortune yet live permanently by evil deeds."

6. *kriminicaya ⁰ anak ta nindā devatā ⁰ vraḥ vleṅ ⁰ guru ⁰ vrāhmaṇa ⁰ mahājñāna ⁰ anak ta pra[d]au dharmma ⁰ anak ta śivabhakti ⁰ ame ⁰ vapā ⁰ suhṛt*
   "[The hell named] Kriminicaya (Mass of Worms): people who despise the gods, the sacred fire, their guru, brahmins, the learned, those who teach religion, those who are devoted to [the god] Śiva, their mother, their father, their friends"

7. *vaitaraṇī nadī ⁰ anak ta didai rūva paṃnāṃ ⁰ kutsita vuddhi ⁰ vañ anak ⁰ taskara ⁰ dhūrtta ⁰ anak ta paṃpat rasa*
   "[The hell named] River Vaitarani (Carrying Across, the river between this world and hell): people who dissemble (separate appearance from behaviour),

who despise knowledge, who deceive others, who steal, who swindle, and people who destroy that which is essential."

8. *kūṭaśalmalī ° anak ta proḥ ta vanyat ° ta rīra ° sākṣī [a]nṛta …*
"[The hell named] Kutasalmali (Sharp-Thorned Silk-Cotton Tree, the so-called torture tree): people who embellish the truth (?), …, untruthful witnesses, …"

9. *yugmaparvata ° anak ta adeṅ vadha vandha ° cakni ° adeṅ pīdā para thve duḥkhaṃ para nu aras*
"[The hell named] Yugmaparvata (Twin Mountains): people who wish to kill or fetter, …, who wish to oppress others, who thrive by cultivating unhappiness in others."

10. *nirucchvāsa ° anak ta mūḍha ° pracaṇḍa ° paṃpat viśvāsa ° saṃlāp strī ° vāla*
"[The hell named] Niruchchvasa (Not Breathing): the deranged, the vehement, those who betray trust, those who kill a woman or child."

11. *ucchvāsa ° anak ta aras nu anyāya ° anak ta thauñ doṣa anak ° cya māṅsa ta aprokṣita °*
"[The hell named] Uchchvasa (Breathing, Sighing): people who act with impropriety, [for example] those who complain about the faults of other people, [yet who themselves] eat unconsecrated meat."

12. *dravattrapu ° anak ta jruṃ anak ° yok bhūmi anak ° yok padaḥ paṅvay sthāna anak*
"[The hell named] Dravattrapu (Molten Tin): people who trespass (?) against others, [for example] those who take another person's land, who take another person's dwelling, house, or residence."

13. *taptalākṣāmaya ° anak ta tut padaḥ anak ° tut vrai ° oy viṣa ta anak*
"[The hell named] Taptalakshamaya (Made of Heated Red Lac): people who set fire to another person's dwelling, who burn forests, who give poison to another."

14. *asthibhaṅga ° anak ta kap ypar padaḥ travāṅ añcan antvaṅ sabhā sthāna phoṅ ° anak ta paṃpat tīrtta anak ° vidharmma*
"[The hell named] Asthibhanga (Breaking of Bones): people who despoil plantations, dwellings, ponds, wells, assembly halls, any kind of residence, people who ruin the watering places of others, who are unjust."

15. *krakaccheda ° anak ta luvdha ta āmiṣa*
"[The hell named] Krakachcheda (Cutting-Off with Saws): people who are greedy for meat (or gluttons in general)."

16. *pūyapūrṇahrada ° anak ta lvac madya ° paradāra ° dau ta bhāryyā guru*
"[The hell named] Puyapurnahrada (Lake Filled with Pus): people who steal liquor, another man's woman, who approach the wife of their guru."

17. *asṛkpūrṇahrada ° anak ta lvac sac ° lvac bhāryyā anak ° yok bhāryyā guru ° kaṃnva ñi ta guru*
"[The hell named] Asrikpurnahrada (Lake Filled with Blood): people who steal meat, who steal another man's wife, who take the wife of their guru, who disturb their guru."

18. *medohrada ° anak ta lobha ° taṃnāṃ ta lobha ° anak ta mān svabhāva (?) ° vikāra °*
"[The hell named] Medohrada (Lake of Fat): people who are avaricious, with deep-rooted desires(?), people who possess a changeable nature (?)."

19. *tīkṣṇāyastuṇḍa ° anak ta yok maha ti anak vvaṃ oy ° lvac pāy*
"[The hell named] Tikshnayastunda (Beaked with Sharp Iron): people who take that which another does not offer, [for example] those who steal cooked rice."

20. *aṅgāranicaya ° anak ta tut sruk nagara ° karol vraḥ go ° anak ta mūtra pur[ī]ṣotsargga ta devasthāna*
"[The hell named] Angaranichaya (Heap of Coals): people who set fire to villages or towns, the stalls of sacred cows; and people who urinate or defecate in temples."

21. *amvarīṣa ° bhrūṇahā ° kat ni ta paradāra dau ta bhāryyā suhṛt*
"[The hell named] Amvarisha (Frying Pan): one who kills a foetus, who cuts another's wife; who approaches the wife of a friend."

22. *kumbhīpāka ° anak ti kamrateṅ phdai karoṃ pre ta kāryya pi krara ° lvac dravya guru ° aras nu adhamakarmma ° lvac dravya nai anak ta dīna ° nai anak ta rac ° nai śrotriya*
"[The hell named] Kumbhipaka (Baking in a Kiln or Cooking Pot): people who, relied upon … and ordered by a lord to perform a task, then delay (?); who steal the goods of their guru; who live by performing low actions [such as] stealing goods belonging to people in distress, belonging to people who are uprooted, or belonging to learned Brahmins."

23. *tālavṛkṣavana ° anak ta kat jhe ta vvaṃ tap pi kata ° kat jhe ta devasthāna ° lmak devasthāna*
"[The hell named] Talavrikshavana (Forest of Fan-Palm Trees): people who cut trees not planned for cutting, who cut the trees belonging to temples, who defile the temples."

24. *kṣuradhāraparvvata ° anak ta lvac tamrya aseḥ yāna ° pāduka ° cap ta vrāhmaṇa nu jeṅ ° avajña ta paṇḍita cap ta yajñopakaraṇa phoṅ nu jeṅ*
"[The hell named] Kshuradharaparvata (Razor-Edge Mountain): people who steal elephants, horses, vehicles, footwear; who touches a Brahmin with his foot, who shows contempt for a Pandit, who touches any ritual objects with his foot."

25. *s … pana ° anak ta thve santāpa anak ° nindā para ° lvac chatra ° upānat*
"[The hell named] S[antā]pana (Scorching): people who afflict others and show contempt for others, [for example by] stealing parasols and sandals."

26. *sūci[mukha] ° anak ta thve … anak vrama … vrama apa dau*
"[The hell named] Suchimukha (Needle-Mouthed): people who cause … "

27. *kālasūtra ° anak ta thve bheda paribhāra kamrateṅ phdai karoṃ ° lobha ta dravya*
"[The hell named] Kalasutra (The Thread of Time or Death): people who create discord among the followers of a lord …, being desirous of wealth."

28. *mahāpadma ᵒ anak ta yok vinya ta …*

"[The hell named] Mahapadma (Great Lotus): people who take flowers …"

29. *padma ᵒ anak ta lvac vnya ᵒ peḥ vnya ta śivārāma ᵒ duk jey sin*

"[The hell named] Padma (Lotus): people who steal flowers, [for example those] who take flowers from the pleasure garden of a Siva [temple] and place them in a little garden pavilion elsewhere."

30. *sañjīvana ᵒ mahāpātaki phoṅ mahāpātaki phoṅ*

"[The hell named] Sanjivana (Bringing to Life, or Living Together): all the very wicked, all the very wicked."

31. . . . .

32. . . . .

33. *śīta ᵒ anak ta lvac maḥ nu kār raṃṅā phoṅ*

"[The hell named] Sita (Cold): people who steal anything that protects against the cold."

34. *sāndratamaḥ ᵒ anak ta lvac canl[u]ḥ (?) ᵒ aśauca ᵒ anṛta*

"[The hell named] Sandratamah (Dense Darkness): people who steal lamps (?), the unclean, the untruthful."

35. *[ma]hāraurava ᵒ … l dravya vvaṃ … anak … ativīta lva … i … p kāla …*

"[The hell named] Maharaurava (The Great [Hell] of Roaring?): …"

36. *raurava ᵒ anak ta patita ᵒ anak ta aras nu paṃroḥha ᵒ dāradāna ta reḥ ta hoc ᵒ vvaṃ pros ṛna anak*

"[The hell named] Raurava (Roaring?): degraded persons, people who live as outcasts, who give little to their wives (?), who do not pay their debts to others."

FOOTNOTES

[1] For the original text, see Appendix 3.1.

[2] For the original text of both inscriptions, see Appendix 3.2(1) and (2).

[3] For the full context of these references, see Appendix 3.3(1) and (2)

[4] For the text and translation, see Appendix 3.4.

[5] On Krishna's transformation and the feat of Garuda in quenching the sacrificial fire, see Appendix 3.5.

[6] For the appearance of Kalanemi as described in the *Harivamsa*, see Appendix 3.6.

[7] For the original text, see Appendix 3.7.

[8] For the original text, see Appendix 3.8.

[9] For the original texts of all the inscriptions on this and the following relief, and their translations, see "Inscriptions of the Kali Yuga" in Appendix 3.9.

BIBLIOGRAPHY

AUBOYER, Jeannine: *Le trône et son symbolisme dans l'Inde ancienne*, Paris, Presses universitaires de France, 1949.

AYMONIER, Etienne: *Le Cambodge. III. Le groupe d'Angkor et l'historire*, Paris, Ernest Leroux, 1904.

BHATTACHARYYA, Kamaleshwar: *Notes d'iconographie khmère. II. Les 'neuf Deva'.* Arts Asiatiques III/2 (1956): 183-193.

BHATTACHARYYA, Kamaleshwar: *Notes d'iconographie khmère. VI. Le Barattement de la Mer de Lait.* Arts Asiatiques IV/3 (1957): 211-216.

BHATTACHARYYA, Kamaleshwar: *Notes d'iconographie khmère. X. Une série de 'neuf dieux'.* Arts Asiatiques IV/3 (1958): 220.

BHATTACHARYYA, Kamaleshwar: *Les religions brahmaniques dans l'ancien Cambodge d'après l'épigraphie et l'iconografie.* Publications de l'École française d'Extrême-Orient, XLIX, Paris 1961.

BHATTACHARYYA, Kamaleshwar: *Notes d'iconographie khmère. XI. Les navagraha et les 'neuf divinites'.* Arts Asiatiques X/1 (1964): 91-94.

BHATTACHARYYA, Kamaleshwar: *Recherches sur le vocabulaire des inscriptions sanskrites du Cambodge.* Publications de l'École française d'Extrême-Orient, CLXVII, Paris 1991.

BHATTACHARYYA, Narendra Nath: *Indian Demonology.* The Inverted Pantheon, Delhi 2000.

BIARDEAU, Madeleine: *Le Mahābhārata. Un récit fondateur du bramanisme et son interprétation* (2 vols.), Paris, Seuil, 2002.

BIZOT, François (ed.): *Recherches nouvelles sur le Cambodge* (É.F.E.O., Études thématiques I), Paris 1994.

BOISSELIERE Jean: *Note sur les bas-reliefs tardifs d'Angkor Wat.* Journal Asiatique 250/2 (1962): 244-248.

BOSCH, F. D. K.: *Le temple d'Aṅkor Vàt, B.É.F.E.O. XXXII – 1932* (Notes archéologiques IV), Hanoi, 1933, p. 7-21.

BROCKINGTON, John: *The Sanskrit Epics* (Handbuch der Orientalistik, 2. Abteilung, Indien, ed. J. Bronkhorst, vol. 12), Leiden-Boston-Köln, Brill, 1998.

CHIHARA, Daigoro: *Hindu-Buddhist Architecture in Southeast Asia* (Studies in Asian Art and Archaeology, vol. XIX), Leiden-New York-Köln, Brill, 1996.

COEDÈS, George: *Les bas-reliefs d'Angkor-Wat.* Bulletin de la Commission Archéologique de l'Indochine (1911): 170-220. Paris, Ministère de l'Instruction Publique et des Beaux-Arts, 1911.

COEDÈS, George: *Études cambodgiennes. VII. Seconde étude sur les bas-reliefs d'Angkor Wat.* Bulletin de l'École française d'Extrême-Orient, XIII-6 (1913): 1-5.

COEDÈS, George: *Études cambodgiennes. XXVIII. Quelques suggestions sur la méthode à suivre pour interpréter les bas-reliefs de Banteay Chmar et de la galerie extérieure du Bayon.* Bulletin de l'École française d'Extrême-Orient, XXXII (1932): 71-81.

COEDÈS, George: *Inscriptions du Cambodge (éditées et traduites par-).* École française d'Extrême-Orient, Collection de textes et documents sur l'Indochine, III. Volumes I et II, Hanoi 1937 et 1943, Volume III, IV, V, VI, VII et VIII, Paris 1951-1966.

COEDÈS, George: *Le date d'exécution des deux bas-reliefs tardifs d'Angkor Wat.* Journal Asiatique 250/2 (1962): 235-243.

COEDÈS, George: *Les Ètats hindouisés d' Indochine et d'Indonésie.* Paris, De Boccard, 3e édition 1989. (Vella, Walter F. (ed.), Cowing, Sue Brown (trans.), *The Indianized States of Southeast Asia.* Honolulu, University of Hawaii Press, 1968.

DAGENS, Bruno: *Les Khmers* (Guides Belles Lettres des Civilisations, 10), Paris, Société d'édition Les Belles Lettres, 2003.

DIMMIT, Cornelia & **VAN BUITENEN, J. A. B**: *Classical Hindu Mythology. A Reader in the Sanskrit Purāṇas.* 1978, repr. Delhi, Sri Satguru Publications, 1998.

FINOT, Louis, **GOLOUBEW,** Victor, **COEDÈS,** George: *Le temple d'Angkor Wat.* 7 volumes [3e partie (3 volumes), préfacées par George Coedès, consacrée à la Galerie des bas-reliefs et aux deux pavillons d'angle]. Publications de l'École française d'Extrême-Orient, Mémoires archéologiques II, Paris 1929-1932.

GITEAU, Madeleine: *Le Barattage de l'Océan dans l'ancien Cambodge.* Bulletin de la Société des Études indochinoises XXVI-2 (1951): 141-159.

GLAIZE, Maurice: *Les monuments du groupe d'Angkor.* 6e édition, notes et addenda de Jean Boisselier, Paris, Jean Maisonneuve, 2003.

GONDA, Jan: *Aspects of Early Viṣṇuism*, Leiden 1954, repr. Delhi, Motilal Banarsidass, 1993.

GONDA, Jan: *Viṣṇuism and Śivaism, A Comparison*, London, 1970.

GROSLIER, Bernard-Philippe: *Les Syâm Kuk des bas-reliefs s'Angkor Wat.* Orients, pour Georges Condominas, Paris Sudestasie/Toulouse Privat, 1981: 107-126.

JACQ-HERGOULAC'H, Michel: *L'armement et l'organisation de l'armée khmère aux XIIe et XIIIe siècles, d'après les bas-reliefs d'Angkor Wat, du Bayon et de Banteay Chmar.* Publications du Musée Guimet. Recherches et documents d'arts et d'archéologie, XII, Paris, Presses Universitaires de France, 1979.

LE BONHEUR, Albert: *Cambodge. Angkor. Temples en péril.* Kodansha International/Paris, Éditions Herschler, 1989.

LE BONHEUR, Albert, **PONCAR,** Jaroslav: *Of Gods, Kings, and Men. Bas-reliefs of Angkor Wat and Bayon.* London, Serindia Publications, 1995.

MAHĀBHĀRATA: *The Mahābhārata Text as Constituted in Its Critical Edition,* Vols. I-V, edited by R. N. Dandekar and the Bhandarkar Oriental Research Institute, Poona 1971-1976.

MANNIKKA, Eleanor: *Angkor Wat. Time, Space, and Kingship*, Honolulu, University of Hawai'i Press, 1996.

MARTINI, François: *La gloire de Râma. Râmakerti Râmâyana cambodgien.* (Traduction), Introduction et notes de Ginette Martini, préface de Solange Thierry, Paris, Les Belles Lettres, 1978.

MAXWELL, Thomas S.: *The Gods of Asia. Image, Text, and Meaning*, Delhi-Calcutta-Chennai-Mumbai, Oxford University Press, 1998.

NAFILYAN, Guy: *Angkor Wat. Description graphique du temple*, avec la collaboration de Alex Turletti, Mey Than, Dy Preung, Vong Von. Publications de l'École française d'Extrême-Orient, Mémoires archéologiques IV, Paris 1969.

POU, Saveros: *Dictionnaire vieux khmer-français- anglais.* An Old Khmer-French-English Dictionary, Paris, Cedoreck, 1992.

POU, Saveros: *Nouvelles inscriptions du Cambodge II & III*, École française d'Extrême-Orient, Collection de textes et documents sur l'Indochine, XXII - XXIII, Paris 2001: 156-163, "Inscription d'Angkor Wat, K. 299".

POU, Saveros: *Choix d'articles de khmerologie.* Selected Papers on Khmerology, Phnom Penh, Reyum, 2003.

ROVEDA, Vittorio and **PONCAR,** Jaroslav: *Sacred Angkor. The Carved Reliefs of Angkor Wat*, Bangkok, River Books, n.d.

RÜPING, Klaus: *Amṛtamanthana und Kūrma-Avatāra.* Ein Beitrag zur puranischen Mythen- und Religionsgeschichte (Schriftenreihe des Sṅdasien-Instituts der Universität Heidelberg), Wiesbaden, Harrassowitz, 1970.

Concept: Jaroslav Poncar
Design: Susanne Annen | Designgruppe Fanz & Neumayer | Marcus Bela Schmitt | Edition Panorama
Separations: Jaroslav Poncar
Printing: abcdruck GmbH, Heidelberg
Bookbinding: Josef Spinner Großbuchbinderei GmbH, Ottersweier

A production by EDITION**PANORAMA**